# LANGUAGE AND POLITICS IN PAKISTAN

# LANGUAGE AND POLITICS IN PAKISTAN

**TARIQ RAHMAN**

Karachi
Oxford University Press
Oxford   New York   Delhi
1998

Oxford University Press, Great Clarendon Street, Oxford OX2 6DP
Oxford New York
Athens Auckland Bangkok Bagotá Buenos Aires Calcutta
Cape Town Chennai Dar es Salaam Delhi Florence Hong Kong Istanbul
Karachi Kuala Lumpur Madrid Melbourne Mexico City Mumbai
Nairobi Paris São Paulo Singapore Taipei Tokyo Toronto Warsaw
and associated companies in Berlin Ibadan

Oxford is a registered trade mark of Oxford University Press

© Oxford University Press 1996

The moral rights of the author have been asserted

All rights reserved. No part of this publication may be reproduced,
stored in a retrieval system, or transmitted, in any form or by any means,
without the prior permission in writing of Oxford University Press.
Enquiries concerning reproduction should be sent to the
Rights Department, Oxford University Press, at the address above.

This book is sold subject to the condition that it shall not, by way
of trade or otherwise, be lent, re-sold, hired out or otherwise circulated
without the publisher's prior consent in any form of binding or cover
other than that in which it is published and without a similar condition
including this condition being imposed on the subsequent purchaser.

ISBN 0 19 577999 1

First published by Oxford University Press, 1997

This edition in Oxford Pakistan Paperbacks, 1998

Printed in Pakistan at
Challenger Paper Products, Karachi.
Published by
Ameena Saiyid, Oxford University Press
5-Bangalore Town, Sharae Faisal
PO Box 13033, Karachi-75350, Pakistan.

*For my father and mother*

# Contents

| | | |
|---|---|---|
| | *List of Abbreviations* | ix |
| | *Glossary* | xi |
| | *Translation and Transliteration* | xii |
| | *Preface* | xiii |
| 1. | Introduction | 1 |
| 2. | Theoretical Preliminaries | 8 |
| 3. | British Language Policies and Imperialism | 23 |
| 4. | The Vernacular-English Controversy | 39 |
| 5. | The Urdu-Hindi Controversy | 59 |
| 6. | The Bengali Language Movement | 79 |
| 7. | The Sindhi Language Movement | 103 |
| 8. | The Pashto Language Movement | 133 |
| 9. | The Language Movements of Balochistan | 155 |
| 10. | The Siraiki Movement | 173 |
| 11. | The Punjabi Movement | 191 |
| 12. | Minor Language Movements | 209 |
| 13. | The Urdu-English Controversy | 228 |
| | *Conclusion* | 249 |

## Appendices

| | | |
|---|---|---|
| A. | Language-wise Publications | 261 |
| B. | Language-wise Allocation of Time on the TV | 262 |
| C. | Language-wise Allocation of Time on the Radio | 263 |
| D. | Grant-in-Aid to Institutions for the Promotion of Languages | 264 |
| E. | Budgets of Institutions for the Promotion of Languages | 265 |
| F. | District-wise Distribution of Languages | 267 |
| G. | Aid by the State to English-medium Schools | 270 |

*Bibliography*   271

*Index*   314

## Maps

1. Provinces of Pakistan with proposed Siraiki Province
2. The Proposed Siraiki Province (as claimed by Siraiki leaders)

between pages 178 and 179

3. Language Map of Pakistan
4. District-wise Language Map

between pages 254 and 255

# List of Abbreviations

Some abbreviations given in the text refer to sources given in full in the bibliography. Others have been explained or expanded in the text and are not given here. The abbreviations below, therefore, refer to dailies and magazines, locations of archives, organizations etc.

| | |
|---|---|
| AC | Assistant Commissioner |
| ANP | Awami National Party |
| BISE | Board of Intermediate and Secondary Education, Hyderabad |
| BM | The British Library (British Museum) |
| BSO | Balochistan Students Organization |
| BO | Bodleian Library, University of Oxford |
| CMG | *Civil and Military Gazette* (English) |
| D | *Dawn* (English) |
| DC | Deputy Commissioner |
| FP | *The Frontier Post* (English) |
| GOP | Government of Pakistan |
| H | *Hurriyat* (Urdu) |
| HP | *Hilal-e-Pakistan* (Sindhi) |
| IDT | *Indian Daily Telegraph* |
| IOL | India Office Library, London |
| J | *Jang* (Urdu) |
| Jsrt | *Jasarat* (Urdu) |
| LWC | Language of Wider Communication |
| M | *The Muslim* (English) |
| MN | *Morning News* |
| MQM | Mohajir Qaumi Movement (Mohajir National Movement) |
| MRD | Movement for the Restoration of Democracy |
| N | *The Nation* (English) |
| NAP | National Awami Party |
| NDC | National Documentation Centre, Cabinet Division, Islamabad |

| | |
|---|---|
| NT | *New Times* (English) |
| NW | *Nawa-i-Waqt* (Urdu) |
| P | *Pioneer* (English) |
| PO | *Pakistan Observer* (English) |
| PNP | Pakistan National Party |
| PPP | Pakistan Peoples Party |
| PSP | Pakistan Siraiki Party |
| PT | The Pakistan Times (English) |
| Punj O | *Punjab Observer* (English) |
| SA | Sind Archives, Clifton, Karachi |
| SNP | Siraiki National Party |
| SU | Sind University Office Record, Jamshoro, Hyderabad |

# Glossary

| | |
|---|---|
| *Bhadralok* | The Hindu middle class which had emerged as a consequence of modernization in Bengal in the nineteenth century. |
| *Biradari* | Brotherhood; clan; extended family; the sub-group to which one belongs. |
| *Maktab* | School. |
| *Maulvi* | Muslim religious figure who leads prayers and performs the functions of a priest. |
| *Mullah* (*moolah*) | Same as *maulvi* but somewhat derogatory. |
| *Moonshee* (*Munshi*) | Clerk, accountant. |
| *Mofussil* | Rural. |
| *Pandits* | Hindu priest belonging to the Brahmin caste. |
| *Sudder* | The part of the city in which officials lived and government offices were generally located. |
| *Raj* | Rule. |
| *Shaheed* | Martyr. |
| *Ulema* | Islamic religious scholars. |

# Translation and Transliteration

Translations from several languages—Balochi, Brahvi, Bengali, French, German, and Sindhi—were made by translators, some of whom have been mentioned earlier. The passages from Hindi, Pashto, Punjabi, Siraiki, and Urdu were translated by the author. All except Urdu were shown for verification to people competent in these languages.

I decided against using all forms of transliteration symbols because I thought the actual pronunciation was unimportant. Moreover, it could only be given through the symbols of the International Phonetic Association which would have made the book unnecessarily complicated.

# Preface

Writing a book in Pakistan is somewhat like undertaking the exploration of the Antarctic in the nineteenth century. First of all, you do not know what hazards and impediments you will encounter on the way; and, secondly, even if you do, there is little you can do about them. In this case, the impediments were firstly financial and secondly intellectual, but there were many who helped me overcome them.

There are hardly any good research libraries in Pakistan but I was lucky to have secured a scholarship to read for the degree of M. Litt. in linguistics at Strathclyde University at Glasgow in 1988-9. I spent most of my time looking for books which were essential reading for my research, and very little time on the course itself.

In 1992, I met Dr Tariq Banuri, Dr Iftikhar Ahmad, and Dr Shahrukh Rafi Khan. All of them were at the Sustainable Development Policy Institute (SDPI) which, under the supervision of Tariq Banuri, quickly developed into a university of sorts. There, I was able to get the latest publications in many fields and often picked the brains of the above scholars. At the Quaid-i-Azam University itself, I used to consult Dr Muhammad Waseem, Professor Fateh Mohammad Malik and Dr Tahir Amin for their ideas on ethnicity and related concepts. Outside the University, I was helped by Dr Inayatullah who is a good scholar and has an excellent library of his own.

These were people whose ideas I benefited from in general. As for the particular languages I was writing about, the number of those who helped me is legion. I will mention only the most important ones I interviewed, while they are all included in the list of interviewees.

Let me begin with the Bengali Language Movement to research which I went to Bangladesh. My deepest thanks go to Mr Omar Hayat who translated most of the important sources on the Movement from Bengali, which made my job in Dhaka easier. I thank Mr Azhar Islam, Deputy Librarian of the Bangla Academy, who helped me locate many important documents. I also thank Professor Kabir Chaudhry who gave me a number of books and took me to his Dhanmandi house which was once a meeting place for the activists of the Language Movement.

In England, where I studied language policies and the Urdu-Hindi Controversy, I found the following libraries very useful: the libraries of the Universities of Cambridge, Oxford, London, Reading, Strathclyde, and Glasgow; The Bodleian Library, Oxford; the School of Oriental and African Studies Library, and the India Office Library, London.

For the Balochi and Brahvi language movements in Balochistan, I found the archives of the magazine *Balochi* and the Balochistan Assembly library very useful. The Balochi Academy also gave me important material and the library of the Command and Staff College, Quetta was especially helpful. Among those who helped me locate research material were Mr Surat Marri, Mr Razzak Sabir, and Professor Abdur Rehman Fikr. Those who translated Balochi and Brahvi documents for me were Mr Munir Ahmed and Mr Hamza Baloch respectively.

The Pashto Language Movement was easy to study because I used to travel to Peshawar as a Visiting Professor in 1993. I thank Dr Rajwali Khattak, Dr Hidayatullah Naeem (both researchers at the Pashto Academy), and Nasir Khattak for their help. I benefited a lot from them and the sources in the NWFP Archives, the Pashto Academy, the NWFP Assembly Library, and in private collections.

The Punjabi Language Movement was easy too, because I often visited Lahore where I met Asif Khan, Secretary of the Punjabi Adabi Board as well as other activists of the Punjabi movement such as Ahmed Saleem. I used the archives of *The Pakistan Times*, the Punjab Public Library, the library of the Punjabi Adabi Board, and the Punjab Archives for my work.

The Siraiki Movement was somewhat more difficult as it involved a research visit to Multan. I am especially indebted to Mr Shaukat Mughal, a dedicated scholar of Siraiki, for having introduced me to the people I interviewed. I am thankful to Mr Omar Kamal Khan and Mr Mazhar Arif who allowed me to use their private collections.

The Sindhi Language Movement was perhaps the most difficult to study because of the insecurity in the province which made travelling risky. I am indebted to Mr Murad Panhwar who helped me meet interviewees and sent me some very useful documents later. I am also indebted to Mr Rafiq Dogar, Research Assistant at the National Institute of Pakistan Studies, who went on a data collection trip to Sindh on my behalf in 1993 and who translated Sindhi documents for me. I used the following libraries in Sindh: the Institute of Sindhology Library, the archives of the Sindh Government at Clifton, Karachi, and the archives of the Municipal Committee, Hyderabad, Sindh

University, and the Board of Intermediate and Secondary Education, Hyderabad.

Urdu, which had to be studied in relation to Sindhi in Sindh and in relation to English for the whole of Pakistan, also proved difficult to come to grips with. Among the people who helped with documents and ideas were Dr Waheed Qureshi, Dr Jameel Jalibi, Dr Farman Fatehpuri, Mr Iftikhar Arif, and Dr Gauhar Naushahi. The institutions I found most useful were the library of the Anjuman Taraqqi-e-Urdu (Karachi) and the Muqtadara Qaumi Zaban.

Among the minor languages of Pakistan I studied Hindko, Gujrati, Burushaski, Shina, Balti, Kashmiri, and Khowar (Chitrali). For my research on the Hindko language movement in Hazara, I thank my friend Omar Asghar Khan, Director of the NGO Sangi, who helped me get in touch with Hindko literary people and language planners. I am especially indebted to Mr Sultan Sakoon whose private collection was very useful.

For Gujrati I am thankful to Ms Farishta Dinshaw who helped me contact some of my interviewees in Karachi. For Burushaski, Shina, and Balti, I am especially indebted to Mr Ijlal, my research student, who carried out some proxy research for me in Gilgit and helped me meet Allama Naseerudin, the Burushaski poet, in Karachi. I thank Allama Naseeruddin for having given me books from his private collection.

As for Khowar, I thank Dr Inayatullah Faizi for giving me material on the language. I also thank the Deputy Commissioner of Chitral and the Commandant of Chitral Scouts for giving me access to their own files and library.

In Islamabad, the following institutions provided me with library and archival material: the National Documentation Centre, Cabinet Division; the National Archives; the National Institute of Historical and Cultural Research; the Census of Pakistan; the National Assembly Library; Library of the Curriculum Wing, Ministry of Education; the American Center; the British Council; and the Quaid-i-Azam University Library.

This brings me to the non-academic aspects of research. In many ways, these are even more important than the academic ones, the latter being impossible without the former. One needs psychological support, board and lodging, money for travelling, photocopying material, and books. These things generally come from universities and other donors in the West, but my research was not sponsored by any official institution.

Some institutions, however, did provide tickets or travel grants. They are as follows:

| | |
|---|---|
| Islamabad-London return fare (1993) | University Grants Commission. I am grateful to Dr Kazi who made this possible. |
| £400/- for stay in London (1993) | The British Council, Islamabad. |
| Karachi-Dhaka return fare (1994) | Hamdard Foundation. I am grateful to Dr Zawwar Hussain Zaidi for having recommended my case to Hakim Said who provided this assistance. |
| Islamabad-Karachi return fare (1994) | The Pakistan Academy of Letters. I am obliged to Mr Fakhar Zaman who gave me the grant. |
| Rs 3000/- for a trip to Multan | The National Institute of Pakistan Studies, Quaid-i-Azam University. |

All the other trips, including my stay at different places in Pakistan and abroad, were financed by myself. Hospitality, however, was provided in some cases by friends and relatives who cannot be thanked adequately for their kindness. I shall mention some people who went out of their way to help me. First, members of my family: my father who helped with mathematical calculations; my wife, who put up with the drainage on our income and helped me in innumerable other ways; my younger brother, Major Ahmad Sami, and his wife Saba who offered me their hospitality and car in Quetta; my brother-in-law, Colonel Azam Jafar, who helped me in matters involving computers and much else; the family of my wife in Lahore, especially her cousin, Manzar Khan; and my uncle in Karachi in whose homes I stayed on my numerous visits to those cities. Also my wife's cousin, Sameena Junaid, and her husband Junaid Athar, in whose house I often stayed in Peshawar.

Then friends such as Major General Malik Saleem Khan who made it possible for me to travel and stay in safety in Sindh; Colonel Khalid Khan and Colonel Iftikhar who helped me in many ways; Colonel Javed Kamal Meyer, the Commandant of Chitral Scouts, who offered me the hospitality of his officers' messes in Drosh and Chitral and facilitated travelling; Major Sohail, his wing commander in Drosh, for his help and warm hospitality; Mr Waseem Altaf of the Income Tax Department, who helped me procure some essential data; Dr Johann

Bart, a linguist from the Summer Institute of Linguistics, who was working on the Kohistani language, and who translated a book from German for me; Dr B. Chandramohan, my friend from Sheffield University; and Mr Fakhruddin Barni, a family friend, who offered me the hospitality of their homes in London.

Some people whom I met through friends or on the strength of institutional affiliation proved very helpful. For instance, Dr Gowher Rizvi and Dr Iftikhar Malik, whom I met through my colleague, Ms Dushka Saiyid, arranged for my stay at Nuffield College, Oxford and offered me their hospitality. Brigadier Ahsan Amin, Defence Adviser of the Bangladesh High Commission in Pakistan, who was my colleague twenty-three years ago in the Pakistan Military Academy, went out of his way to facilitate my visit to Bangladesh. Had his friend Brigadier Sharif Aziz not received me in Dhaka and arranged for my stay, I would have been under extreme mental stress. In the end, I would like to thank Havildars Nasir Ali and Khalid Mahmood Dar who typed the manuscript of this book and all those other silent workers in the press without whose labour this book would not have seen the light of the day. My special thanks go to Ms Sabiah Askari and Ms Zehra Mehdi Barlas of the Oxford University Press for the hard work they put in to bring out this book.

This brings me to the depressing part of research in Pakistan: expenditure. For the most part, one cannot undertake ambitious research projects, such as this book, at one's own expense. There are no research assistants and no research grants to fall back upon. Individuals might be very helpful, but one cannot depend upon luck all the time. Situations such as this force scholars in the Third World to remain peripheral. Money is spent on the elite of power but not on scholarship—at least not on independent scholarship. Does this mean that one should stop research? Perhaps the answer is yes. But if it is a hobby, a source of pleasure, even that is not possible.

Islamabad  
January 1995

Tariq Rahman

You taught me language;
and my profit on 't
Is I know how to curse

> Shakespeare

Hatreds never cease by hatred in this world;
by love alone do they cease

> *The Dhammapada*

# 1

# Introduction

Pakistan is a multilingual country. Based on the percentages for speakers of different languages given in the 1981 census, we can deduce the number of speakers according to the population figure of 127,962,000 for 1993, as follows:

|         | Percentage (1981) | Number of speakers (millions) (1993) |
|---------|-------------------|--------------------------------------|
| Punjabi | 48.17             | 60.9                                 |
| Pashto  | 13.14             | 16.8                                 |
| Sindhi  | 11.77             | 15.0                                 |
| Siraiki | 9.83              | 12.6                                 |
| Urdu    | 7.60              | 9.7                                  |
| Balochi | 3.02              | 3.8                                  |
| Hindko  | 2.43              | 3.1                                  |
| Brahvi  | 1.21              | 1.5                                  |
| Others  | 2.81              | 3.6                                  |

(*Encyclopaedia Britannica Yearbook 1994; Census 1981*)

The language of the domains of power—administration, judiciary, military, education, and commerce etc.—is still English, as it was under British rule before 1947. Urdu, however, is the national language and is used in most state schools, at the lower levels of administration, in the media, and in all the major cities of the country. It was not an indigenous language of the country until the Urdu-speaking immigrants from India, or Mohajirs as they call themselves, settled here.

Pakistan has had many conflicts involving language. Before its creation, when Muslim and Hindu identities took shape, Urdu was part of the former identity and Hindi of the latter. In the struggle for power, the Muslims fought for Urdu, written in the Perso-Arabic script (or *nastaleeq*), to be used in the domains of power while Hindus wanted Hindi in the Devanagari script. This Urdu-Hindi controversy as it was called formed part of the demand for Muslim separatism. The Muslim League continued to use Urdu as a symbol of integration after 1947, in a country whose land masses were separated by more than one thousand miles of Indian territory. The ensuing ethno-nationalist challenge to the domination of West Pakistan and the Urdu-supporting Bengali elite (the *ashraf*) in East Bengal came to be articulated through the Bengali language movement. This movement was counter-hegemonic and involved an emphasis on language and culture, i.e., the Bengali identity rather than the Islamic identity which had been used to counter the domination of the Hindus in Bengal earlier. In a sense it became the prototypical case of ethno-nationalistic assertion in Pakistan.

The state and the supporters of Pakistani nationalism, in their efforts to create a sense of nationhood, have used the sacerdotal idiom of religion, as well as that of modern state-based nationalism. Islam and Urdu have been key symbols in constructing a sense of unity. Ethno-nationalists, by contrast, have emphasized differences, and have also countered the state by using the idiom of secularism. They have evoked language, culture, and myths of racial origin in support of their cause, as well as tangible, instrumentalist factors—the fear of being deprived of jobs, of being powerless, and of remaining underdeveloped.

The major thesis of the ethno-nationalists remains that Pakistan is not just a multilingual but also a multinational state: in the 1960s, the five indigenous nationalities were defined as Punjabi, Pakhtun, Sindhi, Balochi, and, of course, Bengali. After the creation of Bangladesh in 1971, the Siraiki identity emerged, so the number remained unchanged. In the late 1980s, the Mohajirs, who had earlier called themselves Pakistanis, began to assert their distinctive ethnic identity too. The state, of course, denies the existence of these nationalities. It asserts the uni-national thesis—that all Pakistanis belong to one nation, notwithstanding their differences. A corollary of this premise is that a certain uniform culture which is basically that of the Urdu-speaking elite is officially endorsed, the use of Urdu is increased, and the ideal criterion for the distribution of power is merit as defined by the more modernist, more educated ruling elite which is predominantly Punjabi.

The Pakhtun, Sindhi, and Balochi identities are expressed through Pashto, Sindhi, and Balochi/Brahvi. When the proto-elite (this term is defined in Chapter 2) of southern Punjab protested against underdevelopment and lack of power, the Siraiki language became the symbol of their distinctive identity and the claim to a separate province. The Mohajirs of urban Sindh consolidated themselves as an Urdu-speaking collectivity during their resistance to the increase in the use of Sindhi in Sindh even earlier than the language riots of January 1971 and July 1972 (see chapter 7). It was this consciousness of the distinctive Mohajir identity which the Mohajir Qaumi Movement (MQM) overtly articulated in the late 1980s.[1]

The identity of the Pakistani nationalists, which can also be called the official point of view, also has shades of opinion which vary according to differences of circumstances and personalities. An important point is that, whereas members of the Westernized elite support Urdu vis-à-vis the indigenous languages to counter ethnic pressure, they support English vis-à-vis Urdu. Thus, while the Pakistani nationalists, who include members of the Westernized elite, might appear to present a united front towards the indigenous languages, they are divided amongst themselves. This Urdu-English controversy is usually called the medium of instruction debate but it too is part of the political conflict in the country as this study attempts to suggest.

Language is thus at the heart of Pakistan's most significant political problem–ethnicity. It is also important for understanding other patterns of dominance in the country. For example, why does the state appear to support Urdu against the indigenous languages of the country, whereas the ruling elite, which occupies all important positions of power in the state, actually continues to support English? Why does the ruling elite, which is predominantly Punjabi-speaking, ignore its own mother-tongue while increasing the use of Urdu (and English)? Can these observations be related to politics, defined broadly as the pursuit of power? This definition of politics, and other such definitions, is explained in the next chapter. The language issue in Pakistan is about hegemonic and counter-hegemonic movements; about compromises and balances between groups; about strife and equilibrium. In short, it is about what lies behind party politics, elections, and martial laws. Thus, details about party politics and the role of politicians, the military, etc. will be omitted or mentioned in passing in order to make the outline of the argument clear.

It is surprising, considering its importance, that there is no previous scholarly study on the relationship of language to politics in Pakistan. The Indian Muslims and their languages are mentioned in studies of British linguistic and educational policies, which will be examined later. However, the link with power is often ignored. The Urdu-Hindi controversy and the Bengali language movement have received much attention and their links with politics, identity construction, and ethnicity have also been explored (references will follow in chapter 2). Unfortunately, the other language movements of Pakistan have been largely ignored. Even in informed accounts of ethno-nationalism (Alavi 1987, 1991; Amin 1988) the role of language is mentioned only in passing. Moreover, there are no informed reconstructions or analyses of most of the language movements of Pakistan. The only exceptions are Christopher Shackle's articles on the Siraiki language movement, and some work on the role of English in Pakistan which either ignores (Baumgardner 1993), or deals very briefly (Abbas 1993) with questions of power and politics. There are, of course, a large number of pamphlets, articles, and books by the activists of the language movements themselves, but these are partisan, polemical, and mostly uninformed. Their major significance is that they give the points of view of the ethno-nationalists and of their opponents, who may be called the Pakistani nationalists.

These views provide insights into the minds of the actors in language movements. One discovers, for instance, that the construction of reality by the two major opposing camps, the Pakistani nationalists and the ethno-nationalists, differs so much as to place them in different worlds. Between these worlds, communication is impossible. Hence, there is no understanding of each others' position. To illustrate this clearly, these points of view are summarized below.

Both the Pakistani nationalists and the ethno-nationalists evoke simplistic and unsupportable conspiracy theories. The former assert that the ethno-nationalists, who support the multinationality thesis of which the language movements are an expression, are the enemies of Pakistan; that they want to break up the country, despite protestations to the contrary, and that they are inspired, and even supported, by foreign powers (India, Afghanistan, the former Soviet Union, etc.) They are accused of using Communists, Hindus, left-wing intellectuals, and selfish politicians to instigate and support language movements. The nationalists assert that it is gullible people, generally students, who join these movements without realizing what they are doing. In short, the supporters of language movements are marked as either traitors or fools; either enemies of Pakistan and Islam or gullible pawns of such enemies.

In opposition, the ethno-nationalists argue that the Punjabi ruling elite, in collaboration with the Mohajir elite and co-opted members from other ethnic groups, have deliberately conspired to practice internal colonialism. They rule the periphery—the provinces with non-Punjabi majorities—in the name of Islam and Pakistani nationalism. As Urdu is part of the latter, it is imposed on the whole country. The consequence of this policy, they argue, is the exploitation of their resources to increase the wealth of the Punjab; the perpetual subordination of their people to the dominance of the Punjab and the disappearance of their indigenous cultures and languages. In short, the non-Punjabi provinces have exchanged British colonialism for Punjabi—and in the cultural sphere Mohajir—colonialism. Thus, in their eyes, their language movements are part of an ongoing anti-colonial struggle which can only be opposed by selfish colonialists or simpletons who are taken in by the slogans of Islam and Pakistani nationalism. Thus, for the ethno-nationalists, their opponents, the supporters of Urdu, are either exploiters or fools.

The major part of this book consists of a sequential narrative of the events which make up the language movements. Such historical reconstructions, cluttered as they are with data, are tedious reading. Sweeping analytical statements are much more interesting, especially if they support what one already believes. The historical part of this narrative will deny the reader this kind of pleasure and will also take up much space. However, since these facts have not been marshalled in one place earlier, this is imperative. After all, one needs empirical evidence, if only to oppose the conclusions.

Such facts also help us understand highly interesting issues such as identity-formation, ethnicity, and the way language relates to power. The following are the significant questions raised by this study: Do people make efforts and even resort to violence to preserve their language or do they use language as a symbol to get political and economic dividends? Is identity a permanent feature or does it change under varying economic and political pressures? Has language always been a marker of identity? Is it a marker of identity now? Do leaders and intellectuals manipulate language as a symbol of identity to create ethno-nationalism? If so, why? Are language movements and ethno-nationalism created by enemy agents and communists, etc., in Pakistan? These are not easy questions to answer and I doubt if the answers given in this book will satisfy everybody.

To provide answers, it would be necessary to define terms, explain key concepts, and provide a theoretical framework. This is done in chapter 2. After having cleared the decks, so to speak, chapter 3 looks at British language policies with a view to determining whether, and if so how, they were related to the major political objective of the British, i.e., the consolidation of the empire. The next chapter, 'The Vernacular-English Controversy', deals with a question which is hotly debated even now—whether education should be imparted through English or the indigenous languages of South Asia. The continuation of this debate in Pakistan is given in full in chapter 13, but it can only be understood in its historical and political perspective with reference to chapter 4. Chapter 5 discusses the Urdu-Hindi controversy which has been mentioned earlier. Like the chapters on British language policies, this chapter is necessary for understanding the political significance of Urdu in the Pakistan Movement.

Chapter 6, on the Bengali language movement, is crucial for understanding identity construction. It outlines how linguistic identity replaced religious identity in East Bengal and how this relates to an anti-hegemonic movement against perceived internal colonialism.

Up to this point, the book draws heavily on published accounts and does not claim to add anything entirely new to existing scholarship. The next seven chapters, however, present new material on the Pashto (chapter 7), Balochi (chapter 8), Sindhi (chapter 9), Siraiki (chapter 10), Punjabi (chapter 11), and minor language movements (chapter 12). The role of these languages in ethno-nationalist movements will be examined to further an understanding of ethnicity and the degree to which language plays a role in creating, preserving, and expressing it.

The conclusion will examine whether the data from Muslim India and Pakistan supports any specific theoretical positions in the on-going debates on ethnicity, politics, and language. I will also make tentative suggestions about the possibility of reducing linguistic imperialism, language-based exploitation of ordinary

Pakistanis, and the chances of the recurrence of language riots in the country. But these suggestions are, of course, debatable. The basis of that debate are the facts about the language movements themselves. If these facts are marshalled with objectivity, the debate can be informed and fruitful. This is why care has been taken to provide a fairly detailed account of the language movements, while remaining sensitive to the inter-subjective reality of their actors. This may not be the final truth but it will be a step towards discovering aspects of it.

## Notes

1. According to the 1951 census, a Mohajir was defined as 'a person who moved into Pakistan as a result of partition or from fear of disturbances connected therewith, no matter from where, when or for how long a stay' (*Census* 1951: vol. 1). According to the denotative meaning of the word (immigrants), people born in Pakistan cannot be called Mohajirs. However, the word has now acquired a new meaning. It is used only for those Urdu-speaking people who define themselves as Mohajirs and are generally, though not necessarily, resident in the urban areas of Sindh. That is how this word, written with a capital letter and without italics, is used in this book.

# 2

# Theoretical Preliminaries

This chapter defines key concepts such as language planning (LP), its connection with power and politics, identity-construction, and ethnicity. As far as possible, specialized technical terms—the jargon of LP for instance—will be avoided. Unavoidable terms will, however, be explained so that subsequent usage is unambiguous.

**Language Policy and Planning**

The term LP covers many activities involving language. First, the decision as to how language(s) will function in the state is called status planning (Kloss 1969) or language allocation (Gorman 1973: 73). Certain languages will be used in the formal institutions, or state apparatus, which are here called the domains of power. It is part of what will be called language policy in this book. Some understanding of what one means by power is necessary. Power is that which enables one to impose one's will directly or indirectly over others or resist the imposition of other peoples' will. The consequences of the exercise of power would be to increase the tangible or intangible means of gratification of its possessor. In rational goal-seeking terms, this gratification could come from having influence, wealth, prestige, security, the possession of beautiful objects, etc. In extra-rational ones it might mean the enjoyment of passions such as love, hatred, anger, nostalgia, and even such perversions as sadism or masochism. This understanding of power takes into account Lukes' critique of the traditional conception of power as being the imposition of one's will over others, implying that 'the supreme and most insidious exercise of power [lies in] . . . shaping [people's] perceptions, cognitions and preferences in such a way that they accept their role in the existing order of things.' (Lukes 1974: 24; also see Galbraith 1984: 214). The idea of an insidious or invisible power, in the shape of ideas, does not explain the nature of powerfully. Power is also, as Foucault points out, 'something which circulates', which 'is employed and exercised through a net-like organization,' and individuals 'are always in the position of simultaneously undergoing and exercising this power.' (1976: 234). In short, nobody exercises power standing outside the framework, the system, of the distribution of power. Moreover, the perception of power can be culture-bound so that in pre-modern Javanese culture, wealth was seen as 'an attribute of power, not its provenance' (Anderson 1990: 59). However, in order to reduce the complexity of the problem to manageable proportions, let us assume that in Pakistan power is mostly in the hands of the state which has a system by which it controls the distribution of gratifications. The domains of power are the networks of the administration, judiciary, military, education, media, etc., through which the distribution of goods and services and other gratifications is controlled. Other domains of power, not necessarily under direct governmental control but influenced by it, are the domains of culture, research, commerce and ideology. This only leaves the informal domain of private interaction and low-level business which may be called the private sphere. The language(s) used in it may be different from those used in the domains of power. This differentiates state-sponsored language policies from society-sponsored ones. Among the latter are the policies of those who oppose the ruling elite, which will be explained in more detail later.

Once it has been decided which language will be used within the domains of power, that language has to be given uniformity. This is called standardization. It also has to be modernized, new terms have to be added in order to express the new realities of a modern, industrial society. This process is called corpus planning (Fishman 1977a: 36; Cooper 1989: 31). It is this part of LP which early language planners like Uriel Weinreich (who invented the term LP in 1957) and Einar Haugen, who popularized its use, emphasized when they talked of preparing dictionaries, grammars, and standard orthographies, without any reference to the political implication of such activities (Haugen 1959: 8).

The political dimension of these activities has been acknowledged by recent scholars of LP (Cooper 1989:183). If a language is used in the domains of power, the entry to positions of power of those who know it will be facilitated. If the state apparatus is perceived to be controlled by the users of a specific language, their hegemony may be challenged by another pressure group who perceive that they would stand to gain power if their language were privileged. An essentially political struggle for power may thus be expressed in linguistic terms.

Thus, the French Canadians have maintained their separate identity and obtained material benefits through their efforts to increase the use of their language (Esman 1985: 55-9; McConnel et al. 1979: 89-90). Similarly, in Belgium the Flemish movement, led by underprivileged Flemish-speaking leaders, challenged the domination of the French-speaking elite who had made French the sole official language of the country since 1930 (Hartig 1985: 73-4; Geertz 1979: 66).

Sometimes the domination of a language is so overwhelming that the dominated languages start to become extinct. This is a process described as language death (Dressler 1972), language suicide (Denison 1977), and linguistic genocide (Day 1981. For the death of some minority languages of Europe, see Stephens 1976). The re-action to this process is paradoxical. At the pragmatic level, the dominated languages are perceived as ghettoizing, i.e., those which keep their users confined to low powered status and occupations. Thus, people avoid teaching them to their children and even oppose legislation which forces them to do so: witness the opposition to mother-tongue education by Africans in apartheid South Africa (Bunting 1966; Hirson 1981 Troup 1976) and the preference of Hawaiians and Chamorrs (of Guam) for learning English rather than their native languages (Day 1985). This is understandable, considering that people assume that the established order will not change and they do not wish to reduce their children's chances of acquiring power.

At an idealistic level, the reaction of some members of the intelligentsia is more complex as we shall see later. They want to preserve their identity and their cultural heritage (enshrined in their language), and mobilize their community into a pressure group which will force the state to give their language its due share of power and privilege. Whatever their motivation. language becomes important in all such struggles.

Thus, Irish Gaelic was chosen as a symbol of Irish identity although most Irish people neither spoke it nor learnt it. It nevertheless contributed to the anti-British mobilization of the Irish and the establishment of the Irish Free State (Macnamara 1971: 68). In Wales, the Welsh language has served similar identity-maintenance functions since the end of the nineteenth century (Williams 1984: 189-98; Grillo 1989: 83-106). In Spain, the Catalonian and Basque language movements, which had been repressed (Medhurst 1977; Clark 1979), got a reprieve as part of the autonomy process in contemporary Spain (Rial 1985: 102-4; Woolard & Gahng 1990). Noah Webster's spellings, different as they were from British English, were part of the American political articulation of autonomy (Weinstein 1982). And Ben Yehuda's dream of preserving the Jewish identity through the revival of Hebrew (1880-1960), a language used only in the religious and literary domains, made him the father of nationalistic language planning in Israel (Fellman 1974).

Other examples of identity-related and politically-motivated corpus planning are the choice of a script: the Vai syllabry was invented in Liberia in 1883 to privilege the Vai people at the expense of the Negro settlers from America (Dalby 1967). Mustafa Kemal Pasha changed the Arabic-based Turkish script to Roman in 1928 to strengthen the modern European identity of the Turks at the expense of the Ottoman Islamic one (Heyd 1954; Lewis 1981). Hence the use of Arabic linguistic forms such as Arabic pluralization rules—'suggests to some the shadow of Islamic reaction' in modern secular Turkey (Gallagher 1971: 169). The battle for the identity of Central Asia—whether it was to be Islamic and Turkic or Marxist and Soviet was also fought partly through language policies and corpus planning. The Soviets changed the Arabic-based script of the Central Asian languages to Latin in the 1920s and then to Cyrillic in the late 1930s to cut them off from their Muslim past (Shorish 1984). Resistance to the Soviets was expressed through the creation of indigenous technical terms by the Uzbeks (Fierman 1985: 218-9), Mordvinians (Kriendler 1985c: 249), and Belorussians (Kriendler 1985b: 353). Today, with their autonomy, these states give their languages symbolic status as a measure of their national identity (Rashid 1994).

**Language and Power Struggle**

All language is ideological in the sense that it encodes a certain world view; a certain conception of life. As such, language always wields ideological, often covert power (Connolly 1983: 139-50). Thus, language is the site of competing views on how life should be lived. The dominance of a language, then, always favours a certain conception of life and, by implication, those who believe in it. It is not merely at this deep level of ideology that language is part of the struggle for power. It is part of the struggle for possession of the domains of power between different groups, which are here called the elite and the proto-elite. In the previous pages the term 'elite' has been used to indicate those who possess power. The classical elitist theorists, though they differed on several other issues, agreed that a minority takes the major decisions in all societies (Pareto 1935; Mosca 1939; Mills 1956). The core of their argument was that, contrary to the assumptions of democratic theory, a small group of decision-makers, interlinked with each other socially and otherwise, exercise power (Parry 1969; Bachrach 1971). In short, all governments are oligarchies. This theory has been criticized on the grounds that in modern democracies power is dispersed among various groups and institutions. Pluralism, rather than oligarchy, describes the state of affairs (Dahl 1958; 1961). However, social and political change does occur and there is no single satisfactory explanation of why it does. Let us consider some of the major theories explaining events like language movements or language riots.

Functionalist theories, drawing upon the writings of Durkheim (Berger and Berger 1976), view society as being normally in equilibrium. Social changes, including language-based ones, alter the social equilibrium (Parsons 1951, 1966). Conflict theories on the other hand, based on the ideas of Marx and the elite theorists mentioned earlier, focus not on the forces which integrate societies but those which disrupt them to produce domination by a new elite (Dahrendorf 1959). The acceptance or rejection of language(s) is explained by both theories: the desire to accept a dominant language of wider communication because one's own language is ghettoizing; and the desire to create a new order by rejecting the dominant language.

Let us concentrate on language-based conflict in order to understand what role language plays in an overt power struggle between pressure groups, taking the example of such conflicts from contemporary South Asia. The proto-elites of South India protested against the brahmanical, Hindi-speaking ruling elite's policy of making Hindi the official language of the country in 1965 (Tambiah 1967: 231; Nayar 1969: 105). Apart from attachment to the Dravidian cultural tradition—of which language was a part—students from South India felt that they would not be able to compete for employment with students from the North, whose mother tongue was Hindi (Tambiah 231). The compromise solution was the 3 + 1 language formula, according to which English and Hindi share the status of federal languages. The state language must be learnt in school while people from minorities may also learn their own language in addition to all the others (Laitin 1988; Nayar 1969: 200-3). By compromising, Nehru enhanced the legitimacy of his government and promoted the image of the state as a fair arbiter of conflicting interests.

The lack of compromise can result in communal tension. In Sri Lanka for instance, the Sinhalese ruling elite made Sinhala the dominant language in 1956 (Gair 1983) and tried to use the coercive power of the state to create linguistic uniformity. This decision was opposed by the Tamil minority who asserted their own language policy, giving Tamil the status of a national language too. This has been a contributing factor in the acute social tension between the Tamils and the Sinhalese in Sri Lanka (Dharmadasa 1977; Kearney 1978; Abeysekera and Gunasinghe 1987: 243-9).

The situation in India and Sri Lanka (as in Pakistan) is not simply one of conflict between an elite, speaking (or using) one vernacular language, and proto-elites using another. It is complicated further by the fact that the elite of culture and power in these countries actually use English in the domains of power more than any of the indigenous languages. Let us look at this elite a little more closely. During British rule, the state had a virtual monopoly of power at least as far as educated people were concerned. It was the biggest employer and anyone who was even slightly educated depended on it for salaried employment. It is this fact which is given salience in Hamza Alavi's concept of the 'salariat'. He says:

> The 'salariat' is not internally undifferentiated, for its upper echelons, the senior bureaucrats and military officers occupy positions of great power and prestige in the state apparatus, qualitatively different from the status of its lower level functionaries. Nevertheless, they share a common struggle for access to a share of limited opportunities for state employment (Alavi 1987: 226).

Alavi's term is useful in other contexts but not for explaining the struggle between the 'upper echelons' and the 'lower level functionaries' in Pakistan. For the former, the term 'ruling elite' or simply 'elite' is more useful.[1] As La Porte points out, 'a synthesis of several studies' perceives the 'ruling elite' to be 'Western-oriented and Western-schooled' (La Porte 1975: 12). In Pakistan, as Alavi rightly points out (1972), the military and the bureaucracy have always been powerful, even when the country is not ruled by generals as between 1951 and 1958 (Jalal 1990), and after the death of General Zia in 1988.

Since in Pakistan both these elites are trained in English, it is not surprising that the ruling elite remains English-using.[2] They have access to positions of power both within the state apparatus and abroad through their ability to use English. Regarding English as a marker of high status and intellectual ability, they invest in it by educating their children in it. This makes members of the ruling elite supporters of English in their personal capacity, no matter what their official position may be. Such an elite supports the technological and bureaucratic aspects of modernization even if their authority is legitimized through religious or integrative symbols (such as Urdu and Islam).

Feudal lords from the rural areas, who may have political influence or street power, are not part of this westernized elite. They are, of course, always allied to the interests of this elite, since their power is informally upheld by them. There is an anomaly, however, since many feudal lords and their children are also part of this elite, having been educated in English-medium elitist schools.

The lower echelons, for whom English acts as an obstacle, preventing them from competing for positions of greater power on equal terms with the elite, may be called the proto-elite. They may be as a less powerful group who 'are (or feel) excluded from the power and influence that they covet, and . . . [who] . . . possess the personal gifts or material resources to move symbols and masses towards desired sociopolitical regrouping' (Fishman 1972: 15). In order for a group to be defined as a proto-elite, they need to be conscious of their solidarity, or at least the notion that they are a collectivity, and that they can challenge or aspire to challenge the domination of the ruling elite. In Pakistan, this has usually meant the manipulation of certain symbols, language being one of them, to confront the ruling elite. The leaders who move these symbols, or at least those who provide the proto-elite(s) with rationalizations for doing so, belong to the intelligentsia.

The intelligentsia shall be taken to include all educated people, even those who possess traditional, religious education. Most members of the intelligentsia are the products of modernity, and are primarily concerned with the way power and goods are distributed. They have a vested interest in creating pressure groups so as to challenge the power of the ruling elite. This may take the form of ethno-nationalism. In Hamza Alavi's terms this is the 'tendency of the "salariat" to fracture (or align) along ethnic lines' (1987: 226). It is the vernacular-using 'salariat' which uses ethnic symbolism and language which fractures. Hence, we now need to turn to the link between language and ethnicity.

## Ethnicity and Language

The politics of ethnicity is a problematic issue because of conflicting views about its nature and definition (Royce 1982; Isajiw 1974; Burgess 1978; Fishman 1989). The major debate about its nature is between the primordialists and the instrumentalists. The primordialists argue that ethnicity is felt as shared paternity, biokinship, commonality of descent, and blood-relationship (Shils 1957; Geertz 1963; Connor 1993). The instrumentalists suggest that it is a modern phenomenon which helps social groups gain a greater share in power and wealth (Deutsch 1953; Hechter 1971 and 1975; Yinger 1981; Williams 1984); that *interest* is pursued effectively by ethnic *groups* today as well as by *interest*-defined groups (Glazer and Moynihan 1975: 7).

That some feeling of group cohesion, whether based on real or assumed kinship, religion, language, or culture has always been present in human societies is undeniable. Smith has presented many examples of 'the collective cultural units and sentiments of previous eras' which he calls *ethnies* (Smith 1986: 13). This feeling was based on a 'myth-symbol' complex which Smith highlights (1986: 13-6). This brings us to the crucial issue of the imagination of which myths and symbols are a part and through which they can be manipulated. Let us then look at a very powerful theory, that of Benedict Anderson, about the use of myths and symbols to create the modern nation.

> These print languages [the vernacular languages of Europe] laid the bases for national consciousness in three distinct ways. First and foremost, they created unified fields of exchange and communication below Latin and above the spoken vernaculars. Speakers of the huge variety of Frenches, Englishes, or Spanishes, who might find it difficult or even impossible to understand one another in conversation, became capable of comprehending one another via print and paper. In the process, they gradually became aware of the hundreds of thousands, even millions, of people in their particular language-field, and at the same time that only those hundreds of thousands, or millions, so belonged. These fellow-readers, to whom they were connected through print, formed, in their secular, particular, visible invisibility, the embryo of the nationally imagined community (Anderson 1983: 44).

It was not simply the introduction of print which encouraged the development of the mythic or 'imagined community', but the imposition of the ruling elite's own form of language. For example, the French ruling elite made the use of its own variety of French (which it called standard French) compulsory in the political limits of the French king's sovereignty, despite the fact that there were not only other varieties of French but even different languages within these limits (Cooper 1989: 3-11; Jacob and Gordon 1985). When the modern British state was being created (Grillo 1989: 84-96), English too spread in the same way, despite the fact that there was no language academy in England.

As Urmilla Phadnis suggests, if the nation is an imagined community, so are ethnic communities (1989: 259), and language can contribute to the latter kind of reality construction just as it can to the former. If language is part of a perceived identity, does identity change over time or is it an unchangeable primordial given?

Identity is a highly elusive category. First, there is self-perception. A person defines himself or herself in terms of gender; family role (son, daughter, wife etc); occupation (and this may be seen as caste such as *julaha* i.e., weaver); tribe or class, e.g. Mughal, Pathan, Sheikh, or some other self-defining category label (Pakistani, etc.). In the Punjab, for instance, people defined themselves as Arains, Mirasis (singers and entertainers), Jats, Quraishis (claiming descent from the Arab tribe of the Quraish), etc. Thus, in 1942 there was a complaint in the Punjab Legislative Assembly that the 'Arain community is charged at a heavier rate' for the same kind of land as used by the other communities (LAD-Pun 13 March 1942: 316). In the same forum, a deputation of the Jamiat-ul-Quraish (society of the Quraishis) and the Mirasis were mentioned in another context (LAP-Pun 27 Oct 1942: 28). In these cases self-perception is the same as the perception of other people. However, it can be different too. The official census makers of the colonial bureaucracies, says Anderson, classified people by race (e.g., Chinese) whereas they classified themselves 'by rank and status' (Anderson 1983: 167). The Muslim conquerors of India initially called all the inhabitants to the East of the Sindh river 'Hindus' and their language Hindi because they lived in Hind (Rai 1984: 1-2). To make matters even more complicated, identity is made up of several strands. One may be conscious of being a Muslim, a Pathan, and a Pakistani, but one will define oneself differently under different circumstances. In a Pathan tribal conflict, one may call oneself a Mahsud or a Wazir, thus ignoring larger identity labels for the time being. In a Pakistan-India cricket match, one may feel that one is, above all, a Pakistani; while in situations like the Gulf War of 1991, one may define oneself as a Muslim. Thus perceptions of identity may be complicated because they are situation and context-bound. The situations may well be political such as that of 'internal colonialism' in which people feel deprived of jobs and power (Hechter 1975) and people may define themselves linguistically: as Pashtuns, Siraikis, Bengalis, and so on. How does this come about? And has it always been so?

Studies of pre-modern communities suggest that language was not the major symbol of identity (Smith 1986: 27). Many pre-modern 'rural persons, far from being attached emotionally to their mother tongue, do not even know its proper name' (Brass 1991: 70). Most of them, indeed, use local names for their languages. Indeed, they have purely local self-perceptions of identity. For instance, in the case of the Northern Areas of Pakistan, Leitner says:

> As in the case with uncivilized races generally, the Dards have no name in common, but call each Dard tribe that inhabits a different valley by a different name .... The name Dard itself was not claimed by any of the race that I met. If asked whether they were Dards, they said certainly, thinking I mispronounced the word 'dade' of the Hill Panjabi which means 'wild' 'independent', and is a name given them by foreigners as well as 'yaghi' = rebellious .... (Leitner 1889: 58-59).

In short, the Shina-speaking people did not see themselves as a collectivity nor did they define their ethnicity with reference to Shina in the pre-modern era. Foreigners, in this case the British, saw them as a collectivity and gave them descriptive ethnic labels.

Besides being local, identity was also familial and larger groups were seen as the extension of one family, as Fox argues about the Rajput clans of Northern India (Fox 1971). Such was the prestige of this identity that it even cut across religious identity—even as late as the early decades of the twentieth century when most of the Muslim intelligentsia were highly conscious of their religious identity. Thus, according to Rao Rasheed, a Pakistani police officer who was born in an Indian Rajput village:

> We had relationship with Hindu Rajputs. They were part of the brotherhood. In the Panchayats Hindus and Musalmans would take all decisions jointly. Before the Pakistan Movement the prejudice was not that of Hindu and Muslim; it was of Rajput and non-Rajput (Rasheed 1985: 18).

They were, in a real sense *biradaris* (brotherhoods) just as the oldest kinship structures of the Greeks were *phratries* (Smith 1986: 48). However, as suggested by Tajfel's theory of social identity, if a new identity was perceived as being prestigious, or useful, it was appropriated by those who wanted to take advantage of it (Tajfel 1981; Giles *et al.* 1977). Thus the Rajput identity was taken up by many adventurers in North India to raise their prestige (Fox 1971: 37-8). Similarly, in Bengal during the census of 1872, 'the number of Shaikhs and the three other categories [Syed, Mughal, Pathan] increased phenomenally, while the occupational "caste" groups registered a sharp decline' (Ahmad, R. 1981: 115). The occupational castes such as *julaha* or *nai* (barber) were looked down upon and there were many ego-shattering folk sayings and proverbs about them (see samples in Risley 1908: Appendix 1). Identity labels originally belonging to Muslim conquerors and rulers

(Arab Shaikhs, Pathans, and Mughals, etc.) were more prestigious, hence people appropriated them.

In short, even when identity labels were local, tribal, and kinship-oriented, they were changed when possible for instrumental reasons, i.e., prestige. Periods of transition and accelerated social change gave new impetus to this phenomenon. Social change was the most accelerated with the advent of British rule which brought modern education, printing, modern methods of communication—in a word, modernization—to India. In fact, as Gellner argues, the 'general emergence of modernity hinged on the erosion of the multiple petty binding local organizations and their replacement by mobile, anonymous, literate, identity-conferring cultures' (1983: 86). It was modernization which made language an important marker of identity. If the 'core message' of increased communication is that language is important, as those who understand it 'are included in a moral and economic community', then 'merely the possibility of one to many communication is enough to create nationalism' (Gellner 127). If 'it is the interaction of people that creates a sense of identity', as the interactionist theory suggests (Reetz 1993: 119), then the most relevant aspect of modernization would be the enhanced possibility of interaction. Equally important would be the increased role of the state in controlling peoples' lives and the possibility of social mobility through competition (Jeffrey 1986: 3). As all of them are consequences of modernization, ethnic identities may actually be created or asserted under modern conditions rather than forgotten. Thus, mobilization in the name of ethnicity in Pakistan is not so much in the name of the pre-modern local identities which we mentioned earlier, despite the fact that such identities are said to persist in part, especially in the Punjab (Waseem 1994: 102). It is now in the name of new identities constructed on the basis of religion or language, which appeal to large and not merely local groups.

This is so because of the possibility of transcending the local group through print, faster communication in person, or through the electronic media. This in turn makes it possible to mobilize communities through an appeal to non-local symbols. Thus French-men, to give one example, came to feel their 'Frenchness' and transcended local loyalties and identities with the growth of mass education, conscription, and modernization. In the case of France, as mentioned earlier, Parisian French was one non-local symbol which helped to construct the French identity and the 'imagining' of a French nation. In South Asia too, language operated in a similar way. This was not the local, spoken language which was known by local names, but the newly standardized 'vernacular' language(s) created by the British. The census too recognized these languages. In the hands of the bureaucrat, who finds classification necessary for control, language is a convenient classificatory grid because, as Sir Herbert Risley, the Director of Ethnography for India in 1904, pointed out: 'linguistic data are far easier to collect on a large scale, and far easier to examine when collected, than the physical observations which form the main basis of ethnological conclusions' (Risley 1908: 7).

There were, to be sure, other non-local symbols too. In South Asia the most potent was that of religion: Islam, Hinduism, Sikhism, and so on. The position of Islam as the major identity-marker of the Indian Muslims has been researched in detail (Brass 1974; Robinson 1974). Urdu was of secondary importance and was only one part of the identity of the North Indian Muslims in pre-partition India. Both symbols were manipulated by the elite through modern means of increased interaction. In this sense, the creation of a Hindu or a Muslim identity is a modernist phenomenon. Moreover, it is used for modern purposes—to gain strength by creating group-solidarity; to get a higher quota in jobs; to get a separate country (Pakistan). This is an instrumentalist explanation on the lines of Paul Brass (1974; 1979; 1991), though it concedes that the symbols (Islam, Urdu) would not have been chosen in the first place if there were no extra-rational, sentimental attachment to them as argued by Robinson (1974). Before 1837, when Persian was the language of official business and culture, Urdu was not regarded in a sentimental light by the Muslim aristocracy. Robinson's term 'primordial', if it is taken to refer to very old or historical bonds, is therefore not strictly accurate here. The terms extra-rational or sentimental are therefore used in this study for what other such studies call primordial. Both the elites and the masses do share a certain world view and certain symbols are more salient or have the potential to become more salient so that the choice of symbols is limited (Skinner 1974). Thus it is clear, that 'the leaders of ethnic movements invariably select from traditional cultures only those aspects they think will serve to unite the group and will be useful in promoting the interests of the group as they define them' Brass 1991: 74).

The use of the verbs 'select' and 'choose' suggest that leaders consciously and cynically plan how they will mobilize people on the basis of a symbol. This is a simplistic version of the extreme instrumentalist position. More often, there is a feeling of being dominated, being threatened with the loss of one's culture, as well as being politically and economically disadvantaged. In the case of the rise of aggressive

Sikh ethnicity in India, for example, despite many Khalistanis being very prosperous farmers, they felt that the central government had not industrialized the Punjab and had, somehow, been unjust to them as a community (Jeffrey 1986: 35). Thus, groups react to situations for goal-oriented, rational reasons (jobs, power, etc.) as well as extra-rational ones. The latter aspect is a vague desire to protect something intangible which can be described as identity, way of life, or culture. Often the impersonality and homogeneity imposed by modernity (Gellner 1983: 29-38; Banuri 1990: 78-84) creates a 'loss of community' (Smith 1981: 52-8) which is counteracted through an assertion of a distinctive ethnic identity. Thus, movements of cultural and linguistic assertion generally precede overtly political ethnic protests (Smith 1981: 23). Hence, there are extra-rational, sentimental reasons for manipulating symbols of group solidarity in addition to rational ones. While language may not always have been invested with emotional significance, it may come to symbolize intangibles which are primordial givens a sense of community, a desire for solidarity, identity, and the power and security they give us.

Thus, the subjective experience of actors in language movements—that they are struggling for something which has always been the essence of their culture and not merely for worldly goods and power—cannot be dismissed as mere rhetoric. It does have truth and for some people it is important enough to die for and to kill for. Such complications make language movements, the precise link of language with ethnicity, and the role of language in identity-formation extremely difficult to define.

## Notes

1. Hussain gives the following representations of different elite groups, counting presidents, prime ministers, governor-generals, martial law administrators and central cabinet ministers, who have been ruling Pakistan between 1947 and 1978:

|       | 1949-58 | 1958-69 | 1969-71 | 1971-7 | 1977-8 | Total | % of total |
|-------|---------|---------|---------|--------|--------|-------|------------|
| LE    | 40      | 10      | 2       | 6      | 4      | 62    | 25.2       |
| BE    | 15      | 19      | 2       | 0      | 4      | 40    | 16.2       |
| RE    | 0       | 0       | 0       | 1      | 0      | 1     | 0.4        |
| IE    | 7       | 2       | 2       | 1      | 1      | 13    | 5.3        |
| PE    | 52      | 27      | 4       | 10     | 4      | 97    | 39.5       |
| ME    | 1       | 12      | 9       | 0      | 11     | 33    | 13.4       |
| Total | 115     | 70      | 19      | 18     | 24     | 246   | 100.0      |

(* L stands for landed; B for bureaucratic; R for religious; I for industrial; P for professional, and M for military elites) (from Hussain 1979: 36).

It appears to me, however, that the PE and the RE are not elites in the sense of being the actual possessors of power as a collectivity. The RE has never actually held power, but possesses what can be termed as influence. Even this has increased only since 1977 when the opposition parties, which were mostly right wing parties, made an alliance to oppose Z. A. Bhutto. The PE, which has held 39.5 % of the powerful posts, has not held power as a cohesive collectivity. This is conceded by Hussain who agrees that it is weaker than the ME and explains the position as follows:

> For the post of law minister the governing elite always sought men who would rationalize, justify or legalize the political policies of the regime as democratic. The PE who occupied such posts often compromised their political views with the roles prescribed for them, and the more they became involved with the policies of the governing elites the less they identified with their own group. The esprit de corps found among members of the ME and the BE was missing among the PE because they were lacking in strong organizational development (1979: 115).

Since esprit de corps is the essential feature of all pressure groups, especially the BE and the ME, it appears to me that the PE cannot be counted as part of the real ruling elite at all.

2. The officer class of the military is educated in English and cadets are expected to use it even in informal conversation during their training (personal information). Officers use English more confidently than engineers, doctors, lecturers, or school teachers. However, officers are not recruited from the aristocratic elite, nor even from the upper middle class, as they used to be in British days (Janowitz 1975: 154), but are predominantly from the middle class (Cohen 1984: 54; Ahmed, E. 1980: 48-50).

As for the upper echelons of the bureaucracy, which used to be called the Civil Service of Pakistan (CSP), English, more than any other single factor, facilitated direct recruitment to it (Goodnow 1969: 162; Braibanti 1966: 259; Ahmed, E. 1980: 63; Kennedy 1987: 125). As English was the medium of instruction in elitist homes and schools, the system was skewed in favour of educated, upper middle class people. Out of 450 entrants to the CSP between 1950 and 1968, the income of the parents of 311 was Rs 500 or above (Ahmed, E. 1980: 53, Table 2.2). According to Braibanti, upto 1964 the 'middle categories (Rs 800 to 1500) have remained relatively stable' (1966: 272). Considering that the per capita income calculated at current factors was between Rs 242-351 in those years, it is fair to assume that the parents of CSP recruits were quite well off. However, even among the CSP officers the 'performance of those candidates whose parents were in the highest income groups, i.e. Rs 8000 to Rs 16000 and Rs 16000 and above, was highly satisfactory' (Quraishi 1967: 21). Muneer Ahmad also reached the same conclusion and points out that out of the CSP officers in Lahore, 71 per cent had attended colleges held in high esteem and which only wealthy people could afford (Ahmad, 1964: 62). In short, English could only be bought by the elite of wealth or that of power (the military or the civil service which ran elitist schools).

Writing in the mid-sixties Braibanti opined that 'the attractiveness of the service has diminished among Western-oriented families of some means' (1966: 259). This might well be true even now because very rich people go into business or join the international bureaucracy, where English is an asset. However, Kennedy gives the following figures for the monthly income of the parents of the District Management Group (as the CSP is now called) for 1980.

| Parents' Income in Pakistani Rupees | Number recruited in 1980 |
| --- | --- |
| Up to 5000 | 11 |
| 5000 - 10,000 | 19 |
| 10,000 - 15,000 | 20 |
| 15,000 - 20,000 | 13 |
| 20,000 - 25,000 | 19 |
| 25,000 - 50,000 | 19 |
| More than 50,000 | 9 |
| Missing data | 21 |

NB: Average per capita income was Rs 2,837 per month during these years) (Kennedy 1987: 119). Kennedy concludes that 'direct recruits hail from the upper-middle class' (1987: 120). Those who do not are exceptional, having learnt English despite having been educated in the vernaculars in childhood. This supports the view that English prevents, or at least makes it difficult, for vernacular-educated people to join the elite in Pakistan.

The English-using elite is called the anglicized elite up to the Partition. After that, as there is some American influence on the younger members of this elite, it is referred to as the westernized elite.

# 3
# British Language Policies and Imperialism

Language is an important tool of imperialism, defined as the domination of one collectivity over another (Galtung 1980: 107). The term 'linguistic imperialism', defined as the privileging or domination of one language over others, refers to its use by the elites of power, culture, and money in so many domains as to limit the access of speakers of other languages to positions of power and privilege. It also means that the dominant language is used to produce knowledge, cultural artefacts, and discourses which are privileged in a certain social setup. This kind of imperialism is related by Phillipson to social control as follows:

> Linguistic imperialism is also central to social imperialism, which relates to the transmission of the norms and behaviour of a model social structure, and these are embedded in language. This occurs whenever a socializing influence is exerted (Phillipson 1992: 54).

In the light of these insights let us see how imperialists, without distinguishing between those who settled down permanently in the lands they conquered and those who did not, used language.

When the English and Spanish-speaking peoples settled permanently in other parts of the world—the English in Australia, New Zealand, and parts of South Africa (the other settlers being Dutch-speakers); the Spanish and Portuguese in Latin America—and parts of North America they simply ignored the indigenous languages. If linguistic rights were recognized, as they were in North America, they were the rights of Europeans (Heath 1981: 13). In Australia (Ozolini 1985; Ingram 1988) and New Zealand up to the 1970s the dominant language was English. Recently, however, New Zealand's indigenous Maori language has been given some importance (Peddie 1991).

In Latin America, Spanish (or Portuguese in the case of Brazil) 'is both the vehicle of acculturation and the easily identifiable trait for maintaining prestige' (Hornberger 1988: 15). In South Africa, English and Afrikaans (a variant of Dutch) are the languages of power and privilege (Berghe 1968). This language policy kept power firmly in the hands of the European settlers till 1993, when the growing black power had to be accommodated.

Where the Europeans did not settle down permanently, they made language policies in their imperialist interests in order to rule foreign civilizations (Calvet 1974; Phillipson 1992). The French imposed their language on Algeria, Tunisia, and on the other African countries within the French Empire (Alexandre 1972: 77). By doing so, they created a native elite 'to satisfy the needs the colonies had for low-level functionaries and in some cases to satisfy European consciences about the "mission" to Africa' (Wardaugh 1987: 158). The Belgians were less hostile to the indigenous language, but they too used French in the Congo from 1877 onwards, because the area had over two hundred languages (Polome 1968: 296).

The British were apparently more tolerant of the indigenous languages but nevertheless spread English out of policy (Phillipson 1992: 102). That this tolerance too could be the result of certain political policies is illustrated by a study of the British language policies in India between 1780 and 1835 which is the subject of this chapter.

The period between 1820 and 1835 is known as the Orientalist-Anglicist controversy in writings on educational history (Mahmud 1895; Boman-Behram 1943; Nurullah and Naik 1943; Hampton 1947). But the controversy extended far beyond that period—it began in 1780 and, in a sense, has never ended. It was not only an educational matter, but was, indeed, connected with the political domination of India by the British (Spear 1938; Viswanathan 1987, 1989; Pachori 1990) and the philosophical justification of that domination (Majeed 1992).

This chapter argues that the Orientalists who believed that Indians should be educated through Sanskrit, Persian, and Arabic, as well as the Anglicists who wanted the Indian elite to be educated in English, both aimed at consolidating the empire. Their differences are traceable to a change in world view in Britain which made the Anglicists' views fashionable.

## Orientalist and Anglicist World Views

Since the publication of Edward Said's influential book *Orientalism* (1978), it is generally acknowledged that Orientalism—the scholarly study of the East by the West—created knowledge which contributed towards expanding and consolidating the empire. Indeed, as Said argues in his recent book *Culture and Imperialism* (1993), given the pervasiveness of the imperial idea in the Western imagination, there is little in the realm of language and culture which did not contribute to it. This broad thesis will have to be modified in the light of the major intellectual movements and changes in England, if it is to provide insights about the relationship between imperialism and British language policies.

Briefly, the Orientalist world view was partly based upon late medieval and renaissance ideas about a 'mysterious East' with fabulous wealth and esoteric knowledge (Chamberlain 1974: 52; Inden 1990: 48). The German Romantic Movement saw India as the land of the 'origins' of civilization (Halbfass 1988: 435). This attitude changed as Europe's military and technological superiority grew and the Orientalists became convinced of European superiority. But they were not yet unconscious of the past glory of India; indeed, one of the rationales they offered for their own role as mediators and for imperialism itself was that their scholarly reconstruction of the Indian past could regenerate India (Colebrooke 1837: 1-3; for the Asiatic Society's views see Kejariwal 1988). Their leading figures, such as Sir William Jones (1746-1794) and Edmund Burke (1729-1797) were conservatives (Bearce 1961: 17, 11-20, 27-33). However, notwithstanding the political uses of their knowledge, they did produce an appreciation of things oriental. Thus, the historian William Robertson believed in the intrinsic worth of Hindu and Muslim classical languages (Bearce 1961: 20-6) and William Jones praised the Persian poet Jami (Cannon 1970: 85) and the Sanskrit language (Jones 1786: 19-34). This meant that the Orientalist policies, educational and linguistic, were less disruptive of the Indian intellectual tradition than those of the Anglicists.

The Anglicists belonged to an emerging world view in England to which the Evangelism of the 'Clapham Sect' of William Wilberforce, the utilitarianism of Bentham and the two Mills, and the political liberalism of Adam Smith, Ricardo, and Thomas Paine contributed (Stokes 1959: 58; Bearce 1961: 65-78). James Mill's *The History of British India*(1817), argues Javed Majeed, was a major text of the new world view. It was a part of the 'debates about the shape which British rule in India ought to take' (Majeed 1992: 2). This history, boasts its author, was written without any knowledge of Indian languages (1817: 10-23). This statement, even more than Mill's explicit assertion that

Indian civilization was at a lower level not only than the Victorian but even that of medieval Europe (1817: 246-8), indicates how worthless India and its learning were in the Anglicist world view. Equally worthless, because 'romantic', was the Orientalist discourse, with its emphasis on, and worse still, its high valuation of things Indian (Chamberlain 68; Mukherjee 1968: 111). Here then was an imperialism which regarded imposing British culture as part of its moral duty—the 'White Man's Burden' as Kipling was to call it later.

This change in perception about India which took place in England from the 1780s onwards is documented in a number of studies: Stokes (1-47); Chamberlain (66); Bearce (20-35); Kopff; (1969: 236-52) and more recently in Majeed (1992). The change from Orientalist to Anglicist linguistic and educational policies reflects a change in the dominant ideology of British society, a change from 'revitalized conservatism' which 'was itself a response to the threat of the French Revolution' to utilitarianism (Majeed 1992: 2). So, unless all British perceptions of India are subsumed under 'Orientalism', Said's theory will have to take into account the fact that Orientalist discourses about India, although 'constructions', were less contemptuous of India than Anglicist ones. As Girish Chandra Ghosh, a Calcutta journalist, remarked:

> Jones, Colebrooke, Wilson . . . respected our fathers and looked upon us hopefully at least with interest, as you would look on the heir of a ruined noble. But to the great unwashed abroad today, we are simply niggers without a past; perhaps, without a future (in Ghose 1912: 434).

## The Orientalist Phase

Warren Hastings, Governor of India from 1774 to 1785, had Orientalist views and favoured indigenization as a means of governance (Mukherjee 79-80; Spear 1958: 513; Davies 1935: 340-1; Pachori 1990). The cultivation of the Indian classical languages, so as to conciliate the established indigenous elites of culture and learning, was part of this political strategy. Along with this went the idea that the British themselves should learn the Indian vernaculars, so as to control the 'natives' more efficiently. Both policies were political, their ultimate purpose being to help consolidate the empire.

To conciliate the natives, Hastings established the Calcutta Madrassah for Muslims (Hastings 1781; Fisher 1832: 1-10). Lord Minto established the Hindu colleges of Nuddea and Tirhoot (Basu, 1952: 12-13); and the Benares and Calcutta colleges were established. The avowed aim of these seminaries—one which is mentioned again and again in their defence—is that they would win the loyalty of the Muslim *maulvis* and the Hindu *pundits*. Any change in the precarious balance of power could be dangerous. Indeed, the rebellion in Vellore in 1806 was blamed by conservative Orientalists on undue interference with Indian culture in the 'pamphlet war'—the first instance of the Orientalist-Anglicist controversy which came to a head later (Philips 1961: 164).

The directors of the Company kept political expediency in mind when they agreed with the Orientalists, despite mounting Anglicist pressure for change at home. In a policy letter of 3 June 1814, they said:

> We have kept in view the peculiar circumstances of our political relation with India which, having necessarily transferred all power and preeminence from native to European agency, have rendered it incumbent upon us, from motives of policy as well as from a principle of justice, to consult the feelings, and even to yield to the prejudices, of the natives (in Basu 1952: 149).

This became the standard defence of the Orientalists in the General Committee of Public Instruction (GCPI) where the last battle between the Orientalists and the Anglicists was fought. In a letter of 18 August 1824, the GCPI warned the Directors, who were now pressing for change, that the prejudices of the natives 'might very easily be roused by any abrupt and injudicious attempt at innovation' (GCPI 1832: 72 IOL). But this defence was soon to lose conviction when the Indians themselves started learning English.

The policy of learning the vernaculars in order to understand and control the natives was never abandoned. The first link in this chain was Warren Hastings' proposal in 1773 for the establishment of a Chair of Persian at the University of Oxford, so that future bureaucrats could learn Persian and Hindustani before coming to India (Dittmer 1972: 60). The second and more important link was the establishment of the famous Fort William College in Calcutta by Lord Wellesley (Wellesley 1800 IOL). The third was the establishment of a system of language proficiency examinations for both civil and military officers, which continued until the end of the *raj*. So seriously were these examinations taken that the suggestion of the Commander-in-Chief, Sir Frederick Roberts, that army officers should be allowed to write Hindi in Roman rather than Devanagari letters was not accepted by the Secretary of the Board of Examiners (see letters No. 2523 of 27 August 1886 and No.

390 of 1 November 1886 IOL). Consequently, British officers, especially the district officers who represented the government (*sarkar*) for the common people, used the indigenous languages to win their confidence. Thus, the wife of Colonel David Lorimer, political agent in Gilgit, writes that he 'gave pleasure and evoked confidence' when he questioned petitioners in their mother tongue. The following account which she gives of her husband's use of Burushaski illustrates the point clearly.

> Sitting on the dais behind him I saw with amusement an electric shock go through the Hunza Nagir ranks in the usual place of honour on the right of the large audience: bodies tautened and leaned forward, eyes brightened, faces smiled; there was no mistaking the amazement and delight with which the Burushaski speakers heard their language for the first time on the lips of a white man (Lorimer, E.O 1938: 22).

The Fort William College and the Asiatic Society of Bengal gave modern shape to the vernaculars. The college standardized a variety of a vernacular and fixed it in print. In doing so, it gave it a supra-local name and made it an officially recognized language. This created the possibility of transcending local affiliations which we shall examine later. For the British, this knowledge helped them to 'understand' India, however reductively or negatively, and to control it. It is why Wellesley wrote in a letter to David Scott (12 Aug 1802): 'the college must stand—or the Empire must fall' (Pearce 1846: 212). His opponents, the Anglicists, did not quite see why Orientalist scholarship created in the college was necessary though even they did not dispute the necessity of learning the native languages for command.

**Anglicist Pressure**

The first pressure against the prevailing political conservatism came from the Evangelists. Charles Grant (1746-1823), an admirer of William Wilberforce and a Director in the East India Company, attacked the prevalent ethos through his *Observations* (1792). Dismissing Indian civilization and learning, he advocated the imposition of English as follows:

> The first communication [of light] and the instrument of introducing the rest, must be the English language; this is the key which will open to them a world of new ideas, and policy alone might have impelled us, long since, to put it into their hands (Grant 1792: 77).

Grant was writing in response to Orientalist works, such as Crafurd (1790) and Robertson (1791), which suggested that 'the Indian people had a way of life that was valid for them, however different it might be from Western civilization' (Embree 1962: 148).

This was anathema for Grant but he did give thought to the danger of Indians learning British political values and desiring 'English liberty and the English form of government' (Grant 92). He hoped, however, that they would become anglicized as English literature undermined their beliefs.

Grant's peers, however, did not take the risk. When Wilberforce, at the instigation of Grant, forwarded a Bill in 1793, suggesting that schoolmasters and missionaries should be sent to India (the 'pious clause' text in Wilberforce and Wilberforce 1838 vol. 11: 392), members of parliament opposed him. Sir Stephen Lushington and Randle Jackson pointed out that education would give modern ideas—the ideas of the French Revolution—to Indians and that would be the end of the empire in India, as it had been in America (debates in Woodfall 1793: 129-37. Also see Embree 154-55). Grant was defeated although he did manage to get the Haileybury College established in 1905. This was another institution for the training of civil servants, but it was in England, not in India. From now on, young civil servants would be anglicized before they left for India. The Anglicists grew stronger and the directors of the Company grew more and more impatient with Orientalist policies in India.

In 1819, James Mill became the Assistant Examiner of Correspondence at India House, and hence a powerful, practical influence on Indian policy (Stokes 1959:48). As his *History* was already compulsory reading at the Haileybury College, his intellectual influence was great. In India too, the 'westernizing' interlude of Lord Cornwallis, Governor-General between 1786 and 1793, had strengthened the Anglicists. The Directors' letter of 18 February 1824 to the GCPI, attributed to Mill by some scholars, shows this influence. Openly critical of the Orientalist policies, it stated with some acerbity:

> In professing, on the other hand, to establish seminaries for the purpose of teaching mere Hindoo, or mere Mahomedan literature, you bound to yourself to teach a great deal of what was frivolous, not a little of what was mischievous, and a small remainder indeed in which utility was in any way concerned (in Basu 1952: 153).

In another letter dated 29 September 1830 to the Bengal government, the Directors said that the natives were to be 'imbued with the ideas and feelings of civilized Europe' (in Basu 1952: 303. See another letter, ibid., 303-6). The pressure was mounting and it was the pressure of modernity in both England and India, to which utilitarianism contributed.

## Indian Initiatives for Acquiring English

For Indians, the advent of modernity meant that traditional ways of exercising power and obtaining wealth would change. Now power could be obtained by becoming junior partners of the British and for this English was a great advantage. In 1791 the Native Exclusion Act had excluded Indians 'from all higher government posts' (Spear 1958: 532), but a parliamentary committee of 1832 recommended that Indians should be employed in the civil service and taught English (Minutes 1832 in Basu). Thus Indian efforts for learning English, though confined initially to the Bengali Hindus, should be seen in the light of the advent of modernity and the new patterns of power distribution which it brought with it.

In 1774 the Supreme Court was established at Calcutta. This, according to Hampton, was 'the first real stimulus to the acquisition of the languages of the new rulers' (1947: 83). In 1816 the 'native gentlemen of Calcutta' subscribed Rs 113,179 to establish a Vidalaya or Anglo-Indian College (Fisher in Basu 1952: 27). At this college, 'Tytler's *Elements of General History*, Russell's *Modern Europe*, Milton, and Shakespeare were taught' (Fisher 67). This college had been made possible through the efforts of David Hare (1775-1852) and Ram Mohan Roy (1772-1833), both reformers with Anglicist ideas (Hampton 1947: 73).

For Indians, the greatest inducement for obtaining a Western education appears to have been upward social and economic mobility, which came through employment with the new rulers. In 1820, for instance, the inhabitants of the town of Panswell wrote to the Governor of Bombay expressing their desire 'to learn English that we may be employed in your service and maintain ourselves' (Parulekar 1955: 133). In a Minute of 13 December 1823, Elphinstone, the Governor of Bombay, noted that:

> A man with such knowledge of English as we require, would easily get 150 or 200 rupees as a Clerk to a merchant (in Basu 1952: 203).

Thus, it is understandable that Raja Ram Mohan Roy addressed a petition to the Governor-General on 11 December 1823, requesting that modern rather than only traditional subjects be taught in the Calcutta Sanskrit College. Expressing himself rather strongly at places, he said:

> The Sangscrit system of education would be the best calculated to keep this country in darkness, if such had been the policy of the British Legislature (in Sharp 1920: 101; for details about Roy, see Hampton 1947).

In 1827, native princes, chieftains and gentlemen of the western part of India subscribed Rs 2,15,000 for 'founding one or more Professorship for teaching the languages, literature, sciences and moral philosophy of Europe' (Parulekar 1955: 107). There was so much demand for English in the Punjab, which was not yet under British rule, that a schoolmaster had to be attached to the camp for this purpose (Trevelyan 1838: 167). Most of these demands came from Hindus, because the Muslims were still anti-British. The Muslim intelligentsia was probably influenced by a misinterpretation of Shah Abdul Aziz (1746-1824) who, though allowing its study, added that: 'it was abhorrent and, therefore, improper to learn English', either for a better relationship with the English or for employment under them (Mujeeb 1967: 398). In 1872, when Sir Syed conducted a survey of Muslim opinion, he found that English was still considered inimical to Islam by some orthodox Muslims (Khan, S. A. 1872). Even so, as early as 1814 there were Muslim students at Chinsura (Hampton 1947: 35). In fact, in 1835 the local Educational Committee of the Delhi College noted that Persian and Arabic were not regarded as qualifications for employment (Haq 1945: 37). Thus, at least the Muslim students of this college must have started realizing the importance of English. In 1835 according to Trevelyan, the number of schoolbooks written in English sold was 31,649, whereas the number for Persian was only 1,454. The number for Urdu (or Hindustani) was larger, being 3,384, as was that for Bengali (5,754), while the number sold in classical languages was very low indeed: 36 in Arabic and 16 in Sanskrit (1838: 69).

**The Anglicist Campaign in India**

In 1828 Lord William Bentinck came to India as Governor-General. He is alleged to have said to James Mill before leaving England: 'I am going to British India, but I shall not be Governor-General. It is you that will be Governor-General' (Bentham to Colonel Young, 28 December 1827. Quoted in Stokes 51).

Bentinck was receptive to the ideas of the champions of Anglicism. Among these were Francis Warden (see his 'Minute' of 1828 in favour of English in Basu 1952: 221), Alexander Duff, a Scottish missionary in the Evangelist tradition of Grant (Kopff 259-62), and the civil servant Charles Trevelyan. Trevelyan battled hard for the supremacy of Anglicism, and even before Macaulay came to India, he seems to have influenced William Bentinck significantly.

Writing on the political aspects of language and literature teaching, Trevelyan argued that writings in the indigenous Indian languages were likely to be anti-imperialistic. For Hindus, the British were unclean and for Muslims, they were 'infidel usurpers of some of the fairest realms of the Faithful' (Trevelyan 1838: 189). Those who read literature in English, on the other hand, 'almost cease to regard us as foreigners' (ibid., 189-90). English literature was, indeed, one of the most effective means of imperialist control over native thoughts, as Viswanathan points out (1989: 87). For these Anglicized Indians, reasoned Trevelyan, the British would be 'thoroughly necessary'. Thus it was politically expedient to support English and the Western sciences.

It appears that, far from being a passive recipient of other people's views, Lord William Bentinck had a 'system of education' for India (Trevelyan's letter to Bentinck, 18 March 1832 in Philips 1977: 777). This system was Anglicist as other letters suggest. Thus, the debate in the GCPI between the Anglicists and the Orientalists was reported in Manichean terms by Trevelyan to Bentinck. In his letter of 9 April 1838 he tells Bentinck:

> In the Committee [GCPI] the advocates of the old and new system are almost equally balanced. Sometimes Victory is on the side of darkness and at other times light prevails (Philips 1977: 1238-9).

He also tells Bentinck that the Committees of Public Instruction both at Delhi and Agra Colleges are of Anglicist views, as are people outside the GCPI (ibid. 1239).

In his letter of 30 April 1834, Trevelyan informs Bentinck that 'the liberal party has obtained a decided majority' in the GCPI and thus 'the last stronghold of the old system' has fallen (ibid. 1261). He also tells him that the Anglicists sought the help of the Press to defeat the Orientalists:

For nine months we laboured, as it were, under-ground in the general committee and tho' minds of many of the members were no doubt impressed with our arguments and prepared for the coming change, yet we were still in a minority, and it was only when we began to have recourse to the press and to apply a new power to the committee from without, that anything effectual was accomplished (ibid. 1262).

He proudly adds that now the way has been 'completely prepared for the introduction' of Bentinck's 'plan of national education', first mentioned in the 18 March 1832 letter.

**The Advent of Macaulay**

Before Macaulay was sent to India, Charles Grant in his letter of 23 December 1833 recommended him highly to Bentinck, saying, 'I anticipate great results from his appointment' (in Philips 1977: 1177). When he arrived in India, he became a member of the Executive Council of the Governor-General and the President of the GCPI. Meanwhile, differences about the expenditure of educational funds split the GCPI. On 21 January 1834, J. C. C. Sutherland, the Secretary of the GCPI, sent the views of the Anglicists (Bird, Saunders, Bushby, Colvin, and Trevelyan) to the Government (letter no. 2093 in Sharp 1920: 104). The next day he also sent his own views and those of other Orientalists (Shakespeare, H. T. Prinsep, J. Prinsep, and Macnaughten) to the Government (letter no. 2094, ibid. 106).

It was at this point that Macaulay wrote his pro-Anglicist 'Minute' of 2 February 1835. Macaulay's 'Minute' does not present any argument which had not earlier been presented by Francis Warden or Trevelyan. It asserts the supremacy of English and Western culture, holds oriental learning in contempt, hopes for the creation of an anglicized Indian elite, which would uphold imperialist interests, and recommends the use of vernacular languages for the education of the masses. Its virulent tone and the fact that Lord William Bentinck gave his verdict in favour of the Anglicists after having read it, have annoyed generations of Indians, who have quoted it so often that uninformed people consider it the mouthpiece of all Englishmen. Macaulay was forthright about recommending English and prognosticated that the natives would welcome the change if it led to increased employment. However, he cautioned:

All the murmuring will come from the oriental interest which we have, by artificial means, called into being and nursed into strength (in Sharp 114).

Even so, he recommended that Arabic and Sanskrit books should cease publication, the Madrassah and the Sanskrit College of Calcutta be abolished, and no stipends be given for the study of oriental subjects (ibid. 116).

It has been proved that Macaulay's 'Minute' did not suddenly bring about the change from Orientalism to Anglicism (Mayhew 1926, Clive 1973) although some writers hold this highly simplistic view (Nurullah and Naik 1943: 95; Abdullah 1976: 6). Even H. T. Prinsep, Macaulay's main opponent, wrote in his diary that the Anglicists 'entertained high hopes that his influence and authority would turn the scale against me and my supporters' (in Sharp 133). As we have seen, however, Lord William Bentinck's mind was already made up and there were more Anglicists than Orientalists outside the GCPI.

**The Orientalist Response to Macaulay**

According to H. T. Prinsep's *Diary*, Macaulay's 'Minute' was sent to him by the Governor-General, as education was one of his secretarial departments. He circulated it among the concerned officials in due course. As none of the officials responded immediately, he wrote a memorandum, dated 15 February 1835, refuting Macaulay's arguments (in Sharp 1920: 117-29). To Prinsep's annoyance, Lord William Bentinck 'would not even allow my memorandum to be placed on record. He said it was quite absurd that secretaries should take upon themselves to write memorandums' (Prinsep's *Diary* in Sharp 134). Later, 'there was a very hot argument' between Prinsep and Macaulay (ibid. 134). This unpleasantness probably increased because of the response of Indians, who stood to lose their income or social importance as a result of this change. The change from Orientalist to Anglicist language policy came through the Governor-General-in-Council's resolution of 7 March 1835 which said that:

> The great object of the British government ought to be the promotion of European literature and science among the natives of India; and that all the funds appropriated for the purpose of education would be best employed on English education alone (Sharp 130).

The Orientalists did not take this order lying down. H. T. Prinsep opposed it in his 'Minute' of 20 May 1835, citing the memorandums of

W. H. Macnaughten and Colonel Morrison in support (in Sharp 134-9). Brian Hodgson, a student of William Carey, who had died on 9 June 1834, wrote a series of letters in *The Friends of India* advocating the cause of the vernaculars (Kopff 251-2). This position, also favoured by Macnaughten, was against the 'high' Orientalism of those who favoured the classical languages, but opposed Anglicism.

A Despatch prepared by an unknown person at India House on 5 October 1836 (HM 723), but never sent to India, tells us that Macnaughten and James Prinsep retired from the GCPI 'in consequence'. The Asiatic Society called the changes 'destructive, unjust, unpopular and impolitic' (Hampton 101, 99). The India Office Despatch (HM 723) was alarmist, fearing that the changes would alienate the Indian elite from British rule, as were many Orientalists. The Indian response, however, proved that these alarms were exaggerated.

## The Indian Response to Macaulay

According to Prinsep's *Diary*:

> In three days a petition was got up signed by no less than 30,000 people on behalf of the Madrassa and another by the Hindus for the Sanskrit College. T. B. Macaulay took it into his head that this agitation was excited and even got up by me (in Sharp 133-4).

On 18 July 1853, H. H. Wilson commented before a select committee of the House of Commons that the *maulvis* held the view that the Government 'wanted to induce the people to become Christians' by discouraging their indigenous studies (SRSC 1852: 12). The Despatch of 5 October 1836 also attributed the Muslim agitation to extremism and proselytism (HM 723). The fact, however, appears to be that only those Muslims who felt they would suffer if the Calcutta Madrassa was abolished seem to have taken alarm. The agitation had the effect of saving the existing institutions of Oriental learning, though the Anglicist educational policy remained unchanged (Prinsep's *Diary* in Sharp 134).

The Hindu Bengali response was sharply divided between those who approved of westernization and the traditionalists. The traditionalists finally did become articulate and organized enough to get together in the *Dharma Sabha*. However, the immediate reason for this was the abolition of *suttee* (burning of widows) rather than the abolition of Sanskrit (Kopff 266-72). Throughout the British period, the Indian response to Macaulay remained ambivalent and divided, those who approved of modernization, especially those employed by the British, considered Orientalist policies ghettoizing (see Sir Syed's views in Panipati 1962: 29) but even such people condemned the ego-deflating language of Macaulay's Minute (Bose 1960: 66).

## The Death of Persian

The Anglicist policy of increasing the use of English in all domains of power led to its use at the highest level in the judiciary. However, at the lower level the British were concerned with eliminating the use of Persian which had been prevalent in all the courts under Muslim rule. As usual, the Company asked a number of people, most of whom had either served in India or had detailed knowledge of it, for their opinion. The extracts from the proceedings of a parliamentary committee suggest that the main concerns were administrative convenience, convenience for the Indians themselves, and, above all, political expediency. James Mill, when asked whether English could replace Persian, replied:

> There is no doubt that might be done, but I should consider it nearly as great an impropriety as the other. It appears to me, that not only ought the proceedings themselves to be in the language of the parties and their witnesses, but that the record ought to be in that language (Basu 1952: 272).

Most of the respondents did not think that the change would lead to political antagonism though Mackenzie did point out that if many people were deprived of their livelihood as a consequence, there could be discontent (Basu 1952: 280).

Such assurances of practical and political utility made the directors decide on the replacement of Persian. In their letter of 29 September 1830, they recommended that justice should be administered in the languages which people understand (Basu 1952: 170).

It appears that the Anglicists, or at least the more ardent amongst them, wanted to replace Persian with English and not the Indian vernaculars. Trevelyan notes that the Governor-General wanted English 'eventually to be the language of public business throughout the country' (1838: 146). In his letter of 9 April 1834 to William Bentinck, Trevelyan clearly relates the abolition of Persian with the triumph of British imperialism:

> The abolition of the exclusive privileges which the Persian language has in the courts and affairs of court will form the crowning stroke which will shake Hinduism and Mohammadanism to their centre and firmly establish our language, our learning and ultimately our religion in India (Philips 1977: 1239).

For Trevelyan, India was 'merely the stepping stone to the rest of Asia' (ibid. 1239), but this ambitious aspiration—which he wanted Bentinck to keep secret—is a fantasy about which no official response is available.

In the same year, Lord William Bentinck seems to have realized the political inexpediency of imposing English alone in India. In a memorandum on 'Reform in India' dated 1 June 1834 he wrote:

> The substitution of the English language for all the local dialects [is] very desirable, but would be an act of arbitrary power, and quite impossible (in Philips 1977: 1288).

Thus, the Resolution of the Governor-General-in-Council, dated 4 September 1837, replaced Persian with the Indian vernaculars:

> His Lordship in Council strongly feels it to be just and reasonable that those judicial and fiscal proceedings on which the dearest interests of the Indian people depend, should be conducted in a language which they understand (in Malaviya 1897: 3, Appendix 49).

This change too was resented by the Orientalists who saw it as an Anglicist victory. H. T. Prinsep commented thus upon it in his *Diary*.

> It had been yielded to this party [the Anglicist or English lobby] during Lord Bentinck's administration to require the law courts proceedings to be recorded in the vernacular language of the several districts instead of uniformly in Persian in all districts (in Sharp 1920: 132-3).

The Anglicists, of course, celebrated their triumph. Trevelyan, for instance, wrote that Persian had 'disappeared from the collector's office [in Bengal] at the end of a month almost as completely as if it had never been used. It melted away like snow' (1838: 144).

Along with Persian, the cultural ascendancy of the Muslims too melted away. This is why Pakistani writers regard this step as a British conspiracy to do away with the last symbol of Muslim rule (Abdullah 1976: 6; Naushahi 1988:8). However, because Persian was replaced not by English but by the vernacular languages, the vernaculars were officially recognized and strengthened. This means that the groups which spoke these vernaculars could begin to see themselves as nationalities. Whether this was part of a deliberate British policy of divide and rule cannot be ascertained, though individual British officers did suggest that a deliberate policy of creating ethno-nationalism be adopted. Raverty, for instance, suggests that Pashto-speaking people be recruited in all the regiments of the army:

> What would be better still, as tending to secure a praiseworthy emulation and rivalry, and, in case of accident, enabling us to employ one race against the other, and prevent combination—we should form them into distinct corps, according to their nationality (Raverty 1860: IV).

Whether such policies were followed, and if so, to what extent, does not concern us here. What is relevant is that the British policy towards the vernaculars did create identities and mobilization which were partly language-based, as we shall see later.

The results of the changes discussed above were revolutionary. The replacement of the classical languages of India with English symbolized the death of the old order in both England and India. In England conservatism died; in India Orientalist policies came to an end and a new aggressive imperialism began. For the new imperialists (Anglicists), India was not a place of mystery or wisdom, but a backward, ignorant, and superstitious country which they would reform through modernization, for which the English language was a major vehicle. The Indian elite, which the Anglicist policies created, did indeed become the junior partners of their imperialist masters as the Anglicists had predicted. Among them, however, were people who opposed imperialism on the strength of Western ideas, as the Orientalists had predicted.

# 4

# The Vernacular-English Controversy

In a certain sense, the 'vernaculars' of India were a British construct. The Indian languages had, of course, existed from time immemorial, and some had rich literary traditions before the British arrived. However, the dissemination of the written word on a wide scale through printing and marketing was new, and moreover, so was the use of indigenous languages in the domains of power. Language planning activities—the choice of a single dialect, the choice of spellings, the choice of an orthographic system, the writing of dictionaries—were essentially modern phenomena. They were undertaken by the British who, in that sense, created the modern vernaculars. One of their creations, Hindustani, 'would subsume numerous linguistic varieties and their literatures into a single, standard language' This standard language was then used for official purposes (Lelyveld 1993: 668; Cohn 1985:300-7). Linguistic surveys, like Grierson's (1903-21), reflected the classificatory criteria of the surveyors. As Lelyveld correctly points out, the census reports and surveys 'reflect a state preferring to keep order in a society that it considers inherently disunited' (ibid. 1993: 681). Even more importantly, local divisions, vaguely articulated through unrecorded local names of languages, were ignored in favour of larger divisions, contingent upon the newly standardized printed 'vernaculars'. One aspect of this phenomenon was that the vernacular could be used by the indigenous proto-elite against colonial domination.

## The Vernacular as an Anti-Colonial Symbol

This use of indigenous languages, as a symbol of identity and pride can be seen in both Europe and the ex-colonies, In Europe, the Poles took a fierce pride in the Polish language during the occupation of Poland by Russia, Prussia, and Austria. Although the Russians (Rudnyckyj 1976:

15) and the Germans (Niedzielski 1979: 137) tried to suppress the language, it was privately developed and taught to children (ibid. 137-140) and an anti-language, based upon it, was later developed to resist Communist rule (Wierzbicka 1990). In Ireland, despite the use of English by most Irishmen, Irish Gaelic was and is used as a symbol of pride in Irish nationalism and resistance to British rule (Macnamara 1971: 68). This is despite the fact that, at least in Ireland, the language imposed by the state (English) was and is being used in all formal domains.

In Asia and Africa such as part of the anti-colonial struggle were only meaningful when the proto-elite was not divided by language. In Vietnam, which was ruled by the French, language was a weapon though 'hardly the most important one, in the anti-colonial struggle' (De Francis 1977: 258). In Indonesia, Indonesian Youth called for 'one fatherland, one nation, and one language' (Alisjahbana 1971: 180-1). This language was 'Indonesian (revolutionary Malay)' argues which became a national language as Benedict Anderson, only because 'Dutch had become the inner language of the intelligentsia' and Indonesian, being a new and egalitarian language, could express the new thinking (1990: 136-7). In Africa too, according to Pierce Alexandre, linguistic problems played a very minor part in the political struggle for independence, especially in comparison with historical European precedents (1968: 172).

One explanation for this de-emphasis on language in anti- colonial struggles is that they were generally led by Westernized proto-elites. English education had given them the very notions of nationalism, anti-imperialism, and democracy which were crucial to the struggle. Moreover, it was English which had given them elitist status and could art as their weapon in ensuring that power would not pass to the traditional indigenously educated proto-elite which was their rival.

In a sense, this was also the situation in India. Here, languages had a divisive potential. First, there was the vertical division between the westernized English-using Indian elite and the vernacular proto-elites. Then there were the horizontal divisions, between the proto-elites which used or identified with different vernacular languages. The division between Hindi and Urdu, as we will see, contributed to the partition of India. In this chapter, however, we shall see how the vertical division was created through language.

The British policy-makers, including the most ardent of Anglicists, never advocated the teaching of English to the Indian masses (Warden 1828: 221). Even Macaulay had said that such a thing was 'impossible with us, with our limited means' (Macaulay 1835: 116). For some time after 1835, some Anglicists even opposed teaching the masses in the vernaculars.

## The Bombay English-Vernacular Controversy

In Bombay, the Bombay School and School Book Society was created in 1822 'with the sole object of promoting native education through native languages' (Parulekar 1955: xvi). This society, which came to be known simply as the Bombay Native Education Society after 1827, reported as early as 1819 that the 'general design is to teach both the English and native languages' (Parulekar 7). The Bombay Educational Society, established in 1815 to teach poor Europeans and Eurasians, reported that although only English had been taught in its schools earlier, now (in 1820) 'means are taken for introducing the native languages' (Parulekar 21). The vernaculars were becoming established in schools when Sir Erskine Perry, a judge of the High Court, became the President of the Board of Education in 1843. Perry and his supporters championed the cause of English with reference to Macaulay's and Auckland's famous Minutes (Richey 1922: 14-6). The supporters of the vernaculars argued that education could not be disseminated through a foreign language (Sunkersett 1847). Colonel. George Jervis, once the Secretary of the Native Education Society, even argued against the creation of an anglicized elite—the very aim of the Anglicist policy.

> [T]he fruits [of English education will] be restricted to a number of scribes and inferior Agents for Public and Private offices, and a few enlightened individuals,—isolated by their very superiority, from their fellow countrymen (Jervis 1847: 12).

Jervis was an exception in that he expressed humane, if not anti-imperialist sentiments, when he compared the role of English in India to that of Latin in medieval Europe. He argued, that the British rulers should not impose 'the burden of the foreign language of a handful of Rulers on the Millions of our Native Population' (Jervis 12).

The controversy became almost as vehement as the Anglicist-Orientalist Controversy (Richey 1922: 1-25). Colonel Jervis was supported by the native members the Board of Education, Muhammad Ibrahim Muckba (see letter of 1 May 1847 in Richey 16-7) and

Juggonath Sunkersett, while Perry had other member, Escombe and Mc Lennan on his side (Perry's letter of 9 April 1848 in Richey 22). In 1847 the question was submitted to the Government by Perry, the President of the Board (Minute of 14 April 1847 in Richey 14-6). The Governor-General-in-Council did not favour eliminating vernacular education as the following reply indicates.

> The chief and greatest exertions should, however, be directed to the promotion generally of Education, by means of Vernacular classes and schools. Good elementary works in the Vernacular, on science, literature, and morals ought to be provided; while the efforts in English should be confined to a school in each Province, and the College at the Presidency, where moreover the higher branches of learning should be taught also in the Vernacular tongue, as the progress of translations may enable this to be effected. (Richey 1922: 20).

**The Rationale for Vernacularization**

The reply given above was in keeping with the policy which Macaulay's Minute had recommended: the teaching of the elite in English, and of the others in the vernaculars. In view of the fact that many British officers agreed that subordinate positions could be filled by cheap Indian labour rather than expensive British labour (see their statements in Basu 1952: 267-305), it is not surprising that the vernaculars were favoured.

Throughout the nineteenth century one finds reports on education announcing jubilantly that the desire for acquiring English was increasing in Oudh (RPI-O 1869: 112), the Punjab (RPI-P 1871: 3), and even in the present NWFP which was then in the Punjab (RPI-P 1877 and 1888: 52 & 42 respectively). But the policy was to invest money only in the 'good English schools' in the cities (RPI-P 1871: 49) and to make people pay for them (RPI-P 1900: 42). This policy of encouraging English for the few (RPI-O 1869: 112) ensured that English, the major means of becoming a junior partner in the exercise of power, would only be available to a narrow elite with money, (the Indian aristocracy), power (the aristocracy and the higher bureaucracy), and talent (those exceptionally talented Indians who could rise from humble backgrounds because of their special abilities). It was also one of the reasons why the British tended to discourage all demands to vernacularize the universities or the civil service till the last few years of their rule.

## Indian Support of the Vernaculars for Higher Education

The Orientalists who supported the vernaculars—even the humane ones like Jervis—were British officers who did not oppose British imperialism. Thus, while the government was prepared to listen to their views, it did not extend this favour to Indians, who supported the vernaculars with a view to creating or preserving a separate identity. Muslims in Pakistan, were considered generally more aggressive, independent, and susceptible to chauvinism by the British, so attempts at creating a purely Muslim, university-educated elite could only be looked upon with misgivings. Such misgivings were strengthened during the anti-British upheaval of 1857, when some Muslims associated with Oriental education proved to be anti-British. It was pointed out, for instance, that the senior teacher of the Oriental Department at Bareilly was suspected of being anti-British and the Head Moulvi of the Oriental Department at Agra College actually worked one of the guns at Delhi during the upheaval. Thus, these two colleges as well as the Ajmer school were changed in 1858-59 to Anglo-Vernacular ones and their Oriental departments eliminated (GAD-NWP: 1868).

In the light of this background it may be understood why attempts by Muslims to make Urdu the medium of instruction at the higher level in British India did not succeed. Sir Syed Ahmad Khan (1817-99), for example formed the British Indian Association (BIA) in 1866 in order to promote the welfare of Indian Muslims through education. At that time, he was convinced only of the necessity of imparting European learning and did not feel that this could be done through the medium of English. In a memorandum submitted to the Secretary of State on 31 August 1869, Sir Syed wrote:

> Now, it is my firm opinion that even supposing the present system of Instruction, European as well as Vernacular, were to prove successful in educating the Natives up to the desired point—such instruction could not be of the least benefit to India; because as it will ever be found an impossibility for the English language to supersede that of Hindustan, the utmost, therefore, that these English colleges can effect will be to train up a very small number of Natives. But as the Vernacular education is of so low a degree as to preclude any, the smallest, expectation of India being, in any degree, enlightened hereby (Khan, S.A 1869: 115).

As enlightenment of the Indians was not the primary consideration of the British government, this argument could not have carried much weight with the authorities. Sir Syed was also the moving spirit behind the BIA. Hence, he can also be identified with the views of that body as expressed in the following petition:

> We very humbly but earnestly solicit the Government of India to establish a system of public education of the highest class, in which the arts, sciences, and other branches of literature may be taught through the instrumentality of the vernacular; that an examination in the vernacular be annually held in those very subjects in which the student is now examined in English in the Calcutta University; and that degrees now conferred on English students for proficiency in various departments of knowledge, be likewise conferred on the student who successfully passes in the same subjects in the vernacular; and finally, that either a vernacular department be attached to the Calcutta University, or an independent vernacular university be created for the North Western Provinces (BIA 1867 in Malik, H. 1989: 42-3).

The BIA gave the examples of the Thomson Civil Engineering College at Roorke and the vernacular department of the Medical College at Agra, where professional subjects were taught through the vernaculars (ibid. 41). Although the BIA did not oppose education in English but merely desired to extend the scope of education in the vernaculars the British government was not in favour of doing so.

One reason for this was that the Hindus demanded Hindi rather than Urdu for a vernacular university (Gungooly 1868). The other was that at least some Englishmen regarded English as a defence against Muslim activism. Thus in November 1867, Kempson, the Director of Instruction of the North Western Provinces, approvingly quoted in his report the words of a 'native' gentleman from Lucknow who reportedly said that 'the country would either fall prey to the rapacity of a second Mahmud of Ghazni' or to anarchy if English was removed (GAD-NWP 1868). Kempson did not trust the intellectual effect of Hindu studies either. In the same report, he suggests that Sanskrit should be taught under European supervision and that the government should not encourage it.

Possibly for these reasons EC. Bayley, Secretary to the Government of India, wrote to the BIA on 5 September 1867 that whereas the vernaculars could be used for basic schooling, there were not enough translations available in them for undertaking higher education. Since 'the object of university education is not merely or principally to secure a knowledge of certain specified books, but to prepare and fit the mind for the pursuit of knowledge in the wide sphere of European science and literature and for some time to come this can probably be carried on by natives of India only through the medium of the English language' (In Malik, H 1989: 49). This is how the first attempt at introducing Urdu at the college and university level failed.

While presenting the idea of a Vernacular university in 1867, the BIA referred to the Punjab Government's having admission in the same year to 'the necessity of an Oriental University' (in Malik, H. 1989: 43). Such a university was the brainchild of the Anjuman-e-Punjab, which had been created by GW. Leitner, the Principal of the Government College of Lahore, in 1865. One of the aims of this body, in keeping with Orientalist views, was the revival of Oriental learning and the advancement of popular knowledge through the vernaculars (PUE 1933: 41). Sir Donald McLeod, the Lientenant. Governor of the Punjab, was also sympathetic to 'the creation or extension of a vernacular literature' (ibid 41). The Anjuman now put forward the idea of making an 'Oriental University' which would promote modern education through the vernaculars. In March 1868 at a public meeting at Lahore, Sir Donald declared that 'education be conveyed as far as possible through the vernacular' (ibid 41). On 27 May 1868 the Punjab Government asked the Government of India to allow them to establish such an alternative system of higher education. The Government of India declined. The Punjab Government thereupon asked for a university of a lower status than Calcutta. This permission was granted on 22 May 1869 but with the following warning:

> It is also understood that the study of English shall not only form one of the most prominent features of the teaching in any of the schools and colleges which may be connected [with it], examinations in subjects which cannot with advantage be carried on in the vernacular shall be conducted in English (PUE 1933: 43).

Thus, the University College, opened at Lahore on 8 December 1869, began with an inherent contradiction. On the one hand it hoped to promote traditional knowledge in the vernaculars, and on the other, it was tied down by the syllabi of the Calcutta University.

Inspite of the restricted nature of its Orientalist aspirations, the University College was criticized by reformist Muslims (RPI-P 1881: 8 j). Surprisingly, Sir Syed too was critical of it. In 1818. He wrote:

> The University College is even now an impediment in our way. And when it will become a university, and it certainly will, it will be a great catastrophe for the country, for the community [Indian Muslims]; for the progress of the country, and for the advancement of the community. We are told as a favour that our Oriental language and subjects are promoted. But we ask why and with what objective? The answer to this might be given in whatever sweet words but its result is the same: to keep us in a state of slavery (Panipati 1962: 37).

It appears that by this time (1881), Sir Syed regarded the teaching of traditional subjects in the vernaculars as a conspiracy against Muslims in particular, and Indians in general, since English, being the language of power, last the vernaculars ghettoizing. By this time, Sir Syed fully agreed with Macaulay (apart from his strictures against religion) and favoured Anglicist policies in general (Panipati 1962: 77-8).

**The Indian Nationalist Support of the Vernaculars**

While the general trend after 1857 was to manifest loyalty to the British, Indian nationalist sentiment was in the process of being created. Thus, among those who testified before the Public Service Commission of 1866-67, there were many who emphasized the indigenous languages as identity-markers. For example Phirozshah Mehta of Bombay remarked:

> I do not think that Natives of India should be entirely Anglicized and their distinctive nationality lost and submerged in Anglicism (PSC-Bom 1887: 188).

After the partition of the Bengal in 1905, Hindu nationalism increased and the Jaliya Shiksha Parishad (National Council of Education) was created in 1906, with the object of imparting education in the vernaculars of the country (Aggarwal 1984: 32).

However, as the Urdu-Hindi controversy dominated the educational scene, neither Hindus nor Muslims could direct all their energies against English. Hence, English remained dominant in all elitist domains, while the role of the vernaculars increased in non-elitist ones.

M. K. Gandhi (1872-1948), the most influential of the Congress leaders, was a vigorous supporter of the vernaculars. He regarded them as markers of indigenous identity and save the anglicization of Indians as detrinented to the nationalist struggle, since anglicized Indians were totally alienated from indigenous aspirations. Gandhi wrote:

> I know families in which English is being made the mother-tongue It is unbearable to me that the vernaculars should be crushed and starved as they have been But I would not have a single Indian to forget, neglect or be ashamed of his mother-tongue, or to feel that he or she cannot think or express the best thoughts in his or her own vernacular (Gandhi 1922).

Gandhi pioneered a scheme for rural education on the basis of the mother tongue. The Zakir Hussain Committee, working on Gandhian lines, declared emphatically that 'the mother tongue is the foundation of all education' (Hussain 1938: 17). But India had more mother tongues than any system of education could manage and not every nationalist recommended them. Lala Lajpat Rai, for instance, recommended the 'principal vernacular' of every province 'as the medium of instruction' (Rai 1920: 172). The Bengal Council of Education, under the guidance of Gurdas Bannerjee, a judge of the Calcutta High Court, gave first place to Bengali and Sanskrit for Hindus, and to Arabic, Persian, and Urdu for Muslims (ibid. 172). Urdu was not the mother tongue of all Muslims but it became a symbol of their identity which led to Muslims supporting it against Hindi. The Muslims also distrusted Congress, which, despite its secular philosophy and its Muslim members, appeared to represent Hindus only. Thus, many Muslims, especially those who believed in what came to be known as the two-nation theory, reacted against all moves which appeared to favour Hindi at the expense of Urdu. The details of this reaction will be found in chapter 5 on the Urdu-Hindi controversy.

## Economic and Social Incentives for Learning English

The Urdu-Hindi controversy was not the only reason for a lack of opposition to English. The Indian literate population's enthusiasm for English was its facilitation of upward social and economic mobility. It was a symbol of elitism and associated its Indian users with power, modernity, and social prestige. One of the results of the British conquest, as has been mentioned earlier, was:

> the establishment by each of the elites of colonies beyond their regional frontiers, colonies of English-speaking men who dominated the new professional life of the up-country towns (Broomfield 1966).

Those who learnt English managed to get into the apparatus of the state, such as the prestigious Indian Civil Service (ICS). It was to this economic and social valuation that Siva Prasad pointed in his refutation of Sir Syed's early enthusiasm. Writing in 1870, he argued:

> Even the grant of the same degrees by a University cannot extinguish the distinction of the English and Vernacular graduates; the former will be called English B.A and the latter Urdu, Hindi or such like B.A. and if the former gets Rupees 50, Khan Bahadur's [i.e. the ones proposed by Sir Syed] Urdu B.A will not get more than five. It is not the Arts or Sciences which entices the Indian youths to our Universities, it is the English language, the language of their rulers (Prasad 1870 122).

This discrimination against those who had obtained only Oriental education in the vernacular (those I call the vernacular proto-elite) continued throughout British rule and, indeed, continues even today. It is why the Earle Committee (1907-8), the Shamsul Huda Committee (1921), and the Punjab University Enquiry Committee recommended that English should be taught to the Madrassa students, so as to enable them to compete against their English-educated counterparts (i.e., the anglicized elite) in the job market (PUE 1933, Appendix G: xxvi; RMEC 1934: 74-5). The two elites were different, not only academically, they were different in ethos. Since English, not only as a language but as a social symbol, was at the centre of this difference, the next section will focus upon the teaching of English and the vernacular languages in relation to class stratification.

**Making of the Indian Elites**

The educated elite of India, before the arrival of the British, read Persian, the court language, as part of their formal education. Hindus seeking employment under the Muslim rulers and administrators also had to be proficient in Persian. Muslim divines, and even some Hindus, also learned Arabic and the subjects prescribed in Maulana Nizamuddin's *Dars-e-Nizami* (Mujeeb 1967: 407). The Hindus made the transition to the learning of the new rulers, the British, earlier than the Muslims because, for them, both kinds of learning were of foreign origin. The Muslims, guided by people like Abdul Latif and Sir Syed, later also made the transition (Haque 1968; Malik, H 1989).

Under British rule, there were two kinds of elitist schools in India: those for the hereditary aristocracy called the Chiefs Colleges' and those for the newly emerging professional classes called European or English schools (including English-teaching schools and armed forces schools which taught all subjects in English). Both kinds of institutions served political and social purposes. The Chiefs Colleges were meant to anglicize young rulers to encourage loyalty to the crown and preclude events like those of 1857. This was the principle of 'indirect rule' discussed by JM. Mangan in some detail in the context of schooling (1986: 125). In keeping with the 'white man's burden' theory, the idea was, as Captain FKM. Walter—the agent of the Bharatpur Agency—put it in his report of 1869-70, to 'establish an Eton in India' to help the princes come up to the level of the British and thus become 'promoters of peace, prosperity and progress among their own peoples and hearty supporters of British authority' (in Mangan 1986: 125). Five major 'Chiefs Colleges' were established: Rajkumar College (1870) at Rajkot for Kathiawar; Mayo College (1872) at Ajmer for Rajputana; Rajkumar College (1872) at Nowgong for Bundelkhand; Daly College (1876) at Indore for Central India; and Aitchison College at Lahore (1886) for the chiefs of the Punjab. There were lesser schools for the landed gentry too, the most notable among them being: Colvin Taluqedar School, Lucknow; Rajkumar College, Raipur; Nizam College, Hyderabad; Taluqedar School at Sadra, Gujrat; etc (PEI 1918: 183-5; Mangan 1986: 126-7). Here the emphasis was on English as the central symbol, and tool, in the process of anglicization. Lord Curzon, the Viceroy of India (1898-1905), believed that the young chiefs who were supposed to 'learn the English language, and [become] sufficiently familiar with English customs, literature, science, mode of thought, standards of truth and honour' would be allies of the British (Raleigh 1906: 245). The assumption that these English values and norms of conduct were intrinsically superior was, of course, part of Curzon's world view, as it was of most Englishmen. The political motive, of making the chiefs loyal to the Crown and so consolidating the empire was justified on the assumption that it was morally necessary to civilize Indians.

Accordingly, between 1897 and 1902, English was taught on an average of 9 out of a total of 25 hours in class one and two at Aitchison College. In the other Chiefs' Colleges too it was given more teaching hours than any other subject (Mangan 1986: 131). The Chiefs' Colleges, patronized by eminent members of the ruling elite including (governors and the Viceroy), had imposing buildings, excellent facilities for games and sports, paid high salaries to their British administrators (Rs 1250 per month to the Principal of Mayo College), and changed very high tuition fees from their pupils (Rs 4,300 per year at Mayo and Rs 1,250 at Aitchison) (Mangan 128-131). Such exorbitant educational costs excluded all but the wealthiest from such institutions.

Children of the newly emerging professional upper middle class Indian families, sought admission in the European schools. Here too, because such schools admitted only 15 per cent Indians (except in Bombay where 20 per cent were allowed), not everybody could get in. The schools which admitted more than 20 per cent Indian students were called English-teaching schools (PEI 1918: 185). These schools generally granted the Senior School Certificate to pupils at the end of their schooling. According to Sharp, this certificate is 'in the opinion of those who have had long experience of both systems of examination, equal to an ordinary degree of the University of Calcutta' (PEI 1918: 189). Such high educational standards did not prevail in the Chiefs Colleges (where the pupils did not have to compete for jobs) though they were much improved by reforms in the first two decades of the twentieth century instituted by Lord Curzon and his successors (Mangan 140-1).

The English schools—to choose a convenient term for all such institutions which taught most subjects through English—were generally run on the lines of British public schools, whether the administrators were missionaries or others. In the area now comprising Pakistan, such schools existed only in the big cities. In the NWFP, for instance, it was reported in 1938 that 'the Convent Day School is the major English school and Europeans also send their children to the 'Army schools' in the province' (RPI-F 1938: 11). By 1946, besides these schools, the following colleges also used English as the medium of instruction except in the classical and vernacular languages where Urdu was used: Islamia, Edwardes, Vedic Bharati, Sanatum Dharan, and the Government College, Abbottabad (RPI-F 1947: 51). In Sindh, the English schools were mostly in Karachi. By 1939-40, there were three in that city: St Patrick's, St Joseph's and Jufelhurst. There was one in Hyderabad (St Bonaventure's). The tuition fees in these schools were approximately Rs 99 per year, in 1938-39, while the government schools charged Rs 34 during this period. The progress of Education in India report 1932-37 pointed out that there was pressure from the Indian elite to admit more pupils to the English schools than the quota allowed.

> The popularity of these schools among Indian parents is thus obviously increasing. This is attributed mainly to a higher standard of instruction and more efficient discipline generally but there is also a tendency on the part

of the upper class Indian parents to send their children to these schools with the object of helping them to acquire greater fluency in speaking and writing English (PEI 1939: 236).

The number of Indian pupils in European schools, from the area of present-day Pakistan, was as follows in 1938-39.

*Boys*

| Province | Number of schools | Total number of students | Indians |
|---|---|---|---|
| Punjab | 13 | 1,507 | 240 |
| NWFP | 1 | 169 | 97 |
| Sindh | 1 | 281 | 53 |
| Balochistan | 2 | 241 | 85 |
| British India | 146 | 24,51 | 5,590 |

*Girls*

| Province | Number of schools | Total number of students | Indians |
|---|---|---|---|
| Punjab | 18 | 1,477 | 187 |
| NWFP |  |  |  |
| Sindh | 2 | 299 | 89 |
| Balochistan |  |  |  |
| British India | 216 | 28,322 | 6,286 |

(Edn Ind 1941: 110)

In 1939, another European school was established in Sindh which made the figures for 1939-40 as follows: 158 Indians out of a total of 617 (RPI-S 1940: 100).

There was no doubt that their schools were better than the Indian ones. But the 'higher standard of instruction' and 'more efficient discipline' were products of higher investment which the PEI report does not mention although it does provide figures such as teacher pay and cost per pupil which lead to that conclusion. The following figures are taken from government reports on education in British India, especially in Sindh and the NWFP, during the 1930s, when the Indian schools were being vernacularized.

Table 1
Average monthly pay of teachers in schools (rupees):

| Year | Primary | Secondary | European |
|---|---|---|---|
| 1932-1937 | 15-50 | 40-171 | 162 |
| 1938-1939 | 20-63 | 58-186 | 110-189 |

Table 2
Average cost per pupil per year (rupees):

| Year | Primary | Vernacular | Anglo-Vernacular | European |
|---|---|---|---|---|
| 1932-1933 | 13 | 22 | 44 | 251 |
| 1938-1939 | 14 | 21 | 58-107 | 188 |

Table 3
Average tuition fees per pupil per year (rupees):

| Year | Primary | Vernacular | Anglo-Vernacular | European |
|---|---|---|---|---|
| 1932-1933 | Free to Rs 2.0 | 1.4 | 22-48 | 75 |
| 1939-1940 | Free to Rs 1.8 | 1.4 | 25-45 | 87 |

The high cost of European schooling was justified as follows:

> The cost of European Education is high compared with education in India generally, the cost per pupil in Anglo-Indian and European Institutions being Rs. 156 against Rs. 14 only in all types of institutions from a university to a primary school. This, however, is not altogether a valid comparison and it is to be noted in this connection that 69 per cent of this

cost is met from fees and private donations; in other words public funds bear only 31 per cent of the expenditure (Edn Ind 1941: 113).

Even 31 per cent of the public funds (Rs 48.36) however, was Rs 34 more than the average amount spent on ordinary Indian students. Moreover, ordinary Indians were too poor to be able to afford anything but the free or cheap primary schools. The avowed intention of these schools, as the Indian Education Commission of 1882 announced, was:

> The instruction of the masses through the vernacular in such subjects as will fit them for their position in life, and be not necessarily regarded as a portion of instruction leading up to the University (Edn Comm 1883: 586).

The vernacular secondary schools were also designed to offer a 'complete course' in contrast to the Anglo-Vernacular schools, which did teach in English, and could lead up to higher education (PEI 1939: 77). Higher education was expensive—the average yearly fees in the colleges of Sindh in 1936-37 was Rs 153 and the cost per pupil was Rs 246 (RPI-S 1938: 21)—so the anglicized elite remained a narrow aristocracy.

## English and the Indian Westernized Elite

As mentioned earlier, the ICS was considered the most prestigious service in India. The service was initially closed to Indians but in June 1886 a Public Service Commission was appointed to see if the Indian demand for being associated with the governing of their country could be reconciled with the exigencies of imperial control (Seal 1971: 180-8). The Commission did recommend recruitment of Indians through open competition in England (Seal 181), but the examination ensured that only those with high competence in English could get through.

The Commission, headed by Sir Charles Aitchison, referred to T. B. Macaulay's recommendation of 1854 that the Indian vernaculars 'ought not to be subjects of examination' (PSC 1888 Appendix F: 37). It announced that:

> It was intended that the education to be tested in the preliminary competition should be an education of the highest possible English, and not of an oriental, type. In the opinion of the Commission it is necessary to maintain this principle (PSC 1888: 56).

Although a number of Indians requested the Commission to add the vernaculars to the examination (PSC Pun, Bom, NWP & O 1887), this was never done.

Commissioned officers in the army too were equally anglicized, as is revealed by some of their memoirs (Hamid 1988; Khan, G. 1993). They could be trusted to look at the Indian political scene through British eyes, as the following remarks about an incident in the Indian independence movement, by an ex-pupil of the Colvin School, suggests:

> The administration was having trouble with the Congress and troops were called out in aid of civil power (Hamid 1988: 88).

The 'trouble', from the point of view of the freedom-fighters, was an affirmation of the desire for self-rule but the loyal military officer who wrote the above saw this from the British point of view. The fact that this elite transferred its loyalties to the new states, and sometimes not to the state but to the ruling classes after the Partition, does not refute the main point, that they tended to be elitist and were alienated from the masses. A member of this elite, Dom Moraes (1938—), the Indian poet, developed a taste for English poetry when he was in his missionary-administered English school and had 'never known what life in Bombay was really like until Tendulkar' showed it to him (Moraes 1968: 80). The 'Brown Sahib', as V. T. Vittachi, a Sri Lankan writer, calls a typical member of the anglicized elite, was a social and linguistic snob and looked down upon vernacular educated people. In sartorial fashion and mannerism, he was like the English and lived in many ways like the British *sahib* (Vittachi 1987). Yet not all members of this elite were, or are, apolitical, Some, especially intellectuals, including lawyers and those who were not in government service, also absorbed Western ideas of democracy, freedom and socialism from the texts which were prescribed reading—Mill, Burke, Joseph Butler, and the liberals in general (McDonald 1966). Jawaharlal Nehru (1889-1964), the first Prime Minister of India, educated at Harrow and Cambridge was 'vaguely attracted to the Fabians and socialistic ideas' in 1910 (Nehru 1936: 25) while M. A. Jinnah (1876-1948), the founder of Pakistan, believed in parliamentary democracy and liberalism (Wolpert 1984: 12). Their political and social values were Western—secular, liberal, democratic—though they hated being governed by the West (Vittachi 17-9). This contradiction is not surprising since their education, and the texts on which they had been brought up, were 'designed to teach them to lead'. Thus, says McDonald, the 'political consequence of the Arnoldian cirriculum, in the Indian context, could only be frustration' (1966: 465). The most frustrated were the intellectuals and the political activists, who wanted to bring about change. Those who accepted the *status quo* and their own relatively privileged position in it, remained loyal to the British.

## The Indigenous Proto-Elite

The proto-elite in the subcontinent was in government service as well as outside it. Those outside it, especially writers in the vernacular languages, journalists, teachers, etc. were anti-colonial. Sometimes their anti-colonialism was a throwback to the past. In the case of Muslims from UP, it was inspired by the *jehad* (crusade) movements of the *ulema*, especially that of Shah Ismail Shaheed (1781-1831) (Mujeeb 1967: 391). In contrast, the anti-imperialism of westernized intellectuals was inspired by the ideas of individualism, human rights, and the right of self-determination. Sometimes, as in the case of Khan Ghaffar from the NWFP and Ghaus Baksh Bizenjo from Balochistan, members of the vernacular proto-elite fell back upon ethnicity to mobilize the masses. In general, the vernacular proto-elite was antagonistic to most of the ideas of the anglicized elite. It was traditionalist, conservative, or religious. Its inspiration came from sources which were anathema to the anglicized elite: interpretations of religion demanding a theocracy or separatist ethno-nationalism. This tension between the two elites, which would be left to share the governance of South Asia, would influence the way language was perceived later. (For a competent study of this tension in Bangladesh, see Murshid 1985).

## Vernacularization of Education

For the reasons specified in the last section—the policy of spending less money on producing subordinate staff and generating the political support of the nationalists—the British followed a policy of introducing the vernaculars as media of instruction in the schools of India. The Educational Despatch of 1854, generally known as Wood's Despatch, declared that:

> We look, therefore, to the English language and to the vernacular languages of India together as the *media* for the diffusion of European

knowledge, and it is our desire to see them cultivated together in all schools in India (In Richey 1922: 368).

The Despatch encouraged Urdu, since it extended all over India and was considered capable of development. The Education Commission of 1882 linked the progress of Muslim pupils to education with 'Hindustani' (Urdu) and made it 'the medium for imparting instruction to Muhammadans in Primary and upto the middle schools, except in localities where the Muhammadan community desire that some other language be adopted' (Edn Comm 1883: 597). Lord Curzon, a supporter of the policy of vernacularization, held a conference in Simla as a consequence of the Universities Act which was passed in 1904. Curzon noted that 'in the pursuit of English education the cultivation of vernaculars is neglected' (Basu 1947: 63-4). The native intelligentsia, perhaps out of nationalism, supported such sentiments. In 1915, S. Rayaningar moved a resolution in the Imperial Legislative Council recommending the use of the vernaculars up to high school level (Nurullah and Naik Part 2, 1943: 527). In another Simla Conference, however held under the chairmanship of Sir C. Shankarun Nair, the members did not go quite so far (ibid. 528). They did, however, agree to extend vernacular education up to the middle school level (class 8) so that by 1918 the vernaculars were the media of instruction up to the middle level in UP, the Punjab, and the NWFP (PEI 1918: 100). By 1938, the vernaculars came to be used as the media of both instruction and examination even up to high school level in Indian schools (PEI 1939: 98-100).

After the vernacularization of school education, educationists turned their attention to the universities. From 1924 onwards, conferences of Indian universities were held regularly. At the first one, held at Simla, an Inter-University Board was inaugurated. The vernacularization of the universities was often discussed at these meetings. The example of the Osmania University, Hyderabad, which used Urdu as the medium of instruction from 1917 onwards (Dittmer 1972: 124-34), was often quoted. In the Second Conference of Indian universities held at Delhi from 30 October to 1 November 1929, M. Enayatullah, the curator of the Bureau of Translation at Osmania, noted that:

> Most of the visitors must have come to the conclusion that the vernacularization of Indian universities, which is now under discussion in several provinces, is not an idle dream and that with courage and perseverance they can do for their own vernaculars what has been done for Urdu by the Osmania University (SCIU 1930: 65).

The annual report of the Inter-University Board for 1935-36 resolved that 'where a student has an option of taking an Indian vernacular, Hindi should be included in the list of Vernaculars, if it does not already find a place in the list' (ARIB 1936: 73). Later, at the behest of Aligarh and Osmania Universities, Urdu too was included in this resolution (ARIB 1937: 54 and 1938: 15-7). In the meeting of 1939-40, it was resolved that the medium of instruction 'upto and including the degree course' should 'be the mother-tongue of the students' (1940: 40). The universities did not, however, change the medium of instruction from English to the vernaculars despite the rhetoric about vernacularization. In 1940, for instance, Abdul Haq, a champion of Urdu, complained that there was only one paper of Urdu, and that of only 50 marks, at the F.A. and B.A. levels in the University of the Punjab (Haq 1940: 233). In the non-elitist government schools, however, the policy of vernacularization was adopted in earnest.

**Urdu in the Areas now Comprising Pakistan**

It has already been seen that the Indian Muslims regarded Urdu as a symbol of Muslim identity. Thus, the *Punjab Education Code* recognized Urdu, as well as Punjabi and Hindi, as the vernaculars of the Punjab (PUE 1933: 78). Urdu was especially popular among students because there were more books available in it than in Punjabi and because it enabled students to seek jobs all over northern India.

According to the Quinquennial report for education in Sindh (1932-37), despite criticism the government policy was a 'gradual gravitation to the adoption of vernaculars as the medium of teaching in High schools' (RPI-S 1938: 43-4). By 1937 the vernaculars were the media of instruction at the matric level. The number of candidates who chose to answer examination papers in the vernaculars increased in these years, as the following figures indicate:

| Subject | 1933 | 1937 |
|---|---|---|
| History | 75.4% | 88.7% |
| Classical languages | 39.3% | 62.3% |

(RPI-S 1938: 44)

In Sindh, the vernaculars meant Sindhi, Urdu, Gujrati, and Marathi. However, the last three languages were 'confined to Karachi' (RPI -S 1943: 45). Students definitely found mother-tongue teaching more comprehensible, because the survey on education for 1939-40 reported that the results were 'distinctly better' (RPI-S 1943: 40) though the 'standard of English teaching has considerably gone down' (ibid. 37).

In the Punjab, the NWFP, Balochistan, and Kashmir, the mother-tongue was not used for education. In Kashmir, Dogri was the ruler's language but Urdu was in official use (Kaefvi 1979: 15-7). In the Punjab and the NWFP the court language was Urdu from 1855 onwards (Chaudhry 1977) and this was the language which Muslims encouraged as their vernacular. In the Balochistan Agency too Urdu, rather than Balochi or Brahvi, was used as the language of schooling except in some private schools.

From the British point of view, the most important political consequence of educating the Indian elite in English was that language was never used by it as a major symbol of resistance. The westernized elite either served the British as junior partners or opposed them with reference to Western ideas of democracy, human rights, liberty, and legality, but not language. The proto-elites either served the British in subordinate positions or opposed them in the name of religion, tradition, ethno-nationalism, or language. However, language confirmed to remain a minor symbol even in their case, because they used a variety of languages and could never unite on this basis.

# 5

# The Urdu-Hindi Controversy

The use of language for the creation of identity—specifically Hindu and Muslim identities in the nineteenth century—is intimately related to politics. This phenomenon, called the Urdu-Hindi controversy, occurred in British India in the nineteenth century and contributed to the partition of British India into Bharat and Pakistan.

Most of the work on the Urdu-Hindi controversy is in the instrumentalist tradition, insofar as it assumes the pre-eminent cause to be instrumental factors. Thus, Jyotirindra Das Gupta argues that 'the Muslim League and the Aligarh Movement identified Urdu as the symbol of Muslim separatism' (Gupta 1970: 124). Paul Brass also emphasizes manipulation of symbols by the elite (especially the Muslim elite of UP),[1] Urdu being one of them, in order to protect its interests (Brass 1974: 119-81). Francis Robinson, criticizing this instrumentalist bias, argues that, 'it is not just the masses but the elite which understands and pursues its interests within the framework of the ideas it possesses for understanding the world' (Robinson 1979: 81). Thus, primordialist or what we call extra-rational reasons played a role in the choice of Urdu by Indian Muslim leaders as a symbol (Robinson 1974). The most detailed historical account of the controversy, despite its lack of insight into identity-formation and modernization, etc. is by Dittmer (1972). But since it is in German, it remains less well known in English-using scholarly circles than works in English.

The only book in Urdu on the subject (Fatehpuri 1977—now available in English translation (1989)—is unfortunately so polemical, biased against the supporters of Hindi, and uninformed (mainly because it does not refer to primary sources) that it has little scholarly value. A slightly better account is presented by Gilani Kamran (1992: 65-117). However, it also suffers from negative bias against Hindi and lack of reference to primary sources. Scattered references to the controversy are also found in most histories of pre-partition India.

This chapter describes the role of language in the shaping of Muslim and Hindu identities in pre-partition India. Although it was religion which was the main defining feature of Muslim identity, the Urdu language was also an important symbol. For Hindus, except for the religious parties, the symbol of religion had to be played down to avoid alienating other religious groups. However, despite linguistic pluralism, the Hindi language remained an important symbol in the construction of the Hindu identity during the same period. Let us, therefore, turn to the important question of what Hindi was.

## Birth of Modern Hindi

According to linguists, Hindi and Urdu are 'two styles of the same language . . . both have the same inflectional system and a common core of basic vocabulary; they differ in the learned or abstract words used and in the word order' (Gumperz 1977: 252). However, the style which draws its abstract words from Sanskrit, sometimes called 'High' or 'Modern' Hindi, is what is referred to simply as Hindi in the context of the Urdu-Hindi controversy.

As mentioned earlier, medieval Muslim writers used the word Hindi for the languages of north-western India with which they came in contact (Rai 1984: 1-8; Shardadevi 1955: 20-4). This language, however, was different both from modern Persianized Urdu and Sanskritized Hindi. The urge to purge Hindi of many indigenous words was initiated by Muslim literary figures from 1702 to 1755 (Rai 246-57). Shah Hatim in his *Divanzada* (1755), and the Lucknow poet, Nasikh, took Persianization to extremes and old Hindi (Hindavi), or Rekhta, changed to High or Persianized Urdu. By the early nineteenth century it was associated with the Muslims. In 1808, Insha Allah Khan, an Urdu poet of Lucknow, defined it as the language of Muslims in his book, *Darya-e-Latafat*. The more Persianized form of it, however, was really only used by educated middle and upper class males (generally in UP, Bihar, and the Punjab). In other words, it was really a sociolect, though the less Persianized version of it was more commonly used in Northern India (Rai 266-7).

According to John Chamberlain, a missionary who came to Serampore on 27 January 1803, the term 'Hindoost' hanee' (Hindustani) was a covering term for the languages spoken by Muslims as well as Hindus (Periodical 1800: 422). To Shardadevi, the 'first original composition in Khari Boli Hindi appeared in "Rani Ketaki Ki Kahani"' (1803). Insha Allah Khan, a man with considerable linguistic ingenuity, wrote the following preface, explaining the language of his story.

> One day I thought of telling such a story in which there would be pure Hindi words and not of any other tongue . . . There would be no foreign tongue or the tongue of the rustics . . . its Hindviness would remain intact and yet no dialect should be thrust into it (Insha 1803; 10).

And yet Insha could not escape the influence of the Urdu syntax (Shardadevi 1955: 31).

While for Insha this was a linguistic game, it was a serious matter for Hindu intellectuals who wished to assert a distinctive Hindu identity through it. Two people are known for having developed 'Hindi' at Fort William College: Lallujilal Kavi and Sadal Misra. According to Shardadevi, such a language was actually spoken in Agra, Lallujilal's home, and had even been written earlier by people who remained unknown (Shardadevi 82-3). Dittmer asserts that Lallujilal's work, like Insha's, was also a curiosity and he did not create modern Hindi (1972: 61). However, his books, *Sihasan Battial* (1801) and *Prem Sagar* (1803-10) became well known. He also established the first Devanagari Hindi press in Calcutta. Thus, Bengal became the cradle of not only the Bengali renaissance but also the Hindi renaissance, as the first Hindi newspaper *Oodunt Martand* appeared in Calcutta (Shardadevi 215). The first paper to appear in UP, on the other hand, was *Benares Akhbar* in 1845, in Benares (ibid. 221).

While the language of Lallujilal may have actually been in use, his successors used it to create a Sanskritic, specifically Hindu intellectual tradition. Such language planning activities have been reported in many countries including Israel, where the Hebrew Language Council decided to use Hebrew, Aramaic, and Arabic (i.e., Semitic) words to emphasize the Semitic ancestry of the Jews and hence their claim to Palestine (Fainberg 1983; Cooper 1989:124). In India too, the LP activities of standardization and graphization, in the case of Hindi, were carried on by Hindi organizations. The aim of the first was to replace words of Persian and Arabic origin with Sanskritic ones; that of the second was to use the Devanagari script instead of the Persian script of Urdu. This created what is called the New Hindi, High Hindi, or Modern Hindi, about which Rakesh Mohan Bhatt says:

> The policy of Sanskritization resulted in a variety of Hindi which was far removed from everyday usage and became almost incomprehensible to the common man. Second . . . the standardisation process resulted in a

diglossic split between literary/New (High) Hindi . . . and colloquial (low) Hindi (Bhatt 1992: 54-5).

In this process, intelligibility was sacrificed to the demands of politics. Perso-Arabic vocabulary and script were, after all, reminiscent of Muslim rule; thus, from the Hindu nationalist point of view, excessive Sanskritization was an anti-imperialist activity. Its major purpose was psychological: to make the Hindus assert their Hindu identity while decolonizing their minds from notions of Muslim dominance. But from the Muslim point of view, as we shall see, these were alarming developments.

## British Language Policy in Bihar

When Persian had been replaced by the Indian vernaculars in 1837, Urdu was introduced as the vernacular of 'the vast tract of country known as Hindustan, including Bihar, the NWP and portions of the Central Provinces' (see relevant orders in Malaviya 1897: Appendix 49-50). The Government, however, did not want Persianized Urdu to be used as the vernacular. An order of 19 April 1839 stated:

> The pleadings and proceedings be recorded in clear intelligible Oordoo, (or Hindee where that dialect is current), and that the Native ministerial officers . . . do not merely substitute a Hindoostanee for a Persian verb at the end of a sentence . . . (in Malaviya Appendix: 50; No. 33).

Persianization did, however, continue, but it was discouraged again and again by British officials (see orders and letters in Malaviya, ibid. 50-2).

Many British officers were in favour of accepting Hindi as the vernacular language of the people of Hindustan (see John Shore's opinion in Malaviya 11-3). The Director of Public Instruction declared in his report:

> Indo-Persian of the courts has no *raison d'etre* except as a remnant and reminiscence of Mahomedan sovereignty (RPI NWP 1873: 30 ).

Thus, it was not surprising that Sir George Campbell, Lieutenant Governor of Bihar, passed orders in 1872 that Persianized Urdu be replaced by Hindi in the courts of the province (for the orders, see Malaviya 35). This order was strictly enforced in 1880 by Sir Ashley Eden, who found that the subordinate staff had not been following it (for the effects of the orders, see RPI-B 1880: 100).

## Political Determinants of the Language Policy

According to Garcin de Tassy, the eminent French scholar of Urdu and Hindi and a supporter of the former, the British government favoured Hindi in order to conciliate the Hindu majority (de Tassy 1935: 758). He mentions an article in the *Indian Daily News* (reprinted in *Indian Mail*, 27 January 1868) which explains the political benefits of using Hindi in Oudh and the Punjab (de Tassy 758).

The British, however, did not favour only Hindi nor was their policy consistent in this respect. The major determinants of their policy were (1) the conciliation of the Hindu majority; (2) the pacification of the Muslim minority; and (3) the maintenance of public order. The language policy in Bihar was subject to these constraints as the following extracts show. A. C. Bayley, Commissioner of Patna Division, wrote to the Bengal Government on 20 May 1875 as follows:

> Hindi is the language of the people—the language in which accounts, zemindari business, private business, and, as a rule, private communications by letter are conducted; and why the courts should continue to use an absolutely artificial language, . . . I cannot understand (Chaudhry 1977: 426).

Another letter dated 9 July 1875, from C. E. Buckland, the Officiating Secretary to the Bengal Government, written to the Commissioner, Patna Division, indicated that although orders were passed on 2 April 1874 to use Hindi for official work, the Governor 'was strongly opposed to making Hindi the exclusive court language at present, and to this policy Sir Richard Temple [the successor of G. Campbell] desires to adhere' (in Chaudhry 1977: 427). Other letters by government officials express the policy of making the language of the courts intelligible to the masses.

One purpose of this policy appears to have been to make the government more popular by opening up government employment to Hindus who had no knowledge of Persian. Thus, A. C. Bayley, in his letter of 20 May 1875 cited earlier, wrote that 'The change is steadily opposed by this class of people who, as kyests or mussalmans, have almost a monopoly of the court language, and consequently of the court places' (Chaudhry 1977: 425). A. W. Croft, Inspector of Schools, also noted in a letter of 16 June 1875 that the use of Persianized diction:

> is to give the largest section of the people a substantial grievance, by excluding them from the most lucrative form of civil employ. So long as a document read out in court is not intelligible to any person, Hindu or

Mahomedan, of fair education, much remains to be done (Chaudhry 1977: 429).

Croft, however, warned the government against Sanskritized Hindi also. Giving an example of it, he concluded that 'nothing could be more intolerable or more ludicrous' and that 'the danger' which lies before the Government is 'that of committing itself to the cultivation of a language as artificial as the most Persianized Urdu' (ibid. 431). He also pointed out that it was not in the interest of the *raj* to alienate the Muslims while wooing the Hindus.

> The temporary block to public business would be a small matter compared with the political danger involved in the disaffection of a class of men about whom the complaint already is that their means of living are too scanty. The Muhammadans in fact would be ousted from public employ (Chaudhry 1977: 433).

Political expediency—especially the Muslim factor—also played an important part in the British response towards the Urdu-Hindi controversy in UP as we shall see.

## The Birth and Development of the Controversy

In his lecture of December 1864, Garcin de Tassy mentions the publication of Babu Shiva Prasad's history of India in the Devanagari script (de Tassy 1935: 428). Shiva Prasad (also spelled 'Siva' in some documents) was a supporter of the Hindi movement which aimed at replacing Urdu in the Persian character with Hindi in the Devanagari one. This publication may be seen to be the beginning of the movement which led to what came to be known as the Urdu-Hindi controversy. In his lecture of 1865, de Tassy mentions the controversy, pointing out that Hindi is considered the symbol of Hinduism (ibid. 542). In subsequent lectures, he mentions abstracts of articles in favour of Hindi. The supporters of Hindi believed that Urdu, being the language of Muslims, facilitated their entry into employment and maintained the superiority of their culture. Those supporting Urdu countered this, saying that Urdu was the outcome of a composite culture of both elitist Hindus and Muslims and was the lingua franca and not purely a Muslim preserve. The lines of argument were often blurred by claims and counter-claims: that the Devanagari script was more intelligible than the Persian one; that Urdu was intrinsically more refined; that certain words of Perso-Arabic origin could not be expressed through the symbols of Devanagari; that Urdu literature was erotic and hence immoral (de Tassy 539-46; 627; 700-4). As such pseudo-linguistic and moral arguments remained part of the Urdu-Hindi controversy all along. They have been mentioned here at the outset so as to avoid repeating them when they occur later. It should, however, be added that these arguments were born out of ignorance or prejudice. In the final analysis, the conflict was between different ways of life; different perceptions of history; and different aspirations for the future. It was not just a question of language and scripts in isolation.

**Sir Syed's Response**

According to Altaf Hussain Hali, the biographer of Sir Syed Ahmad Khan, the Hindi movement became especially powerful in Benares in 1867, when 'a few distinguished Hindus' made efforts to substitute it for Urdu in the courts of law (Hali 1901: 100). The next year, Shiva Prasad presented a memorial to the Government proposing this change (Prasad 1868). On hearing of Shiva Prasad's activities, Sir Syed wrote to Mehdi Ali Khan (Mohsinul Mulk) from England on 22 April 1870 as follows:

> Babu Shiva Prasad Sahib's initiative has made Hindus enthusiastic about eliminating the Urdu language and Persian script, which are symbols of the Muslims, from India. He has appealed to the Hindu members of the Scientific Society that the bulletin of the society be in Hindi; the translations of books be in Hindi also. This is such a proposal that Hindus and Muslims will not remain united (in Panipati 1976: 464).

It was on the basis of this letter and a conversation with Shakespeare, the Commissioner of Benares, that Hali concludes that Sir Syed had prognosticated the rise of separatism in India (Hali 1901: 100), a point which has led to claims that the Urdu-Hindi controversy created Pakistan (Haq 1961: 22).

**Pro-Hindi Activities and the Muslim Response to Them**

It was after this period that Hindus started supporting Hindi in earnest. A Hindu society at Etawah was especially enthusiastic about Hindi. The society opposed Sir Syed's idea of a university where Urdu would be the medium of instruction and recommended a Hindi one instead (GAD-NWP 1868). Deena Nath Gangooly, a member of the Hindu Society, wrote:

It is not therefore too much to conjecture that with the extinction of Hindi, the death bell of Hindu nationality will begin to ring (ibid.).

W. Kempson, the then Director of Public Instruction of NWP also favoured Hindi. In his letter of 24 July 1868 to the Secretary of the Government he wrote that Urdu and its literature 'are undoubtedly Mahomedan creations' and translations of scientific and other works into it are not 'at all likely to be widely read' (in GAD 1868). In 1877, the Government, however, made either Persian or Urdu compulsory for jobs of Rs 10 and above (Order No 1494 A, 16 July 1877; in Malaviya 1897: 30), thus encouraging the learning of Urdu.

In 1873, the Hindus presented another memorial in favour of Hindi to Sir William Muir, Lieutenant Governor of the NWP (in Malaviya 1897 : 10). In that year, the Urdu Defence Committee was formed with Sir Syed as its Secretary (*Awadh Akhbar* 12 December 1873). The members of this organization realized that Hindi 'will be most harmful to the educated Muslims and a setback to their future progress' (Circular letter in Fatehpuri 1989: 149). To promote the cause of Hindi, on the other hand, the Nagari Pracharni Sabha (the Organization for the Promotion of Nagari), was established in Benaras in 1893 (Nagari Report 1900 IOL; Dittmer 1972: 105). The Hindu version of the case, resting on the democratic principle of majority, was presented by Malaviya (1897). The Muslim response to it, resting on the assumption of Muslim superiority, was written by Hamid Ali Khan (Khan 1900?). The stage was now set for the intensification of the Urdu-Hindi (and Muslim-Hindu) antagonism in the twentieth century.

## The Controversy and the Education Commission

In 1882, the Commission on National Education met to consider educational issues including that of the medium of instruction. The supporters of Hindi submitted 118 memorials signed by 67,000 persons from different parts of northern India. In question and answer sessions before the Commission, a large number of Hindus such as Din Dayal Tiwari and Jai Krishan Dass pointed out that the vernacular of the common people was Hindi not Urdu (in Edn Comm 1883: 175 and 229); that Urdu had acquired prestige under Muslim ascendancy (Haris Chandra, ibid. 213); and that people taught their children Urdu only because the British had made it compulsory for entering government service. Even in the Punjab, where the Muslims, Hindus, and Sikhs all spoke Punjabi, the Hindus supported Hindi and the Muslims Urdu (Edn Comm-P 1884). Language was obviously a highly politicized issue everywhere in northern India by the end of the nineteenth century. In the next century, however, it was to contribute more significantly to Muslim separatism.

**Urdu-Hindi Controversy in UP**

In the early part of the twentieth century the Urdu-Hindi controversy gathered particular momentum in what is now known as UP. In order to understand this, let us refer to the position of Muslims in these areas, the role of the Lieutenant Governor and other British officials, and the supporters of Urdu.

Paul Brass has pointed out that W. W. Hunter's famous description of the impoverishment of the Muslim elite in Bengal (1871) is not applicable to UP but was used for political mobilization by most Muslim leaders (1974: 141). The census figures suggest that the Muslims were not a suppressed group in UP. Consider the figures for urbanization, employment, and education. (These figures are given in the original sources, government reports, and other documents, but here they have been adapted from Brass [1974] for convenience).

*Urbanization*

| Year | Total Population Hindus% | Muslims% | Population Living In Cities Hindus% | Muslims% |
|---|---|---|---|---|
| 1881 | 85.97 | 13.74 | 7.25 | 25.02 |
| 1891 | 85.86 | 13.82 | 8.46 | 23.34 |
| 1911 | 85.05 | 14.38 | 7.2 | 26.9 |
| 1941 | 83.67 | 15.43 | 9.0 | 30.6 |

Adapted from Brass (1974: 143)

For employment, only some categories should be enough to prove that Muslims were not under-represented in jobs. (The total population of the Hindus was 84.48 % and that of the Muslims was 14.28% for the figures given below):

*Employment*

| Kind of Employment | %of Muslims | % of Hindus |
|---|---|---|
| Lawyers | 28.07 | 63.49 |
| Medical Practitioners | 39.83 | 51.17 |
| Instruction | 22.47 | 67.64 |
| Letter, Arts, Sciences | 49.23 | 48.46 |
| Income from Rent | 27.58 | 69.61 |
| Army | 38.36 | 52.51 |
| Police | 49.79 | 48.98 |
| Service of the State | 47.67 | 47.37 |

(Brass 152)

The figures for education in 1871-72 compare favourably with figures in other provinces as far as Muslim representation is concerned:

*Education*

| Province | Muslims % | Muslims at school % |
|---|---|---|
| Madras | 6 | 4.4 |
| Bombay | 15.4 | 8.2 |
| Bengal & Assam | 32.3 | 14.4 |
| N W P | 13.5 | 17.8 |
| Oudh | 9.9 | 25.3 |
| Punjab | 51.6 | 34.9 |

(Brass 146)

These figures suggest that the Muslims of UP were, in fact, not a suppressed community. However, their own perception of their condition was different. They had been a privileged elite and nostalgia rather than realism dominated their worldview. They were convinced that their religion, culture, language, literature, etc. were intrinsically superior to those of other Indians. Thus, Hamid Ali Khan says:

> Though the Hindus, including of course all classes of them, constitute the majority; but it cannot be said that the entire body of them can claim the same political and social importance as the Mohammadans (Khan, H. 1900?: 38).

In a meeting held at Lucknow on 3 April 1914, the Chief Secretary of the UP Government noted that Sahibzada Aftab Ahmad wanted a census of gentlemen (*sharifs*). As the notes of the meeting indicate, there were '28 lakhs and 25 lakhs respectively of upper class Muhammadans and Hindus' (Meeting 1914: 7 IOL). Nawab Ishaque Khan wanted preference to be given to Muslims 'owing to their former political importance' (ibid.).

The Muslims knew that they would suffer in employment if Hindi became the dominant language (Chandra in Edn Comm NWP and O 1884: 200; also see Dittmer 95) but they also felt overwhelmed by the tremendous cultural loss the change would bring about. They were inordinately attached to Urdu literature and felt that their whole way of life was in jeopardy. Thus, for both rational and extra-rational reasons, they opposed Hindi.

## Role of the Lieutenant Governor in the Controversy

Sir A. P. Macdonnell, the Lieutenant Governor of the North-Western Provinces at the turn of the century, is known for his anti-Urdu stance (Fatehpuri 1989: 193; Robinson 1974: 134). On 2 March 1898, a memorial demanding that Hindi in the Devanagari script should be used instead of Urdu in the courts of the province was presented to Macdonnell. He referred it for comments to his staff. The Joint Secretary, Board of Revenue, commented on 16 August 1898 that the 'language which is spoken by educated Hindus and Muhammadans is Urdu' and that spoken Hindi is a group of dialects (GAD-NWP 1900). However, the Under Secretary to the NWP Government made it clear that 'the question of language is not raised. The question His Excellency desires to raise is one of character only' (R. Burn to Joint Secretary Board of Revenue, 12 July 1899 in GAD-NWP 1900).

Macdonnell, however, decided that: (1) petitions could be received in both the Persian and the Devanagari scripts; (2) summonses, proclamations, etc., from courts and revenue offices would also be in both the scripts; and (3) only people knowing how to read and write both scripts would be given government jobs (No 585/111-3436-68 of 18 April 1900 in GAD-NWP 1900).

The condition which could cause real hardship was the last, relating to fluency in both scripts. According to an official survey, nobody employed in any judgeship knew *only* Hindi or had only a slight knowledge of Urdu. There were people, however, who knew no (or very little) Hindi as the following figures illustrate:

| Knowledge of | Muslims | Hindu | Total |
|---|---|---|---|
| Urdu and Hindi | 5 | 111 | 116 |
| Urdu alone | 97 | 45 | 142 |
| Urdu and a little Hindi | 25 | 105 | 130 |
| Total | 127 | 261 | 388 |

(GAD-NWP 1900)

A number of Muslims, including Hamid Ali Khan, sent telegrams to the Viceroy, Lord Curzon, who recommended that rule 3 be relaxed for one year (letter from J. P. Hewett, Secretary to the Government of India, to Chief Secretary NWP, 18 April 1900 in GAD-NWP 1900). This, however, was not enough to appease the Muslims.

The Muslim reaction was predictably acute. Even Sir Syed, who was on his deathbed, wrote an article in favour of Urdu in his weekly *Institute Gazette* (19 March 1898). Other articles appeared in the Press both in Urdu and English (see extracts and references in Fatehpuri 1989: 194-200. Also see Punj O 4 and 22 August 1900, P 12 and 28 May and 1 June 1900; *IDT* 1 April, 10 May, and 5 July 1900). Sir Antony Macdonnell, who had been accused of having reduced the number of Muslims in government service (Punj O 3 June 1899) and of putting them at a disadvantage in competitive examinations by equalizing the marks of Hindi and Urdu (Punj O 21 June 1899), was now openly criticized. Nawab Mohsinul Mulk held several meetings in defence of Urdu in Aligarh and Lucknow in which the audience was brought to fever pitch against Macdonnell's orders (Punj O 22 August 1900; Fatehpuri 1989: 200-2). A number of letters also appeared in the Press against the orders (IDT 14 and P 11 August 1900). Macdonnell wrote in his letter of 31 August to Lord Curzon:

> The Mahomedans have had their field-day at Lucknow over the Nagri-Urdu Resolution, and much steam was let off. About 350 delegates assembled from the Provinces, the Punjab, Hyderabad, and Bombay, but the great bulk of the delegates came from these provinces. Of the 350, about 200 were lawyers, the rest were non-descript (Curzon Correspondence, 1900 IOL).

In Macdonnell's eyes, the lawyers were connected with Western-style reform of what Robinson calls the 'young party' (1974: 139; 358-9). Their opposition was, therefore, 'on theoretic grounds borrowed from English, and not from Oriental, analogies' (Letter from Macdonnell to Curzon, 19 October 1900 IOL). This kind of opposition, he felt, favoured pan-Islamic sentiments and anti-British militancy especially because the lawyers had allied themselves with the Nadwat-ul-Ulema Association in Lucknow (Macdonnell to Curzon, 31 August 1900). Such a policy, he felt, was opposed to Sir Syed's reformism, 'coupled with implicit reliance on, and obedience to, our Government' (ibid.).

Mohsinul Mulk on the other hand was not associated with Sir Syed's policy in Macdonnell's mind. He was seen as a leader of the new policy and his speech was termed, 'fulsome toward myself, insincere, contradictory, and in the end covertly threatening' (ibid.). Macdonnell, therefore, warned the trustees of Aligarh College that they should dissociate the college from politics (Macdonnell to Curzon 3 December 1900). Mohsinul Mulk, who was a trustee, was mentioned by name in a warning issued by the officiating Secretary of the NWP Government to Theodore Morrison, the Principal of the College (enclosure in Macdonnell's letter to Curzon, 19 October 1900). After this, Mohsinul Mulk decided to withdraw from the anti-Hindi agitation. These actions of Macdonnell confirmed Muslims in their view that the Lieutenant Governor was especially antagonistic to them. Simplistic versions of the Urdu-Hindi controversy, like Fatehpuri's (1989), have extended this alleged antipathy to the British in general.

The most significant pro-Urdu step of this period was the establishment of the Anjuman-e-Taraqqi-e-Urdu in 1903. It was first established as the All-India Educational Conference at Delhi and then moved to Aurangabad, Deccan, as the Anjuman (Dittmer 1972: 116-8). Later, under the leadership of Maulvi Abdul Haq it became the most potent organization for the defence of Urdu and was moved back to Delhi (Rabbani 1939; Anjuman n.d.). The Anjuman's most formidable rival, the Hindi Sahitya Sammelan was established by the supporters of Hindi in the Congress and outside it in 1910 at Allahabad (Joshi 1962: 581; Dittmer 148-50). Both the Anjuman and the Sammelan were connected with Muslim and Hindu politicians in informal though significant ways.

Macdonnell justified his actions on grounds of justice and fairplay. Denying that his motives were political, he confessed that British interests would probably be better served by Hindu dominance:

> We are far more interested in a Hindu predominance than in a Mahomedan predominance, which, in the nature of things, must be hostile to us (Letter from Macdonnell to Curzon, 18 May 1900).

However, he argued in the same letter that it was not politically expedient to alienate the Muslims.

> A political danger of considerable magnitude here intervened. The dethronement of Urdu, and the enthronement of Hindi, would mean an embittered war between Mahomedan and Hindu and the excitement of Mahomedan hostility against the Government. The time is not opportune for incurring that difficulty: I, therefore, refused to consider the question of the court language, but after three years consideration, I could not avoid the conclusion that the merest justice required that a man who approached Government with a representation in his mother tongue should be heard (ibid. 227).

Macdonnell also guessed that sentimental reasons motivated the Muslim protestors against his order. He wrote in this letter that the real grievance of the Muslims was that the Hindi script had been 'placed, after centuries of inferiority, on an equality with their own' (ibid. 228). The Viceroy agreed with Macdonnell and wrote back:

> I have not a doubt that you are right, and that the decision is one of equal liberality and justice. The howls of the Mussalmans merely represent the spleen of a minority from whose hands are slipping away the reins of power, and who clutch at any method of arbitrarily retaining them (Letter from Curzon to Macdonnell, 1 June 1900).

## British Policy after Macdonnell

The British did not, however, maintain a consistently anti-Urdu or anti-Muslim policy. Sir J. D. La Touche, Macdonnell's successor, wrote to Curzon on 15 May 1902:

> Sir Antony Macdonnell went too far in acknowledging Hindi as a language. There is no Hindi language, but there are a number of Hindi dialects, of which Urdu or Hindustani is the principal (Curzon Correspondence 1903).

La Touche disapproved of the efforts of 'Hindu purists' to create Hindi which, in his opinion, 'no Muhammadan and no Hindu except a Pandit understands' (ibid.).

La Touche's policy was to avoid all opposition, so that, among other things, the textbooks of primary and secondary education were written in both Hindi and Urdu. This appears to have been the result of official disapproval of the Hindu policy of excessive Sanskritization. Because of this, the influence of the Nagari Pracharni Sabha over the Textbook Committee decreased (Dittmer 114-5). Sir Harcourt Butler, for instance, wrote in a letter of 13 May 1903 to Florence Butler, his mother:

> The Hindus are now very much up and are trying to eliminate all words of Persian or Arabic origin and our text book committee has got under the influence of the ultra-Hindu section and are writing primary text books in Sanskritized Hindi which the people cannot understand. So we are putting our foot down (Butler 1903-IOL).

Thus, the British attitude towards Urdu and Hindi kept changing according to political exigencies and the perceptions of the decision-makers who happened to be in power. The only constant was British political interest, not anti-Muslim or anti-Hindu sentiments.

## M. K. Gandhi and the Controversy

Although the Indian National Congress professed to be non-communal and secular, Muslims felt that it supported the Hindu way of life. The question of language still remained important although religion was the major basis of identity-formation for the Indian masses.

M. K. Gandhi's efforts to conciliate both Muslims and Hindus through linguistic compromise can thus be understood in the context of increasing tendencies towards separatism. Gandhi defined Hindustani as 'that language which is generally spoken by Hindus and Musalmans of the North, whether written in Devanagari or Urdu' (Gandhi 1942: 16). Gandhi, however, aligned himself with the Devanagari movement, the aim of which was 'to have it as the common script of all the languages spoken in the different provinces' (ibid. 16). This could hardly allay the fears of most Muslims, who were apprehensive of and predicted such an assimilation into Hindu culture (Fatehpuri 1989: 257).

The worst fears of the Muslims came true when, on Gandhi's insistence, the Bharatiya Sahitya Parishad changed the term 'Hindustani' to 'Hindi-Hindustani' in its session of 24 April 1936 (Gandhi 1942: 22). Abdul Haq, head of the Anjuman-e-Taraqqi-e-Urdu, the foremost organization for the development of Urdu, opposed the change (Haq 1964: 99, 167) and some prominent Muslims wrote letters to Gandhi protesting against it (in Gandhi 1942: 9-13). Gandhi's response to Haq—that the Muslims could preserve the Urdu script, which was Quranic—appears to have outraged Muslim feelings. In a letter to Gandhi, Haq wrote:

> Mahatmaji, you say you have no antipathy towards Urdu; still you openly called it the language of Musalmans, which is written in the Quranic script. You even said that the Musalmans may take care of it, if they so please (in Gandhi 1942:52).

Even M. A. Jinnah, the President of the All India Muslim League (AIML), had the following to say in his presidential speech at the twenty-sixth session of the League at Patna in December 1938:

> Take next the case of Hindi-Hindustani . . . Is there any doubt now in the mind of anyone that the whole scheme of Hindi-Hindustani is intended to stifle and suppress Urdu? (Pirzada vol 2; 1970: 305).

The response was a passionate chorus of 'No', 'No', and in the end, Jinnah himself spoke in Urdu.

After this, despite the effort of nationalist Muslims and the agreement between Rajandar Prasad and Abdul Haq, accepting Hindustani as the common language of Hindus and Muslims (Gandhi 1942: 38), Hindi and Urdu grew further apart.

**Congress Rule and Widening of the Gulf**

When the Congress ministries of 1937 finally left office, the All India Muslim League formed a committee under the presidentship of Muhammad Mehdi, the Raja of Pirpur to investigate the grievances of Muslims under Congress rule. The report of this Committee (called the Pirpur Report) devoted eight pages to expressing its views about the Urdu-Hindi controversy (Pirpur 1938: 23-30). According to the report, 'although Urdu is allowed in courts [in Bihar] as one of the optional languages, it is always discouraged by the presiding officers and the clerks' (Pirpur 38). In the Central Provinces and Bihar, 'The Muslims generally complain of want of Urdu schools even in districts as Sauger and Mandla' which had a high proportion of Muslims (ibid. 49). In Orissa, the report noted that: 'out of a total number of 181 schools in the province, there is only one institution in which the medium of instruction is Urdu' (ibid. 83).

The Muslim League not only rejected Hindi-Hindustani but was also suspicious of 'the word Hindustani'. Its report on the Wardha scheme declared:

> This change in the meaning of the term Hindustani has not been due to individual caprice but is the result of a definite policy initiated by the High Command of the Congress. Thus under the garb of Hindustani and the cover of the ideal of one language for India, it is Hindi that the Wardha Scheme contemplates to impose on Muslims (Wardha 1939: 7).

This Report also pointed out that, 'A book with technical terms and Sanskrit words will not be any the more intelligible to the Muslims because it is written in the Persian script' (Wardha 1939: 6-7). The newspapers of the period (1934-37)—especially Urdu ones such as *Haqiqat*, *Medina*, and *Hamari Zaban* —echoed similar anti-Hindi and anti-Gandhi feelings (UPINR 1937).

## The Final Separation

It has already been indicated that Islam was the major symbol for the Pakistan movement and that Urdu was also part of this symbolism. As separatist sentiment grew, Urdu was defended by prominent *ulema* such as Maulana Ashraf Ali Thanvi, who declared *ex cathedra*:

> In the present circumstances, therefore, protection of the Urdu language is protection of our religion. Thus this protection is a religious obligation of every Muslim according to his capacity (in Saeed 1972: 25).

Maulana Abul Ala Maudoodi, the pioneer of the religious party Jamaat-i-Islami, also supported Urdu and its script because, in his view, changing them 'can gradually transform it [a nation] into another nation' (Maudoodi 1942: 447). Thus, like Islam, Urdu too became an emotionally charged symbol of Muslim identity, especially in northern India.

The Muslim League, which was the major political party of the Indian Muslims, had always emphasized Urdu as a marker of their identity. In most of its sessions it had opposed Hindi or urged the government to provide facilities to Muslim children, even in non-Urdu-speaking areas, to learn Urdu (for the Bombay Presidency, see Resolution No.7, Second Session of AIML, December 1908 in Pirzada 1969: 80). In the fourth, ninth, tenth, seventeenth, twenty-sixth, and other sessions of the League, several resolutions were passed in favour of Urdu. All attempts at challenging the status of Urdu as the language of the Muslims were termed anti-Muslim activities. Resolution 8 adopted in the fourth session of the League at Nagpur in December 1910 declared:

> The AIML deplores the persistent attempts that are being made in various forms to set up what are called Hindi and Punjabi as the vernaculars of the United Provinces and the Punjab respectively (Pirzada 1969: 194).

The use of Urdu as a symbol of Muslim identity was a conscious identity-building strategy in some cases. For instance, at the third session of the League in Delhi in January 1910, Sir Ghulam Muhammad Ali, president of the session, declared:

> A third way of bringing about the desired regeneration of the community is the extension of Urdu as the common vernacular of all the Musalmans in the country. Community of language is universally admitted to be a powerful factor in securing the unity of a people (Pirzada 1969: 107).

Thus, it was not surprising that the AIML supported Urdu with the fervour that it did.

In the twenty-fifth session of the League (15-8 October 1937), the recognition of Urdu was codified again in the form of a resolution:

> The All-India Muslim League calls upon all the Urdu-speaking people of India to make every possible endeavour to safeguard the interests of their language, in every field of activity with which the central and provincial Governments were concerned, and wherever the Urdu language is the language of the area, its unhampered use and development should be upheld, and where it is not a predominant language, adequate arrangements should be made for teaching it as an optional subject, and in all Government offices, Courts, Legislatures, Railways and Postal Departments, provisions should be made for its use. Efforts should also be made to make Urdu the universal language of India (Pirzada 1970: 279).

Individual leaders of the Muslim League, whether mother-tongue speakers of Urdu or not, also declared their support. At the fifteenth session of the Provincial Education Conference at Aligarh (9 and 10 April 1939), Liaquat Ali Khan said:

> We will speak and write Urdu; educate our children in Urdu and never call our language by any other name except Urdu (*Hamari Zaban* 1 May 1939: 15).

Such sentiments were expressed by Muslims all over India and not only in UP (Gohar 1988; Haq 1964: 143-60).

Meanwhile, Gandhi increased his efforts at propagating Hindi, forming the Hindustani Prachar Sabha (the Society for the Propagation of Hindustani) in 1942 (Gupta and Gumperz 1968: 158). Moreover, the Hindi Sahitya Sammelan, led by P. D. Tandon, moved away from Gandhi's point of view that Hindustani was the common language of Hindus and Muslims (Dittmer 164-9; Gupta and Gumperz 1968: 158). For Tandon, Urdu was a dialect or variant of Hindi (in Gandhi 1942: 63). Because of this Gandhi eventually resigned from the Sammelan on 15 July 1945 (Gandhi in Siddiqui, I. A. 1980: 168). Despite this conciliatory step, Gandhi's own practice remained suspect in Muslim eyes. They pointed out that the language of his own paper, *Harijan*, was Sanskritized (*Harijan Sewak* 12 June 1946 in Siddiqui 194-5; Maudoodi 1942: 446-57). The language of his Hindustani Prachar Sabha, let alone the Sammelan which promoted only Hindi, was also Sanskritized (Siddiqui 141-2). Thus the trend towards separatism, insofar as it was expressed through linguistic symbols, kept increasing in the 1940s till India was partitioned and the state of Pakistan created in 1947. The Urdu-Hindi controversy lingers on in India and *Hamari Zaban*, among others, continues to report all changes in the use of Urdu (for a brief introduction to some post-1947 developments, see Brass 1974: 182-234; Dittmer 1972: 238-62). This book, however, is only concerned with the role of this controversy up to 1947.

To conclude, we have seen that in UP the Muslims were not disadvantageously placed *vis-à-vis* Hindus but, being in a minority, they felt threatened by them. Supporting Urdu was also economically advantageous for the Muslims since the language facilitated access to the domains of authority. Moreover, Urdu being associated with Muslim elitist culture, the Muslims could maintain their cultural elitism as long as Urdu was in a privileged position. As the threats to the economic well-being and to the collective ego (the historic consciousness of cultural elitism) evoked deep sentiment, Urdu was not merely a propagandist ploy; it was a symbol for expressing psychological, social, and economic aspirations. As a symbol, it was invested with so much emotion that it was salient, even without conscious manipulation by the leaders of the Urdu elite. It was chosen, or rather forced itself upon the consciousness of the Urdu elite of UP mainly for extra-rational reasons. The non-Urdu speaking Muslims of India, however, chose it primarily for instrumental ones. For them, after Islam, it was the only identity-marker which could transcend ethnic and local loyalties. Thus, by the time of the partition, Urdu was an important part of Muslim separatism in South Asia. It is arguable that Hindi was a part of Hindu separatism since it was an identity-marker for Hindus. Being Sanskritic in vocabulary and script, as a linguistic symbol, it ignored the Muslim part of the composite Indian culture and emphasized the Hindu one. This aspect of Hindi went against the avowed philosophy of the Congress and alienated the Muslims. The symbol of Hindi, however, is understandable as part of a general Hindu nationalistic reaction against Muslim rule, of which Urdu was reminiscent and symbolic.

The use of Urdu and Hindi as symbols of identity could only be a modern phenomenon. Despite extra-rational appeals and attempts at rationalizations, such assertions of identity could only have been possible in modern conditions. They were part of the creation of identities for political reasons. This issue of identity-formation is also crucial to the next chapter on the Bengali language movement.

### Notes

1. UP stands for Uttar Pradesh today. In 1833, the Bengal presidency was divided into the provinces of Agra and Bengal. In 1836, Agra was renamed the North Western Provinces under a Lieutenant Governor. In 1856, Oudh was annexed and placed under a Chief Commissioner. In 1877, Agra and Oudh were joined together, and in 1902 they came to be called the United Provinces of Agra and Oudh. This was abbreviated to UP during British rule. Thus, for some of the period of the Urdu-Hindi controversy under discussion, UP was not the name of the area where the events described in the text occurred. This name has been chosen only for convenience but specific references to the North Western Provinces in letters etc. are also given.

# 6

# The Bengali Language Movement

The Bhasha Ondolan, the movement which campaigned for the use of Bengali in the domains of power in East Bengal and fought to make it one of the official languages of the state, alongside Urdu, was not merely, or even predominantly, a linguistic one. It was a political campaign of the greatest significance for the new state. It was, in fact, East Bengal's first challenge to the hegemony of the Urdu-speaking Bengali aristocracy (the *ashraf*) and the West Pakistani ruling elite (Alam 1991). The challengers were the vernacular proto-elites: the modern, educated, Bengali-speaking class, and the largely middle-class professionals (Roy 1987), and students who aspired to join the middle class. The subaltern social forces supported the movement from time to time (Alam 1991: 470).

Even more significant, from the point of view of the rise of ethnicity, was the shift from the Islamic image of the Bengali identity to one based on language and culture (Ahmad, R. 1981; Kabir 1987). This change led to the articulation of Bengali ethno-nationalism and contributed to the emergence of Bangladesh (Gulati 1988: 20-36; Roy 1987). So comprehensive was Pakistan's 'failure in national integration', as Rounaq Jahan calls it (1972), that it has only recently been understood by Pakistani scholars (Zaheer 1994).

This chapter does not attempt to offer anything as ambitious as a new explanation of the Bhasha Ondolan, nor does it provide fresh insights into it. Its more modest aim is to provide a brief account of the movement (for details see Umar 1970; Helal 1985) and relate it to politics.

**Changes in the Bengali Identity**

As the Bengali self-image, or concept of identity, changed more than once—and these changes are significant for understanding the language movement—it is necessary to deal with them at some length.

According to the first census of Bengal, that of 1872, Muslims formed 48 per cent of the population of the province (Census-B 1872: Gen. Statement 1B). Most of them were peasants, labourers, and artisans, and their class as a whole was called the *atrap* (*ajlaf* in UP and Bihar). At the other end of the social hierarchy, as mentioned earlier, were the Muslim aristocrats and gentlemen called the *ashraf* (Ahmad, R. 1981: 6-28).

The *ashraf* often spoke Urdu, and official work during the Mughal period was carried on in Persian. In fact, so strong was the feeling that Bengali culture was not Muslim that Muttlib, a sixteenth century poet, believed that translating religious books into Bengali was sinful. He writes:

> Muchalmani sastra katha Bangala Karilum
> Bahu pap haila niscae janilum.
> (I translated Muslim religious books in Bengali. I am sure I committed a grave sin) (Quoted from Dil 1993: 61).

This 'sin', however, was politically necessary because the ordinary Bengali Hindus were very close to their Hindu neighbours in most aspects of behaviour (Mujeeb 1967: 15-6). The Muslim elite attempted to reform them and used the Bengali language for the purpose. However sinful it might appear to them, it could not be avoided.

Out of the necessity of describing Islamic concepts and rituals, the Bengali of the Muslim writers was different from Hindu Bengali. It was Musalmani Bangla or Dobashi which is a 'variety of Bengali which has a heavy admixture of words and some derivational affixes borrowed from the "Islamic" languages: Persian, Arabic, Urdu and Turkish' (Dil 1993: 63). The *puthis* (didactic writing) written in Musalmani Bangla became increasingly Muslimized, i.e., took on Perso-Arabic honorifics and words. Thus, the Hindu honorific *Sri* was no longer used for God and the *nasihat namas* began to use Urdu titles (Ahmad, R. 1981: 109). In short, Bengali was Islamized through the substitution of Sanskritic words by Perso-Arabic ones, i.e., by language planning that was ideologically inspired.

The best-known Islamic reformist movement in Bengal was the Faraizi movement founded by Haji Shariatullah (1781-1840) of Faridpur and carried on by his son Dudu Miyan (1819-1862) (Khan, M. 1965). This movement, supported by several others, such as the Tariqah-i-Muhammadiya, worked towards creating a religious identity among Bengali Muslims.

The coming of the British, the advent of printing, and the increased consumption of the printed word, brought about a literary renaissance in the Bengal. But this renaissance initially resulted in the rise of the Hindu middle class, the *Bhadralok*, and an efflorescence in Sanskritic Bengali literature (Kopff 1969: 193-216).

The Bengali Muslims, including the *ashraf*, lagged far behind in the race for power and wealth under British patronage (Hunter 1871). The army, the higher administration, and revenue were in British hands, and even the lower echelons of the judicial and civil bureaucracy were closed to them because of the change from Persian to Bengali as the court language. According to Hunter, after this change in 1837:

> The Hindus poured into, and have since completely filled, every grade of official life. Even in the District Collectorates of Lower Bengal, where it is still possible to give appointments in the old fashioned friendly way, there are very few young Musalman officials (Hunter 141).

Modern impersonality and uniformity of selectional criteria replaced personal contacts, at least in bureaucratic theory. Jobs were now available by learning the language(s) used in the domains of power.

The Muslim *ashraf*, who were more visible and articulate than the masses, reacted by creating a pressure group—the Muslims. In order to present themselves as distinct from Hindus, the similarities between the two groups were ignored and the differences emphasized. Language was presented as one of the symbols of difference. For the *ashraf* it was Urdu which was chosen as the language of Muslims. Thus, Syed Ameer Ali, a well-known scholar from the *ashraf*, said before the Education Commission of 1882 that 'Urdu should be to the Mahommedans what Bengali is to the Hindus of Bengal' (Edn Comm-B 1884: 213).

Others took the more pragmatic step of resorting to identity-conscious LP. They would make Muslim Bengali diverge as far as possible from Hindu Bengali. The Pandits of Fort William and the *Bhadralok* intellectuals had already Sanskritized Bengali (Das 1966) and chose to call it *Sudhubhasa* (chaste language) (Chatterji 1926: 89). The idea was therefore to create a Bengali purged of its excessive Sanskritic content—'a mean between the highly sanskritized Bengali of the Hindu *Patshalas* on the one hand and the Musalmani Bengali on the other', as Nawab Abdul Latif, the educational reformer, put it (Edn Comm-B: 1884: 213). The British Government, in order to conciliate Muslim opinion, had already agreed that the Bengali taught to Muslims should have 'some infusion of Persian words' (RPI-B 1876: 32). The British officials also recommended that the Muslims of Bengal be taught Urdu, Persian, and Arabic in addition to Bengali (Ahmad, R. 1981: 125). Nawab Ali Chaudhry, among others, tried to create such a reformed language through the establishment of an organization called the Bangiya Sahitya Visayak Musalman Sabha (Muhammadan Society for Bengali Literature) in 1899 (*Muslim Chronicle* 24 February 1900: 854). Muslim identity was emphasized by the introduction of more Perso-Arabic words. The script, however, was not changed, although some Muslims of Chittagong had employed the Perso-Arabic script for writing Bengali in the eighteenth century (Chatterji 1926: 228). This was the beginning of that tilt towards the acceptance of an indigenous Bengali identity which later emerged, when the danger of Hindu domination was removed after 1947.

The threat of Hindu domination is closely related to Hindu predominance in the state apparatus. As a consequence of the warnings of Hunter (1871: 155) and others, the British government increased education amongst Muslims. The following figures illustrate this new trend:

*Progress of Muslim Education in Bengal 1882-1883 to 1912-1913*

| Institution | %Muslims 1882-1883 | % Muslims 1912-1913 |
|---|---|---|
| Arts Colleges | 3.9 | 7.13 |
| Professional Colleges | 2.2 | 5.13 |
| High Schools | 8.8 | 19.45 |
| Middle English | 13.1 | 34.78 |
| Middle Vernacular | 13.6 | 31.19 |
| Primary | 23.3 | 43.18 |
| Total | 27.6 | 40.50 |

(RPI-B 1883 and 1913)

Muslims also occupied more jobs than in 1871 (Ahmad, R. 1981: 153-89). This rising literate group of people aspired for 'gentlemanly' status which, in their world-view, came from foreign descent. Hence, 'the number of Shaikhs and the other categories'—Syed, Mughal and Pathan—'increased phenomenally, while the occupational "caste" groups registered a sharp decline' (Ahmad, R. 1981: 115). This *ashrafization* entailed a denial of everything local, including the language. Modernity thus brought in its wake a Muslim identity which was taken as the antithesis of the Bengali identity.

It has been mentioned that the acceptance of Bengali as part of the Muslim Bengali identity among educated Bengali Muslims, although slow and grudging, started as early as 1899 with the establishment of Nawab Ali Chaudhry's Muhammadan Society for Bengali Literature. In 1906, at the Mohammedan Educational Conference in Dhaka, Abdul Karim, a delegate of East Bengal, pointed out that 'the Muslims of Eastern Bengal cannot do without Bengali . . . they could do without [Urdu and Persian]' (Letter in *The Bengalee* 11 January 1907: 3). The change, however, was slow because of the psychological significance—the snob value—of being able to claim *ashraf* descent. Moreover, as the Muslim League, claiming to represent all Indian Muslims, had made Muslims conscious of the necessity of uniting against Hindus *en bloc* on the basis of a Muslim identity, there was considerable pressure to negate Bengali identity while emphasizing Muslim identity. ·

Thus, two contradictory movements continued simultaneously: the acceptance of Bengali identity and the assertion of Muslim identity. The latter trend, which was dominant, is manifested through such acts as the resolution put forward by the popular politician, A. K. Fazlul Haq, which demanded that an Urdu (and Persian) teacher be appointed in government-aided Muslim schools (Haq, F. 1905). The former trend, though weaker, was strong enough to make the delegates of the Bengal Provincial Muslim League, created in 1912, write the League's resolution in Bengali and not in Urdu (Rashid 1987: 12). Even Maulana Akram Khan, a religious figure and a leader of the Muslim League, declared in 1918 that the question of whether Urdu or Bengali was the mother tongue of the Bengali Muslims was 'the most preposterous question of them all' (Helal 1985: 71).

By the late 1920s, other organized bodies for the promotion of Bengali also came to be formed. One such organization was the Dacca Rationalists. It supported Bengali rather than Urdu as the language of Muslim education in the 1930s (Wadud 1963: 194-5). The threat to Urdu was noticeable enough to make its supporters form an All-Bengal Urdu Association in 1933. They condemned Bengali as a Hinduized language (a view which persisted in West Pakistan till 1971), and said that Urdu alone should be taught to Muslims (Rashid 1987:12, 5-6). In 1937, at the Lucknow session of the All India Muslim League, a resolution recommending Urdu as the *lingua franca* of Muslims all over India was opposed by the delegates of the Bengal (*P* 17 October 1937; Pirzada vol 2, 1970: 279; Rashid 1987: 8). In the same year, the Vice Chancellor of Dhaka University declared in his convocation address of 14 July 1937 that:

The University has also created a Readership in Bengali, and, in view of the increasing importance of the subject, it has been proposed to create a separate Department of Bengali (Mitra and Mitra 1990: 478).

In 1944, the East Pakistan Renaissance Society of Calcutta, formed by radical intellectuals, demanded that Bengali should be the official language of East Bengal (Ahmad, A. M. 1989: 44). The language question came to the forefront when in July 1947, only a month before the creation of Pakistan, Dr Ziauddin Ahmed, Vice Chancellor of Aligarh Muslim University, declared that Urdu would be the medium of instruction in Pakistan. Dr Shahidullah, a Bengali linguist, replied to this by saying that: 'if Urdu or Hindi instead of Bengali is used in our law courts and universities, that would be tantamount to political slavery' (Shahidullah 1947).

In short, the idea that Bengali was not a despicable language, a social stigma to be denied, was gaining ground. It had the potential of coming into its own when the fear of Hindu domination, which necessitated emphasis on the Muslim identity with Islam and Urdu as its major symbols, was removed.

## The Demand for Bengali in East Pakistan

Badruddin Umar, a major historian of the Bhasha Ondolan, recorded the names of the Peoples' Freedom League established in July 1947 and the Democratic Youth League established in August of the same year (Ganotantri Yuvo League) in Dhaka as the first organizations to demand Bengali as the state language of East Bengal (Umar 1970: 21). However, it was the Tamaddun Majlis (TM) which made an impact upon the social scene by demanding Bengali as: (a) the medium of instruction; (b) the language of the courts; (c) the language of administration; and (d) the language of mass communication in East Bengal. Moreover, they demanded that Bengali be taught to everyone serving in East Bengal and that it should be one of the national languages of Pakistan along with Urdu (TM 1947).

The TM has been described as an Islamic and cultural organization by Akash (Akash 1988: 51), but the pamphlet it published had articles by political opponents of the Muslim League such as Abul Mansur Ahmad, the editor of the Calcutta-based *Ittehad* (Ahmad, A. M. 1989: 44). Among other things, Abul Mansur Ahmad pointed out the discrimination which the emerging salariat of East Bengal would suffer.

If Urdu is made our state language then the educated people of East Pakistan will become illiterate overnight and they will also become disqualified for government service (TM 1947. See Helal 1985: 182).

Abul Qasim, an academic from Dhaka University, demanded autonomy according to the Lahore Resolution of 1940, and Qazi Mutahir Husain, another academic, pointed to the fact that Bengali had been developed by Muslim rulers and was not to be associated with Hinduism alone.

The demands of the TM were rational (jobs, power, money) as well as extra-rational (cultural autonomy, pride, identity), and were to occur perennially throughout the Bhasha Ondolan as well as later. At that time, however, the enthusiasm for the Pakistan movement and the Muslim League was such that it relegated the TM to the periphery. Even students were so much in favour of Urdu that the TM was unable to hold its meetings in several residential halls of the University (Umar 1970: 32).

The first educational conference of Pakistan was held in Karachi from 27 November to 1 December 1947. The Minister of Education, Fazlur Rahman, a Bengali, suggested:

There are unassailable grounds for its [Urdu's] establishment as the *lingua franca* of Pakistan (PEC 1947: 39).

Although the conference conceded the mother-tongue principle—that the medium of instruction at the primary stage would be the mother tongue of the child—its bias in favour of Urdu and English was obvious (ibid. 39).

The rumour which spread in East Bengal was that Urdu alone was to be the language of the state (*MN* 6 December 1947). On 6 December 1947, Abul Qasim presided over a meeting held at Dhaka University to protest against the preference for Urdu. It was now that many people, mostly students, openly demanded that Bengali should not merely be a medium of instruction and the official language of East Bengal but also one of the state languages of Pakistan (Umar 1970: 34). Following the meeting, the students went to the Secretariat and to the house of the Chief Minister, Khawaja Nazimuddin. The latter is reported to have promised to make Bengali one of the state languages (Umar 1970: 34). This was the beginning of a pattern which was repeated again and again, since the Secretariat, the houses of ministers, and the provincial legislative assembly were located within the same perimeters as the students' residential halls and complex of colleges (Rahman, A. 1990: 172). The students could easily hold the most powerful decision-makers hostage temporarily and did so on a number of occasions in the early years of the movement (see details in Umar 1970).

The demand for Bengali increased as the days went by. Currency notes, money order forms, tickets, official documents—in fact, all documents of the state—were in Urdu or English. The people of Bengal felt marginalized and alienated. Apart from the memorandums and articles recorded by historians (Umar 1970: 42-54), the rising emotions of the members of the intelligentsia in favour of Bengali were also recorded by eyewitnesses. The following account comes from the journal of an Englishman who was a guest lecturer at Dhaka University:

> 'I believe you'd rather have Hindus in control than Punjabis', I said to a young lecturer who was raging over some provocation. He retorted at once, 'We would indeed, for at least they're our own kind of people. We didn't get rid of the British Raj to be bossed about by these new imperialists'. And on the way to college one morning, two students just in front of me were talking earnestly in a less heated mood: one was saying to the other, 'I am first of all a Bengali, then I am a Muslim, then Pakistani'(Stock 1973: 85).

It would not be fair to make much of such casual remarks but, taken along with evidence from other sources, it appears that by 1948, the shift from Muslim to Bengali identity had become fairly strong among members of the Bengali proto-elite, and that the West Pakistani civil and military personnel had begun to be seen at best as dominant and at worst as internal colonialists.

## The 1948 Language Movement

The Urdu-Bengali controversy was triggered off in earnest when Dhirendranath Datta, a Hindu member of the Constituent Assembly of Pakistan, raised the question of the use of Bengali along with Urdu and English, in the Constituent Assembly. To this, the Prime Minister, Liaquat Ali Khan, replied:

> Pakistan has been created because of the demand of a hundred million Muslims in this subcontinent and the language of a hundred million Muslims is Urdu (LAD-P 25 February 1948: 16).

Khawaja Nazimuddin further provoked the activists of the Bengali movement by declaring that the people of his province wanted Urdu, not Bengali. His province, however, proved to be divided in its opinion.

If strikes, processions, letters to the editor, and newspaper articles are any indication, there is ample evidence that many people opposed Urdu (Umar 1970: 63-81). Eyewitness accounts by Stock (1973: 90-5), Abul Kalam Shamsuddin (1968: 315-22), Abul Mansur Ahmad (1989: 35-44), Ataur Rahman (1984: 56-61), and Ayub Khan, then the General Commanding Officer of East Pakistan (Khan, A. 1967: 29-30) bear witness to the high state of mobilization amongst the students. Finally, on 15 March 1948, Nazimuddin relented and signed an eight-point agreement with the students, including the following major concession:

> In the first week of April on a day reserved for the unofficial business of the East Bengal Legislative Assembly a special motion will be moved recommending that Bengali should also be one of the state languages and given the same status as Urdu in Pak Assembly and in Central Govt. examinations (for Nazimuddin's statement about the agreement see LAD-B 15 March 1948).

Even after this, the movement did not immediately die down. It was in this climate that the Governor-General, Mohammad Ali Jinnah (the Quaid-i-Azam), visited Dhaka.

When Jinnah reached Dhaka airport on 19 March, according to Tajuddin Ahmad who kept a diary of the events, he was welcomed by thousands, but 'no enthusiasm was seen in the people . . . students were indifferent mostly due to the recent police oppression' (Ahmad: Diary 19 March 1948). On 21 March, Jinnah spoke at the Race Course Maidan and declared in peremptory tones:

> Let me tell you in the clearest language that there is no truth that your normal life is going to be touched or disturbed so far as your Bengali language is concerned. But ultimately it is for you, the people of this Province, to decide what shall be the language of your Province. But let me make it very clear to you that the State Language of Pakistan is going to be Urdu and no other language. Anyone who tries to mislead you is really the enemy of Pakistan. Without one State language, no nation can remain tied up solidly together and function (Jinnah 1948a: 183).

According to Tajuddin Ahmad, the 'Quaid-i-Azam's speech hurt every person of this province everybody is disgusted he was expected to be above party' (Diary 21 March 1948). According to other eyewitnesses, people broke down a gate, destroyed a picture of the Quaid and protested against the Quaid's pronouncements (Umar 1970: 108). The 'first reaction of Salimullah Hall students on returning was to tear down the decorations' (Stock 1973: 96).

Five days later, Jinnah expressed similar sentiments at the University Convocation. When he reiterated that the state language 'can only be Urdu' (Jinnah 1948b: 194), some students shouted 'Na! Na! Na'. He paused for some time but then went on to conclude his speech (Rahman 1984: 61; Umar 1970: 110; Shamsuddin 1968: 312). Later, a delegation of students met Jinnah, but the meeting ended in disappointment for the students because Jinnah declared that the eight-point agreement had been signed under duress. His major reason for not agreeing to two state languages was his fear of the disintegration of the country (Ahmad: Diary 24 March 1948; Umar 1970: 112-3).

It should also be remembered that in those days the Bengali intelligentsia was divided in its sympathies. The official view, that the language movement had been created by Communists, Indian agents, and the political enemies of the Muslim League, which Jinnah expressed in both of his speeches in Dhaka, must have been fed to him by his advisers. The West Pakistani Press, especially the *Morning News*, also disseminated this view, and senior Pakistani officials believed in it (Khan, A. 1967: 24-5; also see Ataur Rahman's account of his argument with a senior bureaucrat who held similar views—1984: 108-11). Moreover, a petition supporting Urdu and branding the supporters of Bengali as enemy agents was submitted to Jinnah upon his arrival. With this one-sided propaganda, it is plausible, as one scholar argues, that Jinnah was confirmed in his belief 'that the noise was being created by a bunch of rabble rousers' (Rahman, A. 1990: 171). Soon after Jinnah's departure, Khawaja Nazimuddin proposed in the Legislative Assembly that Bengali would replace English in the province and be used as a medium of instruction (LAD-B 8 April 1948: 165). This was far short of the proposals agreed upon earlier and the language activists felt betrayed.

### State-Inspired LP and the Language Movement

The object of state-inspired LP was to emphasize the Muslim identity of the Bengalis and, by the same token, de-emphasize the Bengali one. One radical proposal, given by the Aga Khan on 9 February 1951 (*PO* 11 February 1951), amongst others, (e.g., Matin 1954), was to make Arabic the state language of Pakistan. More practicable suggestions were to change the Bengali script to Arabic and to purge it of indigenous Sanskritic words, replacing them with Perso-Arabic ones. This was, in short, a way of Islamizing Bengali, an extension of the effort to create a Pakistani nation which had nothing in common but

Islam. From the Bengali point of view, however, it was part of the West Pakistani prejudice that Bengaliness was incompatible with both the Islamic and the Pakistani identity. Thus, these LP efforts were resisted by the Bengalis.

Following the recommendation of Fazlur Rahman, the Education Minister, the central government established 'twenty adult education centres in different parts of East Pakistan to teach primary Bengali through Arabic script' (Islam 1986: 152; *PO* 4 October 1950). The East Bengal government also set up a Language Committee on 7 December 1950 to carry out the Islamization of Bengali. Its members were people who were known for emphasizing the Islamic identity of Bengali Muslims. Even the notable supporters of Bengali among them—such as Dr Shahidullah and Abul Kalam Shamsuddin—were, nevertheless, people who wanted to retain the Islamic identity of Bengali Muslims. The Chairman, Maulana Akram Khan, earned notoriety when he declared in Karachi on 15 April 1951 that those who opposed Urdu in East Bengal were antagonistic to Islam (*PO* 18 April 1951. For opposing opinions, see Editorials *PO* 18 April 1951; 7 May 1951; Letters to the Editor, *PT* 7 May 1951; Shelley 1951). Describing the first meeting of the committee, Abul Kalam Shamsuddin writes that Babu Ganesh Bose, Professor of Bengali at Dhaka University, was the only member who objected to the proposed changes which extended even to the grammar. Shamsuddin, however, snubbed Bose, saying that they wanted to free Bengali from the domination of Sanskrit (1968: 334). The Committee's final report, submitted in August 1951, recommended non-Sanskritized Bengali, and the teaching of Urdu as a second langu-age to make the 'cultural bonds between the two wings of Pakistan closer and deeper' (LAD-B 31 October 1951: 25; Islam 1986: 150).

The Committee's recommendations were, however, not made public, possibly because of its support to state-sponsored policies. Even so, apprehensions that Bengali would be written in the Arabic script were expressed through questions in the Legislative Assembly (LAD-B 1 March 1951: 61). There were also letters in the press, expressing the fear that such a step would alienate the Bengalis from their literature and their cultural heritage, and make them culturally subordinate to West Pakistan (*PO* 10 April 1949).

The students of the Bengali Department of Dhaka University wrote a nine-point memorandum to the Pakistan Education Advisory Board, saying that they would not allow the script of their language to be changed (Umar 1970: 204). Meetings were held in several cities and feelings ran high (for details see Umar 1970: 258-60). The plan never materialized but state LP efforts to Islamize Bengali continued.

## The 1952 Language Movement

The feeling of being exploited and despised by the West Pakistanis kept tempers simmering in East Bengal. In this situation, Khawaja Nazimuddin, now the Prime Minister of Pakistan, arrived in Dhaka and declared that 'Urdu will be the state language of Pakistan'. Like Jinnah, he too emphasized Urdu as a symbol of Pakistani nationhood (*PO* 29 January 1952). The reaction to this was immediate and sharp. Letters and editorials started appearing in the press and on 30 January there was a huge pro-Bengali demonstration in Dhaka (*PO* 31 January 1952).

Khawaja Nazimuddin was condemned as an upper-class Urdu-speaking man, not sympathetic to Bengalis (*PO* 31 January 1952), and Maulana Abdul Hameed Bhashani, a grassroots populist leader, urged the students to come forward and prevent the imposition of 'an alien language upon 50 million people' (*PO* 1 February 1952). Soon, processions became daily occurrences; the one on 4 February was described as 'the biggest demonstration in living memory in East Bengal' (*PO* 5 February 1952). According to Abul Kalam Shamsuddin, the students chanted:

Rashtro bhasha Bangla chai
(We want Bengali as a state language).

On 13 February, the East Bengal government banned the *Pakistan Observer* for expressing anti-Islamic sentiments in its editorial of the previous day. (*PT* 'Editorial' 17 February 1952). Since the *Pakistan Observer* was an active supporter of Bengali, this act was seen by the supporters of the Bhasha Ondolan as yet another attempt at suppressing the voice of the Bengalis (*PT* 17 February 1952). So high-handed was the government's action that Khairat Hosain, a member of the East Bengal Legislative Assembly, was not even given leave to move a motion to discuss this ban (LAD-B 20 February 1952: 14).

On 20 February, there was another strike and Section 144 was imposed on Dhaka. The next day, an incident occurred, which changed the course of East-West politics in Pakistan.

## 21 February 1952 (Ekushe)

On this day, students gathered on the campus of Dhaka University and, after some discussion, decided to defy Section 144. They started to come out in batches of four and five. Accounts of what happened after this vary.

The official version, given in a government circular and in the statement of the Chief Minister, Nurul Amin on the floor of the provincial legislature was that the students used 'filthy language' to policemen, attacked vehicles, and forced shopkeepers to close their shops. It also stated that they threw brickbats at the police, injuring some policemen. The District Magistrate finally ordered the police to open fire. Even then, the crowd did not disperse but attacked the police. Thereupon, 'some more rounds were fired', killing one and injuring nine persons. Two of the injured died later (*Press Release* E. B No. 658; Nurul Amin in LAD-B 21 February 1952: 54-8).

However, in an inquiry held by Justice Ellis of the Dhaka High Court into the firing, the police said that it had used 39 gas grenades and 72 tear-gas shells, and fired 27 rounds, which had led to 'nine casualties of whom three were students and six outsiders' (Ellis 1952: 43, 48). Tajuddin Ahmad wrote in his diary of 21 February that there had been '4 spot deaths of bullets. 30 injured. 62 in jails'. But he had not actually witnessed the deaths. Other accounts, purporting to be those of eyewitnesses, are given in detail by Bashir al-Helal (1985: 310-31).

The accounts of witnesses varied, giving Nurul Amin the chance to ridicule placards at Mymensingh reporting 165 deaths, including those of eleven girls (LAD-B 24 March 1952: 8). In fact, as Abul Kalam Shamsuddin observed, no source could be trusted, but people had died (1968: 331). The coercive power of the state had shed the blood of Bengalis. The deaths were seen as martyrdom and became the most potent symbol of resistance to West Pakistan.

The firing did not cow down the protesters. The immediate reaction was, indeed, the opposite. The protest grew stronger and more bitter (see Tajuddin Ahmad's Diary entries of 22-7 February 1952). Moreover, many people from the Muslim League or of conservative, pro-Muslim League views also became alienated from the ruling elite. For instance, Abul Kalam Shamsuddin, who was working in the office of the *Azad* when he received the news, resigned his membership of the Legislative Assembly immediately (Shamsuddin 1968: 331).

The same evening, the Legislative Assembly held one of the stormiest sessions of its life. Nurul Amin defended the government, while Dhirendranath Datta, Maulana Turkabagish, Khairat Hosain, and

Shamsuddin Ahmad opposed it vociferously. In the end, the opposition walked out of the House in protest. Turkabagish and Shamsuddin Ahmad, who were members of the Muslim League, resigned from the League. The next day was no less stormy. The students held a condolence meeting at which Abul Kalam Shamsuddin delivered a speech, and a monument (*shaheed minar*) was hurriedly erected in honour of the martyred victims (Shamsuddin 1968: 332; Helal 1985: 428-30). The students again clashed with the police who demolished their *minar* (*CMG* and *PT* 23 February 1952). Meanwhile, within the Assembly, Nurul Amin tried to limit the damage by moving the following motion:

> This Assembly recommends to the Constituent Assembly of Pakistan that Bengali be one of the state languages of Pakistan (LAD-B 22 February 1952: 89).

But this motion came too late to pacify the students. They wanted Nurul Amin's insensitive administration to come to an end. Now their favourite slogan was:

> Khuni Nurul Amin Bichar Chai
> Khuner Bangla Khun Chai
> (We want justice, i.e. vengeance against bloody Nurul Amin. We want blood for Bengali blood) (Helal 1985: 372).

The next few days brought violence and agitation. The state's coercive power was used against the protesters again and again (Helal 1985: 334-486). For their part, the protesters too went to the extreme: government installations were stoned and offices of the *Morning News*, which had always opposed Bengali, were burnt (*D* 23 February 1952). The government responded by arresting prominent anti-government politicians and intellectuals. Among those arrested were, Abul Hashim, former General Secretary of the Bengal Muslim League, Khairat Hosain, Maulana Turkabagish, Govindlal Bannerjee, and Monorajan Dhar. All of them had opposed Nurul Amin on the floor of the Assembly and elsewhere (*CMG* 26 February 1952). Newspapers reported 28 more arrests in Dhaka on 26 February (*PT* 27 February 1952), including academics from the University such as P. C. Chakraverty, Munier Chowdhuri, and Mazaffar Hamid Chaudhri (*CMG* 27 February 1952). Even Z. A. Suleri, deputed by the Council of Pakistan Editors to investigate the ban on the *Pakistan Observer*, was arrested by mistake but was freed immediately (*PT* 27 February 1952).

The official point of view of the ruling elite and of West Pakistanis in general was so different from that of the Bengalis that they failed to understand the language movement. They asserted that the movement was inspired by communists, Hindus, and Indian agents. Although a 'Note for Governors' Conference' of the Ministry of Home Affairs dated 1958, marked 'Secret', reported that India had 'not done anything concrete lately at the higher official level' to make East Pakistan secede from West Pakistan (In HBWI 1982: vol 2, 36), most people, even in responsible positions, believed that the prevailing ethnicism was created by India. At the time, this conspiracy theory was disseminated by the West Pakistani Press ('Editorials', *D* 23 February 1952; *CMG* 25 and 29 February 1952), and especially by supporters of Pakistani nationalism, Urdu, and Islam such as the Anjuman-e-Taraqqi-e-Urdu. Abdul Haq declared that the Bhasha Ondolan was inspired by a few 'self-seeking gentlemen', while another writer called them 'traitors to Islam and the enemies of our nation' (Haq 1952: 37). Nurul Amin expressed similar views in detail in the Provincial Legislature on 24 March 1952. He asserted that the language movement was an attempt to overthrow the government and 'deal a blow at the very security of Pakistan'. He also claimed that it was organized by the communists, who claimed to have made it into a mass movement (LAD-B 24 March 1952: 11). Such a claim was, indeed, made by *Swadhinata*, a Calcutta newspaper, in its issue of 11 March 1952. It is also true that the Action Committee of the Bhasha Ondolan had four communist (Youth League) members out of twelve (Muniruzzaman 1973: 229). Moreover, many communists had become teachers and could presumably influence young people (Franda 1970: 596), though probably more were lawyers (figures of 23 and 28 per cent are quoted for the pro-Moscow wing of a leftist party in 1968 by Muniruzzaman 241). Thus, the ideas of the leftists did inspire Bengali nationalism as Muniruzzaman argues. But the Communist Party itself was weak and remained in an embattled position (Franda 1970) because it was suppressed by the government. It operated mainly through other organizations, such as the National Awami Party (NAP) and the Students Union. The ideas which caught the imagination of the intelligentsia as well as the masses were those that related to the distribution of power and wealth. If the people had not been made to feel cheated, exploited, and marginalized, it is arguable that these ideas would have had less appeal for them. As it happened, the government continued to be manifestly unjust, making people more and more receptive to radical ideas. Hence, the official conspiracy theory still widely believed in Pakistan—that the communists cleverly manipulated most of the Bengalis—is simplistic and uninformed.

With such views, the West Pakistanis could hardly be expected to sympathize with the Bengalis. Thus, in the aftermath of the events of 21 February, attitudes hardened: the Bengalis accused the West Pakistanis of insensitivity and the Muslim League of tyranny. The West Pakistanis accused the East Pakistanis of being either traitors or dupes in the hands of anti-state agents.

**Recognition of Bengali as a State Language**

The resentment of the common people of East Bengal against the Muslim League can be gauged by the results of the provincial elections of 1954. The opposition parties—Awami League, of which Bhashani was a popular leader; Fazlul Haq's Krishak Sramik Party; and the Nizam-i-Islam Party—got together in 1953 to form a United (Jugto) Front. In their 21-point manifesto, the points pertaining to language were as follows:

1. Bengali would be made one of the state languages of Pakistan.

2. Education would be imparted through the mother tongue.

3. Burdwan House, the Chief Minister's residence, would be converted into a centre of research for Bengali language and literature (The Bangla Academy is located in this building now).

4. A column (*shaheed minar*) would be erected in memory of those killed on 21 February and their families would be compensated.

5. 21 February, Martyrs' Day, would be a government holiday.

Abul Mansur Ahmad says he had suggested points (3) and (5) above. The total number of points was brought to 21 in order to invest this figure with special significance (Ahmad, A. 1989: 47).

The United Front evoked powerful emotions which contributed to its overwhelming victory—215 out of a total of 237 Muslim seats. Only nine seats went to the Muslim League—the vernacular proto-elite had proved its political power.

The West Pakistani ruling elite, however, did not accept its defeat so easily. On 29 May 1954, barely three months after Fazlul Haq had formed it, the Front's ministry was dismissed. Iskandar Mirza, who was appointed the new Governor, arrested the Front leaders including 35 members of the Provincial Assembly. Sheikh Mujibur Rahman, who was to lead East Bengal to independence in 1971, was also arrested. The allegations against the Front ministry were that it had instigated the Bengali-Bihari riots at the Chandragona Paper Mills in Chittagong; that it encouraged communist infiltration; and that the governor was working for the independence of the province.

After this, the ruling elite made some concessions to the provinces in the Murree Pact of 10 July 1955. A new chapter entitled 'Language of the Republic' was added to the *Basic Principles Committee Report* by the Constituent Assembly, declaring that Urdu and Bengali would be the official languages of the republic (*D* 8 May 1954). However, the majority status of East Bengal was sacrificed to this concession. From that time on, the two wings would have parity representation. In short, the power of numbers was given up for a gain which would prove to be little more than symbolically significant.

Even so, some supporters of Urdu, notably Abdul Haq, protested against the new status of Bengali, repeating that only Urdu could be the 'national and state language of Pakistan' (*D* 11 May 1954). Meanwhile, Fazlul Haq denounced the formula of parity as the surrender of the majority rights of East Bengal, but Suhrawardy, who had handled the negotiations, defended the pact on the grounds that it recognized regional autonomy (LAD-P 31 January 1956).

Consequently, the 1956 Constitution proclaimed both Bengali and Urdu as state languages (Article 214; 1). The language movement ostensibly came to an end. However, the symbol of *Ekushe*, as the twenty-first of February was called, resonated throughout the political and cultural life of the intelligentsia of East Bengal. The essays, poems, and plays on this theme in particular and the language movement in general bear witness to its crucial significance (Chowdhury, M. 1990; Chowdhury, K. 1992; *Poems on 21st* 1992; Islam 1994). In fact, *Ekushe* and the *Shaheed Minar* were (and remain) the most powerful symbols of resistance in the political life of what is now Bangladesh (Umar 1973: 108-10; 263-8). They gave emotional force to political and economic demands which took on the dimensions of resistance to injustice and oppression of the kind first experienced on twenty-first February.

## Major Bengali Grievances in the Ayub Khan Era

Even after 1956, there were complaints from Bengalis that their language was not being treated at par with Urdu. Abul Mansur Ahmad, for instance, pointed out that currency notes, railway and postal signboards etc., were not in Bengali (LAD-P 9 April 1956: 695), and that the state media gave less time to it than to Urdu (LAD-P 27 February 1958: 367; see Farid Ahmad's speech in LAD-P 10 March 1958: 1158-60). Even the *Shaheed Minar*, the major symbol of Bengali identity (Huda 1994: 90-8), had not been completed, though plans for it were 'in the final stages' in 1956. However, 21 February had been declared a public holiday (statement of Ataur Rahman, the Minister of Education, in LAD-B 25 September 1956: 72). The military government of Ayub Khan (1958-1969) merely aggravated the growing East Pakistani feeling of disillusionment with the Centre. This disillusionment was now mainly expressed through the two-economy theory—that the two wings of Pakistan should have separate economies, otherwise the West Wing would keep siphoning off the surplus of East Pakistan to develop itself (Rahman, A. 1968). Along with it went the resentment of the Bengali proto-elite at its lack of power in the state structure.

Let us first consider some figures pertaining to economic disparity. The figures for the total expenditure on both wings are as follows (in millions of US dollars):

|           | East Pakistan      | West Pakistan       |
|-----------|--------------------|---------------------|
| 1950-1955 | 569.10 (20%)       | 2,370.90 (80%)      |
| 1955-1960 | 1,104.00 (26%)     | 3,475.50 (74%)      |
| 1960-1965 | 2,948.40 (32%)     | 7,045.50 (68%)      |
| 1965-1970 | 4,838.40 (36%)     | 8,601.60 (64%)      |

(HBWI 1982: Vol. 6, 811).

The major grievance, that the Eastern wing exported more than it imported, is illustrated by the following figures.

*Percentage of Share of East Pakistan in Imports and Exports*

| Year | Imports | Exports |
|---|---|---|
| 1948-9 | 19.3 | 44.8 |
| 1949-50 | 29.7 | 52.7 |
| 1950-1 | 28.0 | 47.4 |
| 1951-2 | 34.1 | 54.1 |
| 1952-3 | 26.4 | 42.5 |
| 1953-4 | 26.3 | 50.2 |
| 1954-5 | 29.0 | 59.8 |
| 1955-6 | 27.2 | 85.4 |
| 1956-7 | 35.1 | 56.5 |
| 1957-8 | 35.9 | 69.5 |
| 1958-9 | 35.1 | 66.5 |
| 1959-60 | 26.6 | 58.6 |
| 1960-1 | 31.8 | 70.0 |
| 1961-2 | 28.1 | 70.5 |
| 1962-3 | 62.7 | 55.6 |
| 1963-4 | 33.6 | 53.2 |
| 1964-5 | 31.7 | 52.7 |
| 1965-6 | 31.6 | 55.7 |
| 1966-7 | 30.2 | 54.1 |
| 1967-8 | 28.5 | 44.3 |
| 1968-9 | 37.8 | 46.7 |
| 1969-70 | 35.6 | 50.0 |

Source: *Monthly Statistical Bulletin* Central Statistical Office, Government of Pakistan. (Various issues).

Despite some improvement in the 1960s, the continuing disparity between the two wings 'led to the alienation of all the politically relevant sections of Bengali society' (Jahan 1972: 89).

The figures for East Pakistani participation in the power structure of the state during the 1960s are given below:

The East Pakistanis, who formed 56 per cent of the population, are not represented as their numbers warranted, but they are represented better than they were in the 1950s.

| Powerful Offices | East Pakistan | West Pakistan |
|---|---|---|
| Chief Executive (Prime Minister) | 5 years | 19 years |
| C-in-C (Army, Navy, Air Force) | | 24 years |
| Finance Minister | | 24 years |
| Chief of Planning or Minister | | 24 years |
| Defence | 8.1 % | 91.9 % |
| Home Dept. | 22.5 % | 77.5 % |
| Education Dept. | 27.3 % | 72.7 % |
| Information Dept. | 20.1 % | 79.0 % |
| Health Dept. | 19.1 % | 81.0 % |
| Agriculture Dept. | 21.0 % | 79.0 % |
| Law Dept. | 35.0 % | 65.0 % |

(HBWI 1982: Vol. 6, 810-811).

However, as Rounaq Jahan observes, the 'civil service could accommodate only a fraction of the Bengali vernacular elite, and hence could hardly be regarded as an adequate substitute for an "integrative" political institution like a political party, where recruitment is broader, more rapid, and less selective' (1972:107). Because of the virtual absence of Bengali representation in the military, Bengali civil servants could hardly redress the balance of power which, in the absence of popular institutions, remained firmly tilted in favour of West Pakistan.

## Linguistic and Cultural Grievances

Although after 1956, the main emphasis of the Bengalis was on overtly economic and political matters, cultural and linguistic matters also remained important. They were especially significant insofar as they contributed to identity formation. Thus, Abul Kalam Shamsuddin, who supported a Muslim identity, condemned the literary conferences held in Dhaka in 1954, Mymensingh in 1956, and Chittagong in 1958, in which some people supported the unity of Muslim and Hindu Bengali language and literature (Shamsuddin 1968: 344-8).

On 31 December 1958, Ayub Khan, who favoured modernization and centralized rule, suggested in the Cabinet that 'the introduction of roman script for all the languages of Pakistan would help increase literacy and could result also in the creation of a common language' (Khan, A. 1967: 85). This suggestion was passionately opposed by almost everybody. Students chanted slogans on 21 February 1961 that the writing of Bengali in the Roman script would not be tolerated, and the Intelligence Branch confirmed that:

> A direct reaffirmation of the popular demand for more positive identification of Bengali as the State Language of Pakistan and outright rejection of the proposal for adoption of the Roman Script were the main features [of the events of 21 February] (IB: East Pak 28 February 1961).

The idea had to be abandoned. However, the government continued corpus planning to try to de-emphasize the distinctiveness of the Bengali identity, which the ethno-nationalists promoted. The report of the Commission on National Education declared that:

> The supreme need should be recognized by bringing Urdu and Bengali nearer to each other by increasing the common element in their vocabularies and by putting such common elements to extensive use (Edn Comm 1959: 293).

The Bengali Academy, set up in 1955 (Helal 1986; LAD-B 3 April 1957) with the major function of promoting 'the culture and development of Bengali language and literature' (The Bengali Academy Act, 1957 in Helal 1986: 215), now came under pressure to make this development subservient to the requirements of Pakistani nationalism. Dr Shahidullah, who was known for his pro-Muslim bias and who had been advocating the use of Perso-Arabic morphemes for creating new Bengali terms since 1950, when he was a member of the Bengali Reform Committee, was made the chief editor of a Bengali dictionary project in 1960 (Dil 1966: 17). Although he was highly respected, Dr Shahidullah's views about corpus planning were not popular among identity-conscious Bengalis.

Other governmental institutions meant to carry out integrative LP were the Central Boards for the Development of Urdu and Bengali, the Pakistan Writers Guild, the Linguistic Research Group of Pakistan, and the Pakistan Council for National Integration (Dil 1966: 191). The Central Board for the Development of Bengali completed the first phase of the Bengali renderings of technical terms of different science and arts subjects (11 sciences and 10 arts), keeping most of the international terms intact while other were 'rendered with the help of Sanskrit, Bengali and Perso-Arabic roots and endings' (Hai 1971: 191). However, Sanskritic terms were emphasized by the Bengali nationalists, in order to express their Bengali identity. Some of them were:

| | |
|---|---|
| television | *doordorshon* |
| telephone | *door ala poni* |
| radio | *betar* |
| book | *grokonthor* |
| pen | *jharna kolom* |

(Chowdhury Int: 30 September 1994).

Some English words of common usage, such as TV and telephone, remained in use, but *betar* had become current, as in *Bangladesh Betar* (Bangladesh Radio), till President Ziaur Rahman changed it to radio again. Attempts to impose *kitab* for *grokonthor* or *khush amded* (welcome) for *shagatam* were resisted, and identity-conscious language planners kept using Bangla words despite governmental efforts to substitute Urdu/Persian words for them (Chowdhury Int: ibid.).

The official policies of integration did not produce the desired result, in the absence of equitable power and resource sharing. The East Pakistani rejection of a unitary form of government—56 per cent respondents from the Eastern wing said they wanted a weak Centre, in their response to a questionnaire of the Constitution Commission (RCC 1961)—was not heeded. The Governor, Monem Khan, unleashed a reign of terror and even created a government party among the students (Jahan 1972: 164-6).

Once again, Bengali was one of the bones of contention. Monem regarded it as a non-Muslim language and felt that it promoted cultural unity with Calcutta (*PO* 4 January 1944, 8 and 16 September 1967). Another measure of resistance, which has been noted earlier, was the observance of the Shaheed Day. The Confidential Report of the Intelligence Branch reports that in 1961, it was 'more vocal this year. The procession in Dacca on Shahid Day was about a mile long' (IB East Pak 27 and 28 February 1961). Again in 1966, the enthusiasm was said to be 'unprecedented'. According to the newspapers, it was the biggest mass meeting since 1954 (*PO* 22 February 1966). The Bengali new year (*Pahela Baishakh*), which was condemned as anti-Muslim, was also celebrated enthusiastically (Rashiduzzaman 1982: 129). Moreover, in February 1966, there was a campaign to increase the use of Bengali and name plates, signboards, posters, and street signs were changed to Bengali throughout Dhaka (*PO* 15 February 1966).

Another bone of contention, to mention only cultural ones, was the poetry of Tagore. The government banned it for being non-Muslim, but the Bengali nationalists agitated against the ban, because Tagore was a symbol of their distinctive Bengali culture (Rashiduzzaman 1982: 123).

In February 1966, Sheikh Mujibur Rahman presented his famous Six Points, which gave practical shape to the Bengali demand for autonomy. Though none of the points were about language as such, the Awami League's activists, and indeed Sheikh Mujib himself, made it quite clear that the autonomy they desired would be used to preserve Bengali language and culture. Indeed, the East Pakistan Students League—the student wing of the Awami League—forced people to use Bengali, at least as far as signboards etc. were concerned. Thus, according to Rounaq Jahan, 'there were hardly any English or Urdu signboards left in any public place in Dacca' (1972: 168). The students also demanded, *inter alia*, the use of Bengali in education, in the courts of law, and in administration during their anti-Ayub agitation in 1968 and early 1969 (Islam 1986: 158). Thus, the mass emotion evoked by the Bhasha Ondolan now fed anti-West Pakistan, counter-hegemonic demands, such as the demand for a confederation based on the Six Points. Hence, references to the martyrs of 21 February and to the Bengali language were salient in the agitation against Ayub and during the election campaign during General Yahya's regime. On 31 December 1970, for instance, Mujib said:

> I appeal to our writers to express themselves freely for the benefit of the people and for the enrichment of the Bengali language and culture. I can assure them that any attempt from any quarter to suppress the creative urge of the artists, poets and writers will be resisted by me and my party (PO and MN 1 January 1971).

The political and military events which actually created Bangladesh in December 1971 are well known (Zaheer 1994) and are not the focus of this chapter. Now that Bengali nationalism was being expressed openly and militantly, Bengali no longer occupied centre-stage. It was taken for granted as an essential part of Bengali nationalism.

To sum up, the Bhasha Ondolan was significant for its effect on West Pakistan too. It was the first time that the domination of the Centre was successfully challenged through ethnic appeals and a pattern was set for similar developments in the future. But the lesson the ruling elite drew from the rise of Bengali ethno-nationalism was that expression of ethnicity should be suppressed. In short, the conspiracy theories that leftists and foreign agents create such movements—continued to be as strong as ever and attitudes remained inflexible.

# 7

# The Sindhi Language Movement

The Sindhi language is an important aspect of Sindhi identity and is viewed as an essential part of their cultural heritage by Sindhi ethno-nationalists (Syed 1990 ?: 99). The movement to promote its use in the domains of power is associated with Sindhi nationalism (Sangat n.d.: 7 and 8; Sath 1990: 2; Aslam n.d.: 8; Syed 1990: 398). And that is also one reason why the ruling elite has opposed it.

The necessity of upholding and strengthening Pakistani nationalism used to be the rationale of the Urdu-speaking Mohajirs in their opposition to Sindhi. After the emergence of the Mohajir ethnic identity, the Mohajirs claim a place for Urdu as one of the languages of Sindh or of a separate province to be carved out of Sindh. This is one of the impediments in the development of Sindhi, one which makes Sindh a conflict-prone province. Because of the politicization of the issue, there are few serious treatments of the evolution of the Sindhi language movement, though there are references to its role in studies of Sindhi nationalism (Amin 1988: 126; Ahmed, F. 1992a: 168-70).

The aim of this chapter is to place the Sindhi language movement in its historical perspective. More importantly, it attempts to relate the movement to the question of the distribution of power and resources.

### British Policy towards Sindhi

Sindh was conquered by Sir Charles Napier in 1843 (for his account, see Napier 1843). At this time the Baloch tribe of Talpurs, who had seized power from the Kalhoras in 1783, used Persian as the court language, though this Persian had Sindhi words in it (Khuhro, H. 1978: 242). Sindhi was also taught in some schools but, according to B. H. Ellis, Assistant Commissioner in Sindh in the 1850s, this was 'Hindoo-Sindee, written in the Khudawadee and other varieties of the Sindee character', and there were only 23 such schools with 803 pupils (Ellis 1856: para 6). Most Muslims as well as Hindu (clerks) who functioned as bureaucrats under the Muslim rulers studied in schools where Arabic and Persian were taught. There were said to be 609 such schools with 6,479 pupils (Ellis 1856: para 5). However, according to Lieutenant (later Sir) Richard Burton (1821-1890), at that time a military officer and spy in Sindh (McLynn 1990: 52-4), even in these Perso-Arabic schools the pupil 'is nine years old before he proceeds to the next step—the systematic study of his mother tongue, the Sindhi' (Burton 1851: 135). This, it should be pointed out, was a departure from Muslim educational practices in the rest of South Asia where the mother tongue was not taught. Thus, besides numerous poetical and religious works in Sindhi, there were also textbooks in the language, such as the seventeenth century work called *Abul Hasan Jo Sindhi* (Baloch 1971: vii), even before the British conquest.

In 1847, R. K. Pringle, Commissioner of Sindh, submitted a report on the language situation in Sindh to George Russell Clerk, Governor of Bombay, suggesting that education may be encouraged. Apropos the language he wrote:

> It may also be for consideration whether the vernacular language of the people may not with advantage be introduced in business; but I have not yet had an opportunity of ascertaining its capabilities for this purpose (Pringle 1847: 58).

Most British officers favoured the use of the vernacular language at the lower levels and Sir George Clerk wrote in his Minute of 24 April 1848:

> We should introduce the language of the country (namely, Sindhee) as the medium of official intercourse. I do not see in what way our revenue and judicial officers (however their offices and courts may be constituted) can work effectually through a foreign medium of communication, such as Persian or English (Clerk 1848: para 68).

The Bombay Government finally issued a circular (No. 1825 of 6 September 1851) requiring all officers to undergo an examination 'to test their proficiency in a colloquial knowledge of Sindhee' (Ellis 1856: para 35).

## Controversy over the Script

The major controversy between the British officers concerned the script. Burton was in favour of the Arabic script as, in his opinion, the eight orthographic systems of the Hindus were 'equally useless', for 'want of a sufficient number of vowel signs' (Burton 1851: 152-3). The Arabic *naskh* (or *nashki* as he called it) was preferable because:

> 1st. That all the literature of the country has been for ages written in this hand.

> 2nd. All educated Muslims are able to read it and most of them to write it.

> 3rd. Although the Hindoo Amils throughout Sindh are at present unable to read it, their knowledge of the *Nastaliq* or Persian hand would render the difficulty of learning it nugatory (Burton 1851: 156).

Captain George Stack, the only other authority on the Sindhi language, advocated the cause of the Hindu *khudawadi* script which had the merit of being indigenous. Stack also modified the proposed script and R. K. Pringle favoured this modified form of *khudawadi* (Khuhro 1978: 254). The Governor of Bombay, Lord Falkland, also agreed with the use of this script because of its indigenousness, although he did point out that it was not well known (Falkland's Minute of 28 July 1849 in Khuhro 1978: 256).

A number of British officers had, indeed, pointed out the same difficulty in response to questions addressed to them by the Commissioner in 1847 (Pringle 1848). Thus, the Court of Directors of the Company decided in favour of the Arabic script through Resolution No. 48 of 1852 (Khuhro 1978: 257). This decision was political in that it was meant to conciliate the Muslim majority of Sindh so that it would not oppose the British government. Evidence in support of this suggestion will be adduced later.

Once the choice of *naskh* was made, it was necessary to agree on orthographic symbols. Up to that period, writers had used different symbols, especially for sounds that were not common between Arabic and Sindhi. The government now appointed a committee, headed by the Deputy Commissioner of Sindh, B. H. Ellis, to agree on the graphemes of Sindhi. The Committee had five Muslims and four Hindus and they agreed on 52 graphemes of Sindhi orthography and 'a sheet containing the alphabet revised was published in July 1853' (Ellis 1856: para 42). It should be emphasized here that, contrary to popular opinion in Pakistan, the Sindhi alphabet was not invented by the Committee but only standardized by it.

## British Political Considerations

Apart from fleeting references to Muslim opinion in Burton's writings and elsewhere, there is no direct documentary evidence that the conciliation of Muslims through the choice of *naskh* was an objective of British language planners. However, conciliation was a general policy and there is no reason why it should not have influenced the choice of the script in Sindh. Moreover, Ellis showed a keen understanding of the Hindu-Muslim antagonism in Sindh and writes in his report:

> there can be no doubt but that this, or any other character in ordinary use by Mussalmans, will not be adopted by the Hindoo community. While the great majority of the population of Sindh consists of Mahomedans, it is imperative on us that we should not deter them (the Hindoos) from entering the public service, and debar them from the means of instruction in their own language, by the universal adoption of a Hindoo-Sindee character, which Mussalmans would never adopt; yet the Hindoos are a sufficiently numerous and influential community to demand that their interests should not be overlooked (Ellis 1856: para 43).

The point that the Muslim interest was secured first—as they were more numerous and prosperous than the Hindus—is implied here.

Direct evidence that the Muslims were conciliated comes from other matters such as the distribution of jobs. The following letter of H. B. E. Frere, the Commissioner of Sindh, to the Acting Collector of Hyderabad, states:

> I have the opportunity of begging your attention to the great preponderance of Hindoos in all offices except that of Kardar, to an extent that shows that in a very few years there will be none but Hindoos in the district offices. This is a result by no means desirable, and there can be but little difficulty in averting it; at towns like Tatta [sic] there are numbers of well-educated Mahomedans capable of and anxious for employment as Government servants, and where proper care has been taken I have found a fair proportion in comparatively subordinate positions (Letter No. 743 of 3 April 1852 in SA).

The Arabic Sindhi script was adopted in the same spirit, although the Hindu script was also used in order to win over the Sindhi Hindus to British rule.

The Hindu Sindhi script was recommended by Englishmen like B. Ellis and Sir Bartle Frere, who felt that alienating the Hindus would not be conducive to the consolidation of British rule in Sindh. According to the Education Commission of 1882, the 'Hindus held aloof from the Government school, because it taught Sindhi through the Arabic character' (Edn Comm-Bom 1884: 24). Sir Bartle Frere had a standard alphabet prepared from Hindu orthographic symbols in 1856, but it was not introduced immediately (ibid. 25).

The moving spirit behind the efforts to spread the use of Hindu Sindhi was Narayan Jaganath Mehta, 'a Deccani Brahmin gentleman whom the Bombay government appointed to be Deputy Educational Inspector in Sindh' (Dow 1976: 55). Mehta's reasons were probably nationalistic—the Hindu script was a symbol of the Hindu identity for him—and it was among identity-conscious Hindus that the script became popular when it was introduced in 1868. However, once this grievance of the Hindus was removed, they turned their attention to Arabic Sindhi which, being used for employment widely in Sindh, was less ghettoizing than Hindu Sindhi.

In any case, as many British officers reported, Hindu Sindhi and even the Devanagari script 'itself [was] one may say, quite unknown to the natives of Sindh' (Dunsterville 1857). Frere felt that the Devanagari 'character is more better known than Dunsterville allowed', but recommended the publication of a dictionary in Arabic Sindhi (MS letter to the Governor of Bombay, 20 July 1857, No. 201 of Karachee in SA). Thus, despite all efforts at promoting Hindu Sindhi, Fultun, an Educational Inspector, reported a falling off in the study of this script between 1875 and 1877 (Edn Comm-Bom 1884: 39). Political expediency prevailed and the Education Commission reported that it had not been given up 'as it is believed to be a concession to Hindu sentiment, which may one day attain its purpose' (ibid. 39). However, in 1881 Dayaram Gidumal, an Assistant Collector in Sindh also recommended its abolition. This was supported by Giles, the Commissioner, and 'official support was withdrawn and the script soon died a natural death when it ceased to be pushed by government agency' (Dow 1976: 55).

The Muslims saw Hindu Sindhi as a British-Hindu conspiracy, and even recent reports assert that the idea behind Hindu Sindhi was to cut off the Muslims from the adjoining Muslim civilizations using Arabic-based scripts (Barelvi 1987: 35). It was, however, an attempt to promote Hindu culture by people for whom, according to Dow, 'any sign of the predominance of Muslim culture was anathema' (1976: 56).

The conclusion which one reaches after a study of British efforts at promoting Sindhi, in both the Arabic and the Hindu scripts, is that this was a way of conciliating public opinion in Sindh and thus consolidating the empire.

## Muslim Attitude towards Sindhi in Pre-Partition Days

One of the demands of the Muslims of British India, also included by M. A. Jinnah in his fourteen points, was the separation of Sindh from the Bombay presidency so as to create another Muslim majority province in western India. Sir Ghulam Husain Hidayatullah, a representative of Sindhi Muslims, pointed out at the Indian Round Table Conference (12 November 1930 – 19 January 1931), that Sindh 'is racially, geographically and linguistically a separate province' from Bombay (Proceedings of the First Meeting of Sub-Committee No. ix on 12 January 1931 in Khuhro, H. 1982: 330). Coming to the question of the Sindhi language, he said:

> I come to the Director of Public Instruction . . . Does he know Sindhi? Even some of my Inspectors of Education do not know Sindhi, the language of the place, though most of the Civilians are required to pass the examination (ibid. 336).

During a debate in the Sindh Legislative Assembly, Pir Ilahi Bakhsh complained that 'Every Sindhi who goes to the Bombay University complains that he is not being heard', and argued that Sindh should have a separate university (LAD-S 28 March 1945: 20). This university, according to Ghulam Murtaza Syed, who was then a member of the Sindh Legislature and was later to become the leader of the Sindhi ethno-nationalist movement, was for the following purpose:

> We wanted to get rid of the intellectual dominance of the Bombay university and with a view to achieving that aim, and creating such an atmosphere under which the cultural homogeneity of the province might be maintained and developed, we appointed a Committee to investigate the possibility of establishing a university of Sindhi language whereby the literary talent in the province might be encouraged and properly guided (Syed 1949: 58).

In short, the Muslims emphasized the distinctiveness of Sindhi culture from that of Bombay—language being a major determiner of this distinction—in order to create a separate Muslim majority province. However, Dr Moonje, a Hindu leader, argued that language could not be a basis of separation because, if that were admitted, then in principle, the Bombay presidency alone would have to be split up into Gujrati, Marathi, Karnatki, and other linguistic administrative units

(Proceedings of the Third Meeting of the Sub-Committee on Sind, 14 January 1931 in Khuhro, H. 1982: 416). However, the Sub-Committee on Sind, of which Jinnah was a member, recommended that 'the social and linguistic differences between the inhabitants of Sind and those of the Presidency of Bombay proper' provided an impressive case to separate Sindh from Bombay (Report dated 16 January 1931 in Khuhro, H. 1982: 447).

Muslim politicians prevailed and Sindh became a province in its own right in 1936. Sindhi was now the major language of basic schooling in the province. According to the annual report on public instruction (1939-40), this was a sound step. The report said:

> The results after the adoption of this medium [mother tongue] are distinctly better. This in itself shows that the step taken is psychologically sound and is on the whole natural (RPI-S 1943: 40).

The provincial government also outlined the steps it had taken to promote Sindhi. These included the compilation of a dictionary along the lines of the *Oxford English Dictionary* and the creation of scientific terms (LAD-S 18 December 1941: 20-1). The Sind University Act also was debated again and again in the Legislative Assembly.

Sindhi was also the language of official correspondence and records at the lower level. There was, indeed, an office of a Sindhi Translator 'so that circulars, Laws and Acts issued in English could simultaneously be translated into Sindhi' (Baloch, N. 1993: Preface). According to N. A. Baloch, as many as 734 laws were translated into Sindhi, of which the Indian Contract Act of 1872 was an early example (ibid. For a reprint of this Act see Baloch, N. 1993). The Sindhi Press too was flourishing and there were 87 Sindhi newspapers—not counting Hindu Sindhi, English, and Urdu Sindhi ones—in the province (LAD-S 7 August 1937: 8-12).

Hindus, despite being Sindhis, tended to identify with Hindi. The provincial government, which was Muslim-dominated, had ceased to recognize Hindi as a language for primary education on 25 November 1931, though Urdu was recognized as one (LAD-S 30 January 1940: 12-3). Sindhi thus became the dominant language of schools and even Gujrati, Marathi, and Urdu schools had to teach it after 1942 (LAD-S 26 February 1941: 60). The antagonism between Hindus and Muslims also extended to other dimensions, the most important being political. G. M. Syed complained that 'The Hindus who formed 27% of the population were given 40% representation in the Sind Legislative Assembly' (Syed 1949: 4). They also dominated business and commerce and formed a majority of the population of Karachi (see Table 1, below). However, on the eve of Partition, when Sindh had a Muslim government, Durgadas B. Adwani wrote a letter to M. A. Jinnah (23 June 1947), complaining against the Sindh University Act and the conduct of the Education Minister, who was alleged to have shut out even first class Hindu students from the Government Medical College, and declared 'that Urdu shall be the medium of instruction in the Sindh University' (Zaidi 1994:418). As in the rest of India, Urdu was a Muslim identity symbol to confront Hindus. But, whatever members of the Sindh government might have said in their battle against their Hindu opponents, they did not make Sindhi subservient to Urdu.

**Advent of the Mohajirs in Sindh**

Partition brought an influx of immigrants to the cities of Sindh as Table 1 indicates:

Table 1

*Change in Religious Composition in Karachi*

| Community | 1941 Persons (1000s) | Per cent | 1951 Persons (1000s) | Per cent |
|---|---|---|---|---|
| Total | 365.3 | 100 | 1006.4 | 100 |
| Muslims | 153.3 | 42.0 | 967.5 | 96.1 |
| Caste Hindus | 173.9 | 47.6 | 4.4 | 0.4 |
| Scheduled Castes | 11.9 | 3.3 | 11.8 | 1.2 |
| Christians | 10.0 | 2.7 | 16.7 | 1.7 |
| Parsees | 3.7 | 1.0 | 5.0 | 0.5 |
| Jain | 3.2 | 0.9 | - | - |
| Sikhs | 4.8 | 1.3 | 1.0 | 0.1 |
| Others | 4.6 | 1.2 | - | - |

Source: Census 1951: Chapter 5, Statement 5-B

Although Ayub Khuhro declared in the Legislative Assembly that 45,000 refugees were sent to Tharparkar, 30,000 to Nawabshah, and 25,000 to Hyderabad (LAD-S 18 February 1848: 2) to cultivate 'abandoned fields' (ibid. 11 February 1948: 23), most of the refugees settled down in the major cities of Sindh. In the whole of Pakistan, refugees formed 9.8 per cent of the population, but in Sindh and Khairpur state they formed 11.7 per cent of the population. However, as they were concentrated in the cities, the demographic composition of urban Sindh (including Karachi, which was then the federal capital area) changed as follows:

Table 2

*Proportion of Mohajirs in the major cities of Sindh in 1951*

| City | Population | Mohajirs | Mohajirs as percentage of population |
|---|---|---|---|
| Karachi (Corporation) | 10,64,557 | 6,12,680 | 57.55 |
| Hyderabad | 2,41,801 | 1,59,805 | 66.08 |
| Sukkur | 77,026 | 41,791 | 54.08 |
| Mirpurkhas | 40,412 | 27,649 | 68.42 |
| Nawabshah | 34,201 | 18,742 | 54.79 |
| Larkana | 33,247 | 11,767 | 35.39 |

Source: Census 1951: Vol. 1, Table 2 Section 2 and 3; District Census reports.

The Mohajirs were better educated than the local Sindhis as the following figures show:

Table 3

*Years of Education*

| Place | Total Population | Received Schooling | Received over 10 Years of Schooling |
|---|---|---|---|
| Pakistan | 7,29,93,118 | 1,02,94,704 | 5,86,151 |
| Karachi | 11,22,404 | 2,76,602 | 30,914 |
| Sindh & Khairpur | 49,25,342 | 3,79,375 | 17,202 |
| Punjab & Bahawalpur | 2,06,36,702 | 25,88,870 | 1,78,656 |
| NWFP | 32,22,172 | 2,15,304 | 25,052 |
| Balochistan & States Union | 7,29,93,118 | 1,02,04,704 | 5,86,151 |

Source: *Census 1951: Vol. 1 Table 9-A*

112    *Language and Politics in Pakistan*

The figures for Karachi represent the higher percentage of Mohajirs who were educated. Their literacy rate was 23.4 per cent, whereas that of Sindh as a whole was only 13.2 per cent.

This led to Mohajirs taking up technical, bureaucratic, and professional jobs, as the following figures illustrate.

Table 4

*Occupation of the Non-Agricultural Labour Force*

| Occupation | Sindh and Khairpur | Karachi |
|---|---|---|
| Non-Agricultural labourers | 4,57,942 | 3,73,796 |
| Professional and technical | 17,634 | 10,449 |
| Engineers and architects | 243 | 1,119 |
| Transport managers, pilots | 17 | 36 |
| Professors and teachers | 7,923 | 2,995 |
| Religious workers | 2,061 | 918 |
| Physicians and surgeons | 2,519 | 1,427 |
| Nurses and other health workers | 1,170 | 1,123 |
| Authors, writers, journalists, judges and lawyers | 390 | 498 |
| Chemists and metallurgists | 17 | 112 |
| Other professions | 2,898 | 1,927 |
| Administrative | 41,832 | 75,330 |
| Business executives | 4,503 | 7,209 |
| Government Services | 439 | 1,344 |
| Office workers | 30,380 | 66,777 |
| Manufacturing (Skilled) |  | 58,032 |

Source : *Census 1951: Table 11-A*

Thus, the Mohajirs were the largest urban-based pressure group in Sindh, even in the 1950s. The tangible symbol of their identity was the city of Karachi, where the culture of UP held undisputed sway. The cultural implications of this were grave. The Mohajirs, who already felt that their urban Mughal culture was superior to the indigenous culture of Sindh, now got a physical locale in which that culture could take root and flourish. As Urdu was an important aspect of the aesthetic sensibility of Lucknow and Delhi, the two centres of UP culture, it assumed the role of an evocative cultural symbol in urban Sindh too. In fact, since Urdu had been an important symbol during the Urdu-Hindi controversy days, it was perpetuated by the Mohajirs and the ruling Punjabi elite as a marker of Pakistani Muslim identity.

Since Mohajirs were concentrated in cities where they did not come across many Sindhi speakers, they were not under pressure to learn Sindhi. Indeed, even those who wanted to, found it hard to do so, because it was so easy to get by with Urdu. If the Mohajirs had been spread thinly everywhere and local languages had been encouraged, they might have become an assimilated minority. Why the government allowed their concentration in urban Sindh in the first place is a question which has not been satisfactorily answered. The Sindhi nationalists assert that Liaquat Ali Khan, the first prime minister of Pakistan (who had himself come from India), settled them there so as to create an electoral constituency. G. M. Syed, while asserting this, also adds that the Punjab did not accept them (Syed's interview in Ali, M. 1987: 25). Hamza Alavi also claims that the Punjab did not accept the Mohajirs.

> Forty years ago the Punjabi-ruling oligarchy ensured that refugees from East Punjab (and only those) were settled in West Punjab so that Punjab in Pakistan remained ethnically homogeneous. All other refugees, mainly Urdu-speaking refugees from Northern and Central India, were settled in Sind. They were kept out of the Punjab although Punjab is a much larger province and had a greater capacity to absorb the refugees (Alavi 1987: 271).

But this assertion, as well as those claiming that communal riots were instigated to drive out the Hindus, are not supported by credible evidence. It appears that Karachi, being an industrial city and the capital, attracted Mohajirs, who therefore settled down there initially. After that, these settlers, having created their own culture, naturally attracted others of their kind from India. Whatever the reason the Mohajirs concentrated in the cities of Sindh, the political consequence of this, in M. Waseem's words, was the emergence 'of a new Punjab-urban Sindh axis of power which dominated the Muslim League, the bureaucracy and the army' (Waseem 1994: 34).

In any case, the conditions of urban Sindh, combined with their own cultural history and the pro-Urdu policies of the government, made the Mohajirs a resistant, non-assimilationist collectivity. The evolution of the Sindhi Movement in Pakistan can be seen in the light of the resistance offered to it by the Mohajirs and the ruling Punjabi-dominated elite.

## Sindhi and the Separation of Karachi from Sindh

The first major setback to the progress of Sindhi was caused by the separation of Karachi from Sindh. When the proposal was first put forward, it was opposed by the Sindh Legislative Assembly. Hashim Gazdar, one of the members of the Assembly, said:

> Such a step could not only cripple Sind economically and politically, but would constitute a flagrant contravention of the Pakistan Resolution passed by the All-India Muslim League at Lahore, in 1940, which emphasizes the sovereignty and the territorial integrity of the autonomous units constituting Pakistan (LAD-S 10 Feb 1948: 17-18).

It was felt that the Mohajirs, who had been given refuge by the Sindhis, were appropriating the soil of Sindh. Moreover, even in that early period, misgivings were expressed about Sindh being dominated by the Punjabis (ibid. 18-24; G. M. Syed in Siddiqui, J. 1987: 65).

As a consequence of the decision to separate Karachi, the University of Sindh was moved to Hyderabad which was less developed than Karachi. In 1952, a separate university was established in Karachi which was clearly more inclined to encourage Urdu than Sindhi. The Sindhi language movement, which had been going on since the anti-Bombay days, took the form of the Sindhi-Urdu controversy because of the decision taken in 1957-58, by the University of Karachi forbidding students from answering examination questions in Sindhi. To this, Hyder Baksh Jatoi, President of the Sindh Hari Committee, reacted as follows:

> It is obvious to anyone that a Sindhi-knowing student cannot answer papers in Urdu as ably and efficiently (other considerations being equal), as an Urdu-knowing student. The disadvantage to the Sindhi-knowing student in relation to the Urdu-knowing students is at least of 20 per cent marks.

His pamphlet ends on a note of alienation.

> This order of Karachi University amounts to a call to the Sindhi students: 'Leave Karachi, go to Sind if you want to retain Sindhi, Karachi is none of yours' (Jatoi 1957: 13).

Later, when the provincial minister of education was questioned about the situation, he confessed that 'everyone knows that the emphasis is greater on Urdu than on Sindhi' (LAD-P 9 March 1958: 1103).

However, as 500,000 people in Karachi were Sindhi-speaking, this discouragement of the language was resented by the Sindhi Press which had 'five dailies and a number of weeklies' (Bughio 1991). Sindhi now became a major symbol of the sense of deprivation—cultural, educational, economic, and political—which Sindhi leaders and the emerging middle class intelligentsia felt.

**One Unit and Sindhi**

In 1954, the provinces of West Pakistan were amalgamated to form one administrative unit. As this did away with the separate identity of Sindh, it was opposed by the Sindhi nationalists (see editorials in *Mehran* 30 December 1956 to 2 January 1957). Sindhi was now merely a regional language and the Sindhi Adabi Sangat, referring to the 14 national languages of India, appealed to the government to make Sindhi one of the national languages of Pakistan. The Sangat gave economic arguments, saying:

> If the intention is not to see 5 million Sindhi speaking people handicapped and put at a disadvantage in the field of education, trade and commerce, and public services as against Urdu-knowing fellow citizens then it is absolutely essential that Sindhi is made to serve as an official language at least for Sind and its adjoining Sindhi speaking areas (Sangat n.d. 7).

The Sangat, in common with the rest of the Sindhi intelligentsia, was aware of the relationship between economic and political power and language.

The Sindhi Press expressed similar views, although, the Karachi-based Urdu Press gave the impression that Urdu rather than Sindhi was acceptable to all the inhabitants of Sindh. The Sindhi Press objected to these statements, and *Al Wahid*, a Sindhi daily, declared in its editorial of 25 April 1954 that the bias of the Urdu papers was 'only with a view to stopping the news to reach the government and the people of Pakistan that besides Bengalis, other Pakistanis including Sindhi people, also opposed the honour of national language to only Urdu' (Quoted from Bughio 1991: 11).

In the Sindhi Adabi conference of Larkana, I. I. Qazi, a well-known intellectual of Sindh, warned the Sindhis that their culture would cease to exist if Sindhi was allowed to fall into disuse (Qazi

1956). In fact, most Sindhi nationalists opposed One Unit on cultural, linguistic, economic, and political grounds.

## Ayub Khan's Martial Law and Sindhi

One Unit continued to exist during Ayub Khan's ten-year rule, and the indigenous languages of the country, which were given the marginalizing label of 'regional languages', were slighted. Among other things, the report on national education in 1959 reduced the importance of Sindhi. It agreed that the mother tongue should be used up to class five as the medium of instruction but went on to prescribe that:

> Urdu should be introduced as the medium of instruction from class VI from 1963 and should continue progressively in the higher classes. It is necessary to give Urdu the same position in Sind as in the rest of West Pakistan (Edn Comm 1959: 284).

The supporters of Sindhi submitted a memorandum to Ayub Khan pointing out that the proposals reduced the role of Sindhi which was a medium of instruction up to matriculation, and which had been a medium of examination up to BA (quoted in Rashdi 1984: 3).

Among other forms of protest, a 'Sindhi Day' was celebrated throughout the province on 9 November 1962, and eminent political and intellectual personalities issued a communique in which they demanded that the former status of the language be restored. 'It is of some significance' notes one writer 'that only one Urdu-speaking politician, Mahmudul Haq Usmani, was a signatory to that statement' (Jafar 1992). However, as it was Urdu which was taking the place of Sindhi, this was only to be expected in such a situation of conflict.

President Ayub, finding the reaction of Sindhis alarming, tried to conciliate them by deciding that 'Sindhi will continue to remain a medium of instruction as heretofore' (Ministry of Education and Information, Notification, in Rashdi 1984: 4). However, Sindhi was discouraged during this period and the number of Sindhi medium schools decreased. The latter was, of course, the inevitable consequence of the Mohajirs having become a majority in Karachi, but it was seen by Sindhi nationalists in the light of a conspiracy. The number of primary schools teaching in Sindhi and other languages on

23 August 1948, when Karachi was separated from Sindh, was as follows:

Table 5

| Year | Language | Number of Schools | Number of pupils |
|---|---|---|---|
| 1948 | Urdu | 69 | 18,440 |
|  | Sindhi | 57 | 6,965 |

(ABE 1950: 59)

Replying to a question, Dur Muhammad Usto, the Sindh Minister of Education in 1972, told the Assembly that in 1954 there were 76 Sindhi-medium and 187 Urdu medium schools in Sindh (LAD-S 20 December 1972: 53). The Minister also said that 11 Sindhi schools for girls had been converted into Urdu ones because there were not sufficient Sindhi pupils in them (ibid. 53). Later, another Education Minister, Pyarali Allana, told the Legislative Assembly that 30 primary schools had been closed down during Ayub Khan's days (LAD-S 29 May 1974: 30).

In other domains too, Sindhi suffered during this period. After the formation of One Unit, only a few laws such as the West Pakistan Ghulam Muhammad Barrage Betterment Tax Ordinance, 1964, were translated into Sindhi, whereas earlier, all laws were printed in it. In this period, records and registers, which used to be kept in Sindhi, began to be printed in Urdu (LAD-S 19 November 1973: 15-6). Even in the municipality of Hyderabad, for instance, it was resolved on 11 June 1965 that Urdu would be used for official work because that was also the policy of the West Pakistan Government (MCH 1965). The administrators of the municipal committee, who were Mohajirs, were reputed to be anti-Sindhi according to Sindhi nationalist circles (Aslam n.d.: 5).

Sindhi nationalists also complained that in this period Sindhi was replaced by Urdu on official buildings such as railway and bus stations; Sindhi writers were discouraged, whereas those writing in Urdu were patronized; Sindhi publications were denied advertisements and Sindhi radio broadcasts were reduced (Aslam n.d.: 2). The last issue was also discussed in the National Assembly and the government's statement (in LAD-P 13 December 1963: 900) failed to satisfy the Sindhis, because the programmes from Karachi and on the 'national hook-up' were allotted much more time than Sindhi ones. The issue was, of course, of symbolic significance as it reflected the perception of the Sindhis that their language and culture had become peripheral, not only in Pakistan but even in Sindh itself.

In 1966, there was another bitter debate on the medium of instruction and examination. A group of students tried to persuade the University of Sindh to adopt Sindhi as the medium of instruction and examination at the university level. The Sindhi Press supported the students and the newspapers wrote editorials in their favour. Among these were the editorials of *Ibrat* (12 May 1966), *Mehran* (16 May 1966), *Nawa-e-Sind*, *Khadim-e-Watan*, *Hilal-e-Pakistan* (all of 18 May 1966). Among other things, the Press pointed out that Sindhi students would secure higher marks if they were permitted to answer questions in Sindhi rather than in Urdu (*Hilal-e-Pakistan* quoted in Baloch, K. n.d.: 20).

The alienation of Sindhis from both the Mohajirs and the Ayub Khan government kept increasing during the 1960s. Finally, on 4 March 1967, when Masroor Hasan Khan, an Urdu-speaking Commissioner of the Hyderabad Division, ordered the arrest of some students of Sindh University, the nationalists found a symbol of resistance, just as the Bengali students agitating for the Bengali language had found one on 21 February 1952.

### General Yahya's Policy towards Sindhi

Ayub Khan's government fell in March 1969 and General Yahya Khan imposed martial law once again. The new government circulated tentative proposals for a new educational policy. One of these proposals was that Urdu should be made the sole medium of instruction and the official language in the western wing of the country, while Bengali would enjoy the same status in the eastern wing (PNEP 1969: 3-4). All the ethno-nationalists of West Pakistan were opposed to this. In Sindh, the *Jeay Sindh Naujawan Mahaz* (the Young People's Movement of Sindhi nationalists inspired by G. M. Syed) responded with a list of eight points, one of which noted that this would entail the closing down of schools and loss of jobs for teachers of Sindhi.

The eight points were rather alarmists. They suggested that the new policy, if implemented, would entirely annihilate Sindhi culture and thus do away with the distinctive Sindhi nationality. The economic and political consequences were also made explicit.

Apart from the loss of economic and social privilege that this inability to compete on equal terms with others would impose upon the Sindhi-speaking youth of the country, it would keep them deprived of their legitimate share in all state services and thus would deny them full sense of participation in the governance of their country (Talpur 1969: 8).

The *Mahaz* felt that Urdu was at par with English, not being the language of the masses, and that it should not be imposed in the name of 'national cohesion'. Finally, it was proposed that all the 'recognized mother tongues of Pakistani people, including Bengali and Urdu, should be declared as national languages' and all should be used as the media of instruction (ibid. 13).

## Ideological Antagonism between Sindhis and Mohajirs

The view that Sindhi should be the national language of Sindh had been expressed by G. M. Syed, the father of Sindhi nationalism, and by other Sindhi nationalists earlier. More recently, Syed eloquently expressed his views in *Sindhu Desh*:

> To discard the national language of Sindh, thrust a foreign language upon them so that the Sindhis may lose their thousand years old language, which was the foundation for their unity; to refuse to recognise the separate existence of the Sindhi nation, and thereby to forget their thousand years old separate existence. This has resulted in Sindhis losing their sense of self-respect, their past glory and have begun to feel helpless and at the mercy of outsiders (Syed 1990?: 115).

This, in Syed's view, was because the Punjabi ruling elite, in collaboration with the Mohajirs, wanted to colonize and exploit Sindh so that the Sindhis would not have 'separate governments of their own' (ibid. 99) and the Urdu-speaking Punjabis and Mohajirs would dominate the province politically, economically, and culturally. The official point of view, shared by the Mohajir intelligentsia roughly up to 1985, was that Urdu could unite Pakistan: if any other language were given the status of the national language, the country would break up (Barelvi 1987: 2). The point at issue, as mentioned in the Introduction, was whether Pakistan was a multi-ethnic state or not.

Government officials and the Establishment intellectuals took up the same position as they had in the case of the Bengali language movement and dubbed all expression of Sindhi nationalism as a communist and Indian conspiracy, while Sindhi itself was associated with Hinduism just as Urdu was associated with Islam (Piracha 1970: Part 2; Barelvi 1987: 113).

While many nationalists denied these charges, pointing out that there was much Islamic literature in Sindhi (Saib n.d.: 8-9; Appeal 1983: 4), most of them advanced secular arguments inspired by G. M. Syed. The main apprehensions of the Sindhis were that they would lose their identity and culture and be left behind in the race for goods, services, and power in the country (Baladi 1990; Magsi 1990).

It is true, of course, that the Sindhi nationalists were partly inspired by socialist ideas of multinationalism. (Socialist ideas are expressed by Jeay Sindh Taraqqi Pasand Party [JSTPP] of Qadir Magsi. See his interview by Mujtaba 1992: 51-5; and Magsi 1990). However, it does not follow that they were the pawns of the Soviet intelligence agencies sent out to seduce people from their allegiance to Pakistan. Similarly, G. M. Syed himself confessed in an interview that he had asked the Government of India to help him to create an independent Sindhu Desh (Siddiqui, J. 1987: 19) but Indira Gandhi refused. There are reports that material published in Bombay is smuggled into Sindh, but this literature would only be effective if there were existing grievances. In Sindh there were (and are) grievances and Sindhi has become one of the symbols that the intelligentsia has used to mobilize a pressure group to express them.

We have seen that the Sindhi and Mohajir attitudes towards the language issue were antagonistic. Rumours and ill-will against each other intensified as the newly-educated Sindhi middle class competed for jobs and power—leading to the language riots in Sindh.

## Language Riots in Sindh

The tension between the supporters of Urdu and those of Sindhi has led to riots twice: in January 1971 and July 1972. The events leading up to the riots have never received detailed description or analysis, though the riots of July 1972 have been placed in the context of the historical tension between the Mohajirs and Sindhis (Ahmed, F. 1992a). The first riots, those of 1971, have always been ignored, though the polarization between the Mohajirs and Sindhis which has made Sindh so violent a province became manifest then.

In 1970, G. M. Syed gave the name of the Sindh United Front to his Sindhi Awami Mahaz so as to participate in the elections. Like Sheikh Mujibur Rahman of East Pakistan, he too made an appeal to sentiments of ethnicity. The Mohajirs, who had emerged as a modern skilled workforce earlier, still dominated white-collar jobs and academic institutions, but this domination was now in jeopardy. Punjabis were taking over businesses and bureaucratic positions; Pakhtuns had started pouring into Karachi as labourers; above all, the Sindhis had been exposed to modern education and were aspiring to permeate the state apparatus.

Until the 1970s, however, after the Punjabis, it was the Mohajirs who were predominant in both the elite groups of society—the military and the civil services of Pakistan—as the following figures bear out:

Table 6

| | Ethnic Origin of the Top Military Elite in 1959 | | Ethnic Origins of the Top (Class 1) Bureaucracy | |
|---|---|---|---|---|
| | Number | Percentage | Number | Percentage |
| Punjabis | 17 | 35.4 | 1,727 | 48.89 |
| Pakhtuns | 19 | 39.6 | 287 | 8.12 |
| Mohajirs | 11 | 23.0 | 1,070 | 30.29 |
| Sindhis | 0 | 0 | 90 | 2.50 |
| Baluchis | 0 | 0 | 9 | 0.25 |
| Bengalis | 1 | 2.0 | 349 | 9.95 |
| | 48 | 100 | 3,532 | 100 |

Source: Sayeed 1968:278    Source: GOP, *Fourth Triennial Census of Central Government Employees, 1973.*

However, being migrants and cut off from their roots, they felt deracinated, threatened, and insecure to the point of paranoia. In conversation with each other, they repeated myths about discrimination which reinforced these feelings. Moreover, Mohajirs from urban Sindh, especially the middle and lower middle classes, resented the quota system which, in their view, discriminated against them.

The quota system, which had been developed in 1949 to fill vacancies in the Central Civil Service, was meant to allow people from the less developed areas to get a share in the Service. Twenty per cent of all vacancies were to be filled on merit, while the remaining eighty per cent would be filled according to the following formula: 40 per cent were reserved for East Pakistan, 23 for the Punjab, 15 per cent for Sindh, NWFP, Balochistan, and Azad Kashmir, the Northern Areas, Federally and Provincially-Administered Tribal Areas. Karachi's share was 2 per cent, rising to 7.6 per cent (including Hyderabad and Sukkur, i.e., urban Sindh) after 1973 (Kennedy 1984: 693). The Mohajirs condemned the quota system as unjust, and Nawab Muzaffar Khan, Convener of the Sindh Mohajir Punjabi Pathan Mahaz (MPPM), articulated such issues when he decided to contest elections from Hyderabad on 11 February 1970 (*J* 12 February 1970).

Meanwhile, Sindhi nationalism, inspired by G. M. Syed and Sheikh Mujib's autonomist rhetoric, had gathered much support amongst the students. The Jeay Sindh Naujawan Mahaz decided to contest elections on the issue of full autonomy for Sindh (*PT* 4 February 1970). In these circumstances, the syndicate of the University of Sindh decided on 21 August 1970 that 'Sindhi be adopted as the official language and language of internal correspondence' (Resolution No. 7 of 21 August 1970, SU). Other voices were also raised in support of Sindhi. In October, 108 Sindhi writers and intellectuals challenged the attempts by the ruling elite to make Urdu the dominant language of West Pakistan. The leading intellectuals of Sindh, notably Sheikh Ayaz, also demanded that Sindhi be made the dominant language of Sindh (*PO* 5 October 1970). The Sangat, among others, praised the University for having made Sindhi its official language and also demanded that the names of railway stations, parks, gardens, etc., should be written in Sindhi (*D* 21 October 1970). The Urdu Press, in its turn, wrote against Sindhi, branding its supporters as leftists, anti-Islamic, or anti-Pakistan dissidents (Piracha 1970: Part 2; 3 and 11 January 1971). By the end of 1970, Sindh was in ferment. Although the SUF lost the elections, nominating no candidate for the National Assembly, and only some for the provincial one, its ideology had gained ground. The idea that Sindhi should gain its rightful place in Sindh was one which all Sindhi political parties, including the Pakistan People's Party (PPP), supported in principle.

Tension suddenly increased when the Board of Intermediate and Secondary Education, Hyderabad, resolved on 21 December 1970 that:

> Sindhi be adopted as the official language of the Board. Resolved further that the subject of Salis [easy] Sindhi be introduced as a compulsory subject for the students whose mother-tongue is Urdu from the year 1971-72 and who are appearing at the Secondary School Certificate part-I Annual Examination held in the year 1972 (Resolution No. 21) BISE.

This created a crisis which resulted in the breakdown of law and order.[1]

Nawab Muzaffar Hussain, Convener of the MPPM, led the Mohajir protest against the decision of the University and the Board. Mohajir students brought out processions in Nawabshah, Mirpurkhas, and Hyderabad from 9 January 1971 onwards. Sindhi students in their turn brought out processions; violence began and Jeay Sindh students burnt pictures of the poet Iqbal. As Iqbal was one of the major symbols of Pakistani nationalism, this was seen as treason by the Urdu Press. Mohajir students burnt books in the prestigious Institute of Sindhology and there were further reprisals and counter-reprisals. In Karachi, events took an ugly turn on 27 January 1971 when buses were burnt and unruly crowds, demanding that all signboards should be in Urdu only, destroyed English ones. The army was called out in Hyderabad and parts of Karachi were placed under curfew. Even then, the violence continued until the middle of February. All over the country the supporters of Urdu and of Pakistani nationalism condemned the Sindhis, while the Sindhis and ethno-nationalist political parties condemned the non-assimilationist attitude of the Mohajirs.

## The Second Language Riots

The polarization between the Mohajirs and Sindhis, created by the riots of January 1971, increased as time went on. While the PPP tried to conciliate the nationalists by supporting Sindhi, the Mohajirs held meetings demanding that Urdu should be one of the official languages of Sindh (Barelvi 1987: 126). The Mohajirs were now a firmly non-assimilationist collectivity who saw Urdu as their identity-marker. At the same time, the more aggressive pamphlets of the Sindhi nationalists kept declaring: 'Non-Sindhis! Learn Sindhi or Leave Sindh'.

In these conditions, after the 1971 war and the emergence of Bangladesh, Zulfikar Ali Bhutto and his PPP came to power. The Chief Minister of Sindh, Mumtaz Ali Bhutto, now declared that he would fulfil the promise he had made to his Sindhi electorate to give Sindhi the same role in the province as it had enjoyed before the One-Unit period. Threatening those who would create disorder in the province, he declared that if he 'had ten lives, all those' would be sacrificed 'over the name of Sindh' (LAD-S 26 June 1972: 123).

Meanwhile, the Mohajirs in general, and the students of Karachi University in particular, had demanded that Urdu should be an official language of Sindh along with Sindhi. On 29 June 1972, the Governor of Sindh, Mir Rasul Bux Talpur, assured the Mohajirs that their demands would be met (Mahmood 1989: 96).

The Language Bill was presented in these difficult circumstances. Its main significance was symbolic, for both the Mohajirs and the Sindhis. If Urdu was accepted as a provincial language, as the Mohajirs demanded, Sindh would be accepted as a multi-ethnic province. If it was not, as the Sindhis desired, it would retain its Sindhi identity. The question was no less than the division of Sindh, something which was anathema to the Sindhi nationalists. The Sindh (Teaching, Promotion and Use of Sindhi Language) Bill of 1972 was given to members of the Legislative Assembly on 3 July. It provided *inter alia* that:

**Clause 4**
(1) Sindhi and Urdu shall be compulsory subjects for study in classes IV to XII in all institutions in which such classes are held.

(2) The introduction of Sindhi as a compulsory subject shall commence at the lowest level namely class IV and by stages to be prescribed, be introduced in higher classes upto class XII.

**Clause 6**
Subject to the provisions of the Constitution, Government may make arrangements for progressive use of Sindhi language in offices and departments of Government including Courts and Assembly.

The bill was discussed on 5 July at the house of Dr Ishtiaq Husain Qureshi, a former Vice Chancellor of Karachi University and an active member of the pro-Urdu lobby. The Mohajirs feared that Sindhi would be used everywhere in Sindh and this would be against their interests. Thus, they suggested an amendment, making Urdu as well as Sindhi the official languages of Sindh (Qureshi 1972; Munir 1972; Muzaffar 1972). The Urdu Press was also sensitive to the Bill. Feelings ran so high that on 7 July, even before the Bill had been passed, the supporters of Urdu rose against Sindhi. Referring to this, Mumtaz Bhutto told the Assembly that 'there have been disturbances in parts of Karachi today [i.e., 7 July], where innocent by-passers [sic] were molested and attacked' (LAD-S 7 July 1972: 70).

Within the Legislative Assembly, too, feelings ran high. No sooner was the Bill read out than Nawab Muzaffar objected to it, saying that adequate notice (three days) had not been given. The Speaker pointed out that the Bill had been known since 3 July and had even been published in the papers on 5 July. There were emotional and, at times, bitter and acrimonious speeches on both sides. When the amendments suggested by the Opposition were not accepted, the Opposition staged a walkout and the motion was carried (LAD-S 7 July 1972: 5-114).

On 8 July, the Urdu newspaper *Jang* carried lurid headlines proclaiming the death of Urdu. The following line from the poet Rais Amrohvi, written in another context, was splashed across the page.

> Urdu ka janaza hae zara dhoom say niklay
> (This is the funeral procession of Urdu; let it go out with fanfare.)

Soon the whole of Sindh was aflame and the bloodiest language riots witnessed in Pakistan followed. The Mohajirs attacked Sindhis in Karachi and the Department of Sindhi at the University of Karachi was burnt. Crowds defied Section 144 and police vehicles were damaged in Karachi and Hyderabad. Curfew was imposed in Karachi and Hyderabad, but sporadic incidents of violence and arson were reported. Mumtaz Bhutto explained the Language Bill on 12 July, claiming that Urdu, being the national language, would not be harmed. The Mohajir leadership claimed that the national language was always ignored and that they would be forced to learn Sindhi in the province to get employment. Meanwhile pro-Urdu and pro-Sindhi processions continued to clash with each other and violence spread all over Sindh.

**Resolution of the Conflict**

The confrontation between the Mohajirs and the Sindhis ended only when Z. A. Bhutto intervened to resolve their differences. The demands presented by the two communities made it apparent that, besides the sentiments involved in the preservation of their respective languages, what they were interested in was power in the province.

The Sindhis wanted Sindhi to be the official language of Sindh as well as one of the national languages of Pakistan, while the Mohajirs reiterated their demand that both Urdu and Sindhi should be the provincial languages of Sindh. The other demands pertained to jobs and powerful offices. The Mohajirs wanted an equal share (despite forming only 22 per cent of the population of Sindh, according to the Census of 1981) of all important posts, and the assurance that power would be equally divided. For instance, they wanted either the governor or the chief minister of the province to be a Mohajir; similarly that the posts of district and police officers should be evenly distributed to maintain the balance of power between the two communities. Another of their demands was that Karachi should have a city government with a wide range of powers (Barelvi 1987: 132-3).

The compromise solution was a twelve-year reprieve for the Mohajirs through the following Ordinance issued by the Governor of Sindh on 16 July. It said:

> No person, otherwise qualified for appointment or promotion to any civil service, or a civil post in connection with the affairs of the province of Sind, shall be discriminated against only on the ground of want of knowledge of Sindhi or Urdu language (The Sind Government Gazette, Extraordinary, 22 July 1972).

The twelve years have elapsed but government jobs can still be obtained without any knowledge of Sindhi, and with knowledge of Urdu alone, which all children have learnt at school.

**Consequences of the Conflict**

The official figures for loss and damage, as announced in the National Assembly by Qayyum Khan, the Federal Interior Minister, were as follows:

| | |
|---|---:|
| Number of persons injured (this included 133 police personnel) | 319 |
| Number of deaths | 2 |
| Value of property robbed | Rs 68,998 |
| Value of property damaged | Rs 1,671,427 |
| Value of property damaged in Karachi | Rs 223,354 |
| Value of property damaged in the rest of Sindh | Rs 517,116 |
| Number of cases registered | 143 |

(LAD-P 28 August 1972: 506).

The most ominous consequence of the conflict is its legacy of bitterness. Potentially even more explosive is the rise of Mohajir ethnicity. The demands of the Mohajirs, referred to earlier, indicate that they not only rejected the possibility of assimilation but were not even prepared to accept minority status. They wanted equal power in Sindh, and language was one way of securing it. As the Jeay Sindh activists saw it,

> If Urdu is accepted as an official language of Sindh, the rights of Sindhis will be undermined. As soon as Urdu is accepted as the second language of Sindh, it would amount to accepting the existence of two nationalities in the province. And if this is accepted then the Sindhis' claim that Sindh belongs to them is wrong . . . In this manner Urdu-speakers will create a *Mahajiristan* (JSSF n.d.: 15).

And, indeed, many Mohajirs began calling themselves a separate nationality ('Editorial' *MN* 5 August 1972) and the Mohajir Action Committee threatened to launch a popular movement to make a separate province of Karachi so as to protect Urdu (H 13 January 1972). This was the beginning of that shift away from the Pakistani or New Sindhi identity to the Mohajir identity which became manifest with the rise of the Mohajir Qaumi Movement (MQM) in the late 1980s. As Mohajir ethnicity has in fact divided Sindh, there is always the possibility of an ethnic civil war, one of the potentially dangerous legacies of the language riots. Equally dangerous from the point of lasting peace in Sindh is the formation of G. M. Syed's Jeay Sindh Mahaz in 1972 and its hold on students in the form of the Jeay Sindh Students Federation (JSSF) (Syed, A. 1988: 52-3). Syed's hold on the intelligentsia of Sindh through literary and cultural bodies is not dangerous because many members of the intelligentsia do not see violence as a solution to the problems of the Sindhis. However, it does help to disseminate the point of view of the Sindhi nationalists.

## Sindhi after the Riots

During the Ziaul Haq era (1977-88) all democratic movements were suppressed. The suppression of the Movement for the Restoration of Democracy (MRD) was so violent in Sindh, where anti-Punjabi and anti-military feelings ran high, that it took on the nature of a civil war (Mahmood 1989). Language became a secondary issue but continued to be mentioned in the Sindhi nationalist struggle against the Establishment. On 25 April 1980, for instance, the SGA organized an All Sindh Educational Conference in Hyderabad, in which a number of papers were read out in support of Sindhi. Ibrahim Joyo pointed out that Sindhi primary schools were not being encouraged and that basic education should be in the mother tongue (Joyo 1985: 43). In 1983, Sindhi intellectuals appealed to the government not to project Urdu as being as important as Islam itself. This was in response to the regime's use of Urdu as a symbol of legitimization and national integration (Appeal 1983: 6).

On 2 February 1988, a Sindhi Adabi Conference was inaugurated at Jamshoro. It passed several resolutions demanding an increase in the use of Sindhi. One of them was that all teachers in Sindh should know Sindhi and that Sindhi should be taught in urban Sindh also (for details, see Kamal 1988: 27-8). On 4 February, the day the conference ended, the Sujag Bar Tahreek (Movement for the Awakening of Children) 'carried banners in support of Sindhi' (*D* 5 February 1988).

Other organizations for the promotion of Sindhi, such as the Sindh Sujan Sabha and the Sindhi Boli Sath, also kept working to increase the use of the language. The Sath is very active and its declared aims are:

1. To get the Sindhi language recognized as a national language.
2. Within the framework of the state constitution to get the ratification of the Sindhi language as the sole official language of Sindh and the adoption of Sindhi language in all spheres of official as well as non official levels [*sic*] (Sath 1990: 2).

The Sath's stance is anti-Urdu and its code of conduct enjoins upon members to support the other indigenous languages and even English as a link language, while eschewing the use of Urdu (ibid. 29). The Sath has pointed out instances of discrimination against Sindhi. The Convener of the Sath, for instance, condemned the decision of the Karachi Municipal Corporation banning the use of Sindhi in official correspondence (*N* 6 January 1988).

### Sindhi Identity and Corpus Planning in Sindhi

One of the resolutions of the Sindhi Adabi Conference in 1988 demanded the setting up of a Sindhi Language Authority on the model of the National Language Authority (Kamal 1988: 27). This institution, the SLA, was set up in 1990 in order to develop Sindhi. In order to make the language suitable for use in modern life, the SLA was also supposed to 'arrange translation and publication of Technical Terms in science subjects and humanities' (SLA 1991: 5).

This aspect of corpus planning had, indeed, been going on ever since the British days when new terms had been introduced into Sindhi in order to translate laws and other modern concepts. In 1962, the Sindhi Academy, first established at the old campus of Sindh University, and now well known as the Institute of Sindhology, also had a bureau of translation for such language planning activities. It also published the monthly scientific journal called *Makhzan* which used newly devised Sindhi terms. A recent pamphlet published by the SLA gives the following terms for motor vehicles and their parts:

| | |
|---|---|
| air brake | *hawai brake* |
| air horn | *narghat* |
| automatic | *khudkar* |
| right hand drive | *sajir* |
| left hand drive | *kabir* |

(Baloch, K. M. 1993).

Many of the terms in this pamphlet use Arabic, Persian, Urdu, and English roots but they are pronounced and pluralized according to the rules of Sindhi (see lists in Sindhi 1980: 502-7). One such example is *soteo* which is used for *phoneme* and comes from *saut*, the Arabic for *sound* (Sindhi Int: 24 November 1993). Perhaps, as the SLA is a governmental institution, it does not manifest the tendency to use only indigenous roots for coining new words.

The Sindhi nationalists tend to use words of an indigenous origin more often than other educated Pakistanis who tend to use words of Urdu and English in their place. One such word was *phetho* (a measurement tape) which came to be used for audio cassette, but has now fallen into disuse (Sindhi Int: ibid.). Some of these words are often unfamiliar and their function is to emphasize Sindhi identity rather than to facilitate communication. The religious language planners, such as the Jamiat Shoora Sindh, use Arabic and Persian roots while the Sindhi nationalists use Sindhi ones.

## Rise of Mohajir Ethnicity and the Sindhi Response

As mentioned earlier, Mohajir ethnic identity rose some time in the 1970s and was first articulated during the language riots of that period. However, by the 1980s the Mohajir identity crystallized as separate from the Pakistani identity. The emphasis was no longer on Urdu, though it was assumed as a necessary part of this identity. According to Hamza Alavi:

There was an overnight ethnic redefinition. They [the Mohajirs] abandoned the Islamic fundamentalist Jamaat-i-Islami and the traditionalist Jamiat-i-Ulema-i-Pakistan and massively rallied behind the new MQM. Instead of moving towards an end to communalism, however, the rise of the MQM signified a further consolidation of communalism in Pakistan (Alavi 1987: 243).

The rise of the Mohajir identity has been written about in the Press and in academic publications (Alavi 1987; Zaidi 1992 b). It will, therefore be mentioned only in passing here. The consensus of most serious studies is that the domination of Punjabis over industry, bureaucracy, and the military challenged Mohajir domination of the institutions after the late 1960s (Zaidi 1992b: 338-9).

By the 1980s the Mohajirs no longer dominated the higher echelons of the civil bureaucracy, as the figures given below indicate:

Table 7

*Ethnic origins of DMG officers as percentages (1989): based on domicile*

| Grade | NWFP | Punjab | Sindh Urban (Mohajirs) | Sindh Rural (Sindhis) | Baloch-istan | AJK | Northern Areas | FATA |
|---|---|---|---|---|---|---|---|---|
| Total | 17.5 | 53.7 | 7.1 | 8.5 | 6.9 | 1.7 | 1.4 | 2.8 |
| BPS 22 | 0 | 13.6 | 0 | 0 | 0 | 0 | 0 | 0 |
| " 21 | 27.7 | 57.1 | 5.5 | 0 | 0 | 0 | 0 | 0 |
| " 20 | 34.2 | 48.5 | 0 | 5.7 | 8.5 | 2.8 | 0 | 0 |
| " 19 | 27.6 | 42.8 | 6.6 | 5.7 | 12.3 | 0.9 | 0.9 | 2.8 |
| " 18 | 14.2 | 60.0 | 6.6 | 7.1 | 5.2 | 1.8 | 0.9 | 3.7 |
| " 17 | 11.7 | 51.5 | 9.5 | 13.2 | 6.3 | 2.1 | 2.6 | 2.6 |

(BPS: Basic Pay Scale)
Source: Adapted from the Establishment Division
Graduation List 1989. In Senate 1989: 19.

Moreover, as Karachi is a large city with many educated young people, the Mohajir youth are extremely frustrated. According to many scholars, they do not find jobs and even business is no longer in their hands. Also, the army, which is '85 per cent of Punjabi origin and, since 1977, has developed very lucrative business interests' keeps money away from the Mohajirs as well as from other ethnic groups (Ali, B. 1992: 184-5). In these circumstances, Mohajir youth were attracted to the MQM, which appeared to offer them a sense of direction, through a new ethnic identity and, of course, the power of a well-organized group. What was unforeseen was that this group would become so militant as to alienate some sections of the Mohajirs themselves in the late 1980s, when the MQM was at the height of its power.

The Sindhi nationalists did not accept the Mohajirs' claim to being an ethnic group, on the grounds that they came from different areas of India and included even Gujrati-speaking people. G. M. Syed said that even the older nationalities of Pakistan had not been accepted as such, so there was no question of accepting the Mohajirs' claims in this regard (Siddiqui, J. 1987: 33). G. M. Syed and the other Sindhi nationalists advised the Mohajirs to accept Sindhi identity and to assimilate themselves with the Sindhis. He said:

> The national language of Sindh will be Sindhi which can intermingle with Urdu. Ultimately our object must be that all persons residing in Sindh will have the same language, same culture and same ideas (Syed 1990?: 105).

For Syed and some other Sindhi nationalists, the real enemies of the Mohajirs as well as of the Sindhis were the ruling elites of the Centre—i.e., the Punjabi-dominated elites.

Some Sindhi nationalist groups were reputed to be confrontationist even before the rise of the MQM. However, now it is the MQM which has the image of being the most violent party in Sindh. The MQM's policy has been to compete for power through political means and street power, a strategy in which language plays a minor role only. However, in its alliance with the PPP in 1989, Article 12 gave security to Urdu. It read:

> Culture has central importance in our everyday life. It is the essence of the whole experience of the community. Those inhabitants of the province whose culture and language are different have the full right to preserve them and promote them.

This compromise, which was unacceptable to the Sindhi nationalists, is still adhered to in practice, even though the MQM and the PPP soon parted ways. Even the Special Committee of the Senate, which presented its report on Sindh in December 1989 said:

> In Sindh both Urdu and Sindhi should be taught in all educational institutions and used as the official languages. Enough resources should be mobilized for the development of both at all levels and in all departments of public life. Efforts must be made that every child studying in Sindh and every official serving in the province is in a position to understand and speak both these languages (Senate 1989: 46).

A document called 'A Declaration for Peace and Amity in Sindh', signed by Ibrahim Joyo among others, accepted both Urdu and Sindhi as the languages of Sindh (CAPS 1993). This, said one writer, 'amounts to testifying to the bilingual nature of the province' which the Sindhi nationalists were not willing to do earlier (Siddiqui, M. 1993). It should, however, not be assumed that the more committed Sindhi nationalists have accepted this position, though Hamza Alavi, generally a cautious scholar, feels that Sindhi-Mohajir friendship is a real possibility (1991: 175-87).

There has been no substantial change in this state of affairs to date. Although the Army pledged that it would purge the MQM of its terrorist element in its action of June 1992, it only suppressed the terrorists of the MQM Altaf group while encouraging those of the Haqiqi faction. No government has risked provoking the Mohajirs by changing the status of Urdu in Sindh. Perhaps Urdu serves to keep Sindhi, and hence separatist Sindhi nationalism, at bay, which is in the interest of the Punjabi-dominated ruling elite. In other words, Sindh is in fact a divided province. Its major cities, especially Karachi and parts of Hyderabad, are Mohajir-dominated, and hence Urdu-speaking enclaves. Rural Sindh is Sindhi-speaking and the urban-rural cleavage which was the Hindu-Muslim cleavage in pre-Partition Sindh is now a Mohajir-Sindhi cleavage. The Sindhis feel that they are being turned into a minority in their own land like the native Indians in America and are not prepared to accept this ethno-linguistic division. The Mohajirs, some of whom (the MQM Altaf Hussain group) desire a geographical division of Sindh to create a Mohajir enclave, also complain of unemployment, a discriminatory quota system, and fear of violence.

Given this intransigence on both sides, Sindh is in danger of violence, riots, and perhaps a civil war. Language may no longer be the symbol chosen to mobilize hostile sentiments by either community but its role in creating a situation in which confrontation is more pronounced cannot be ignored.

### Notes

1. These narratives of events are based on newspaper reports supplemented with the description of events in other sources. In general, the Urdu newspapers were anti-Sindhi, and Sindhi newspapers anti-Urdu. The English Press was better informed and somewhat more objective. Among the newspapers relied on were: *Hilal-e-Pakistan, Dawn, Hurriyat, The Pakistan Times, Jang, Sun, Jasarat, Nidai Millat*, etc.

# 8

# The Pashto Language Movement

Hallberg's sociolinguistic survey of Pakistan's Pashto-speaking communities reveals that they 'have very positive attitudes toward their own language. Not only is it virtually the only language of use in most domains, but also it is seen as a strong mark of identity and pride' (1992a: 42). Hallberg, however, does not trace the history of the Pashto movement—the efforts made by modern Pakhtuns to promote the use of Pashto in the domains of power. (The spellings used here are Pashto and Pakhtun though they are also pronounced Pakhto and Pashtun). The only information available about these efforts is in the form of articles, generally in Pashto, which are polemical and use conspiracy theories by way of explanation. This chapter provides an account of the efforts to promote the use of Pashto and to investigate how these LP efforts are related to ethnicity and politics.

**Pashto and Pakhtun Identity**

According to Gankovsky, the 'fundamentals of the Pashtun original culture and the peculiar psychological make-up of Pashtuns' evolved by the second millenium AD (1964: 129). These fundamentals are summed up as *pakhtunwali*, and they emphasize vengeance (*badal*), hospitality (*melmastia*), and forgiveness (*nanawati*). The ideal of *pakhtunwali* privileges autonomy, egalitarianism, and chivalry (Ahmed 1976: 56-8). One who lives up to this ideal is said to possess or do Pashto, and not merely speak the language of that name (Barth 1969b: 119). The Pakhtuns do not seem to have emphasized their language, Pashto, as much as the ideal of *pakhtunwali* as an ethnic identity-marker in pre-modern days. Thus, Khushal Khan Khattak (1613-89), a great Pashto poet, identifies himself as a friend of Farid Khan (Sher Shah Suri), a person of Pakhtun ethnic origin but no longer a speaker of Pashto, who defeated the Mughal King Humayun (1508-56) and ruled India from 1540 to 1545.[1] Khushal says:

*Va Mughal va ta ba hase kar Khkara karam*
*che razi rasakha rooh da Farid Khan Shai.*

(The Mughal I will show such deeds
that the soul of Farid Khan will be pleased with me).

Conversely, Shabbir Hasan Khan Josh, an Urdu-speaking poet of Pakhtun origin from Malihabad (UP, India) tells us that the Pathans of India took pride in their ethnicity and considered bravery and aggressiveness a part of it. He himself is almost obsessed with his *pathanwali* as he calls it (Josh 1964: 341 *et passim*). From the late nineteenth century onwards, the Pathans of India did not speak Pashto, though, according to Raverty, 'in the territory of the Rampur Nawwab, whole towns and villages may be found in which the Afghan language' was spoken up to 1860 (Raverty 1860: ix). Their genealogical tables, in common with their Pashto-speaking counterparts, were in Persian, which appears to have been the language of literacy among the Pakhtuns.

Persian was so much the language of sophisticated discourse that it seems to have been used by Pakhtun aristocrats, those who wielded power, and even by the kings of Afghanistan. Khan Abdul Ghaffar Khan, the famous ethno-nationalist leader of the Pakhtuns, reports that when he went to Afghanistan in the 1920s at the height of the *Hijrat* movement—migration to Afghanistan because India was declared a non-Muslim country (Baha 1979—he found that Amanullah Khan, the ruler of Afghanistan, did not pay attention to the development of Pashto. During a conversation with the King, Ghaffar Khan said:

'What a pity it is that you, who know so many languages, do not know Pashto, though it is your mother tongue and your national language!'
The King agreed with me and soon he began to learn Pashto (Ghaffar 1969: 51).

He also claims to have had a similar encounter with a student of Habibia College in Kabul whom he exhorted to speak Pashto (ibid. 52). Later on, as we shall see, Pashto was promoted by Amanullah and his followers in Afghanistan.

Barth discusses this indifference to Pashto in relation to the maintenance of identity. He argues that nearness to centralized authority makes the assertion of autonomy and egalitarianism, the focal Pakhtun values, impossible. Hence:

The elite and urban middle class in this purely Afghan kingdom have shown a strong tendency to Persianization in speech and culture, representing I would argue a sophisticate's escape from the impossibility of successfully consummating a Pathan identity under these circumstances (Barth 1969b: 129).

But this ideal-type society is almost non-existent in the urban areas, and even in the tribal townships of Pakistani Pashto-speaking areas. According to Akbar S. Ahmed:

Pakhtun society may be divided into two categories: acephalous, egalitarian groups, living on irrigated lands, usually within larger state systems. *Nang* ('honour') is the foremost symbol of the former society, as *qalang* ('taxes', 'rents') is of the latter (Ahmed 1991: 7; for the original explanation of the concept see Ahmed 1976: 73-83).

However, it is in the *qalang* societies, the urbanized Pakhtuns of Afghanistan and Pakistan in the 1920s that the Pashto movement rose. The Swat state, where Pashto was used as an official language, was also a *qalang* area, a bureaucratic centralized state, argues Akbar Ahmed (1976: 122-8), and not an acephalous tribal society as Barth suggests in his well-known study of the Swat Pakhtuns (1959 a and b). We have already mentioned—and details will come later how King Amanullah, who himself could not speak Pashto, promoted the language in the 1920s. In British India, Ghaffar Khan himself pioneered the trend of emphasizing Pashto as a symbol of Pakhtun identity.

In short, the Pashto movement rose when Pashto could no longer be taken for granted, as in pre-modern times. It rose when the modern state was being created in Afghanistan and Swat, and the dominant Pakhtuns, who could have afforded to be indifferent to it earlier, now needed to extend their power-base by creating a Pakhtun nation-state. Then, to promote 'official nationalism', they needed such symbols of statehood as a state language.

In British India too, a symbol was needed to confront the state. But here, the need for creating a community with as many bonds of solidarity as possible was an anti-colonial enterprise. Thus, the Pashto movement was suspect in the eyes of the colonial power and, as we shall see later, of its successors.

## Pashto during the British Period

The British took over the governance of the NWFP as part of Ranjit Singh's dominions when they annexed the Punjab in 1849. It was, therefore, ruled from Lahore till 1901 when it was made a separate province under a commissioner. In 1932 it was given the status of a Governor's Province (Obhari 1938; Baha 1978).

British language policies were influenced by the imperatives of imperial rule. Hence, the use of Pashto was also subject to this factor. As with other languages in other parts of the empire, British officers learned Pashto in order to understand the natives and control them more effectively through this understanding. After the events of 1857, the Pakhtuns were considered reliable and were recruited in large numbers in the army. Their European officers were especially instructed to learn the language of their troops and were examined in it. Scholarship in Pashto, in common with orientalist learning elsewhere (Said 1978), helped British officers make and implement imperialist policies (Cohn 1985). Thus, Raverty, the compiler of a Pashto dictionary, says that his 'researches into their language and literature during the last twelve or fourteen years' have led him to the conclusion that 'the Western Afghans are desirous of cultivating our friendship and would be glad to see a British force again located at Kandahar' (1860: v). Moreover, the Russians, who were suspected of having imperialist designs on Afghanistan and the North West Frontier of British India, were reported to have given attention to Pashto. According to Raverty, 'Pashto is now taught, as well as other Oriental tongues, at St Petersburgh, although the Russians do not hold an inch of land where it is spoken. The Russian capital is, indeed, the only city in the world where the Afghan language is made a branch of study' (Raverty 1860: vi).

Raverty, perhaps because of his expertise in Pashto, recommended that Pashto be taught in schools, and hoped that the missionaries of Peshawar would 'evangelize the Afghans' through it (Raverty 1860: vi). However, senior decision-makers neither took the risk of converting Afghans to Christianity, nor that of using Pashto in the domains of power at any level. The reasons for this are again political and the letters of British officers give some insight into them. For instance, the Commissioner and Superintendent of the cis-Sutlej states wrote to the Secretary of the Punjab Government on 17 June 1862:

> In 1853 when I first took charge of the Commissionership of Peshawar, the language of the Courts was Persian; and I altered it to Oordoo for two reasons. Firstly the extreme slipperiness of Persian, and extreme Provision of Oordoo as a Judicial language. Secondly the Political advantage of hastening the amalgamation of our provinces (in Chaudhry 1977: 43).

The idea that the Pashto-speaking people of the Frontier should look towards India, where Urdu was predominant, and not towards Afghanistan, certainly influenced the choice of the vernacular in this region. This is further supported by the following letter of 22 July 1862 from the Director of Public Instruction to the Secretary of the Punjab Government.

> Even in the frontier Districts of Peshawar, and the Derajat, where Persian may be considered the vernacular of the educated classes rather than Urdoo, and Pushtoo a distinct language from either, is commonly spoken by the masses, I would recommend that Urdoo be continued as the Court Vernacular. On the annexation of the Punjab political motives, I dare say, had a great share in giving the superiority to Urdoo over Persian, which was commonly used in the Courts in the Frontier, and the desirability of making the union of the wild tribes with the adjoining population in our territories more complete, and their intercourse more convenient, by the use of a common tongue, is obviously very desirable. All our Education efforts tend to this object among others and they will be greatly aided by the currency of Urdoo, in all our Courts, as the standard language (in Chaudhry 1977: 38).

It appears then that the British policy towards Pashto—learning it themselves for control, while denying its use in the domains of power for the natives—was based on their imperialist interests. That could be the reason why they discouraged all attempts, especially by anti-imperialist politicians, to promote it.

## Khan Ghaffar's Efforts to Promote Pashto

Pashto was used as an identity-marker by Khan Abdul Ghaffar Khan (1890-1987), the founder of the anti-British, pro-Congress Khudai Khidmatgar movement, which began in the NWFP in 1929 (Ghaffar 1969: 96). The members of this movement wore red clothes—a colour chosen arbitrarily for reasons of convenience as 'white clothes got easily dirty' (Tendulkar 1967: 59)—and were very nationalistic. The 'Red Shirts' were seen as Soviet-inspired revolutionaries and supporters of Afghan irredentist claims (Pakhtunistan) by the British and the Pakistani governments. Hence Pashto, which was one of the symbols manipulated by Ghaffar Khan, also came to be tainted with these anti-government, indeed anti-state, perceptions. For these reasons, British intelligence agencies reported all the activities of Ghaffar Khan and movements for the promotion of Pashto (see Abstracts of Intelligence of the NWFP Police in NDC).

When Ghaffar Khan returned to British India from Afghanistan, he reopened 'the old schools in the tribal areas' (Ghaffar 1969: 57). Such schools were called the Azad (free) or Islamia schools and Ghaffar Khan is reported to have said that in them Pashto and Arabic would be taught in primary classes (Para 418 of NWFP Police Abstract, 1929, Acc 479 in NDC). These schools, which are mentioned in Ghaffar Khan's biography, are not in the Police records which only show schools located at Utmanzai, Swabi, and Charsadda (see Paras 320, 410, and 697 of the Police Abstract for the year ending 31 December 1921, Acc No. 472 in NDC). In all the Azad schools, according to Ghaffar Khan's son, the Pashto poet Ghani Khan, the language of instruction for beginners was Pashto (Ghani Int: 2 November 1993). Ghaffar Khan also began the publication of a magazine called the *Pakhtun* in 1928 (Ghaffar 1969: 88-90; also see Para 337 in Acc 479). Emphasizing the importance of Pashto, he wrote:

> A nation is known and recognized by its language and without a language of its own a nation cannot really be called a nation. A nation that forgets its own language will eventually disappear from the map altogether (Ghaffar 1969: 88-9)

Characterized by such ideas, the late 1920s and 1930s are significant for the development of Pashto nationalistic prose and poetry. According to Ghani Khan, Makhfi of Charsadda, Abdul Malik Fida, Abdul Akbar Khan, and Ghani Khan himself wrote nationalistic literature (Ghani Int: ibid.).

The first anti-imperialist newspaper to be launched in this area was *Islam*. It was started in 1854 by Abdul Ghafoor of Saidu and was published and distributed secretly. It raised consciousness of Pashto as a marker of an identity which was Islamic and anti-imperialist (Sabir 1986: 188). In 1925, Allah Bakhsh Yusufi launched *Sarhad* in Urdu, though it did have twelve pages in Pashto too. Another publication, the fortnightly *Angar*, had more Pashto than Urdu and was published by the rebel Khudai Khidmatgar, Amir Nawaz Jalia (ibid. 189).

However, it was the *Pakhtun* which gained the widest popularity and which influenced Pakhtuns most of all. The *Pakhtun* raised the issue of language planning in Pashto. It also emphasized Pashto as the marker of Pakhtun identity and exhorted the people and the authorities to use it in all domains. In the August and September 1929 issues, for instance, Khan Ghaffar wrote that the British system of schooling was only meant to perpetuate British rule and that the people were alienated from it. He also demanded that Pashto should be made the medium of instruction at the primary level (Ghaffar 1929 a and b; Also see Para 417 of the Police Abstract of Intelligence, Acc 479, NDC).

Another contributor suggested that the people themselves should conduct their daily affairs—writing letters, maintaining business records and accounts, conversation—in Pashto. The Government, too, was asked to establish a Pashto Academy with a perpetual grant of Rs 40,000 per year. It was also suggested that non-Pakhtuns should be asked to learn Pashto, especially if they wanted to be employed in the NWFP (Shah 1945: 21-4).

Some contributors believed that the use of foreign words or sentences from a commonly used language such as Urdu (i.e., the phenomenon called code-switching by linguists), was a sign of mental servility, and that the Pakhtun identity could only be maintained through the use of correct Pashto (Babar 1945). In short, Pashto was seen as a necessary ingredient of Pakhtun ethnicity and its development was supposed to lead to the progress of the ethnic group (*Pakhtun* 21 March 1940: 35-7).

## Pashto and Politics in Pre-Partition NWFP

The NWFP Legislative Assembly was not the equivalent of the legislature in other provinces, but Sahibzada Abdul Qayyum Khan (1864-1937 [for a biography, albeit sympathetic, see Ahmed, S. 1989]) had been nominated the Minister of Transferred Departments in the 1932 Legislative Council. He had already contributed to a survey which the Primary Education Committee had conducted in 1929-30 regarding the problems of basic schooling (Ahmed, S. 1989: 158-9). On the medium of instruction, he wrote:

> Among the Pushto-speaking people, we came across a remarkable solidarity of opinion in favour of instruction being given in Urdu rather than in Pushto. Pushto was recommended to be used only colloquially in the lower classes of the school in the course of explanation by the teacher. The Pushto-speaking population was practically unanimous in favour of instruction throughout in Urdu. Accounts and every day conversations are usually in Urdu and never in Pushto (LAD-F 12 October 1932: 132)

In 1935, however, Sahibzada Abdul Qayyum presented certain letters pertaining to the medium of instruction. It was now conceded that:

Education of the 1st and 2nd classes should be imparted in the mother tongue of the student; that is to say, in Pushto speaking areas in Pushto and in Hindko speaking areas, in Hindko. (Letter from the Secretary NWFP Government to the Director of Public Instruction, dated 4 September 1935 in LAD-F 13 November 1935: 250).

The non-Pashto-speaking and predominantly non-Muslim members of the Assembly objected to this memorandum, which came to be known as the anti-Hindi-Gurmukhi circular or the Black Circular. The Hindu and Sikh members, who opposed it vehemently, did not attend three days of sessions of the Legislative Council. A 'Black Day' was also observed and processions were brought out. Dr Khan Sahib, the elder brother of Ghaffar Khan, who was Sahibzada Qayyum's political opponent, expressed his sympathies with the non-Muslims and declared, on 7 August 1936, that when the Congress came to power, this circular would be repealed (LAD-F 28 September 1937: 674).

The main objection of the non-Muslims was that their language and culture would be under threat (see Lala Ladha Ram's speech in the Legislative Assembly in LAD-F 6 November 1935: 69). Although the Government did point out that Pashto would only be used in predominantly Pashto-speaking areas, the opposition continued to oppose the idea.

After the 1937 elections, Sahibzada Qayyum, who now led the United Nationalist Party, won the support of the non-Muslims by conceding certain conditions, one of which was that the Pashto circular be withdrawn (Shah, S. W. 1992: 30). His ministry lasted from 1 April 1937 till September 1937, when Dr Khan Sahib's Congress, with the help of the Hindu-Sikh Nationalist Party and the Hazara Democratic Party, passed a no-confidence motion against it (Rittenberg 1977: 236-7). Dr Khan Sahib's government, which lasted for two years and six weeks, reopened the Pashto language issue. In 1937, Mian Jafar Khan, the Minister of Education, moved the following motion.

> This Assembly recommends to the Government that Pushto be made the medium of instruction in the primary schools in the North West Frontier Province (LAD-F 28 September 1937: 602).

Once again the opposition came from the non-Muslim members, with the support of the Hindko-speaking members of Hazara. The non-Muslim members felt that making Pashto compulsory would be an imposition (see the speeches of Rai Bahadur Ishar Dass and Rai Mehr Chand Khanna LAD-F 28 September 1937: 610-4). Sarwar Khan of

Haripur (Hazara) also added the argument that improvement in the status of Pashto would lead to extra-territorial loyalties. He said:

> Let us pause to see whether the people of the Frontier Province are going to federate with Kabul or with India (ibid. 606).

This argument was refuted by Sardar Aurangzeb Khan (a member of the NWFP Legislature) but it was certainly kept in mind by British decision-makers. In any case, despite Dr Khan Sahib's wish to teach Pashto 'to the Pashto-speaking boys' (ibid. 622), he did not want to antagonize his anti-Pashto supporters. Thus, Pashto could not immediately be made the medium of instruction.

In 1938, however, Dr Khan Sahib's government did manage to introduce Pashto 'as a compulsory medium of instruction for primary education' (Tendulkar 1967: 229) but, explained Qazi Ataullah, the Minister of Education, it would only be taught in Pashto-speaking areas (LAD-F 25 March 1939: 582). The Minister also added that Pashto literature would be promoted. Even then, Pashto did not become the medium of instruction as the *Report on Public Instruction* (1940-41) noted:

> Pashto continues to be taught in primary schools in Pashto speaking areas as an additional subject (RPI-F 1942: 61)

Meanwhile, the Speaker of the Assembly had ruled that those who did not know English could speak in Pashto or Urdu and they would be responded to in the same languages (LAD-F 8 November 1938: 342-4). However, the Acts of the Legislative Assembly were not printed in Pashto (LAD-F 24 March 1939: 583-4) nor were members allowed to use Pashto if they knew English. In fact, the use of English was not curtailed, although Pashto was tolerated to a greater extent than formerly (LAD-F 21 March 1946). The maximum the colonial government was prepared to do for Pashto was to tolerate it in order to conciliate public opinion. This toleration never went beyond recognizing Pashto in certain peripheral domains, in order to give it symbolic importance.

**Pashto outside British India**

Since the British showed only reluctant support towards Pashto, the supporters of the language looked outside British India for inspiration. The two states which did support the language were Afghanistan and

Swat. Although Swat was a princely state within India, it was not directly ruled by the British. Thus, it did appear to have some autonomy in the eyes of Pakhtun nationalists.

In Afghanistan, Pashto was promoted by King Amanullah who founded the *Pashto Tolane* (the Pashto Academy) in the mid-1920s (Poullada 1973: 73), and the 1923 Constitution was also written in Pashto (ibid. Appendix A: 277-89). However, it was later that 'Pashto was by royal decree of 1936 also declared to be the national language of Afghanistan' replacing Persian (Mackenzie 1987: 547). Today Pashto is one of the two national languages of the country, the other being Dari (Afghan Persian). Developed through language planning activities, Pashto is now used for higher education. The Pashto Academy (Kabul) branch of lexicology has published glossaries of technical terms, using indigenous Pashto morphemes (Pashto Tolane 1911-12). Sufficient terms are now available for imparting higher education in Pashto, and research articles are written in all subjects, including scientific and technical ones (for some of these articles see *Poha*, the journal of Nangarhar University).

The Afghan elite has traditionally used Dari, but as it is Pashto-speaking, it uses Pashto as a symbol of Afghan unity and to consolidate its dominant position *vis-a-vis* the Dari-speaking Tajiks, etc. Thus, the Afghan Academy, of which the Pashto Tolane is now a section, was established in 1967 (Dupree 1973: 93). This policy makes 'government officials claim support for Pashto; although in fact, almost all of them function in Dari' (Miran 1977: 69; also see Dupree 1978.) However, Pashto has gained far wider acceptance in all domains in the second half of the twentieth century than it had earlier. At the moment the situation is too uncertain to be commented upon. It does appear, however, that the five television stations controlled by warring commanders give more time to Pashto or Persian in order to appeal to different ethnic support groups (*News* 27 November 1994).

The Swat state was recognized by the British in 1926 and Miangul Abdul Wadud, the grandson of the Akhund of Swat who had gained power in Swat at the expense of the feuding chiefs or Khans in the nineteenth century (Ahmed 1976: 94-6) was accepted as the *de jure* ruler or Wali (Husain 1962: 94). The new Wali, in his own words, took the following language policy decisions about Pashto:

> I declared Pashto to be the official language of the state and adopted the Urdu script as the style of writing. Special forms and registers were prepared in Pashto for use in offices and courts. Both officials and the public were directed to employ simple, everyday language in all their

writings, and express themselves briefly and to the point; especially avoiding lengthy salutations and adulatory phrases. Experience proved that I had decided rightly : Yusufzai Pathans of Swat find it convenient to conduct their personal and official business in Pashto (Husain 1962: 117).

Schools, however, used Urdu and English as they did in the NWFP. There was also an Anglo-Vernacular school and a number of primary schools run under the direction of British officers, as letters and reports on the Dir and Swat state prove (for these reports see Acc 772 in NDC). The Wali also got a number of books translated from different languages into Pashto (for a list see Husain 1962: 188). When Swat was amalgamated with Pakistan in 1969, this experiment in Pashto came to an end. However, the Islamic leader Sufi Muhammad, who wants the *Shariat* (Islamic law) to be used in the Malakand Division, of which Swat is a part, does not accept Urdu as the language of the Islamic courts as the government wanted. In his words 'Urdu is fine but people understand Pashto better' (*News* 2 December 1994). This means that in this case, the people see no contradiction between Pashto and Islam.

**Pashto and Pakhtunistan**

The attitude of the Pakistani ruling elite towards Pashto can be understood better in the light of Afghanistan's irredentist claim to parts of the NWFP (see Afghan Minister Sardar Tarzi's statement of June 1947 in Zaidi 1994:395-6). This area was called Pakhtunistan, the land of the Pakhtuns, and the ethno-nationalist leaders of Pakistan were suspected of being its supporters (for the Pakhtunistan issue up to the late sixties see Dupree 1973: 485-94; 538-54).

The Muslim League wanted a referendum in the NWFP on the question of whether the people of the province 'want to join Pakistan Constituent Assembly or the Hindustan Constituent Assembly' (Jinnah 1947: 183). The Congress accepted the League's demand but Ghaffar Khan decided to boycott the referendum saying that if it 'was to be held at all it should be a referendum on the question of "Pakhtunistan" or Pakistan?' (Ghaffar 1969: 178). Pakhtunistan was initially defined as 'a free Pathan state' (Ghaffar Khan on 24 June 1947 in Tendulkar 1967: 439) but on 4 September 1947 he said he would accept a loose confederation (i.e., agreement on defence, external affairs, and communications) with Pakistan of the 'six settled Districts of the North-West Frontier Province which may wish to join the new state of their own free will' (in Tendulkar 451). Later, the terms 'Pakhtunistan' and 'Pakhtunkhwa' were also used by Khan Wali Khan, as a substitute for the British name 'NWFP' for this Pakhtun-dominated province. This change of stance from demanding independence to mere symbolic assertion of cultural autonomy reflects the decline in separatist tendencies in the NWFP (Amin 1988: 187).

However, as the Afghan government used the Pakhtunistan issue for irredentist claims on Pakistani territory (examples of such claims can be seen in statements of officials [like Tarzi's in Zaidi 1994: 395] and pamphlets [Pazhwak 1960]), the Pakistani ruling elite developed a deep mistrust of even the words Pakhtunkhwa and Pakhtunistan. One part of this claim—about the 'national entity of the people of Pakhtunistan, as a people apart from the peoples of the subcontinent' (Pazhwak 1960: 16)—was also based upon Pashto. Moreover, at least during the 1950s, many supporters of Pashto also supported Pakhtunistan. Some of them even collaborated with Afghanistan and India, as the facts given below will bear out.

According to intelligence reports, Anwarul Haq Gran, the supervisor of the Pashto Unit of the All India Radio in New Delhi, was also the Chief Organizer of the Pakhtunistan movement in India (Pakistani Charge d'Affaires in Kabul to Chief Secretary NWFP Government, 4 March 1950, Memo No. PEK/21/2 in NDC). Moreover, Nasrullah Khan Nasr, Secretary of the Adabi Tolae (Literary Group), an organization for the promotion of Pashto, used to meet the Afghan Consul at Peshawar, ostensibly to give him news about the NWFP (ibid.).

At least one attempt at opening a Pashto school, the Pashtoon Hala Maktab in Gangi Khel (South Waziristan), was said to have been initiated by the Afghan allowance holders (Chief Secretary, NWFP Government to Assistant Secretary, Government of Pakistan, Ministry of States and Frontier Regions, 17 April 1950, No. 823/STB/128 at NDC). These allowance holders were reported to be one thousand five hundred and seventy eight in number and received 'Rs 6,80,424 annually', from Kabul (Political Agent, South Waziristan to the Chief Secretary, NWFP Government, 19 January 1950, D. O. No. 12/S-8/49 in NDC).

The Afghan Consul was once reported to have announced a special fund for the upkeep of the tomb of the Pashto poet Rahman Baba, after a poetry session held on 31 March 1950 in the poet's honour. The descendants of the poet went to the Consul to claim the money on 17 April and these events were reported by the Police (Special Diary of the NWFP Police, Para 8, 18 April 1950 in NDC).

The Pashto Tolane of Kabul, too, was reported to be working in the interest of Afghan irredentism. As a secret report said:

> [The Pashto Tolane] is the main organisation responsible for the development and propagation of the Pashto language and literature for the dissemination of Pathan culture in Afghanistan. Actually it serves the double purpose of a Pashto Academy and a mighty machine that is zealously advocating the Pathanistan ideal.

The report went on to give the names of all the Afghan journals, most of them in Pashto, which advocated this ideal in Pakistan (note on 'Pathanistan propaganda' by the Local Administration, 22 August 1950 in NDC).

Not only the Pashto publications of Afghanistan but even those of Pakistan, at least before 1958 when martial law was imposed, were reported to have 'contained highly objectionable matter advocating the cause of Pakhtoonistan and the disintegration of West Pakistan' (Director of Information, Peshawar, to the Resident and Commissioner, Frontier Regions, Peshawar, 14 October 1959 No. 30/122/ID in NDC). Such reports made government officials so mistrustful of Pashto that all Pashto publications and all efforts to develop the language were monitored by the police. For instance, when the Pashto weekly *Jamhuriat* published a poem on 8 April 1960 entitled 'Rahman Baba and Pashto', exhorting the Pakhtuns to promote their language, it was reported at once, as were all other such efforts (Director of Information, Peshawar 1960 No. 7815/ID in NDC). Indeed, at the height of the Pakhtunistan issue in the fifties and the sixties, the government was almost paranoid about Pashto, which it took to be the major visible symbol of Pakhtun ethno-nationalism. It is in the light of this background that the Pashto Movement in Pakistan can be understood.

## The Politics of Pashto

As Pakhtun nationalists, the supporters of Khan Ghaffar Khan and his son Wali Khan gave primacy to their Pakhtun identity over the Muslim or the Pakistani one, discussions on the issue often grew bitter. Once, Qayyum Khan refused to even shake hands with Samin Jan Khan, because the latter had said that he was a Pathan as well as a Muslim (LAD-F 7 March 1952: 35). Pashto, being a symbol of this identity, was always supported by the Pakhtun nationalists. Thus, Wali Khan off and on gave statements in support of Pashto (*PT* 1 August 1962). His elder brother, Ghani Khan, also voiced similar views. However, he clarified that he was not against Urdu, but that there was a reaction to its imposition in the NWFP (*FP* 22 October 1989).

The NWFP was merged in West Pakistan by a resolution passed by the Provincial Assembly on 25 November 1954 (LAD-F 25 November 1945: 23). Soon after this, Ghaffar Khan spoke bitterly against Punjabi domination on the platform of the Anti-One Unit Front (see his speech of 24 April 1956 in the Police Report in Acc No. 234 NDC).

The National Awami Party (NAP) supported Pashto throughout the period of One Unit, and during Yahya Khan's government. However, when it came into power in the NWFP, in coalition with the Jamiat-i-Ulema-i-Islam (JUI), from April 1972 to February 1973, it moved away from Pashto. The Education Minister, Ameerzada Khan, who was from the NAP, is said to have turned down the request of members of his party to give Pashto a higher status (*NT* 4 May 1972; Khattak, R. Int: 1 November 1993). Instead, he chose to declare Urdu the official language of the NWFP and assured the PPP leadership that it would support Pakistan's integrity and that it had left the Pakhtunistan issue behind (*NW* 12 May 1972; Amin 1988: 125). Thus, the NAP leaders, keen to prove their loyalty to Pakistan and to avoid confrontation with Hindko speakers, in order to stay in power, chose to ignore ethnic symbolism. Even so, they held power for a brief period only.

Pashto did, however, remain an issue in the Legislative Assembly. Although the text of the debates held during the seventies is in Urdu, many people actually spoke in Pashto and a translation was made. Moreover, the translation of the verses from the Holy Quran is generally in Pashto. The fact that members of the NAP took their oath in Pashto and delivered speeches in that language politicized the language issue. In the session of 3 May 1972, some members from Hazara demanded that the translation of Pashto speeches be provided to them (LAD-F 3 May 1972: 7). The debate became so acrimonious that, on 14 June 1972, the Opposition, led by the PPP's Hayat Muhammad Khan Sherpao, staged a walkout (LAD-F 14 June 1974: 17-9) and there was much discussion of the issue in subsequent sessions (LAD-F 15 January and 16 June 1972: 30-51). The point was that, despite Urdu being the official language of the NWFP, the PPP saw the NAP as a supporter of Pashto in its role as a Pakhtun identity-marker. And this, indeed, was the way in which members of the NAP saw it themselves; hence the significance of the use or non-use of Pashto in the Legislature.

Noting the contradiction in the NAP's attitude towards Urdu, its opponents sought to embarrass the NAP with accusations of not promoting it. Thus, Maulana Habib Gul asked the government what was being done to make Urdu the official language of the NWFP and pointed out that boards outside the offices of the ministers were in English (LAD-F 28 June 1973: 15-6). The Chief Minister, Inayatullah Gandapur, replied that three committees were working on the issue. Habib Gul, however, repeated his question later as he was not satisfied with the work of the committees (LAD-F 21 November 1975: 48). During the Ziaul Haq era, the Martial Law Administrator and Governor of the NWFP, Lieutenant General Fazle Haq, discouraged Pashto, at least during the initial phase of military rule. He often told the members of his council, the equivalent of the legislative assembly in that period, to use Urdu (LAD-F 6 July 1980: 103; 27 February 1983: 90) and once declared that only in Mardan did most people speak Pashto. As for the other cities, he presented the following figures (*only* for the cities, not the areas around them):

| Peshawar | 70 per cent people spoke Hindko |
| --- | --- |
| Kohat | 70 per cent people spoke Hindko |
| Dera Ismail Khan | 90 per cent people spoke Hindko |
| Bannu | 40 per cent people spoke Hindko |
| Abbottabad and Mansehra | 100 per cent people spoke Hindko |

From this he concluded that the medium of instruction could not be Pashto unless the teachers were first trained in the use of the language (LAD-F 5 October 1980: 75-8).

In the NWFP anti-Zia circles, Pashto was used to express opposition to authoritarian federal rule, martial law, and Islamization. This role was evident at the World Pashto Conference held at Peshawar on 22 April 1987. Renowned anti-establishment figures like Ghaffar Khan and Wali Khan expressed satisfaction with the conference. Representatives of left-leaning political parties like the PPP, Mazdur Kisan Party, Pakhtun Students Federation, and of course the ANP (the new name of Wali Khan's NAP) attended it. The conference expressed solidarity with the communist revolution in Afghanistan, and the poet, Hamza Shinwari, made the demand that Pashto be introduced at a high level and its use promoted in all domains (30 April 1987).

At the present point in time, despite the populist rhetoric of the PPP (which is in power again), there is no change in the status of

Pashto. Attempts are, however, being made to initiate changes and it is to the history of these attempts that we turn now.

**Promotion of Pashto**

Soon after the birth of Pakistan, the NWFP Legislative Assembly, dominated by Khan Abdul Qayyum Khan's Muslim League, proved its Pakistani credentials by moving the Urdu Resolution. This was meant to make Urdu rather than English or Pashto the language of the Courts (LAD-F 29 September 1950: 39-40). It was later reported that Urdu was used in the lower Courts though the higher Courts kept functioning in English. Pashto, however, was given no official status though it was of course used informally, since most people who thronged the courts understood no other language (LAD-F 7 November 1952: 8-9). As for the domain of education, Mian Jafar Khan, the Minister of Education, replied as follows to a question in the Legislative Assembly:

> Pashto is a subject of study in all schools in the Pashto speaking areas of the province. It is also an official subject in the middle and high schools as well as in the university (LAD-F 13 March 1952: 21).

This, however, was merely the letter of the law. In practice, Pashto could not be introduced in elitist schools at all. For instance, replying to a question about a recently opened public school in Peshawar cantonment, the minister said:

> It is a Military school and is directly under the supervision and control of the Military authorities. The Provincial Government has nothing to do with the affairs of this school (LAD-F 22 November 1952: 29).

In addition to the elitist schools controlled by the army and the air force, the provincial government was also unable to dictate to private schools. Thus, the English medium schools of the NWFP never included Pashto in their curricula.

Even schools controlled by the government, where Pashto was supposed to be the medium of instruction in class 1 and 2, and a compulsory subject up to class 5, did not teach Pashto thoroughly. Sometimes, there were not enough teachers for it (as stated in LAD-F 17 November 1952: 5-6) and at other times, students were not encouraged to take it as an optional subject from the sixth to the tenth class (Editorial *Pakhto* February 1970: 2-3).

Even in the Tribal Agencies, where hardly any language but Pashto is understood, the children are not always taught in it. A USAID survey of the Kurram Agency tells us that the formal medium of instruction remains Urdu (USAID 1991a: 82). This is rather surprising in view of the fact that as far back as 1922-27, Pashto was taught in this Agency. The *Report on Public Instruction* of 1922-27 states:

> An interesting feature of the Kurram schools is the prominence given to Pushtu, which forms part of the school course for primary classes. The subject is said to be well taught (RPI-F 1927: 89).

But this was perhaps exceptional since it was the initiative of the incumbent Political Agent, who also encouraged the publication of a Pashto newspaper, the *Kurram Times* (ibid. 89). The *Frontier Boy Scout* magazine was also published in both Urdu and Pashto (RPI-F 1939: 107).

The USAID report on the Kurram Agency notes that the use of Urdu may increase attrition by discouraging the students (USAID 1991 a: 82). In South Waziristan too, the medium of instruction in primary schools 'appears to be primarily Urdu' (USAID 1990: 69). In this case the report adds:

> Sources say that is mainly because the Pashto textbooks in use in the settled areas of NWFP are written in the Yusufzai dialect, which is not the dialect in use in the Agency (USAID 1990: 69).

This problem was taken note of in the Evaluation Report of the Primary Pashto Textbooks Translation Project (Edn Dept-F 1991: 28), but it did not prevent Pashto from being used in the settled areas. The Assistant Director of Education (FATA) also mentioned that the northern dialect was opposed by the speakers of the southern one, but he conceded that the major impediment in the way of Pashto was that no jobs were available in it (ADEF Int: 22 December 1993).

The teachers were said to be the source of the problem, as 'many of them are Hindko speakers from D. I. Khan and accordingly either do not speak Pashto or are not very comfortable in that language' (USAID 1990: 69). However, this too has not been proven and, as existing surveys suggest, most teachers can use Pashto for instruction (NWFP 1991 a and b).

Pashto was not introduced as a medium of instruction, even at the primary school level (i.e. class 1 to 4) till 1984, when the country was under martial law and many Afghan leaders were fighting against the Soviet army with the support of the Pakistani government. By then, most Pakhtuns, although expressing sympathy with the Afghans, had moved away from the demand for Pakhtunistan (Amin 1988: 192). The members of the Pakhtun elite too had been co-opted by the Pakistani ruling elite and 'Pathan domination in the provincial power structure has been far greater than that of the Baluch' (Phadnis 1984: 189). Despite these facts, even in 1984 Pashto was only introduced in schools in selected areas of the NWFP (Edn Dept-F 1991: 1). Simultaneously, a Pashto Textbooks Translation project was launched. This project was evaluated by a committee in 1989 which pointed out, *inter alia*, that:

> 1. Pashto was not introduced simultaneously in all primary schools nor was it being taught as a subject in Urdu-medium schools.
> 2. Achievement tests showed an improvement in Pashto medium schools as compared to Urdu medium schools.
> 3. The drop-out rate from the Urdu medium and the Pashto medium schools was the same (Edn Dept-F 1991: 1-4).

In other words, the use of Pashto in the primary classes was a success in pedagogical terms. There are, however, numerous other problems which were revealed by responses to the questionnaires given to teachers, parents, and administrators. The major problem was a fear of the ghettoizing potential of a language. If a student had to switch over to Urdu or English and employment was available only in those languages, Pashto education appeared wasteful to parents (ibid. 38). Perhaps because of the devaluation of Pashto in the domains of power, ordinary people felt that it could not be used by them. As the report put it:

> Psychologically, the people are not used to be convinced [*sic*] of the fact that Pashto should acquire a privileged place in the school curriculum (ibid. 40).

In short, because Pashto is still not used in the domains of power, it occupies a peripheral position even where it has been introduced. However, it remains an identity-marker. Let us, therefore, turn to LP attempts to understand this.

## Pashto LP and Identity

Apart from Ghaffar Khan and the journalists of the 1930s, Nasrullah Khan Nasr, the person who was earlier reported to have been an informer of the Afghan Consul, also devoted himself to promoting the use of Pashto. He began work in 1940 by opening a school for adult education, using Pashto as the medium of instruction (Khaleeq 1966: 50). Later, he established the Pashto Adabi Tolae, which promoted Pashto literature by holding poetry sessions and distributing pamphlets and books in Pashto (ibid. 51). Notwithstanding the covert aims of Nasr and his literary organization, he did contribute towards making people aware of the need for developing Pashto.

A number of other literary organizations have been established since the early fifties. Among them are the Olsi Adabi Jirga (1949); the Abasin Arts Council (1955); and the Sahu Likunko Marka (1962). The latest, Pakhtune Likwal, established in 1990, reiterated the demands for a change in the status of Pashto made time and again by its predecessors (Rehman Said's letter to the editor, *FP* 22 February 1993). Another such organization, Peshawar Adabi Jirga, came into being in 1991 and issued a constitution in 1994, stating that its major aim was developing Pashto and increasing its use. It too demands that Pashto should be officially patronized. These demands have, of course, been made through other forums such as literary gatherings (*PO* 16 March 1966) and letters to editors (*FP* 7 March 1990 and 26 May 1993) and, despite disclaimers, have been perceived as part of the ethno-nationalist endeavour for giving the Pakhtun identity greater prominence.

Both the modernization of Pashto vocabulary and the standardization of its script have a political dimension. That is why, for purely non-linguistic reasons, they have remained controversial, and several scripts are still in use in Pakistan (Taizi 1989). It appears that the first authentic manuscript in Pashto, the *Khairul Bayan* of Bayazid Ansari (1526-74), was written in the *nastaleeq* script, in 1560. The second, the *Makhzanul Islam* of Akhwand Darweeza (1533-1615), was written in *naskh*, between 1603 and 1612 (Pashto Academy 1991: 7-8). The *nastaleeq* script, however, appears to have been favoured up to the eighteenth century, while *naskh* has dominated thereafter (Khattak, P. 1977 b: 32-43).

During the debate on the script in the magazine *Nan Parun* in 1942, Maulana Abdul Qadir proposed that *naskh* be replaced by *nastaleeq*, so that Pashto could be written like Urdu; moreover that in order to facilitate readers of Urdu, the distinctive orthographic symbol or graphemes of Pashto should also be replaced by Urdu ones (Qadir 1942: 20-5). These symbols, or at least some of them, have been used since Bayazid Ansari's time; in fact, he is credited with having invented them (Pashto Academy 1991: 8). They have served many functions: at the linguistic level, they represent the sounds of both the dialects of the language; more importantly, they differentiate Pashto from other languages and function as identity-markers. Thus, there was almost unanimous opposition to the proposal to change to *nastaleeq* and the distinctive graphemes were retained (Shaido 1942 and 1943 sums up the views of the participants in the debate).

Other such suggestions were also opposed (*Pakhtun* 24 October 1945), as was the proposal that the Roman script be adopted for Pashto (Ali, M. 1942). Thus, when the Pashto Academy held a conference of both Afghan and Pakistani Pakhtun language planners in March 1957, there was consensus on this issue (Pashto Academy 1957 b). This consensus has also emerged in the Pashto conferences at Bara Gali in 1990 and 1993 (Pashto Academy 1991; Khattak, R. 1991). The distinctive graphemes of Pashto are, therefore, still a part of the Pashto script and continue to serve to differentiate it from Urdu and Punjabi.

Other areas of standardization—diacritical marks, shapes of graphemes, and spellings—have also been controversial. Despite agreements in 1957 and in 1990 on usage, differences do persist. The word lists issued by the Kabul Pashto Tolane, containing spellings of words, have also been ignored in Pakistan (Ulfat 1961). Thus, either because the government of Pakistan covertly wishes that differences should persist between Afghani and Pakistani Pashto (Khattak Int: 1 November 1993), or because of inefficiency, Pashto still lacks standardization.

The modernization of the vocabulary is equally controversial. Those who want the new terms to be coined from Perso-Arabic morphemes are generally the supporters of either an Islamic or a Pakistani identity. They point out, and quite rightly, that Perso-Arabic diction is more familiar and intelligible (Akbar 1957), but their real aim is to give primacy to the Islamic rather than the Pakhtun identity of the Pakhtuns (Naseeruddin 1984).

The supporters of the Pakhtun identity, on the other hand, use indigenous roots for neologisms, thus purging Pashto of its Perso-Arabic content, though, according to one researcher, Islamic literature has been informally taught in Pashto at the lower level (Naeem 1986). Such people, according to some informants, are generally the supporters of the ANP and the Pakhtunkhwa Qaumi Party (Khattak Int: 1 November 1993). They are influenced by Sadiqullah Rishtin's movement for *soocha* (pure) Pashto (Dupree 1973: 93) and advocate the use of words coined in Kabul. Among these words are the following:

| English | Pashto Neologism | Words commonly used |
|---|---|---|
| submarine | *dub mako* | *sumreen* |
| aeroplane | *alvatak* | *vai jaaz* |
| university | *pohintun* | *universtae* |
| professor | *pohand* | *propesar* |
| hospital | *roghtun* | *aspatal* |
| signature | *las lik* | *dast khat* |
| script | *lik dud* | *rasmul khat* |
| rocket | *torghunday* | *rakut* |

These English words or their Urdu equivalents pronounced with a Pashto accent are what ordinary Pakistani Pakhtuns commonly use. The emphasis on the Pashto terms is part of the need to emphasize the distinctiveness of the Pakhtun identity from the non-Pakhtun one.

The official LP organizations, like the Pashto Academy, do not go to this extreme. A glossary of technical terms and modern concepts is being prepared under the supervision of Raj Wali Khattak at the Academy according to the following principles:

> (a) The retention of words in common use even if they are borrowed from foreign languages, e.g., operation (for surgery); radio, actor, etc.
>
> (b) Using Pashto as well as morphemes of other languages for coining new terms (Khattak Int: 1 November 1993).

Sometimes, a word of Pashto origin is combined with English ones, to form new word: *palwasha* (ray), combined with 'laser', forms *laser-palwasha* (laser ray). In short, official LP places less emphasis on the distinctive Pakhtun identity than do the more outspoken Pakhtun nationalists in their private capacities.

At present, despite comparative freedom in some aspects of language planning, Pashto is still not used in the domains of power. It is peripheral in non-elitist schools and non-existent in elitist ones. It is used on signboards etc., and there are some publications in it, including two dailies (see Appendix A). These steps make the Pashto-speaking people less critical of the ruling elite than previously, when their language was totally ignored. However, they still cannot aspire to positions of power in Pakistan without a knowledge of Urdu and English.

To conclude, Pashto was chosen as an identity-marker by Pakhtun nationalists in modern times for political reasons: to create a pressure group in Pakistan and to consolidate Pakhtun rule over non-Pakhtuns in Afghanistan. Pakhtun nationalism, varying from aspirations to independence or autonomy to mere assertions of cultural distinctiveness, has been expressed through Pashto. However, as the Pakhtuns have become more prosperous and better integrated in the economic and power structure of Pakistan, the Pashto movement has decreased. Nowadays, Pashto is an identity-marker and the efforts to increase its use in formal domains no longer come from those who want secession from Pakistan. These efforts are, however, part of the Pakhtun nationalist demand for greater autonomy, the right to preserve the indigenous way of life, and pride in the Pakhtun identity.

## Notes

1. Sir Olaf Caroe says that the former Chief Minister of the NWFP, Dr Khan Sahib, also considered Sher Shah his hero because 'he was such a true Pathan' (1957: 141). For the significance of the symbol of this ruler for the Pakhtuns and a brief biography, see Caroe 1957: 134-50.

# 9

# The Language Movements of Balochistan

Balochistan is a multilingual province in which Balochi, Brahvi, Persian, Pashto, Siraiki, Jatki, Punjabi, and Urdu are spoken in addition to the elitist and official English. The Balochi-speaking areas extend outside the borders of Pakistan into Afghanistan and Iranian Balochistan. The Baloch, however, do not only comprise speakers of Balochi: the Brahvi-speaking tribes are also called Baloch and certain Siraiki-speaking tribes, such as the Jamalis, perceive themselves as Baloch.

This makes both ethnic origin and language, which are the primary markers of ethno-nationalism elsewhere in Pakistan, less important than other factors. Even so, there are movements to increase the use of the indigenous languages—Balochi, Brahvi and Pashto—in the domains of power in Balochistan. The aim of this chapter is to study the historical evolution of the language movements of Balochistan and to relate them to politics, especially to Baloch nationalism and the Centre's response to it. The main language movement is the Balochi language movement and efforts to promote Brahvi are subsumed under it for reasons given below. The Pashto language movement in Balochistan is part of the Pakhtun identity and will not be touched upon here except where it relates to Baloch politics.

### Linguistic Composition of Balochistan

The present borders of Balochistan are a colonial legacy. The 'districts of Kurram and Pishin and Sibi' were taken from Afghanistan under the treaty of Gandamak dated 26 May 1879 between the British and the Amir of Afghanistan. It was, however, provided that these districts 'shall not be considered as permanently severed from the limits of the Afghan Kingdom' (Article 9 of the Treaty in Ahmad, S. I. 1992: 405). Zhob and Loralai, between the Amir's borders and British India

(Adm Rep-B 1888: 5), were inhabited by 'Afghan tribes'. This area was, and is, predominantly Pashto-speaking.

The Baloch nationalists exclude these areas from Balochistan. According to one of them:

> The Pakhtoon areas in Balochistan were never claimed by Baloch. Their insistence on redemarcation of the provincial boundaries on the basis of language and culture means the exclusion of these areas from Balochistan and the inclusion of the Balochi-speaking districts of Khan Garh, now Jacobabad and Harand and Dajal, now Dera Ghazi Khan, into their country (Janmahmad 1989: 287).

Janmahmad claims that Mir Khudadad Khan, the Khan of Kalat, opposed the merger of the Pashto-speaking areas with Balochistan, a merger which the British desired (1989: 288). Moreover, when the government of Pakistan wished to merge the Pakhtun districts with the Balochistan States Union in 1954, some Baloch sardars (tribal heads) did not agree. They drew up a memorandum on 16 February 1954, proposing that the Pashto-speaking areas be separated from Balochistan. The government, however, decided to merge all of these areas in the Balochistan States Union on 16 June (Janmahmad 288). Whether this was done intentionally to weaken the Baloch nationalist struggle cannot be ascertained. However, this was certainly one of its results. The Pakhtun factor remains as one of the irritants in the way of promoting Baloch nationalism in the province. The strongest political organ of the Pakhtuns in Balochistan was the Wrore Pakhtoon of Abdus Samad Achakzai which was formed in 1954. Achakzai, like the Baloch nationalists mentioned above, wanted a Pashto-speaking province which would include some of the areas of Balochistan (Achakzai's statement before the Lahore High Court, 26 Oct 1956 in Janmahmad 1989: 289). However, this did not come about and the Pakhtuns, now led by Mahmud Khan Achakzai, have been demanding an equal share in power (and jobs) in the province (LAD-B 29 June 1972; *J* [Quetta] 20 November 1984). The Baloch nationalists have often resisted these demands (BSO Unit Secretary's statement issued at NED University, Karachi, July 1985) and this has led to conflict and ill will (Janmahmad 1989: 285-94).

This background of Baloch-Pakhtun politics explains why Pashto is seen as an identity-marker by the Pakhtun minority of Balochistan. It is a way of preserving Pakhtun identity in the face of the power of the Baloch majority and Baloch ethno-nationalism which appears threatening to the Pakhtuns. The Pashto language movement then is part of this political struggle. The Pashto Academy, first established in 1971, promotes Pashto folk literature, language, and history. Although its ex-president Abid Shah Abid denies its political role (Abid Int: 7 June 1994)—that of identity preservation—its activities have created a consciousness of the Pakhtun identity among Pashto-speaking intellectuals and have also contributed to keeping Pashto on the agenda of language planners in Balochistan. That is why Pashto has never been ignored in any of the language policy decisions of the Balochistan government as we shall see.

As for the Baloch who moved into Sindh or the Siraiki-speaking areas, most of them have assimilated into these cultures and play no role in the politics of Balochistan. The Langahs, some of whom are active in the Siraiki ethno-nationalist movement, were Baloch, though they ruled Multan. Others, such as the Jamalis, see themselves as Baloch though most of them speak Siraiki now. There are also Balochi-speaking people in the Punjab as Ranjit Singh, the ruler of the Punjab, had 'seized Horrund and Dajal' (D. G. Khan) (Khelat Affairs 1977: 170). The Baloch in Sindh, especially in Karachi, have moved there recently in search of jobs and are fast losing their Balochi identity.

This brings us to Balochi and Brahvi speakers. The area of the Kalat state, where these people predominate, was described thus by Captain R. G. Sandeman, the officiating Deputy Commissioner of Dera Ghazi Khan, in 1872:

> The state of Khelat itself, before we interfered in her affairs, extended in the north to Shaulkot, or, as called by us, Quetta; to the sea on the coast of Mehran; from the Frontier of Persia beyond Kharan and Punjgur, on the west; to Sind and the Punjab on the East (Khelat Affairs 170).

Nowadays Balochi and Brahvi speakers predominate in districts given in Map 4 (see Appendix F).

**Balochi-Brahvi Controversy**

According to European scholars such as Bray, Brahvi 'reveals a clear and unmistakable resemblance to the Dravidian languages of Southern India' (Bray 1913: 178). But even Bray was not sure whether the Brahvi people are also Dravidians (ibid. 181). This controversy continues (see Emeneau 1962), but what is significant from the point of view of politics—specifically the articulation of Baloch nationalism—is the manifest desire of both Balochi and Brahvi speaking intellectuals and politicians to emphasize unity and similarities rather than differences.

According to the *Encyclopaedia Britannica,* there is a nucleus of eight Brahvi tribes to which other people have been affiliated so that the number of tribes has swelled to twenty-nine. These tribes were loosely united under the rule of the Khan of Kalat, whose family rose to power under Mir Nisar Khan (1750-1795) until 1947 when the Khanate became a part of Pakistan (*Britannica* 2: 464). The origin of the Brahvis, even more than their language, is an enigma. However, Mir Ahmed Yar Khan, the Khan of Kalat, calls the Baloch and the Brahvis two groups of the same people. The 'group which was originally called "Ibrahimi Baluches" is now pronounced as "Brahvi Baluches" ' (Yar 1975: 56). Justice Khudabaksh Marri asserts that the Brahvis are 'one of the many early tribes of Baloches' (Marri 1974: 110) and that many of them, including the ruling family of Kalat, use the term 'Baloch' with their names (ibid. 230). However, he opines that there is some Dravidian blood in them (ibid. 13). This is disputed by many, including Nasser Brohi who wrote a book passionately arguing that the Brahvis are not Dravidians, and that the Baloch and the Brahvis 'must have a common origin' (Brohi 1977: 101). More recently, *Koord Gal Namik,* a book written in 1659 by Akhund Saleh Mohammad, a minister in the court of Mir Ahmad Khan I, the Khan of Kalat, has been held up as proof by both Baloch and Brahvi intellectuals that they are one people. The book asserts that the Baloch are Kurds and that the Brahvis, called Brakhuis, are one of the tribes of Kurds (Mohammad 1659).

However, the book merely asserts its claims without offering any proof of events which are supposed to have occurred several centuries earlier. What it does prove is that there was a desire in the seventeenth century to emphasize the common origin of Brahvi and Baloch tribes. Perhaps the reason then was that, at that time, a Brahvi ruler was ruling over Balochi-speaking people and the myth of common origin could help in consolidating his rule. Today, both Baloch and Brahvi speakers also stand to gain if they are treated as one people. Hence Baloch nationalists, both Balochi- and Brahvi-speaking, angrily reject the idea of antagonism in the Brahvi and Balochi language movements.

According to Janmahmad, the demand for the recognition of Brahvi was raised 'with official patronage' at the Regional Languages Conference in Lahore in 1961 (1989: 260). Later, in 1972, the Brahvi Students Federation, made efforts for the promotion of Brahvi. Today, merely anecdotal evidence is available of their efforts. However, according to Abdullah Jan Jamaldini, Brahvi was promoted as part of the Balochi language movement from the 1950s. Even at the time, some pages of the monthly *Balochi* were devoted to Brahvi. Later, when Radio Pakistan Quetta started functioning in 1966, Brahvi was given time on it, along with Balochi. In the same year the Brahvi Academy was formed. It had, and continues to have, members who are also active in the Balochi Academy (Jamaldini Int: 5 June 1994).

There is, at present, a Brahvi Literary Society and a Brahvi Orthographic Committee as well as the Brahvi Academy in Quetta. However, they work in partnership with the institutions meant for the promotion of Balochi. *Eelam*, a Brahvi-Urdu weekly which started publication in 1960 (Brohi 1977: 113), exhorts the government to promote both Brahvi and Balochi (*Eelam* 17 May 1994). Another example of co-operation is the establishment of the languages section within the Department of Pakistan Studies at Balochistan University. MA courses in Balochi, Brahvi, and Pashto were started in 1987, and academics make efforts to promote research in both Balochi and Brahvi (Sabir Int: 08 June 1994).

The Baloch nationalists regard attempts at promoting language as the only criterion for nationality as a conspiracy of anti-Baloch forces (Bizenjo 1992: 110-3; Janmahmad 1989: 260-1). These attempts, they argue, come from anti-Baloch forces i.e., the government of Pakistan or neo-imperialist foreign scholars; they do not come from the Brahvis, who see themselves as Baloch. How much of this is true cannot be ascertained but it is difficult to agree with Harrison who says that 'there is likely to be a continuing element of tension in the cultural arena between Brahvi and non-Brahvi Baloch intellectuals' (1981: 185).

What this means is that Baloch identity is defined more by a certain cultural similarity, a way of life, rather than language alone. This obviously makes language less important as a symbol of Baloch nationalism than it is in similar movements among the speakers of Sindhi, Pashto, and Siraiki.

## Language and the Islamic Resistance

The coming of British rule to Balochistan appears to have evoked a less antagonistic intellectual response than the earlier arrival of the missionaries. The missionaries printed the Bible in Balochi written in the Persian script, as early as 1815 (Catalogue 1832: 105). Later, in 1884 A. Lewis translated St Matthew's Gospel and, from 1899, T. J. Lee Mayer's series of translations from the Bible started appearing in the Roman script (Grierson Vol. 2: 334-5). In response to these translations, which made the Baloch *ulema* feel that the Islamic faith of their people was in danger, the first anti-British intellectual movement in Balochistan started in the 1880s.

This movement, the Darkhani movement, was inspired and pioneered by Maulana Mohammad Fazil who was from Darkhan, a village near Dhadar which is now called Fazil Abad. The Maulana is said to have called a gathering of the *ulema* in Dhadar in 1883 and it was decided that they would translate religious books into Balochi and Brahvi. Such books were in Persian or Arabic, but it was now felt that they would be more effective in countering missionary propaganda if they were available in the indigenous languages of the Baloch (Qambrani 1990: 18-21; Shahwani 1993).

Maulana Huzoor Bakhsh Jatoi translated the Quran into Balochi (written in the Arabic rather than the Persian script) in 1902-3. Other books too were written in the same script and the *ulema* spread throughout Balochistan, teaching the rudiments of Islam to villagers. The Maktaba-e-Darkhani (the Darkhani school) is said to have produced a fairly large number of books. Exact numbers are disputed, but Shahwani lists 339 books, out of which 210 are in Brahvi and 91 in Balochi. In this list, there are also 15 books in Persian, 10 in Arabic, 5 in Urdu, and 2 in Sindhi (Shahwani 1993: 63).

**Language and Secular Resistance**

By the 1930s the first modern Baloch political groups had been organized and Balochi newspapers began to appear. Their concerns were secular—identity, freedom, control over resources, jobs, power, etc.—and were expressed in the idiom of political debate. Abdul Aziz Kurd's Anjuman-e-Ittehad-e-Balochistan (Organization for the Unity of Balochistan) published *Al-Baloch*, a weekly from Karachi, which demanded an independent state comprising the Kalat state, British Balochistan, Dera Ghazi Khan, and Iranian Balochistan (*Al-Baloch* August 1933). In 1935, the Kalat National Party, inspired by similar nationalist ideas, was formed. It was partly because of such aspirations that the Khan of Kalat issued an 'Announcement' on 11 April 1947 to the effect that Kalat would be a sovereign state and all foreigners who chose to stay in it would have to integrate with the indigenous people (In Zaidi, Z. H. 1993: 551). This document was sent to Jinnah by the Khan on 14 April 1947, requesting him to make a statement 'in support of the Kalat Government announcement' (ibid. 549).

As the Muslim League did not deny the Khan's claims, the Khan declared independence on 12 August 1947. We are not concerned with the controversy over the case but it does appear that the most articulate political leaders outside British Balochistan, such as Ghaus Baksh Bizenjo, were genuinely sympathetic to Baloch nationalism (see Bizenjo's speech in the Kalat National Assembly on 14 December 1947 in Harrison 1981: 25).

Balochi and Brahvi were not an important part of this nationalism. However, when the Khan went to Karachi in October 1947, the meeting was reported by Karachi's leading newspapers to have been 'exclusively Baloch, and both the address of welcome and reply was made in Balochi language' (*D* 17 October 1947). Moreover, according to historians, 'the Balochistan Parliament in its meeting of 14 December 1947 recommended that Balochi be declared the national and official language of Balochistan' (Janmahmad 1989: 261). In practice, however, most of the work of the Kalat state was carried on in Urdu, while correspondence with outsiders was in English. The 'Announcement' mentioned earlier was in Urdu, which seems to have gradually replaced Persian after the coming of the British. Notwithstanding administrative necessities, it is significant that Balochi nationalism was expressed through Balochi during the 227 days of the independence of the Kalat state.

Eventually, hearing of the movements of troops in Pasni and Jiwani and fearful of further problems, the Khan acceded to Pakistan on 27 March 1948. Even so, the Pakistan Army moved to Kalat on 1 April 1948, with orders to overcome resistance from the nationalists (Harrison 1981: 25). Prince Abdul Karim, the younger brother of the Khan, rebelled and crossed over into Afghanistan. However, finding no help there, he came back and was imprisoned. Thus began the conflict between Baloch nationalists and the government of Pakistan, which was to cause much bloodshed later. As Baloch antagonism was expressed overtly and militarily to begin with, language remained only a subsidiary symbol of nationalism. In a sense, therefore, the pattern of Baloch nationalism is the opposite of that of Bangladesh, where it was language which first became a major symbol of a separate Bengali identity.

## Beginning of the Balochi Movement

Soon after the establishment of Pakistan, Karachi became the focus of intellectual activities. The Lyari Adabi Board, the Balochi Academy, and the Fazil Academy were all private bodies which sprang up in Karachi after 1947 (Hashmi 1973: 9 January). It was in Karachi that members of the Baloch intelligentsia, who were conscious of culture and identity, and of political and economic issues were concentrated. Thus, the first monthly periodical in Balochi, called *Oman*, was published in 1951 from Karachi by the Baloch Educational Society (Jahani 1989: 25). Azat Jamaldini, his brother Abdullah Jamaldini, and Gul Khan Naseer, the most famous modern poet of Balochi, started what was called the Lathkhana Movement—a literary renaissance in the fifties influenced by famous leftist intellectuals such as Faiz Ahmad Faiz and Sajjad Zaheer. Their organization, called the Balochi Zaban-e-Diwan (Organization for the Balochi Language), was established privately in 1951 and, according to Abdullah Jamaldini, it was for the promotion of both Balochi and Brahvi. The Jamaldini brothers applied for permission to publish a monthly Balochi magazine to be called *Sob* (Victory) but permission was denied. However, in 1956, Azat Jamaldini did succeed in publishing *Balochi*. The monthly magazine was forced to close down in 1958, because it was denied advertisements and official patronage. It was revived in 1978 and continued publication till 1981. In 1986, it started publication from Quetta, this time under the editorship of Abdul Wahid Bandiq (Bandiq Int: 8 June 1994; Jamaldini Int: 5 June 1994).

The fifties also saw the resurgence of nationalist aspirations in politics. Prince Abdul Karim, who was released in 1955, laid the foundation of Ustaman Gall (Peoples' Party) in the same year. Its nucleus was the former Kalat National Party and its manifesto declared that it would establish a 'Baluch Province on linguistic and cultural lines' with Balochi as the official language (*Oman* August 1955: 3; Janmahmad 1989: 196). In 1956 the Ustaman Gall joined the Pakistan National Party which merged in the NAP. The forces of ethno-nationalism, as we know, were represented by the NAP in both East and West Pakistan.

The most sensational event of the fifties, however, was the arrest of the Khan of Kalat on 6 October 1958 on the charge of gathering 80,000 tribesmen 'to revolt against the Government' (Yar 1975: 181). The Khan denied these allegations and many people, including some Pakistani officials, opined that President Iskander Mirza had encouraged the Khan to assert his autonomy, giving Mirza a pretext to impose martial law (Rasheed 1985: 36-7; Yar 1975: 181-5; Harrison 1981: 28). On 10 October 1958, Nauroz Khan, a chief of the Zehri tribe, led 1000 guerrillas against the Pakistan army. Nauroz Khan is believed to have agreed to a truce after military officers took an oath on the Quran to treat him with honour and justice (Yar 1975: 186; Harrison 1981: 28-9). It was taken as a great betrayal when his sons were hanged and he himself was jailed. This version of events is denied by Pakistani officials but it is widely believed by the Baloch (author's interviews).

The significance of these events for the language movement, though indirect, was notable. One result was that nationalist feeling became deeper and was expressed more clearly in the literature. Nauroz Khan emerged as the archetypal hero and the Baloch were depicted as being exploited by the anti-Baloch forces of the Centre (Janmahmad 1989: 132-4).

**The Language Movement in the Sixties**

The 1960s were characterized by two apparently paradoxical developments. On the one hand, the government suppressed the Baloch tribes, especially the *Pararis* led by Sher Muhammad Marri, with military force (Harrison 1981: 33). On the other, it gave some concessions to the linguistic and cultural aspects of Baloch nationalism. Perhaps these concessions were given to appease the Baloch intelligentsia or to create a better image for the Ayub Khan government, which was engaged in suppressing the militant expression of Baloch nationalism.

Among the concessions given by the government was the agreed publication of a monthly magazine called *Ulus*, in Balochi and Pashto from 1961. The Balochi edition had a Brahvi section, but the main emphasis was on Balochi. In the same year, the weekly *Nokeen Daur* started publication from Quetta and ran till 1971, when financial stringency forced it to close down (Jahani 1989: 25). Also in 1961, the Warna Wananda Gal was created. Its aim, like other linguistic and literary organizations of the 1950s, was to promote Balochi and Brahvi language and literature (Marri Int: 2 June 1994).

Efforts to create an officially backed Balochi Academy started in 1958, and one was finally established in 1961 in Quetta (*Balochi* April-May 1958: 5). It was, indeed, Quetta rather than Karachi which became the centre of the Balochi/Brahvi language movements from the sixties onwards. From the late fifties onwards, the radio also started relaying programmes in Balochi from Quetta, and more publications came to be centred in Quetta. With the establishment of the Brahvi Academy in Quetta in 1966, that city became firmly established as the centre of the Baloch linguistic and literary renaissance.

The above, however, were minor concessions because the use of Balochi or Brahvi was never permitted in the domains of power. Yet the members of the Baloch intelligentsia regarded them as victories. The Baloch identity and way of life had, after all, better chances of being preserved now than it had had before. As for the Ayub Khan government, it too had cause for satisfaction. Through its partial patronage of linguistic and literary activities, the bureaucracy could mollify the Baloch intelligentsia and control it, thus preventing the intelligentsia from becoming as alienated from the Centre as the militant nationalists were.

## Urdu in Balochistan

In the nineteenth century, the court language of the Kalat state was Persian, but there was a thriving oral poetic tradition in Balochi (Sardar 1977) and Brahvi (Qambrani 1990). Basic education was imparted by *mullas* in *maktabs*, and explanations were given in the local languages. However, in some areas, as in Kech, the Gazetteer tells us that 'There is, indeed, only one Baluch *mullah* . . . a few of the remaining *mullahs* are Afghans' (Gazeteer-B 1907: 263).

Mullah Muhammad Hasan (d. 1855), who was a poet of Balochi and Brahvi, also wrote poetry in Urdu (Kausar 1986: 7-9). The subordinate bureaucracy of the British, which was from northern India, used Urdu. Because of them, a British Survey reports that 'Urdu, being the language of officials, is beginning to make some headway' (Bray 1913: 15). As the Balochistan Agency was placed under the Punjab Government, where the officially recognized vernacular language was Urdu, it was Urdu which came to be used in schools and the lower levels of administration and the judiciary. Thus, not only in British Balochistan but even in Kalat, where British officials influenced and controlled aspects of administration, Urdu was used for official correspondence from 1907 onwards (for copies of such documents, see Kausar 1986).

The government of Pakistan, which used Urdu as a symbol of integration, continued to encourage the use of Urdu, so that by 1972, when the coalition government of the NAP and the JUI took power in Balochistan, all educated Baloch knew Urdu. The Baloch poet and nationalist, Mir Gul Khan Naseer, was the Minister of Education, while Ataullah Mengal from the NAP was the Chief Minister. Thus, the order of the Governor, who was none other than the well-known Baloch nationalist, Ghaus Baksh Bizenjo (Harrison 1981: 52-61), declaring Urdu as the language of official correspondence and routine office work appears paradoxical (Order in Kausar 1986: 15-6). The order was issued after a discussion in the cabinet but not in the Legislative Assembly. The paradox has never been fully explained, but it is a significant landmark in ethno-nationalist politics, and opinions about it need to be recorded. According to Janmahmad:

> The Baloch leaders, mindful of the Pathan role, proceeded very cautiously. They reluctantly decided to declare Urdu the official language of the province, not because they had any love for the language or because Urdu had any place in the province's social and political life at all, but because adopting Balochi as the official language would have been severely opposed by the Pakhtoons, who would have demanded that their tongue should also be given official status (1989: 292).

Harrison's opinion is different. According to him it 'was partly to deflect Brahvi pressures that Bizenjo and Mengal agreed to the designation of Urdu . . . [as the official language of Balochistan] . . . thus providing a pretext for temporarily setting aside the choice between Baluchi, Brahvi, and Pushtu' (1981: 185). But Harrison presents no evidence and his explanation is rejected by Baloch nationalists (Bizenjo 1992: 113). Some of them claim that Balochi was not developed enough, nor did it have a standard script, and for these reasons could not be used as an official language (Bizenjo 1992: 113; Malik and Akram Int: 4 June 1994). Others, such as Abdullah Jamaldini, point out that jobs were available for speakers of Urdu, so that the choice of Balochi would have made the Baloch unable to compete with other Pakistanis. Moreover, he adds, as Urdu was symbolic in upholding the federation, the NAP adopted it so as to remove the impression that it was secessionist (Jamaldini Int: 5 June 1994). If this was a consideration, it did not work because Z. A. Bhutto dismissed the NAP-JUI ministry on 12 February 1973, after it had been in power for just nine months.

## Politics and the Script

The need for a standard script for Balochi and Brahvi was felt from the beginning of the language movement, in the early 1950s. Both Brahvi and Balochi had been written earlier but, in the absence of language planning bodies and the pressure of commercial printing, spellings and script had not been standardized.

The earliest known handwritten manuscripts are in the Arabic script. In Brahvi, the earliest work is said to be *Khidmat Deen*. It contains religious and moral precepts and is dated between 1293 and 1294 (Qambrani 1990: 14). The best known work is Mulla Malik Dad Kalati's *Tuhfat ul Ajaib*, again a religious work, written some time between 1759 and 1760 and printed by the Darkhani school in 1882 (Sabir 1990: 37; Qambrani 1990: 16).

The oldest manuscript in Balochi, *Codex Oriental Additional 24048*, was compiled circa 1820, probably by Usman Kalamati (Elfbein 1983: 78). Other manuscripts are dated 1873 (*Oriental 2439*) and 1877 (*Oriental 2921*) (Jahani 1989: 23). They were written by Kamalan Gichki and, in Elfbein's view, at least one of them was 'written for the enlightenment of a British officer' (Elfbein 1963: 364).

All these manuscripts, as well as the works of the Darkhani school, were in *naskh*. However, the Darkhani language planners created 53 graphemes for Balochi and 54 for Brahvi, some of them especially modified to express the sounds of these languages (Sabir 1990: 38). Other graphemes, numbering from a total of twenty-five to forty-nine, were also decided upon (Sabir 1990: 39-42). An attempt at standardization was made in a private meeting of Baloch language planners at Magsi House, on 22 July 1955. Muhammad Hussain Anqa, Gul Khan Naseer, Sayyid Hashmi, and Khair Muhammad Nadvi were the most active of these planners (Jahani 1989: 136). They made joint and private efforts at creating a common, standard script. The Jamaldini brothers published *Balochi* in a standard script, which involved the rewriting of all contributions (Jamaladini Int: 5 June 1994), and Sayyid Hashmi (1962), Gul Khan Naseer, Abdul Qayyum, and Akbar Barakzai devised orthographic systems of their own (Jahani 1989: 138-40). As none of these systems had been accepted by everyone, Gul Khan Naseer called a convention to settle the question of the Balochi script, in September 1972 at Quetta (*D* 3 September 1972).

The convention became a battleground of ethno-nationalist and Pakistani-Islamic world views. Gul Khan Naseer favoured the adoption of a phonemic Roman script with 36 letters. The students of the left-leaning Baloch Students Organization (BSO) and Baloch intellectuals supported him (Hameed 1972 b). Although they gave quasi-linguistic arguments, they appeared to favour Roman as a reaction to the Pakistani state's emphasis on an Arabic-based script(*naskh*or *nastaleeq*) as a marker of Islamic and Pakistani identity. For them, the Arabic script would not symbolize the distinctiveness of the Baloch identity, since it was common to all the languages of Pakistan. More pragmatic people supported the Arabic script, precisely because it was common to everybody and would not alienate the Baloch from other

Muslim societies. The right wing religious parties, which opposed the secular ethno-nationalism of NAP anyway, attacked Romanization as a conspiracy of the socialists against Islam and Pakistan (see editorials in *J* and *NW* 6 August and *NW* 8 September 1972; Bhutto 1972). Even Anqa, a Baloch intellectual, pointed out that the Baloch would not agree to exchange the Arabic script for any other because of religious sentiments (Anqa 1973: 46-52. Also see Hameed 1972 a).

The acerbity in the debate on standardization was ideological and political. In fact, nobody except Lal Baksh Rind actually wrote Balochi in the Roman script (Jahani 1989: 146-7). At present, most Baloch intellectuals prefer the Arabic script, and the Balochi and Brahvi Orthographic Committees have adopted *nastaleeq*, with most of the graphemes of Urdu, as the standard script of these languages.

Apart from asserting its concern for the preservation of Baloch identity through its stand on standardization, the NAP did not do much to promote the use of Balochi. Perhaps the only other event of note is the passing of a resolution in the Legislative Assembly that Radio Pakistan Quetta should give two-thirds of its time to the local languages and one-third to Urdu (LAD. Bal 11 January 1973: 102). But this was a meaningless gesture, as Urdu continued to grow stronger at the expense of the local languages in all domains.

The seventies are better known for the escalation of the conflict between the Baloch nationalists and the Pakistani state than for linguistic changes. From April 1973, soon after the dismissal of the NAP government, till 1977, the Pakistan Army and Baloch tribes, especially the Marris, were involved in hit-and-run battles which are estimated to have claimed almost 600 lives: 446 army personnel and 125 tribesmen (Harrison 1981: 38-9). This time, too, there were heroes who were depicted in Balochi and Brahvi literature. The most notable hero was Mir Luang Khan, the lame elder brother of Gul Khan Naseer, who fought the army rather than submit to a search (Harrison 1981: 37). The triumvirate of Khair Baksh Marri, Ataullah Mengal, and Ghaus Baksh Bizenjo also emerged as nationalist heroes. As in the sixties, this militant expression of Baloch nationalism made mere linguistic expression peripheral. Linguistic and literary expression, however, became a permanent symbol of nationalist aspirations.

**Indigenous Languages in Primary Schools**

As noted earlier, the martial law regime of General Ziaul Haq increased the use of both Urdu and Islam as symbols of integration. Thus.

according to an official survey, the use of Urdu increased in Balochistan up to 1984 as follow:

| | |
|---|---|
| Official work in government offices | 90 % |
| Official work at the district level | 70 % |
| Divisional offices (judicial level) | 50 % |

(Circular No. S.O. Cabinet V 84/103-4 of 13 March 1984).

Heads of institutions were asked to extend the use of Urdu; technical terms in Urdu were disseminated; and Urdu typing was officially encouraged (Kausar 1986: 20-7).

After Ziaul Haq's death, when Benazir Bhutto's PPP formed the government at the Centre, Nawab Akbar Bugti became the Chief Minister of Balochistan. Now, the supporters of Balochi expressed themselves more freely. Ayub Baloch presented a resolution for increasing the time given to Balochi on television and radio. Terming Balochi a symbol of Baloch identity, he presented fifteen points, aimed at disseminating Baloch culture and literature, and for the protection of local artists, (LAD-Bal 6 July 1989: 50-2).

The most significant step taken in support of the indigenous languages was a bill to make them—i.e. Balochi, Brahvi, and Pashto—compulsory media of instruction at the primary level (i.e., classes 1, 2, and 3) in rural schools (LAD-Bal 21 June and 15 April 1990). The bill, called 'The Balochistan Mother Tongue Use Bill, No. 6 of 1990' provided that these three indigenous languages would be used as compulsory media of instruction in 'institutions in the areas prescribed by the Government'. A letter of the Education Department (Letter No. 3-6/79-E of 3 August) exempted elitist schools from the Act, so that they could continue to use English as before. In short, the experiment was to be confined to the rural areas, the peripheries, the under-privileged, and would not extend to the elite. Moreover, as these languages would not open up the possibilities of jobs, they were ghettoizing. This could hardly motivate parents to be enthusiastic about them.

The activists of the language movements were, however, very enthusiastic. They sat on committees to prepare textbooks for classes 1 and 2, using words from both the Eastern and Western dialects of Balochi. Teachers were trained and the Balochistan Textbook Board published textbooks for primary classes. On 8 November 1992, during the chief ministership of Taj Muhammad Jamali in a Pakistan Muslim

League government, a cabinet decision resulted in the discontinuation of the experiment. The order is as follows:

> It was unanimously decided by the cabinet that the local languages shall be adopted as optional subjects in education institutions throughout the province (No. SO. CAB-4-359/92 [SRGAD]/827, Government of Balochistan).

The order merely made instruction in MT optional, but in practice it stopped altogether, since parents did not want their children to spend their time and energy on languages which would ghettoize them. Moreover, the Textbook Board was asked not to produce any more books in these languages; nor were the teachers imparted any further training (information given by officials of the Board and interviewees). The experiment was suddenly stopped.

Baloch intellectuals reacted vehemently. Saba Dashtiari, an academic and supporter of the Balochi language movement, wrote open letters to politicians, journalists, writers, and editors, exhorting them to protest against this unjust decision (1992; 1993a; 1993b). The January 1993 issue of the Brahvi magazine *Tawar* was dedicated to this subject and carried interviews of Bahadur Khan, Nadir Qambrani, Razzak Sabir, Gul Bangalzai—all supporters of Balochi and Brahvi—in which the speakers protested against the decision. Most writers called this decision a conspiracy of the bureaucracy which had never favoured the development of a Baloch identity (Tigri 1993).

The opponents of MT education pointed to multilingualism and lack of standardization in Balochi as the main impediments to teaching in it. The use of words from both dialects of Balochi and lack of standardization in the textbooks of classes 1 and 2, as pointed out by Kalgi (1992) and Ghamshad (1992) among others, was seen as a major hurdle. The supporters of MT felt strongly that language planning and official support was needed to overcome these problems (Mengal 1993: 24-8). The supporters of Pashto supported mother tongue education in principle, since it would also contribute to the preservation of the Pakhtun identity.

This debate continues today. The activists of the Balochi/Brahvi language movements are trying to mobilize public opinion in favour of making education in the mother tongue compulsory again. Notwithstanding the lack of enthusiasm on the part of parents, all MT supporters feel that the very existence of young people educated in Balochi and Brahvi will improve the future prospects of their languages, as these people will have access to literature written in these languages. Above all, future generations may then eventually form a pressure group, which could increase the use of the mother tongues in other domains. This is at present probably the most compelling argument in favour of MT education.

**Balochi Movement in Iran**

In Iran, the most obvious identity-marker of the Baloch, the Balochi language, is emphasized more strongly than in Pakistan. The Iranian ruling elite has generally suppressed it openly and ruthlessly. Reza Shah's government not only banned the use of Balochi in schools, but even made it a crime to 'publish, distribute and possess Baluchi books, magazines, newspapers etc.' (Harrison 1981: 95). Later, the policy of conciliating the moderate Baloch was adopted and Radio Zahedan increased its broadcasts in Balochi. This was necessitated by the fact that the Iranian Baloch could listen to such broadcasts from Pakistan, Afghanistan, and India (Harrison 1981: 101-3). The Islamic revolution was initially tolerant of Balochi newspapers and magazines, but the language is still not used in schools. Nationalist organizations try to increase the use of Balochi because it is an identity symbol. However, they have met with much more resistance than there has been in Pakistan, even for language planning activities.

**Achievements of the Balochi-Brahvi Movement**

In Pakistan, although the ruling elite has used the coercive power of the state to suppress Baloch nationalism, the language movements have been marginalized and ignored rather than suppressed. This is a major grievance of the Baloch intelligentsia who point out that adequate time is not given on radio and television (Shad 1991: 9-13); that Balochi publications are not given official patronage, so their number is meagre (see Appendix A); and that Urdu, as well as the alien culture of Urdu-speakers, has been imposed upon them (Hasanabadi 1991). They are aware that Balochi and Brahvi will remain ghettoizing languages until such time that they are used in the domains of power, and jobs are given through them (Hasanabadi 21; Dashtiari 1993 a: 9). Above all, they are aware that their languages are part of their identity and language planning, especially standardization and modernization of the vocabulary, is required in them (Jahani 1989; Hashmi 1962; Dashtiari 1993 a: 9-10; Badal 1990).

Standardization of the script is in progress, as we have noted earlier. Modernization of the vocabulary, which has been going on since the sixties, is still impeded by ideological differences. The religious school of Maulvi Khair Muhammad Nadwi and Abdul Rahman Sabir, editors of *Saughat* and *Sada-e-Baloch*, want to retain the Arabic spellings of words as well as words of Arabic origin (Jahani 1989: 138-9), while Sayyid Hashmi wants to purge the language of them, creating new words from Balochi roots. Among the neologisms of Sayyid Hashmi are:

| Neologism | English | Word commonly used |
|---|---|---|
| *bungapp* | subject | *mauzu* |
| *dastunk* | a poetic form | *ghazal* |
| *gal* | word | *lavz, labz* |
| *galwar* | dialect | *lahja, boli* |
| *gidgush* | television | television |
| *wanagi* | book | *kitab* |
| *tamur* | film | *film* |
| *nimdi* | letter | *khat, kagad* |
| *laccha* | poetry | *sher, nazm* |

(See Hashmi 1962: 140-143; Jahani 1989: 233)

Most of the commonly used words are from Urdu and English which makes the nationalists aware that, without stimulus, their language will die out (Hamdam 1992). As the words of Balochi origin emphasize Balochi identity, they insist on using them even in place of familiar words from other languages (Shad 1991: 19; Badal 1990). Some of the words of the purists, especially those relating to the world of letters, which is dominated by identity-conscious intellectuals, are commonly used nowadays. Among them are: *labzank* (literature), *azmanak* (drama), *kasmanag* (short story), *dastunk* (hemistich), and *nimdi* (letter) (Badal 1990: 12). Other words, such as the ones for television and radio, are not used. It seems that habit and convenience, and even mere pragmatism, are stronger for ordinary people than they are for the intelligentsia, the mainstay of the Balochi-Brahvi language movements.

Apart from creating new words and publishing a number of books and journals, the activists of the language movements have at least once introduced the languages in schools. Even at present, Balochi and Brahvi are used for the religious diplomas of *Adeeb Alim* and *Adeeb Fazil*. They are optional subjects in the provincial and central civil services examinations and can be taken as a subject of examination in matriculation though they are not taught in schools. They have, however, been taught at the MA level in the University of Balochistan since 1987.

Above all, perhaps, the activists of the language movements have succeeded in removing the cultural shame that was felt about using Balochi and Brahvi, which existed before the movement started. This cultural shame is attested to through many sources. In the case of Brahvi, Bray writes:

> There is a very general feeling among his [the ordinary Brahvi's] neighbours that Brahvi is a strange language, a jargon too uncouth for 'gentility', and the feeling is shared in some measure by the Brahvis themselves, who do not hesitate to employ Baluchi or Pashto on the slightest excuse (Bray 1913: 176).

Of Balochi, Nimatullah Gichki told Carina Jahani that 'he and his Baloch fellow students were even ashamed of speaking Balochi to each other', let alone using it in writing, and that it is only in the past twenty to twenty-five years that this negative attitude towards Balochi has changed (Jahani 1989: 97).

Whatever the veracity of these and other such statements, it is obvious that now the Baloch are no longer ashamed of their language. However, because they are educated in Urdu, the language used in the cities, they are prone to expressing themselves more often in Urdu than in Balochi and Brahvi. This is something which increased use of these languages can change. The significant achievement of the language movements in Balochistan is that they have made people conscious of their identity.

# 10

# The Siraiki Movement

Southern Punjab is known as the Siraiki area. The area is, on the whole, underdeveloped and the Siraiki language movement started in earnest only in the 1960s. The language of Multan, Muzaffargarh, Bahawalpur, Leiah, etc. has not always been called Siraiki. The names Multani, Muzaffargarhi, Uchi, Riasati, Derewali, Hindko, Thalchari, Lahnda, Jaghdali, Jatki, and Belochki have been used by local people for the language which is now called Siraiki (Wagha 1990: 5-7).

Some scholars, such as Abul Fazal, the courtier of the Mughal emperor Akbar (1554-1605), neither used the all-inclusive name of Hindi for the language of this area, nor distinguished between the various dialects in the manner of the locals. In his *Ain-e-Akbari* Abul Fazal mentions the language of Multan, Sindh, North Afghan (between Sindh, Kabul, and Qandahar), Balochistan, and Kashmir among a total of twelve languages (Fazal n.d.: 98). Hindi, however, remained the generic term for Indian languages, so that even in the nineteenth century Maulvi Khuda Baksh of Taunsa (D. G. Khan) termed his rhyming dictionary from Persian to Siraiki a 'Hindi' dictionary (Baksh 1960: 15).

The first Europeans to become interested in Siraiki were missionaries. William Carey (1761-1834), working at Serampore, got a respondent from the Siraiki area, which he called Wuch, in 1813 (Fuller 1815: 31) and printed a grammar—perhaps the first (Shackle 1983: 5)—in the Kirakki script, though Muslim poets had been writing earlier in the Arabic and then the Persian script (Rasoolpuri 1976: 8).

Richard Burton also wrote a grammar of what he called 'Siraiki' (Burton 1849: 84-5). He thought it was a dialect of Punjabi, a view shared by most British officers who administered the Punjab. However, some of them did note that it was different from the Punjabi of Lahore (for their letters see Chaudhry 1977: 43, 57: and Steedman 1882: 58).

One such officer was Edward O'Brien, who emphasized that Multani was, indeed, different from Lahori (1882: 72). A missionary,

Andrew Jukes (1847-1931), agreeing with him, used the word 'Western Punjabi' for it (Shackle 1983: 22). This word was also used by Trevor Bomford, another missionary, and is important because it was used by George Grierson in his linguistic survey (Bomford 1895; Grierson: vol IV, 233-332). Grierson chose the word *Lahnda* (Western Punjabi) for this language, but his division of languages into circles, with Siraiki and Punjabi falling into different circles, is not satisfactory (Gankovsky 1964: 110).

**Creation of a Siraiki Identity**

The process of the creation of a Siraiki identity in south-western Punjab involved the deliberate choice of a language, called Siraiki, as a symbol of this identity. This involved the renunciation of both the local names of regional dialects (e.g. Multani or Riasati) as well as the all-inclusive label of Punjabi. The term 'Siraiki' probably came to be used for all dialects of the Siraiki-speaking areas through consensus amongst the Siraiki nationalists in 1960 (Rahman, U. Ltr: 6 February 1993). Accordingly, Mehr Abdul Haq, one of the early researchers on Siraiki, called his thesis on the Multani language in 1963 a study of Siraiki, because Multani was associated with a city, whereas Siraiki could appeal to all the ethno-nationalists of southern Punjab (Haq Int: 26 December 1992). He also claimed that Siraiki was the mother of Urdu (Haq 1967: 679-91). The term Siraiki had, of course, been used earlier but probably for a different language. Ayub Khuhro, for instance, used it to describe the language of northern Sindh, which is a dialect of Sindhi (Khuhro 1930: 206) and which Shackle calls Sindhi Siraiki (1976: 7) and Gankovsky merely a dialect of Sindhi (1964: 110).

There are claims that this was the language of the sun-worshipping Asury people who ruled Multan three thousand years ago; or that it was the language of the village Sarwa in Rahim Yar Khan district (Wagha 1990: 4). Another explanation is that it was the language of the Kalhoras, the rulers of Sindh, who came from Multan (Lambrick 1975: 213). But the most plausible explanation is that it is the language of northern Sindh (Shackle 1976: 2). *Siro* means head or the north in Sindhi and, since Multan was north of Sindh, this was the Sindhi term for the language of this area. The only difficulty is that *ji* not *ki* is the Sindhi post-position for *of* (language of the head or north should be *Siroji* and not *Siroki*) (Wagha 1990: 4). However, whatever the origin of the term, it was being used among activists of the Siraiki Movement by 1962.

LP activities in Siraiki were meant to promote Siraiki as a linguistic ethnic identity-marker. Hence, the major emphasis of the Siraiki language planners, who were private individuals, was on identity.

First, they termed Siraiki a language in its own right, and not a dialect of Punjabi. This was opposed by the Punjabis and a debate ensued which is still going on (for the Punjabi point of view, see Shahbaz, M. 1977; Khan, A. 1973: 32-40. For the Siraiki view, see Haq, M. 1967; Wagha 1990: 63-8 and 89-92. For the view that Punjabi is a dialect of Siraiki, see Kalanchvi 1974: 7-10). Shackle rightly suggested that 'even the terms in which the polemic is conducted between the two seem to display remarkable similarities' (1985: 322). This is inevitable because both Siraikis and Punjabis use the functional definition of language, according to which language is 'a superimposed norm' (Haugen 1972: 243) and all mutually intelligible varieties of it are deviations from it. If they were to use the 'structural' definition of Haugen (ibid. 242), a language would be the sum of all intelligible varieties of it, with the prestigious norm being a variety too. In that case, we could call both Siraiki and Punjabi (and Hindko etc.) varieties of what some sociolinguists call 'Greater Punjabi' (Rensch 1992b: 87). Alternatively, it could be called 'Greater Siraiki' or by some other name.

The linguistic fact seems to be that Siraiki and Punjabi are mutually intelligible. There are, to be sure, phonological, phonetic, and grammatical differences given by Shackle (1979: 153-4). Punjabi does not have the implosive consonants which Siraiki and Sindhi possess, and the pattern of rhythm and stress is different in ways which no linguist has studied. The politeness marker of Sindhi (*sain*) is used with a slightly different pronunciation in Siraiki. Despite these facts, Shackle is right that 'many shared morphological details, as well as overall agreement in much of the vocabulary and syntax, link it quite closely to Panjabi, with which it has a higher degree of mutual intelligibility' (1979: 154).

However, because of the lack of prestige of the term 'dialect' and the absence of the 'structural' definition of it, Siraiki speakers stress the antiquity of their language and the presence of written literature in it. The label of 'dialect' is seen as stigmatizing by Siraikis. Moreover, the Siraikis emphasize their differences from Punjabis, in order to stress their specific cultural and ethnic identity. Thus, for them to accept their language as a dialect of Punjabi, even on a structural definition, would be counterproductive. Such cases of political definitions of language are to be found elsewhere in the world too. The case of Hindi and Urdu being called different languages, despite mutual intelligibility, is one. Another example is that of the mutually intelligible dialects of the Scandinavian countries being called languages for nationalistic reasons (Hudson 1980: 35).

As a consequence of having decided to create a standard language, by accepting a dialect of south-western Punjab as the standard, the next task was to establish its script and orthographic norms. These norms, too, were dictated by the desire to differentiate the script from that of Punjabi, to emphasize a distinct identity.

Siraiki was probably written in variants of the Brahmi script before the Muslim conquest of Multan in the eighth century (Rasoolpuri 1976: 7-8; Shackle 1983: 5, 55). The Arabic *naskh*, which came to be used at that time, was replaced by the Persian *nastaleeq* after the eighteenth century. The first known attempt at creating new orthographic symbols to express the distinct sounds of the language, that is, the implosives it shares with Sindhi, was that of Qazi Fakhruddin Razi in 1893 (Rasoolpuri 9). Following that, a number of people—Azizur Rahman (Rahman, A. 1944: 5), Khurram Bahawalpuri, Zami Bahawalpuri, Dilshad Kalanchvi, Nazeer Ali Shah, Mehr Abdul Haq, and Aslam Rasoolpuri—proposed systems of modifying the letters of the alphabet by adding diacritical marks (Rasoolpuri 10-3).

Two LP committees, one established by the Siraiki Sangat of Karachi and the other by the Siraiki Conference held at Multan in March 1975, also proposed some changes. The Multan Committee proposed the use of circles under or over certain letters (Kamal 1975: 12), while the Karachi Committee suggested dots instead of circles. Both did, however, agree on using the *naskh* (Rasoolpuri 23). Nowadays, most Siraiki publications employ dots for the implosives and other distinctively Siraiki sounds.

The other area of identity-conscious LP was the invention of new technical terms. Such terms are presently being coined by private language planners, but there is no agreement on their use, nor even a standard glossary of them. The overriding imperative for the Siraiki intellectuals has been identity formation (Kamal 1975: 19-21). Thus, when they use words for literary or learned writing, they fall back upon that indigenous word stock, which is only partly shared with Punjabi. (Some examples are given below:)

All of these newly-coined words use indigenous, mostly Sanskritic, morphemes. They have not only not been accepted by the public in general, but many Siraiki literary figures do not even use most of them in their writings.

| Word commonly used | Siraiki coinage | English |
|---|---|---|
| *ilm* | *bhum* | knowledge |
| *alim* | *bhum val* | intellectual, erudite person |
| *lisaniyat* | *boli bhum* | linguistics |
| *intikhab* | *chunar* | election |
| *qutub shimali* | *ubheejar dharti dhur* | North Pole |
| *qutub janubi* | *lamuchar dharti dhur* | South Pole |
| *rasmul khat* | *likkhat reet* | script |
| TV | *moorat vaja* | television |
| radio | *sur vaja* | radio |
| atom bomb | *suth gola* | nuclear bomb |
| grammar | *akhhar mool* | grammar |
| *dast khat* | *akhhar huth* | signature |

(Faridi n.d.)

## The Siraiki Area

With the claim of Siraiki being a different language from Punjabi came similar claims about the distinctness of the Siraiki area from that of the Punjab. For instance, in the *Ain-e-Akbari* of the Mughal administrator Abul Fazal, fifteen provinces are mentioned, and the province of Multan, which is distinct from that of Lahore, is described as follows:

> This province is included in the first, second, and third *aqleem* [a division of land]. It stretches from Ferozpur to Sevistan which is 408 *kos* [unit of distance] and from Khanpur to Jaisalmer which is 408 *kos*. Now that Thatta has also been included in it, it stretches from Ferozpur to Kej Makran almost 606 *kos*. Towards the east it meets Sirhind; on the north with Shor; on the south with Ajmer and on the west with Kech and Makran (Fazal n.d: vol 1: 1036-7).

Abul Fazal's description is cited by Azizuddin Ahmed among others (Ahmed, A. 1988: 142), while other researchers point to even earlier sources suggesting that it was not considered a part of the Punjab till the Sikh conquest in 1818 (Ganadiah 1984: 7). In fact, the history of Multan suggests that what was called Sindh in prehistoric times and even up to the seventh century had an area extending from Kashmir to the Arabian sea, i.e., almost that of present-day Pakistan (Kalichbeg 1900: 11). Later, for most of known history, Multan remained an independent centre of power (Khan, N. 1983). Even after the British annexation of the Punjab, when Multan and its surrounding areas were included in this province, Bahawalpur remained a quasi-independent princely state. It was only in 1971 that it was included in the Punjab. These factors provide Siraiki intellectuals with arguments for separating the Siraiki areas from the Punjab.

Nowadays, the Siraiki area is defined roughly as the area where this language is spoken. But this is a very vague definition because common people still give either local names for their language or use all-inclusive names such as Punjabi or Hindko. Hence, the figures given by the census are not accepted by the Siraiki activists. The British, too, had put what is now called Hindko under Western Punjabi, i.e., Siraiki. Andrew Jukes sent a letter to the Church Missionary Society claiming that Western Punjabi was spoken in the districts of south-western Punjab, Shahpur, Jhelum, and Montgomery. It was even spoken in the cities of the North West Frontier Province such as Peshawar, Kohat, and Bannu, i.e., 'over 60,000 square miles' (CMS 1895). Grierson called it the language of the western Punjab and gives its area in such a way that Hindko speaking areas are included in it (vol IV: 233). Nowadays, this area is disputable. The first printed map of the Siraiki *suba* (province), Siraiki *waseb* (homeland), or Siraikistan was given on the front page of a book by Riaz Hashmi arguing the case of the ex-state of Bahawalpur as a province. Hashmi wrote:

> The time is now set that a province known as SARAIKISTAN be established forthwith by adding the districts of Multan, Muzaffargarh and Dera Ghazi Khan in the former state of Bahawalpur (1972: 22).

The present heads of the Pakistan Siraiki Party (PSP), Taj Muhammad Langah, and the Siraiki National Party (SNP), Abdul Majeed Kanju, agree with this, though with minor modifications. Langah believes the province should include: 'Multan division, Bahawalpur division, Dera Ghazi Khan division (DGK), Sargodha division, district Jhang and district Dera Ismail Khan (DIK)' (Langah 1990: 21). Kanju too agreed with this area in an interview with the author (Kanju Int: 6 February 1993). DIK is in the NWFP, but these leaders do not claim areas of Sindh and Balochistan, even though some activists claim that they are Siraiki-speaking (Wagha 1990: 24; Zami 1970: 21-2). Map 1 shows the area of the Punjab while Map 2 shows the proposed area of the Siraiki province; Map 4 gives the districts in which the majority of speakers are Siraiki-speaking according to the census of 1981 (see Appendix F).

# MAP 1
## PAKISTAN

THE SHADED AREA BELOW IS THE
PROPOSED SIRAIKI PROVINCE (SEE MAP 2)

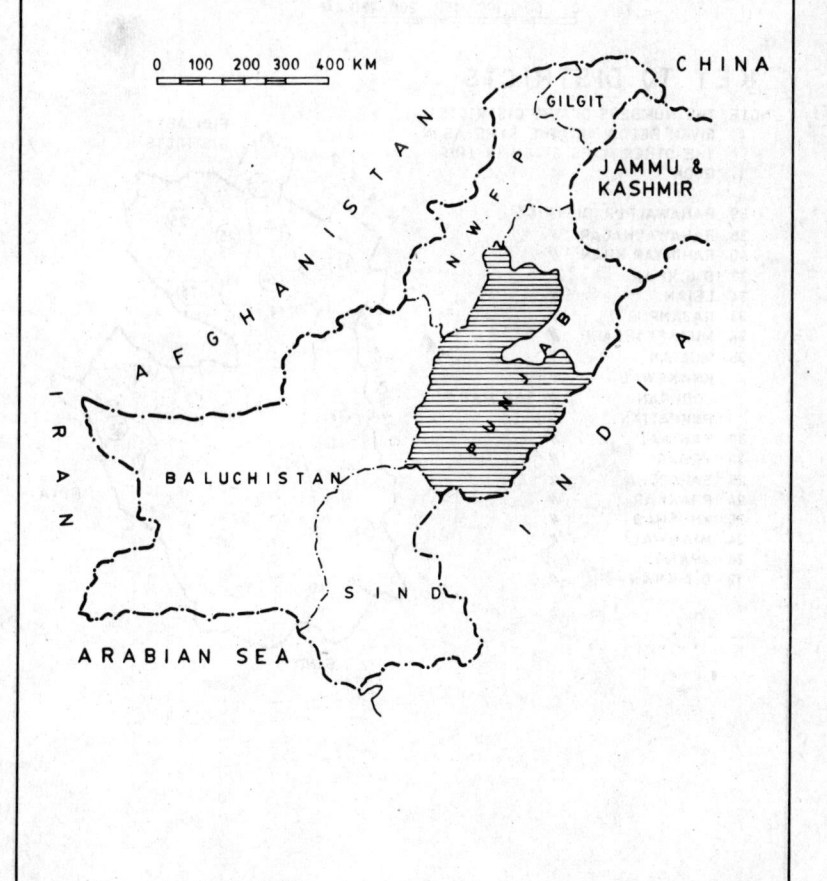

# MAP 2

## THE PROPOSED SIRAIKI PROVINCE

0  50  100  150  200  250 KM

### KEY TO DISTRICTS

NOTE: THE NUMBERS OF THE DISTRICTS GIVEN BELOW ARE THE SAME AS IN THE OTHER MAPS GIVEN IN THIS BOOK

- 39. BAHAWALPUR DISTRICT
- 38. BAHAWALNAGAR  ⁄⁄
- 40. RAHIMYAR KHAN  ⁄⁄
- 33. D.G. KHAN  ⁄⁄
- 34. LEIAH  ⁄⁄
- 33. RAJANPUR  ⁄⁄
- 34. MUZAFFARGARH  ⁄⁄
- 35. MULTAN  ⁄⁄
-     KHANEWAL  ⁄⁄
-     LODHRAN  ⁄⁄     } SEE MAP 4
-     PAKPATTAN  ⁄⁄
- 37. SAHIWAL  ⁄⁄
- 36. VEHARI  ⁄⁄
- 25. SARGODHA  ⁄⁄
- 24. BHAKKAR  ⁄⁄
- 25. KHUSHAB  ⁄⁄
- 24. MIANWALI  ⁄⁄
- 26. JHANG
- 12. D.I. KHAN  ⁄⁄

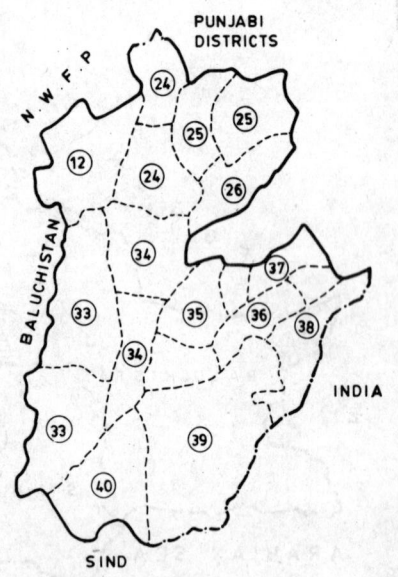

Siraikis, however, claim that the bureaucracy has conspired to decrease their number (Ahmed, A. 1988: 170). The Punjabis, on the other hand, claim that these figures have been exaggerated (Kahut 1992: 188-90).

**Cultural Distinction**

The Siraiki area has always had, geographically, culturally, economically, and even racially, more in common with Sindh than with the Punjab (Gankovsky 1964: 107). Population was sparse and the river Sindh provided fish and agricultural goods. Farming required the presence of all the available males as did the semi-nomadic way of life in the desert regions. Thus, Siraiki culture, like the Sindhi one, discouraged travelling for employment. The Siraikis were far more homebound than the Punjabis (Ahmed, A. 1988: 145; Ganadiah. 1984: 8). The British created great feudal lords in this area so that the common people were probably more oppressed here than in the Punjab. Perhaps this was another reason why they were less enterprising than their Punjabi counterparts (Ahmed, A. 149). Thus, when canals were dug in the Punjab in 1886-88, the British brought settlers from other areas of the province to the Siraiki areas in the new canal colonies (Marani 1991: 31-3). The Sutlej Valley Project brought canals into Bahawalpur too in 1925 and, as usual, settlers from outside were brought in to cultivate the new area (Ahmed, A. 149; *Kanayat* 1972: 48). This practice continues and is one of the major grievances of the Siraikis even now.

The differences mentioned so far do not necessarily lead to assertions of separate identity as they did in this area after the 1960s. The main reason why they were emphasized was the lack of development here. According to comparative studies of the development of districts by independent economists—Helbock and Naqvi (1976); Pasha and Hasan (1982): and Khan and Iqbal (1982)—most of the districts of the Siraiki-speaking areas are placed lower on the basis of development indicators than those of the Punjabi-speaking areas. Despite problems of interpretation and discrepant criteria, these studies do indicate that the Siraiki districts are less developed than the Punjabi ones.

**Cultural Renaissance in the Siraiki Area**

As we have seen, ethno-nationalism is generally a response to perceived injustice. Lack of development, providing less access to power, goods, and services is seen as injustice. Thus, the conditions in south Punjab were ripe for the development of such an ethno-nationalist movement. Like many other such movements—such as the 'celtic revival' in Ireland (Davies 1845: 73; Beckett 1966: 417)—the political assertion of ethnicity came later. What came first was a cultural, linguistic, and literary assertion, the creation of a unique tradition. Siraiki literature, which was mostly in verse, was mystic and religious, rather than secular and political till the present century (for detailed histories see Jampuri 1969; Haideri 1971; and for a brief English introduction, see Wagha 1990; and Shackle 1976: 8-9). In the princely state of Bahawalpur, Azizur Rahman published the *Diwan-e-Farid*, the mystical poetry of the saint Ghulam Farid, in Siraiki. As the language of the state was Urdu, the translation and the commentary were in that language. Azizur Rahman also wrote books on the family of the ruler, Nawab Sadiq Ali Abbasi. Later, his son, Hafizur Rahman translated the Quran into Siraiki. In 1950, a Siraiki magazine called *Panjnad* began publication from Karachi and, in 1953, a grammar of the language was published in Multan. At that time, there was nothing like a clearly politicized or even a consciously motivated Siraiki movement, but writing in Siraiki was beginning to emerge and, along with it, an incipient consciousness of a distinct identity was also in evidence.

Cultural activities began in earnest in 1960 when Riaz Anwar, a lawyer from Muzaffargarh, celebrated the Jashn-e-Farid (a fair in the honour of Ghulam Farid) at Muzaffargarh. As the saint was becoming a symbol of the distinctive cultural identity of the Siraiki people, this celebration helped to create a sense of identity. The anniversary was celebrated every two years and contributed to the movement. In 1961, Riaz Anwar formed his *Bazm-e-Saqafat* (cultural organization) which arranged conferences such as the Khwaja Farid Conference in Multan. According to the antagonists of Siraiki, a powerful bureaucrat in General Ayub's government, Qudratullah Shahab, patronized the writers of Siraiki, asking twenty of them to claim that their language was different from Punjabi (Aslam 1987: 91). There was also a Siraiki Conference in Hyderabad Sindh in 1963, according to Langah (Int: 27 December 1992). This connection with the highly mobilized Sindhi ethno-nationalism is documented in a later publication about Sindhi-Siraiki friendship, *Sindhi-Siraiki Dosti* (n.d.). However, at the time, this conference did not succeed in mobilizing Siraiki nationalism.

A number of literary and cultural forums began functioning in Multan and Bahawalpur in the sixties. The Siraiki Academy of Multan began publishing a newsletter which came to be called the weekly

*Akhtar* and which continued publication till 1971. The monthly *Siraiki Adab* was published from Multan and the quarterly *Siraiki* from Bahawalpur (Barelvi 1987: 240-1). Siraiki was also distinguished from Punjabi and this consciousness led to the formation of a separate Siraiki identity (for details of cultural activities and the people involved in them, see Ganadiah 1984: 18).

The rights of the north-western Punjab were asserted in many forums, whether at the behest of the Siraiki activists or otherwise. Muhammad Sajjad Makhdum, a member of parliament, said in the National Assembly on 19 June 1963:

> Multani is spoken in 10 districts of West Pakistan and so far there is no provision for a radio station at Multan. There is no road link between Karachi and Multan and Lahore. This strip of 800 miles [is] lying as it is, without any modern means of communication (LAD-P 19 June 1963: 767).

This radio station was established in 1970 but the Siraiki activists have not ceased complaining that programmes in their language are not being given enough time (Kanju Int: 6 February 1993; Javed 1992).

**The Bahawalpur Province Movement**

The politicization of the Siraiki Movement began with what is called the Bahawalpur Province Movement. This was a movement for the creation of a separate province in the former princely state of Bahawalpur. The state had an area of 17,508 square miles and a population of 2,574,066 (Census 1961: II-66). It had been ruled by the Abbasi nawabs since 1749. The state acceded to Pakistan in 1947. In 1954, Nawab Sadiq Ali Khan, the ruler of Bahawalpur, agreed to merge the state with the newly created province of West Pakistan. (For the original treaties of 1947, 1948, 1949, 1951, 1952, and the 'Merger Agreement', see Hashmi 1972: 183-235).

Punjab, being the largest province, was perceived by the nationalists from the other provinces of West Pakistan as the dominating province in One Unit. Riaz Hashmi from Bahawalpur also joined the anti-One Unit Front. He insisted that the province of Bahawalpur should be created when West Pakistan was broken into separate provinces (Hashmi 1972: 126). The Front was in favour of dividing Pakistan into linguistic provinces (Hashmi 1972: 126) and the present leaders of the Siraiki movement see this as the first entry of Siraikis into politics, as well as the first demand for a Siraiki area

(Kanju Int: 6 February 1993). In 1957, when West Pakistan was supposed to be broken up into its constituent units, the twelve members from Bahawalpur in the National Assembly declared that their area would become a separate administrative unit (Shahbaz 1972: 21). However, before this could be done, Ayub Khan imposed martial law and West Pakistan remained as it was until the new military ruler, Yahya Khan, decided to restore the provinces in November 1969.

The government now decided to amalgamate Bahawalpur with the Punjab, a decision which the leaders of the former state did not accept. Several groups for the defence of the rights of Bahawalpur were formed, among them being the Bahawalpur Mutahadda Mahaz (the Bahawalpur United Front, abbreviated as Mahaz). In February 1990, the Mahaz started bringing out processions protesting against the government's decision. By the end of March, the activists of this group started courting arrest and, on 30 March 1970, the important leaders, among them Chaudhry Farzand Ali, Mian Nizamuddin Haider, Sardar Mahmud Khan, and Seth Ubaidur Rahman were arrested. The women were led by Tahira Masood, daughter of Nizamddin Haider, who was nicknamed 'Joan of Arc'. The Urdu-speaking Mohajirs who had settled in Bahawalpur, led by Tabish Alwari, also supported the movement.

On 24 April 1970, the police opened fire on a procession, killing two persons and wounding many. The leaders were arrested and the inquiry conducted by the government was not accepted by the Mahaz (Sajid 1972: 51-2).

All this suppressed emotion was expressed in the elections of December 1970. The PPP, being left-wing and populist (Afzal 1987: 115-9), won 81 seats out of 138 in the National Assembly and 113 out of 181 in the provincial one. In Bahawalpur, however, it did not win many seats (Ahmad, I. 1976: 90). Most seats went to the sympathizers of the Mahaz, whether they stood as independents or as candidates of a political party (for details of elections, see *Kanayat* 1972; and *D* 8 December 1970).

Once elected, the leaders of the Mahaz did not pursue the case of Bahawalpur forcefully. They did issue declarations in support of a separate province (*Sun* 10 April 1973), and Chaudhry Farzand Ali, the Convener of the Mahaz, wrote letters to Yahya Khan and Z. A. Bhutto (23 February 1972), but to no avail. In fact the Mahaz split into factions (*Musawat* 14 April 1972), and Prince Saeedul Rashid Abbasi declared that the demand for a new province was no longer a priority issue, as Pakistan had lost East Bengal in the 1971 war (*M* 17 April 1972; J 6 and H 10 June 1972). Later, Ghulam Mustafa Khar, the PPP Governor of the Punjab, claimed that the Mahaz leaders had compromised with his party and they did not press their demands (Malik, M. 1975: 15).

The Bahawalpur Province Movement had fizzled out by 1972 and the Siraiki Movement started. Riaz Hashmi and Seth Ubaidur Rahman now started working for the Siraiki province. However, some people in Bahawalpur were 'suspicious of such an arrangement because it will place them in a subservient position relative to Multan' (Nadira 1989). That is why an organization calling itself the Bahawalpur Suba Mahaz kept operating in Bahawalpur and, as late as 1988, declared itself opposed to the Siraiki province ('Roohi Rang' in M 18 February 1988). However, Seth Ubaid and Majeed Kanju are of the opinion that most of the political activists in Bahawalpur now support the formation of the Siraiki province, leaving questions of power sharing between Multan and Bahawalpur for the future (Rahman, U. PC; and Kanju.Int: 6 February 1993).

**Politicization of the Siraiki Movement**

The Bahawalpur Movement did not mention Siraiki except as a local language (*Kanayat*: 37). Its affairs were conducted in Urdu. It was, however, supported by Siraiki nationalists in general and such organizations as the Siraiki Adabi Majlis (Siraiki literary society). However, it was the first significant attempt at politicizing the issue of economic and cultural underdevelopment in the Siraiki area, and Riaz Hashmi made it quite clear that this demand was connected with that of creating provinces on linguistic lines, and that it 'seeks to secure for different linguistic groups political and economic justice' (1972: 25). The figures for economic and other realities presented by Hashmi (1972: 101) and other supporters of this movement later provided the rationale for the Siraiki Movement as a whole.

The watershed in the Movement was the Siraiki Literary Conference held at Multan between 14 and 16 March 1975. This was supported by twenty-three Siraiki literary and cultural organizations (for names, see Kamal 1975: 1). The conference was, however, not just literary or linguistic. These aspects of it were subordinated to its political ends, which were ethno-nationalistic. It was for this reason that the ruling PPP government discouraged it and, according to Taj Muhammad Langah, even forbade Ghulam Mustafa Jatoi, the PPP Chief Minister of Sindh, from participating in it (Langah Int: 27 December 1993). However, Sindhi nationalists like Rasul Baksh

Paleejo participated, giving the conference a distinct political tone (Kamal 1975: 13-4). Seth Ubaid connected the conference with the demand for a separate Bahawalpur province. He argued that the Siraiki movement had started because of the Bahawalpur movement which had wanted to create a Siraiki province (Kamal 1975: 15). The conference also brought together literary and cultural activists, because of which Shackle calls it a very significant development in consciousness-raising of the Siraiki identity (Shackle 1977).

## Cultural Organizations

Except in Bahawalpur, the Siraiki movement has been cultural in its major manifestations as we have seen. This did not change even after the Multan conference of 1975. Political aims continued to be expressed directly and through literary works. Thus, a number of publications notably *Sanhiya, Sanjh, Sochan, Siraiki Sangat, Parchol, Siraiki Majlis*, etc., were launched. A number of writers are contributing to Siraiki culture and literature. Their most important contribution, identity-conscious language planning, has been mentioned in detail earlier. Here, only the role of cultural organizations will be taken up.

The most active cultural organization of the Siraiki movement is probably the Siraiki Lok Sanjh (Siraiki People's Co-operative Society). The Sanjh was created on 7 November 1985 in Rajanpur at Bangla Korai. The resolution passed there stated the aims of the Sanjh as follows:

a. To promote the cause of the Siraiki language and culture.

b. To create consciousness of rights and promote social education among the Siraiki people.
c. To make the Siraiki area a powerful unit of the federation of Pakistan (Charter-S 1989: 6-7).

The Sanjh established its units in town and cities of the Siraiki area including D. I. Khan. Among the major cities outside this area, it chose to establish its offices in Lahore and Islamabad. The Sanjh tries to make people aware of their Siraiki identity and other problems through fairs (Charter-S 8). According to Mazhar Arif, the founding General Secretary of the Sanjh, 'our strategy was to go to the fairs and sing and dance. The people would respond enthusiastically' (Arif Int: 19 January 1993).

The Sanjh is anti-feudal and left-leaning, because of which it is accused of being the front organization of a socialist party. Like Paleejo's Awami Tehrik (the People's Initiative) in Sindh, it is highly critical of the present feudal leadership and feels that a separate Siraiki province would be dominated by similar people (Aslam 1989: 89). In this context, Mazhar Arif in an interview told the present writer:

> We want to end exploitation but are not the front organization of any political party. We do have contacts with the PNP and the ANP as they accept ethno-nationalism. There was a meeting with the PNP in 1986 with Ghaus Bakhsh Bizenjo and our own President Fida Husain Gadi. The PNP agreed with our stand that Siraikis formed a separate nationality. They made a unit called PNP Siraiki for southern Punjab. The ANP also made their Siraiki Unit in 1987 and Paleejo was part of it. All this made us appear close to these two left-leaning parties but we were in no sense their front organization (Int: 19 January 1993).

The Lok Sanjh does, however, hold leftist views and has a number of middle and lower middle class intellectuals in it. Fida Husain Gadi, a retired schoolmaster, remained its head till 1988; he died in January 1993. The Sanjh has also been associated with other leftist organizations and participated in the Progressive (i.e., left-leaning) Writers' Conference of 1986. In this, Siraiki, was acknowledged as one of the ethnic languages of Pakistan (Arif Int.).

The demands of the Sanjh are similar to those of other Siraiki parties. The principal demands are that Siraikis should be acknowledged as a nationality, official documents should be written in Siraiki, and Siraiki areas should vote on the basis of ethnicity (Charter-S 1989: 34). The Sanjh leaders' awareness of under-development and cultural deprivation, the demands for using Siraiki as the medium of instruction at the primary level and improving educational facilities and job opportunities, are no different from other Siraiki intellectuals, as Mazhar Arif's speech at the seminar on Southern Punjab held in Multan on 24 June 1992 clearly shows (1992; also see Charter-S 1990: 38-42).

The supporting organizations of the Sanjh are the Shagird Sanjh (Students Association) established in 1986; Siraiki Lok Tamasha (Siraiki People's Theatre) which staged its first play in Multan in 1987 and has branches in D. G. Khan and Kot Addu, etc.; and the Siraiki Trimit Sanjh (Siraiki Women's Association) which was formed in

1989. All of them work towards making people conscious of their Siraiki identity and the problems of the area (Arif Int.). The Sanjh may not call itself a political party, but it does have a political ideology and its supporters—such as the Shagird groups contesting elections in university students unions against right-wing Islamic student parties—have to take sides on all issues.

**Political Aspect of the Movement**

Siraiki political organizations have generally been divided, short-lived, and less popular than national political parties even in their own areas. The first such organization was Riaz Hashmi's Siraiki Suba Mahaz (Front for Creating a Siraiki Province). This was probably formed in 1973 in Bahawalpur after the failure of the Bahawalpur Province Movement. Omar Ali, a Siraiki activist, told the author that he was a member of the Siraiki Students Federation which was also inspired by Riaz Hashmi. In 1973, he was part of a group of ten activists who 'made the map of Saraikistan on the walls of Bahawalpur at night' (Ali Int: 18 January 1993).

Like all rulers at the centre, Ziaul Haq was in favour of a strong centre. Being a military ruler, he could afford to be much less sensitive to ethno-nationalistic demands than ruling elites which claim to be democratic. Thus, Siraiki politics was a matter of covert nocturnal scrawling of slogans, and mild public meetings during the Zia period. Muhammad Hayat Bhutta's Siraiki Qaumi Mahaz indulged in this kind of political activity in 1977 and later. In 1979, however, Mian Sajid Pervez formed the Siraiki Conference but it fizzled out after Mian Sajid himself joined the Movement for the Restoration of Democracy (MRD), the only significant political opposition to General Zia, which provided 'the major impetus for Siraiki nationalism' (Aslam 1987: 90). The MRD, however, was crushed in Sindh and fizzled out elsewhere and, along with it, this political party also died.

It was only in 1986 and 1987, when General Zia had decided to withdraw martial law and to appoint Muhammad Khan Junejo as a civilian prime minister, that the ethno-nationalist movements became overtly expressive. The PNP and the ANP, as has been already indicated, formed Siraiki units. The PNP Siraiki unit was headed by Wilayet Gardezi and the Siraiki Qaumi Wahdat Committee of the ANP was headed by Abdul Majeed Kanju (Kanju Int: 6 February 1993). The major Siraiki political party, however, was the Siraiki Suba Mahaz which had tenuous links with the earlier political organization of that name in Bahawalpur. According to Taj Muhammad Langah, Seth Ubaidur Rahman of Bahawalpur was asked to lead it but he declined. Thereupon, a new Siraiki Suba Mahaz was created on 5 March 1984 under the leadership of Qari Nurul Haq, while Riaz Hashmi had his own party of that name in Karachi (Langah Int: 27 December 1992). In 1987, Taj Langah himself became the president of the new Mahaz, which became the most powerful Siraiki political party.

Another party which emerged during this period was the Siraiki Qaumi Movement (SQM, not to be confused with the Siraiki Qaumi Mahaz of 1977 with the same initials). This was based on the successful model of the Mohajir Qaumi Movement (MQM) of Karachi. The SQM had three centres: Karachi, Khanpur Katora, and Ahmadpur Sharqia. It was led by several people, including Hameed Asghar Shaheen, Azam Saeedi, Shahid Karim, and Shahida Naz. It continues to survive, publishing pamphlets which list the grievances of Siraikis, and sometimes by supporting other parties for political reasons (Kanju Int: 6 February 1993 and relevant pamphlets).

## Siraiki Politics after Zia

The death of Ziaul Haq in 1988 brought elections in November of that year. In the same year, the socialist Saraikistan National Front of Comrade Manzur Ahmad Bohar was also formed. In general, Siraiki parties did not put up their candidates in the elections, though they did support Benazir Bhutto's PPP. According to Langah, this may have given the PPP about fifteen seats in the National Assembly (Langah Int: 27 December 1992). However, this claim is unsupported by proof and is refuted by other political parties.

The PPP, however, did not form a separate Siraiki province, for fear of alienating the sympathies of the Punjabi ruling elite and the army. On 2 March 1989, Langah dissociated his party from the PPP, and on 6 March he formed the PSP, Pakistan Siraiki Party, (*N* 8 April 1989). The PSP continued to criticize the PPP for not redressing the grievances of the Siraiki people (*N* 8 July and 3 October 1989). In the October 1990 elections, the Siraiki parties did not do well. One reason for this could be that the conflict of the PPP versus the IJI, occupied the electorate's attention, and other matters became peripheral. Moreover, the Siraiki parties did not present a united front. A party calling itself the Siraiki National Alliance (SNA) opposed the PSP. The SNA was supported by the SQM, Lok Sanjh, and other smaller Siraiki organizations. Thus, the Siraiki parties got very few votes, and it seems probable that the PPP never took them seriously.

On 29 January 1993, the Siraiki Suba Mahaz, which had lingered on in Bahawalpur under the leadership of Seth Ubaidur Rahman, changed its name to the Siraiki National Party (SNP). Abdul Majeed Kanju, who had joined the Mahaz in January 1992, became the President of the newly formed party while Seth Ubaid remained its Chief Organizer (Kanju Int: 6 February 1993). However, neither Nawaz Sharif's government (1990-93) nor the second government of Benazir Bhutto fulfilled the demands of the Siraikis, despite the fact that southern Punjab voted for the PPP in the 1993 elections (Waseem 1994: 164).

## Grievances of the Siraiki Activists

Pamphlets issued by the Siraiki organizations such as the SQM and the Sanjh (Charter-S 1989: 9-33); learned disquisitions (Ahmed, A. 1988; Marani 1991; Hashmi 1972); and political parties point out that the Siraiki areas are not treated fairly. The following points have been collected from different sources and are an indication of what the Siraiki proto-elite claims and what many ethnically-conscious members of the Siraiki intelligentsia believe.

> 1. Siraiki activists point out that their area is being economically exploited. The advocates of the separation of Bahawalpur from the Punjab point out that Bahawalpur produces much of Pakistan's cash crop of cotton (Salah-uddin 1972: 32-3); that its budget was in surplus when it was amalgamated in West Pakistan (Hashmi 1972: 101-2) and that it was not developed later (Rashdi 1970).

The same arguments were later used for the Siraiki area as a whole, which also produced cotton and, according to the Siraikis, generated more money than was spent on it (Ahmed, A. 1988: 141-72; Arif 1992). The Siraiki activists point out that the budget allocation for the Siraiki districts of the Punjab is less than that for the Punjabi-speaking part of the province (pamphlets and interviews). The figures quoted by the activists may not be reliable. However, the figures quoted by Azizuddin Ahmed, suggesting that the Siraiki areas are less developed, are more reliable (Ahmed 1988: 249-50). Independent studies of the development of districts, which have been mentioned earlier, also suggest that there is a lack of development in this area.

2.  Land from the Siraiki areas is given to non-Siraikis. The names of officials to whom land has been allotted are given by Azizuddin Ahmed among others (1988:251-6). Marani estimates that about 600,000 acres of it were given in the Thal Development scheme alone (1991: 62). The Siraiki Action Committee has produced its own figures, accusing ex-Prime Minister Nawaz Sharif, among others, of giving away Siraiki land to non-Siraikis (*N* 29 May 1991).

3.  Siraiki leaders oppose the settlement of Biharis (Urdu-speaking people from Bangladesh who opposed Bengali ethno-nationalism) in Siraiki areas anywhere in Pakistan. To oppose this move, an All-Parties Siraiki Alliance was formed on 6 May 1992 (Kanju Int: 6 February 1993). The move was also condemned by the PSP leadership (*J* 14 January 1993).

4.  Other demands, such as an increase in the time given to Siraiki language programmes on radio and television, increased quotas of employment, admission to educational institutions, and the formation of a Siraiki regiment in the army are made by political parties and others (Kanju Int: 6 February 1993; Arif 1992; Javed 1992).

**Reaction to Siraiki Demands**

As we have seen earlier, Pakistani nationalists have always suspected ethno-nationalist movements of being inspired by India. In the Siraiki case too, the Indian connection has been asserted. Kahut claims that the area is full of Indian female spies and that India is trying to break up Pakistan (1992: 202). The 22 May 1992 conference in India and the publication of the journal *Siraiki* by Jagdesh Chandar Batra from New Delhi in the same year might increase these suspicions. However, the Siraikis have never demanded an independent geographical unit nor have they ever been violent. They generally hold conferences—there was a conference in London in 1992 (*D* 20 Oct 1992) and another one in Multan on 4 December 1992—and demonstrate peacefully. Only rarely does one hear of violence: some SQM activists, for instance, criticized the President of the Khanpur Bar Association, a Punjabi, for being critical of the Siraiki movement. Another time, processionists tried to set fire to the house of a Punjabi member of the National Assembly from Rahim Yar Khan (*N* 11 October 1989). These are minor deviations from the peaceful course which the movement has followed so far.

The Siraiki language movement is a response to underdevelopment. The emerging Siraiki intelligentsia feels that it is dominated by the Punjabi ruling elite which does co-opt some Siraiki establishment figures, but does not distribute resources and power more widely among Siraikis. This sense of deprivation has led to the assertion of a separate identity of which language is the most powerful symbol. The symbol has not yet acquired much evocative power. Perhaps the reason for this is that many members of the Siraiki intelligentsia feel that they have good chances of acquiring power by retaining their Punjabi identity. However, the consciousness of there being a distinct Siraiki identity is more widespread now than it was before. The Siraiki language movement can be said to have been successful in creating that identity.

# 11

# The Punjabi Movement

The activists of the Punjabi movement want Punjabi to be used for educational, administrative, and judicial purposes in the province of the Punjab. As the Punjab is the most populous and prosperous province of the country, notorious for its dominance in the army and the bureaucracy, many people find this language movement incomprehensible. Indeed, most Punjabis of the upper and the middle classes do favour Urdu, and submerge their Punjabi identity in the Pakistani one. What is difficult to explain is why the activists of the Punjabi movement do not do so. Would the Punjabi activists gain power? Considering that most of them are generally competent in Urdu (and some even in English), they could choose the easier way of joining the Punjabi elite rather than opposing it. Moreover, some of them such as Hanif Ramay—who was the chief minister of the Punjab under Z. A. Bhutto's PPP rule in 1972-76 and is the Speaker of the Punjab Legislative Assembly at the time of this writing—possess political power; nor is it difficult for others to join mainstream politics and rise to eminence as Pakistanis (as Ramay asserts in his book: 1985: 29). Does the lure of the movement extend only to the less successful, as Christopher Shackle suggests?

> It is much easier to become an office bearer in a Punjabi organization than in a respectable Urdu one; in a society where men love to toll off their sonorous titles, this pull should not be underestimated (1970: 259).

This hypothesis may explain why some young men preferred to join Punjabi rather than Urdu literary organizations in the 1960s when Shackle was in Lahore, but it does not explain why obviously talented people like Asif Khan, Sharqat Tanwir Mirza, and Najm Hosain Syed—all men of letters in their own right—should join the movement. Moreover, a hypothesis based ultimately on snobbery does not explain why people should put their careers at stake or risk political persecution for a cause. Ramay, for example, says he was jailed and kept in the Lahore fort, which is notorious for torture, because of his espousal of the Punjabi cause (Ramay 1985: 149-50).

It appears then that this is a question that should be addressed in an account of the movement. Accounts of the activities of Punjabi organizations are available (Khan, A. 1994; Mirza 1994), but there is no scholarly account of the whole movement. Its historians have generally been activists who are polemical and resort to conspiracy-theory explanations, noting that Punjabi was never used by the British or the Pakistani governments in the domains of power, even in the Punjab itself.

**Punjabi in the British Era**

The British annexed the Punjab in 1849. The official language used by the Sikhs, whom they had defeated, was Persian, though religious schools did teach Punjabi in the Gurmukhi script (Adm Rep-P 1853: 98). The question of a language policy became evident as the vernacular terms used by the officers in correspondence were often unintelligible to their superiors (Letter of the Secretary, Board of Administration to Commissioners under the Board, 11 April 1849 in Chaudhry 1977: 1). The Board proposed that Urdu should be used as the official language of the Punjab, since it was already being used in Northern India where they were established (Chaudhry 1977: 3). The Deputy Commissioner of Dera Ghazi Khan said that, whereas the 'Moonshees, Moolahs, and other educated persons write Persian', not a man out of his 'sudder establishment understand[s] Oordoo' (Letter to the Commissioner of Leiah, 24 July 1849 in Chaudhry 17). The Assistant Commissioner of Muzaffargarh also argued that 'the native officers both Sudder and Mofussil, composed chiefly of Mooltanee are unable to write Oordoo while with Persian they are familiar' (Letter of 25 July 1849 to Commissioner of Leiah, ibid. 17). The Commissioner of Multan, therefore, recommended the use of Persian since 'in Mooltan none but the Hindoostanees who have lately been employed, are able to read the Oordoo without the greatest difficulty' (Letter to Secretary of the Board of Adm, Lahore, 27 July 1949, ibid. 19). The Commissioner of Leiah Division did, however, recommend the use of Urdu to the Board of Administration, despite the problem of the clerical staff, in his letter of 1 August 1849:

> Native Omla if they had a voice in the matter would give Persian the preference to Oordoo and it is known how unpopular among that class the order was which substituted the latter language for Persian in all the courts of our old Provinces (Chaudhry 1977: 21).

In his opinion, the staff could learn Urdu in a few months. The Board, however, recommended the use of Persian for Leiah as well as Multan, Peshawar, and Hazara. For the divisions of Lahore and Jhelum, however, Urdu was recommended (Orders are in the form of a letter in Chaudhry 26-7).

The question is then why did the British not recognize Punjabi as the vernacular of the Punjab? Why did they choose Urdu instead? Punjabi activists assert that this was done for political reasons or because of the influence of the lower staff who were mostly from northern India (Mirza 1989). The documents of that period, mostly letters of British officers, do not corroborate these assertions.

There were, of course, many Hindustanis in the *amlah* till 1857, at which time they were suspected of being sympathetic to the mutineers and were consequently dismissed (Adm Rep-P 1853:100). In 1854, Sikhs were not recruited to the army for political reasons and there were not many Punjabis in the other services either. However, there was no bias against Punjabis as such, as the *Report* says:

> There are sixteen [Hindustani] tehseeldars and fifty-three thanedars. We would gladly have filled these sixty-nine appointments with Punjabis exclusively, had fit men been procurable (Adm Rep-P 1953: 208).

But whether these Hindustanis actually influenced policy decisions is yet to be proved and is highly unlikely. It is, however, likely that the British officers, like their clerks, also knew Urdu and as Leitner, Principal of Government College, Lahore, reports (1882: ii), they found it more convenient to carry on administration with their existing skills. It is also possible that many among them shared the prejudices of Hindustanis. As Leitner, who was a supporter of Punjabi, wrote:

> The fact is that the direction of the Educational Department has long been in the hands of men, both European and Native, connected with Delhi (Leitner 1882: 47).

But even if this is true, it only confirms that both Englishmen and Indians were prejudiced against the Punjabi language. This prejudice is further confirmed by letters. Letter after letter reveals that most British officers assumed that Punjabi was a rural patois of which Urdu was the refined form (for this opinion see letters in Chaudhry 1977: 52, 55, 181, 183, 191, 208, 218, et passim. Also see Leitner 1882: ii and 29). There is no indication that Punjabi, written in the Persian script by Muslims, was considered politically dangerous.

The British officers were, however, against Gurmukhi because it was symbolic of the Sikh religious identity. In a letter of 16 June 1862, the Commissioner of Delhi wrote to the Punjab Government that, 'Any measure which would revive the Goormukhee which is the written Punjabee tongue, would be a political error' (Chaudhry 1977: 67). As Sikh children learned Gurmukhi in school (Leitner 1882: 33-7), it might have been considered politically expedient not to support it officially. There were, to be sure, popular folk songs against Mughal rule, which may be called anti-colonial (Saleem 1986: 16-23), but they were no longer a part of any active anti-British movement. Thus, there is no mention of this oral literature nor of any political apprehension from the Punjabi language or its literature, which was mostly mystical, in the official records of that period.

### Pro-Punjabi Movements in British Days

By 1854, the whole province of the Punjab (which included the present NWFP) used Urdu in the lower levels of administration, judiciary, and education. This position was challenged first by the British and later by the Hindus and Sikhs, while the Muslims continued to support Urdu.

In a letter of 2 June 1862, Robert Cust, a British officer in the Punjab, advocated the use of Punjabi written in the Gurmukhi script, on the grounds that it was the vernacular language which the British should support in principle (letter No. 318 in the Punjab Archives). This suggestion was repudiated by the other officers who felt that Punjabi was merely a dialect of Urdu. The Deputy Commissioner of Gujrat wrote to the Commissioner of Rawalpindi on 23 June 1862 that:

> Even a Punjabee villager will more readily understand simple Oordoo than indifferent Punjabee talked by us foreigners and by such of our Moonshees as may be Hindustanee (Chaudhry 1977: 52).

The Deputy Commissioner of Jhang also wrote to the Commissioner of Multan that the introduction of Punjabi would be confronted with the difficulty that, the 'Hindustanee Amlah understand the language imperfectly' while the Punjabis 'among them are well acquainted with it colloquially' but do not know it 'as a written tongue' (Letter of 24 June 1862 in Chaudhry 58). However, it was not the convenience of the staff which finally made the British officers dismiss the suggestion of Mr Cust. Their prejudiced views about Punjabi being an uncouth dialect, or patois as some of them called it, prevented them from taking the suggestion seriously.

By the 1880s, as we have seen, the Urdu-Hindi controversy had started agitating the minds of the Hindus and Muslims of the Punjab. Thus, when the Hunter Commission was formed to recommend educational changes in India, the question of the medium of instruction at the lower level had to be settled. The Sri Guru Singh Sabha (Sikh National Association) of Lahore petitioned Sir Charles Aitchison, the Governor of the Punjab, on 28 April 1882 to make Punjabi, in the Gurmukhi script, the medium of instruction at least for their community. The Governor, however, replied that such a step would harm the Sikhs. He said:

> To exclude the children of the Sikhs from instruction in Urdu would be to place them under very serious disadvantages. Without a knowledge of Urdu it would be impossible to advance beyond the most elementary education, and to continue their studies in the middle and high schools. They would be shut off from access to an excellent, large, and daily increasing literature, and they would be placed at a great disadvantage with their countrymen in the business of life (Edn Comm-P 1884: 106-7).

The Governor's point, that Punjabi would have a ghettoizing effect on its speakers, was valid on the assumption that positions of power and prestige would not be made available in that language. The Sikhs submitted memorials to the Commission in favour of Punjabi, while the Hindus submitted petitions in favour of Hindi (Memorials in Edn Comm-P 1884: 457-602). The Muslims, as individuals and in organizations, opposed Hindi and favoured Urdu (Memorial of the Anjuman Islamiaya [Amritsar], ibid. 147; Fateh Beg, ibid. 209-10).

In the Urdu-Hindi controversy, Urdu had become a symbol of Muslim identity while Hindi was the symbol of Hindu identity. Under these circumstances it was not surprising that Muslims chose to ignore their mother tongue(s). This attitude persisted till the creation of Pakistan and one finds many instances of Punjabi Muslims complaining in all forums, including the legislative assembly, that adequate arrangements did not exist for the teaching of Urdu to their children (for instance see LAD-Pun 5 and 22 March 1943: 31, 426). The main positions were clearly delineated along communal lines: Urdu for the Muslims; Hindi for the Hindus; and Punjabi for the Sikhs. Thus, when the British did allow the Local Bodies to establish Gurmukhi classes in the late 1890s, most of the students were Sikhs

(RPI-P 1897: 45). Yet, in fact, Punjabi was not popular even among the Sikhs, because it was 'not a bread-winning language' (RPI-P 1899: 42).

During the ongoing Urdu-Hindi controversy, the position of Urdu was challenged yet again. This time the challenger was not a Hindu or a Sikh but a British officer, J. Wilson, who was the Deputy Commissioner of Shahpur. He wrote a note in 1894 arguing that Punjabi was the vernacular of the people of the Punjab, so that one dialect of it should be standardized and used as the medium of instruction in primary schooling in the Punjab. He also argued that the Roman character, 'being a character developed by speakers of Aryan languages' is more suitable for Punjabi than the Arabic character, which is of Semitic origin (Wilson 1894). He did concede, however, that Gurmukhi or Nagari is even more suitable for writing Punjabi than Roman but, since 'it would never be adopted by the Mussalman portion of the population' (Wilson 1894: 172), the only practicable alternative was that of using Roman.

Wilson's proposals were condemned even more savagely than those of Cust. Most of his colleagues were still of the view that Punjabi was a dialect or patois, despite Leitner's details about Punjabi literature and the indigenous tradition of education in the province (1882). Indeed, some Englishmen even felt that Punjabi should be allowed to become extinct. Judge A. W. Stogdon, the Divisional Judge of Jullundur, wrote in his letter of 3 August 1895 that:

> As for the encouragement of Punjabi, I am of the opinion that it is an uncouth dialect not fit to be a permanent language, and the sooner it is driven out by Urdu the better (in Chaudhry 1977: 208).

Others felt that the cost of such a change would be exorbitant (Chaudhry 187) or that such a change would be a backward or reactionary step (Chaudhry 181, 183, 191, 218). Still others pointed out that the political repercussions of such a change, in the context of the Urdu-Hindi controversy, could be alarming. The Commissioner of Rawalpindi wrote in his letter of 27 May 1895 to the Junior Secretary to the Financial Commissioner, Punjab, that the proposed change of script was especially problematic. In his words:

> Under the change [to Roman] the Mullah might lose scholars and bigots might raise an agitation that Government was causing the Arabic (Persian) character to be disused in favour of English in order to help Christian Missionaries by discouraging the teaching of the Koran (in Chaudhry 1977: 240).

The same opinion was expressed in different words by other officers (for their letters, see Chaudhry 1977: 268, 277, 317). The proposals were, of course, dropped.

Since the Urdu-Hindi controversy was part of Hindu-Muslim antagonism, any attempt at supporting the cause of Punjabi was interpreted by the Muslims as an attack upon them. Thus, when Dr P. C. Chatterjee, a Bengali Hindu educationalist, proposed in his convocation address at the Punjab University, in 1908, that Punjabi should replace Urdu, the Muslims opposed him vehemently. On 29 December 1908, a meeting was held in Amritsar to condemn Chatterjee's proposals.

Sir Muhammad Shafi, a prominent Muslim leader from the Punjab, condemned Chatterjee's views and called him an enemy of the Muslims. It was especially pointed out that Chatterjee was a Bengali and not a Punjabi and thus, it was reasoned, his real interest lay not in promoting Punjabi but in opposing Urdu, which was now symbolic of Muslim identity and separatism (Barelvi 1988: 27). Such reasoning was based on the leading role of the Bengali Hindus in supporting Hindi against Urdu throughout the Urdu-Hindi controversy (Jones 1966: 383-85). Thus, the support of Punjabi by a Bengali Hindu was perceived as an expression of his anti-Muslim bias. As mentioned in the chapter on the Urdu-Hindi controversy, the Muslim League condemned the demand for Punjabi in its December 1910 session, and Sheikh Zahur Ahmed gave the following highly provocative statement against it:

> Delhi, the home of Urdu, is in the Province of the Punjab and it would be a very sad day, indeed, if the birth-place of Mir, Ghalib and Zauq should be vulgarized by the Babylonish jargon, by courtesy called Punjabi (Pirzada 1969: 196).

But such was the feeling against Hindus and Sikhs, with whom Punjabi was identified, that the Punjabi Muslims were not provoked.

## Punjabi Movement Before Partition

As has already been mentioned, by and large it was only the Sikhs who promoted Punjabi language and literature and since the British started to enrol the Sikhs in the army after 1857, they 'unwittingly helped to shape an identity that was already recognisable to other peoples of northern India' (Jeffrey 1986: 49). Thus, soon after the Hunter Commission, Punjabi was no longer officially discouraged. Even in

1877-78 'Punjabi, in the Gurmukhi character' had been 'introduced in the Oriental colleges' (RPI-P 1879: 29) and by 1906-7 inspecting officers were 'instructed to encourage the use of Punjabi colloquially in all Lower Primary classes' (RPI-P 1907:24). However, the number of Gurmukhi schools rose slowly (RPI-P 1911: 5; 1912: 28; RPI-F 1907: 11). Under the Muslim-dominated provincial governments, the Sikhs complained that Punjabi Muslim ministers discouraged their children from studying Punjabi (see Sardar Lal Singh's statement in LAD-Pun 6 March 1942: 407). Thus, while there were 1,245 Urdu medium primary schools in the major cities of the Punjab in 1940, there were only 13 such Punjabi medium schools (LAD-Pun 1 April 1940). In the same year, 13,342 students offered Urdu, 626 Hindi, and 96 Punjabi as their first vernacular in the Matriculation and Vernacular examination (LAD-Pun 1942: 354). Urdu was also most in demand for making adult literacy programmes, as 255,000 primers were printed in Urdu whereas the number printed for both Punjabi and Hindi was 35,000 (LAD-Pun 4 December 1941: 69-70). One reason for the lack of interest in Punjabi, even amongst the Sikhs, was its ghettoizing effect. Ordinary Sikhs did not want to sacrifice social mobility to a linguistic symbol. However, identity-conscious Sikhs did promote Punjabi as we have seen.

The first daily newspaper in Punjabi was published by the Sikh Sabha of Lahore (Khurshid 1986: 381). The Sikhs also published a number of papers in the Gurmukhi script among which the *Khalsa Samachar* and *Panj Darya* are well known (Qaisar 1992: 18-9).

While the majority of educated Punjabi-speakers, both Hindus and Muslims, promoted Hindi and Urdu, among the Hindu organizations, the Sat Sabha, founded in 1866 and modelled after the Brahmo Samaj by its founder, Lala Behari Lal, also used Punjabi for its work (Jones 1966: 380). Some Muslims also tried to promote Punjabi, though they were not part of mainstream Muslim political culture.

The first Punjabi newspaper in the Persian script was called *Amrat Patreeka* and was published in Jhelum in 1896 (Khurshid 1986: 381) by a Hindu called Bhola Nath. The first publication with which many Muslims were associated, and which was edited by a man who later became one of the leaders of the Punjabi movement in Pakistan, was *Punjabi Darbar*. This was published from Lyallpur by Joshua Fazal Din (a Punjabi Christian) (Khurshid 1986: 382). A Punjabi Society was established at Government College, Lahore in 1926. This Society staged many plays in Punjabi and promoted the language in other ways (Hameed 1964). Another private literary organization, the Doaba Kavi Sabha, was organized by Umar Din Ulfat Varsi in 1931 at Jullundur

(Faqir 1956: 3). In general, however, educated Muslims associated themselves with Urdu rather than Punjabi. But this, as we have noted before, was because of political expediency. The Muslim intelligentsia had formed a pressure group against Hindus and Sikhs, and Urdu was part of this Muslim identity. Meanwhile, the common people of the Punjab, less conscious of the exigencies of modernity, continued to enjoy oral Punjabi literature. The mosque schools taught moral stories in Punjabi and Punjabi stories were sold in the bazars (Saleem PC: 8 December 1994).

## The Beginning of Activity

Soon after the creation of Pakistan, Punjabi 'vanished as a university subject' (Shackle 1970: 243). Because of its association with Sikhs and due to the state's promotion of Urdu, Punjabi was relegated to the periphery. In 1948, however, some activity did begin, when a meeting of some Punjabi intellectuals was held at the Dyal Singh College under the presidentship of Syed Abid Ali Abid. All the participants were distinguished men of letters, M. D. Taseer and Faqir Muhammad Faqir amongst others. They decided to work towards making Punjabi the language of education in the Punjab and to encourage publications in Punjabi. The first objective remained an aspiration, but Abdul Majid Salik did start publishing the monthly *Punjabi* in 1951 (Qaisar 1992: 20). Its editor, Faqir Muhammad Faqir, was successful in persuading eminent Punjabi literary figures, who had made their name in Urdu literature, to write for it. The Punjabi League and the Punjabi Cultural Society were formed in early 1952 and a number of minor Punjabi organizations, such as the Punjabi Morcha (Punjabi trench), created in 1954 by Sardar Iqbal Dillon (Int: 23 November 1994) proliferated. But none of these organizations were able to get Punjabi accepted as even an optional language in the University of the Punjab in 1953 ('Editorial' *Punjabi* March-April and November-December 1953).

The first significant event of this period was the Punjabi Conference held on 9 March 1956 at Lyallpur. It was sponsored by the Punjabi Bazm-e-Adab (literary society) and its main purpose was consciousness-raising ('Editorial' *Punjabi*, March 1956: 3-5). This Bazm-e-Adab was the Pakistani version of Umar Din Ulfat Varsi's organization, which has been mentioned earlier. Having migrated from Jullundur to Lyallpur, Varsi organized his society under an acceptable Persian name (Faqir 1956: 3). The major impediment to the acceptance of Punjabi, as perceived by Punjabi intellectuals, was that most literate Punjabis (and perhaps also the illiterate) exhibited various degrees of cultural shame about their language. In his presidential address at the conference, Abdul Majid Salik pointed to this and the fact that Muslim Punjabis had always served Urdu. He was, however, quick to add that the progress of Punjabi should not be at the expense of Urdu which should remain the national language of Pakistan (Salik 1956: 8).

The Conference demanded that Punjabi be used as the medium of instruction at the lower level. This was accepted in principle, although no real change was made. In fact, since all the provinces of West Pakistan had been amalgamated into One Unit by this time, the ruling elite was less supportive than ever of the indigenous languages of the former provinces.

## Punjabi During Martial Rule

According to Shafqat Tanwir Mirza, an activist of the Punjabi movement and later the editor of the Urdu daily *Imroze*, Ayub Khan's martial law was anti-Punjabi. In his words:

> To support Punjabi language and literature was labelled an anti-state act and in 1959, under Ayub's martial law, the Punjabi Majlis, a Lahore based literary organisation was declared a political party and banned. So much so that from 1959 to 1962, no one dared to form a literary organization in Lahore lest it be declared a political organization (Mirza 1985: 43).

This was true as far as the political aspects of the movement were concerned, but after 1962, it appears that the state did make some concessions to the cultural aspirations of Punjabi intellectuals. Radio Pakistan started its Punjabi programme 'Ravi Rang' in 1960, and the Board of Intermediate and Secondary Education, Lahore, agreed to teach Punjabi from the sixth to the twelfth classes (Rasalu Int: 1 February 1993). The monthly *Punjabi Adab* also began publication and there was a literary efflorescence in which some outstanding works on the Punjabi identity were produced (for resistance literature in Punjabi, see Saleem 1986).

Among the most significant works on the Punjabi identity is Najam Hussain Syed's 'Dullah di Var'. The 'var' is an 'epic poem', a ballad of resistance or 'the versified narrative of an armed conflict' (Malik, F. 1988: 22-3). Dullah (or Abdullah) Bhatti of the poem's title was a rebel against the Mughal emperor Akbar (1554-1605) and was the subject of many a folk song in the Punjab (Saleem 1986: 17-20). The significance of Najam Syed's poem is explained by Fateh Muhammad Malik:

> Najam has picked up this legendary figure from folklore and made him a major symbol of Punjabi identity. He has portrayed Dullah as a working class revolutionary. Dullah's struggle has been projected in proletarian colours. His rebellion is not only aimed at the change of the government but also at the change of the exploitative socio-economic system (Malik, F 1988: 31).

The other folk heroes who resisted exploitation and foreign dominance were Ahmed Khan Kharal (1803-1857), Nizam Lohar (nineteenth century), and Bhagat Singh (1907-1931), who were all anti-British (Ramay 1985: 111-30).

Another Punjabi writer who used the symbols of Dullah Bhatti and Shah Hussain (1539-1593), a famous saint of Lahore (Krishna 1977: 12-26), was (Major) Ishaque Mohammad (1921-82). In his play *Quqnus* (phoenix) he uses these two figures to signify a distinct Punjabi identity which, unlike the Punjabi elite, resists exploitation. Ishaque's play *Musalli* was perhaps the most well-known anti-colonial work. In this, the original pre-Aryan inhabitants of the Punjab are shown to be marginalized (Ishaque 1972; 1976). As the plays of both Syed and Ishaque were inspired by socialist thought, and as Ishaque was the founder of the leftist Mazdoor Kisan Party (Afzal 1987: 115), the literature of the Punjabi Movement was labelled as being leftist or anti-Pakistan (Malik, S. 1985: 245).

The Punjabi Group of the Writers' Guild was formed in the early 1960s with Shafqat Tanwir Mirza as its first secretary. The Punjabi Adabi Sangat, the Punjabi Majlis of Government College Lahore, the Punjabi Adabi League, an irregular private society of Lahore, Majlis Shah Hussain, and a number of smaller organizations provided forums for the activists of the Punjabi Movement to interact with each other. The Sangat met at the YMCA at Lahore on Sunday evenings, though, according to Shackle, its attendance was thin, while that of the Halqa-e-Arbab-e-Zauq, an Urdu literary forum, was much greater. The Punjabi Majlis, which had a majority of left-leaning intellectuals (Saleem 1986: 35), nevertheless welcomed everybody, while the Halqa was selective (Shackle 1970: 248-51). The Majlis Shah Hussain, which was formed in 1962, was perhaps 'the most dynamic of the Punjabi institutions' in the late sixties (ibid. 252-3). In 1962, the Punjabi Guild arranged a literary and musical function on 'Mela Charaghan' (the fair of the lamps) which marks the death anniversary of Shah Hussain (Malik, F.

1988: 18). It also began publishing a monthly magazine called *Lahran*, in 1965. Another magazine called *Haq Allah* started publication in 1962, but only lasted until 1965 (Khurshid 1986: 384).

The main purpose of the Punjabi organizations was to make the Punjabi language the focus of the Punjabi, as opposed to the Pakistani, identity. The Punjabi Group of the Writers' Guild, under the inspiration of Shafqat Tanwir Mirza, held symposiums on the future of Punjabi writers (*PT* 22 February 1962) and was actively concerned with consciousness-raising. As this assertion of the Punjabi, rather than the Pakistani identity was seen as being ethno-nationalistic, it was condemned as being anti-Pakistani. Thus, in a speech Syed Abdullah, Principal of the Oriental College of Lahore and a great supporter of Urdu, accused the Punjabi activists of being anti-Pakistan and anti-Islamic (*PT* 15 March 1962). Altaf Gauhar, a senior bureaucrat, believed that the Punjabi—Urdu controversy which was going on in Lahore could harm national unity (*CMG* 20 April 1963). Hamid Ali Khan, the representative of Punjabi in the Central Language Board, declared that he loved literary Punjabi but condemned 'political Punjabi' (Chikna Choor 1963: 3). By 'political Punjabi', he meant the demand for making Punjabi the language of basic schooling, administration, and the judiciary in the province.

The term 'political' also referred to the opposition to Urdu (and in some cases mother-tongue speakers of Urdu), by some of the activists of the movement. The older generation of Urdu speakers did look down upon Punjabi which they, like the British, regarded as a rustic dialect. However, the younger generation is generally bilingual in Urdu and Punjabi though, like mother-tongue speakers of Punjabi, it too regards Punjabi as a rustic and ghettoizing language (Mansoor 1993: 108, 121). As the older generation of Urdu speakers supported Urdu against Punjabi in the sixties, the Punjabi activists were often critical of them. This was one political aspect of the movement, which raised government apprehensions. What alarmed them most, however, was the interest the Punjabi activists took in the development of Punjabi across the border, in India. Some activists, like Dillon of the Punjabi Morcha, were so appreciative of Sikh culture, that government officials and Pakistani nationalists feared they would undermine the two-nation theory on the basis of which Pakistan was created (Dillon Int: 23 November 1994).

Finally, on 6 April 1963, the Punjabi Group of the Writers Guild was banned, on the grounds that it had started the Punjabi-Urdu controversy, which could harm the interests of Urdu and strain relations between the supporters of Urdu and those of Punjabi. Moreover, the Group had discussed the Gurmukhi script and been in touch with the Sikhs. For some time, the issue was hotly debated. The greatest opposition to Punjabi was articulated in the Urdu Tarweej Conference of 26-28 April 1963, and the usual allegations against the Punjabi Group—that of being anti-Pakistan and anti-Islam—were repeated (Yar, M. 1963: 49-54). After this, the Punjabi Movement became very subdued on the political front, though its literary and cultural activities continued.

## The 1969 Educational Policy and the Movement

Air Marshal Nur Khan's proposals of 1969 were anti-English and were welcomed in pro-Urdu and anti-elitist circles. However, they were opposed by the supporters of the indigenous languages of West Pakistan. The activists of the Punjabi movement also opposed them. Rather surprisingly, a retired lieutenant general, Bakhtiar Rana, also urged the government to accommodate Punjabi in the new educational policy (*PT* 7 August 1969). The Punjabi Adabi Sangat presented a Memorandum to Nur Khan, proposing that the following steps be taken:

1. Open the doors of our seats of learning to Punjabi by:
   a. Adopting it as a medium of instruction at the primary level.
   b. Making it an elective subject up to the secondary classes.
   c. Establishing separate departments for it in higher academic institutions.
   d. Creating a separate chair for it in the Punjab University and other Universities to be opened in this area.
   e. Using Punjabi as the medium of instruction for the adult literacy programmes in the province.
2. Encouraging Punjabi writing by enabling the libraries to buy books in the language (Memorandum 1969).

Safdar Mir, an eminent journalist and a supporter of Punjabi, pointed out that whereas Sindhi and Pashto could be used at the primary level under the proposed policy, Punjabi was not even mentioned. 'This', in his view, 'aroused the suspicions and apprehensions of the protagonists of the Punjab' (Zeno 1969). A number of organizations—Punjabi Adabi League, Punjabi Durbar,

Majlis Shah Hussain, Punjabi Society, Majlis Mian Muhammad, Majlis-e-Bahu, Majlis Waris Shah, Majlis Shah Murad, and Rahs Rang (a drama group in Lahore)—supported these demands for Punjabi. Dr Waheed Qureshi of the Oriental College and Lieutenant General Rana also demanded the establishment of a Punjabi Department at the University (Memorandum 1969: 13-7; also see Mirza 1969). Despite all this opposition, however, the *New Education Policy* of 1970 did not deviate from its proposed policy of not altering the position of Punjabi.

## Activities in the 1970

The 1970s opened with one positive achievement for the Punjabi movement: the setting up of the department of Punjabi at the Punjab University under the chairmanship of Najam Hussain Syed. However, Najam's secular and leftist reputation made the department suspect in the eyes of his ideological opponents. During Ziaul Haq's martial law, when these opponents came into power, syllabi were changed, the literature of the Sikhs was tabooed, and the faculty was purged of certain members. This was, and remains, an impediment to the study of Punjabi literature and its interpretation (Humayun 1986: 227-33).

In 1970, the Punjabi Adabi League translated the Quran into Punjabi (*NT* May 1970). General Rana himself organized the Punjabi Ittehad Tehrik (Punjabi Unity Movement), which was reported to have over 1000 members, and published a weekly called *Punjab di Avaz* (the voice of the Punjab). The Tehrik reiterated the demand for using Punjabi in education, administration, and the judiciary at the lower levels.

After the emergence of Bangladesh in December 1971, the Punjabi movement became somewhat subdued although these were the best years for the production of consciousness-raising literature. The relationship between identity and literature also received direct expression at different forums. No less a personage than the poet Faiz Ahmad Faiz said at a convention of the Sangat that only Punjabi could express the true self most authentically. Ustad Daman, the Punjabi poet, made much of Faiz's remarks, concluding that speaking Punjabi was tantamount to telling the truth (*PT* 13 January 1972).

Another important issue was language planning. The issues of choosing a script and making dictionaries available had to be addressed by the Punjabi activists and they used the newspapers to express their views. The main issues involved changes in script and the compiling of a good dictionary. After a long debate (see *PT* 10 and 17 September and 5 October 1972), the script was not changed. However, even now there are people who want to use the Gurmukhi script for writing Punjabi (Dillon Int: 23 November 1994). This, perhaps, is a reaction to the perceived dominance of Urdu, which shares its present script with Punjabi. But this is a minority opinion since many Punjabi activists do not want to abandon the Arabic-based Urdu script, which symbolizes their Muslim identity. A good dictionary, however, was published by the Urdu Science Board in 1989 (Bukhari 1989).

## The 1980

As we have seen earlier, General Ziaul Haq's military regime was not sympathetic to the indigenous languages, since they were regarded as symbols of ethno-nationalism. On 2 January 1985, however, a Charter of the Punjabi-speaking people was signed by 139 prominent people. A press conference was addressed by Masood Khaddarposh, Convener of the Punjabi Forum, and Fakhar Zaman, a well-known writer and former senator. Besides the activists of the Punjabi movement, leftist members of the PPP like Mairaj Khalid and Mubashir Hasan also signed the Charter (*M* 3 January 1985). The prominent English language journalist and editor of the left-leaning weekly *Viewpoint*, Mazhar Ali Khan, also signed the Charter. In short, the opposition to General Zia's right wing government took this opportunity to support Punjabi and the multi-nationality thesis. The Charter did not make any new demands; its main thrust was to make Punjabis proud of their language and cultural identity (Charter-P 1985). The most significant step in that direction was the Punjabi Conference of 1986.

This conference took place in Lahore from 25-9 April, in the wake of the lifting of the martial law. The new-found freedom encouraged Fakhar Zaman to arrange the conference and invite participants from India and other countries of the world. The delegates from India, however, were denied visas, so that Amrita Pritam, the famous Punjabi poetess, could not preside over the Conference as originally intended. The supporters of Punjabi protested over this (Shah, B. 1986), and like most other ethno-nationalistic debates, this matter took on the character of a left-right debate. The right wing writers pointed out that well-known leftists: Abdullah Malik, the famous Urdu novelist; Tariq Ali Khan, the Trotskyite student leader of Ayub Khan's days now living in London; Ajmal Khattak of the ANP; and Ghaus Baksh Bizenjo had either participated in or sent messages to the conference (Rahman, A

1986; Qasmi 1986). Even Benazir Bhutto, Ziaul Haq's main political opponent with known liberal views, sent a message (Qaisar and Pal 1988: 9). The atmosphere of the Conference was undoubtedly progressive and anti-establishment. The religious faction was accused of censoring Punjabi literature (Humayun 1986: 227-33). Aftab Naqvi, a college lecturer, was hooted when he emphasized the Muslim identity of Pakistani Punjabis (Naqvi 1986: 118-19), and it was proposed that the Punjabi movement should try to ally itself with the working class, rather than the middle class, which had always been indifferent to it (Saqib 1986: 127). Among the resolutions passed by the delegates, the most important one was, predictably, that which pertained to the use of Punjabi in the educational, administrative, and judicial domains (Qaisar and Pal 1988: 457-84). The delegates also supported the ethno-nationalist movements in the other provinces of Pakistan, as well as the socialist revolution in Afghanistan. One typical comment by the right-wing Press about these activities was:

> This is not serving one's mother tongue. This is only finding ways for the progress of socialist thought and politics under the banner of progressivism (Rahman, A. 1986).

On 8 May, a procession was brought out in Lahore under the auspices of the Punjabi Writers Board, the Punjab Naujawan Mahaz, etc. All the other Punjabi organizations participated and chanted slogans: 'Punjabi Parho, Punjabi Likho' (read Punjabi, write Punjabi) (*M* 9 May 1986). While the Punjabi activists asserted their distinctive identity (Zeno 1986), the supporters of the Pakistani identity, like Fateh Muhammad Malik, argued that this identity was in a hierarchical and not a mutually exclusive relationship with the Pakistani identity (Malik, F. 1988: 20-35).

As in the cases of the other language movements, Punjabi language planners are also motivated by the imperative of creating an authentic Punjabi identity through language planning. Many Punjabis, and not only the activists, complain that ordinary spoken Punjabi is too full of Urdu words to be authentic (Agha Babar in Zaidi, M. A. 1993). This appears to be a threat to the Punjabi identity, because of which some Punjabi activists use words of indigenous origin, even at the cost of intelligibility, in their writings (though to a lesser extent in conversation). Examples of new coinages and words commonly used are given below.

The Punjabi daily *Sajjan* (1989-90) used many such words. A critic of such usage claimed that it became so unintelligible that it lost readers. It was also argued that some of these words were Sanskritic or Hindi rather than the well-known Persian or Arabic equivalents already in use (Iqbal 1991: 12).

| Word commonly used | Punjabi coinage | Meaning |
|---|---|---|
| lafz | akhar | word |
| sailab | harh | flood |
| aqvam-e-muttahidda | ik muth qauman | United Nations |
| salana | varhe var | yearly |
| khususi | achecha | special |
| taqreeb | ikath | gathering |
| bhejna | ghalna | to send |

(Khalid 1993)

The stress on indigenization appears anti-Islamic to its critics because it involves purging the language of its Arabic and Persian roots. Thus the use of the word *chinta* for worry rather than *fikr* is reminiscent of the Urdu-Hindi controversy, when the supporters of modern Hindi substituted this word for worry, while the supporters of Urdu retained the Persian *fikr*.

## The Present

During Benazir Bhutto's first tenure, Nawaz Sharif, the Chief Minister of the Punjab, used Punjabi nationalism to confront the centre. Fakhar Zaman, a supporter of the PPP, called this policy 'Punjabism' and stigmatized it as a 'political stunt' (*D* 20 December 1988).

The 1990s have seen the rise of younger people to the forefront of the movement. Saeed Farani Kammi (1990) and Nazir Kahut (1992) have written books which, though polemical and based upon conspiracy theories, contribute towards making educated Punjabis conscious of the need to take pride in their language. Alyas Ghumman writes on technical and scientific subjects in Punjabi (Ghumman Int: 31 January 1993) while a number of journalists bring out the fortnightly *Ravael* and the monthly *Maan Boli*. The attempt to bring out a daily, *Sajjan*, failed after twenty-one months (3 February 1989 to October 1990), but it inspired Punjabi activists because the journalists who worked in it devoted themselves selflessly, on a voluntary basis, and kept publishing the daily, despite a crippling lack of funds (Qaisar

1992; Ali, N. 1992). Thus, *Sajjan* became a legend which inspires the Punjabi movement even now.

The PPP came to power again ir 1993 and Fakhar Zaman became the Chairman of the Academy of Letters, while Hanif Ramay became the Speaker of the Punjab legislature. Fakhar did give the indigenous languages, and especially the theme of anti-establishment resistance, importance at a national conference of writers held in Islamabad between 9-11 October 1994, but the Punjabi Sangat's major demand, that Punjabi should be made the medium of instruction at the primary level, has not yet been fulfilled (Mirza 1993).

## Reasons for the Movement

We have seen that Punjabi is given very little patronage by the state and has never been the medium of instruction or the language of administration in Pakistan, despite the fact that the apparatus of the state is dominated by Punjabis. This is explained by some people with reference to character qualities: that the Punjabis are generous and therefore tolerant of Urdu; that they are ashamed of their language and impressed by Urdu; that they are insensitive to cultural imperialism. But such explanations only indicate the emotional attitude of the speaker. A more likely explanation is that Urdu serves to extend the power base of the ruling elite. Indeed, as Shafqat Tanwir Mirza argued in a recent interview, Punjabi is given less importance than other ethnic languages, so as to impress upon their supporters that the sacrifice of one's mother tongue, which only the Punjabis give so willingly, is the real criterion of Pakistani nationalism (Mirza 1994: 91).

But these rational, instrumentalist explanations do not explain the behaviour of the activists of the Punjabi movement, nor the Punjabi speakers' emotional response towards their language. We have seen how all activists claim that Punjabis despise their language or, at best, hold it in affectionate contempt. A survey of students' attitudes, referred to earlier, concludes that:

> The majority of Punjabi students (59%) display negative attitudes to Punjabi. They generally do not approve of studying Punjabi and there is no commitment to practice. It is also considered economically unimportant (Mansoor 1993: 119).

A similar survey of attitudes towards Punjabis settled in England also suggested that it was 'poorly evaluated even by its users' (Mobbs 1991: 245). But does this mean that the Punjabis consider their language a social stigma as the Lapps do theirs? (Eidheim 1969). For the Lapps, the fact that they 'habitually used Lappish in their daily life' was a 'secret', and some families 'even made the drastic decision to prevent their children from learning Lappish' (Eidheim 1969: 43; 55). The Punjabis do not appear to shun Punjabi in private domains to this extent, but educated ones do teach Urdu and English to their children and consider these languages more sophisticated and cultured than Punjabi. However, unlike the Lapps who are a minority *vis à vis* the Norwegians, the Punjabis are a self-confident majority. Perhaps it is their confidence in all other spheres of life which makes them negligent of their language. They do, however, enjoy Punjabi songs and jokes. Moreover, written tales in prose and verse in this language are still in circulation at the popular level. This is regarded by some intellectuals as part of the resistance to alien cultural domination (Saleem PC: 8 December 1994). However, it does not seem to be part of an active anti-establishment resistance movement, rather an indication that Urdu is still alien for popular Punjabi culture. Punjabi is certainly a marker of intimacy and informality. This means that the language is taken for granted as an intimate part of identity, though it has not been used to create a pressure group to obtain more goods or power, i.e., for instrumental reasons.

This is understandable, because Punjabis already have power which ethnicity would only threaten. This is why the Punjabi movement mobilizes people not for instrumentalist but for sentimental reasons. The pre-modern sentimental attachment to a distinctive way of life, conveniently symbolized by Punjabi, is really what is at stake. The domination of Urdu, no matter how useful for the elite, does take away the language and literature of the Punjab from the Punjabis. The activists feel that this is a price which should not be paid; the others do not take it seriously. Hence, the movement is a weak, middle-class phenomenon, concentrated mainly in Lahore. It is unique among all the language movements of Pakistan because it is the only one which is not motivated by rational, goal-directed, instrumentalist reasons. But for all that, it is a modern phenomenon. Had the use of Urdu and English in the domains of power not alienated the Punjabi intelligentsia from its cultural roots—something which could only have happened under modern conditions of formal schooling, ubiquitous media, and the constant use of other languages—the Punjabi language movement would not have started at all.

# 12

# Minor Language Movements

The census gives the figure of 2.91 per cent for what it calls 'other' languages, i.e., languages other than Punjabi, Pashto, Sindhi, Siraiki, Urdu, Balochi, Hindko, and Brahvi. These languages include Gujrati, which is confined mostly to Karachi and the urban areas of Sindh, and the languages of the Northern Areas, Kohistan, Chitral, and Kashmir. This chapter, however, deals with the minor language movements, so that it gives very little attention to languages in which there is no conscious movement, desire, or attitude towards the language. The languages it deals with in some detail are as follows:-

| Language | Where Spoken | Number of Speakers |
| --- | --- | --- |
| Hindko | Hazara, some cities of the NWFP | 3.1 million. |
| Gujrati | Mostly in Karachi, and in the Indian state of Gujrat. | 200,000-680,000. in Karachi.[1] Over 42 million in India (*Britannica*). |
| Shina | Gilgit, Diamer district, parts of Baltistan, Kohistan, Kashmir, and parts of NWFP | 450,000 to 500,000 in Pakistan and 20,000 in Indian-held Kashmir (SSNP-2: 93). |
| Burushaski | Central Hunza Valley, Nagar River Valley, Yasin Valley. | 55,000 to 60,000 (SSNP-2: 37). |
| Khowar | Chitral district and parts of Gilgit, Northern Swat Valley etc. | 188,000 to 222,800 (SSNP-2: 32) |

| | | |
|---|---|---|
| Kashmiri | In the Vale of Kashmir in India and pockets in Azad Kashmir. | Figures for Azad Kashmir are not available: 4 million speakers in Indian-held Kashmir (*Britannica*). |

Other languages such as Wakhi, Domaki, Kohistani, Kalasha, etc. are briefly touched upon.

## Hindko

Compared to many of the minor languages, Hindko is fairly widely spoken. Hindko, Siraiki, and Punjabi are mutually intelligible and Grierson used the term Hindko and Hindki to designate certain dialects of what he called Lahnda, i.e., Western Punjabi (Vol. 4: 554-65. Also see Shackle 1980 and Rensch 1992b: 3). Recently, however, the idea that it is not a dialect of Punjabi but a separate language has been promoted by Hindko-speaking intellectuals (Nayyar 1977: 55-6; see *Hindko Zaban* etc.).

Hindko speakers live in four districts of the NWFP (Mansehra, Abbottabad, Peshawar, and Kohat) and in one district of the Punjab (Attock) (see Appendix F). In Peshawar and Kohat it is spoken in the old cities, but in Hazara it is used by all indigenous people. In Attock, only 0.6 per cent of the people reported Hindko as their mother tongue but this is because of 'the local use of more than one name for the same language' (Rensch 1992 b: 6). However, Shackle gives details of the Hindko of this region, as well as that of other areas (1980: 482-7).

There are two main centres of the Hindko language movement: Peshawar and Abbottabad. In Peshawar and some other cities of the NWFP, the inhabitants of the old city were Hindko-speaking. According to Mukhtar Ali Nayyar and other Hindkowan intellectuals, they were the original inhabitants of this area who were later dominated by the Pakhtuns who moved down from Afghanistan (Nayyar 1965; Shaukat Int: 3 January 1995). Hindko was used in the old city in all informal domains: poetry sessions, fairs, entertainment, etc., before a conscious language movement began. Some religious preachers such as Maulana Gul Faqir and Ghulam Ahmad even delivered sermons in Hindko. A politician, Muhammad Gama, is said to have used it in the political sphere to represent the Hindkowans (Nayyar. Interview. 3 January 1995).

It was poetry, however, which was the focus of the cultural life of the Hindko-speakers of Peshawar. The first literary organization, the Bazm-e-Sukhan, is said to have started functioning in 1903. Mukhtar Ali Nayyar has written about many pre-partition poets of Hindko such as Haji Gul (1760-1825), Shafiq Mian (1790-1884), and Abdullah (1861-1930) in a series of articles in *Hindko Zaban*. The most famous poet is Ahmad Ali Sain (1842-1937) to whose memory special numbers of *Hindko Zaban* are devoted (March-April 1991; April-May 1992; etc.). The poetry sessions associated with the poets of the 1930s were lively. The poets, called *ustads* (teachers), came with their supporters, who cheered their champions and sometimes even clashed with their rivals (Shaukat. Int). The sessions were oral, with much public participation, and the Urdu weekly, *Hamdard-e-Sarhad*, published from Bannu in 1941, also printed material on Hindko poetry. Likewise, the Urdu weeklies *Shahab* and *Sang-e-Meel*, published from Peshawar in 1938 and 1948, also carried material on Hindko (Naseem 1991: 20; Khan, S. 1990: 37). After Partition, the Bazm-e-Khayal and Bazm-e-Shaura-e-Hindko, both literary organizations, were established in Peshawar. In 1956, the Urdu daily *Anjam* published pieces of Hindko verse, and after 1963, it started devoting first half a page and then a full page to the language (Khan, S. 1990: 39-40).

Mukhtar Ali Nayyar, Farigh Bukhari, and Johar Mir were the pioneers of the modern Hindko language movement in the mid-1960s in Peshawar. Mukhtar Ali Nayyar, who has been called the Father of Hindko (Baba-e-Hindko), made the script of the language by modifying some of the letters of the Urdu script as early as 1955. He published the script in his book *Hindko Nasr di Kahanri* in 1965. In 1976, he also wrote a grammar and a dictionary of 22,000 items, out of which 14,000 have been published in *Hindko Zaban*. Farigh Bukhari, another pioneer, established the Hindko Literary Society and published his book *Navian Rahan* (new paths) in 1964.

In 1972, Sheen Shaukat, then a young man, established the Hindko Arts Council, which made the Hindko-speaking intelligentsia conscious of the need to promote their language (Shaukat. Int: 3 January 1995). Later on, despite disagreements on the script (Imdad Int : 3 January 1995), books were written, plays were produced, and the government was asked to give time to the language on radio and television. The monthly *Hindko Zaban*, which began publication in 1973, as well as the dailies *Surkhab* and *Nusrat* established Hindko journalism on a firm footing (Khan, S. 1990: Chapter 4) and provided a forum for the activists of the movement who wanted their language to be used in the media, for primary education, and for competitive examinations.

There are several organizations for the promotion of Hindko in Peshawar now, of which Idara Farogh-e-Hindko (organization for the promotion of Hindko) is notable (IFH Report 1992). There is also a Parchol Adabi Baithak, a literary group which meets every week and has recently started publishing a Hindko journal called *Parchol*. Perhaps because of the domination of Pashto, the activists of the Hindko movement in Peshawar are extremely dedicated to their language and produce a substantial amount of writing without official patronage. They claim that they have succeeded in making young people conscious of the necessity of preserving their language and using it without the cultural shame which existed earlier.

Even in the fifties and the sixties in Abbottabad, the Urdu daily *Jamhoor* carried articles on Hindko and the culture of Hazara (Manglori 1959; Pema 1960). At the time only a handful of intellectuals were conscious of the need to preserve the language and culture, while ordinary people were ashamed of it. As in Peshawar, some of these intellectuals established organizations such as the Hindko Adabi Jirga (Hindko Literary Committee) in 1978; the Hindko Adabi Sangat (Literary Association) in 1979; and in the early 1980s, Ghulam Jan Tahirkheli's Hindko Academy (Interview with Hindko writers of Abbottabad, 19 August 1994).

Even before the formation of these organizations, people had started writing in Hindko, both in Peshawar and Abbottabad. Sultan Sakoon, a leading Hindko writer from Hazara, published the first *ghazal* in Hindko in *Nasheman* (an Urdu weekly) on 14 May 1976. Later, Yahya Khalid started contributing a column in Hindko (Gal Kath) in *Jamhoor* (17 June 1980:5). It was at this time that Hindko writers became concerned about the lack of a standard script for their language. In 1980, the Hindko Academy appointed a committee to prepare such a script (*Nasheman* 9 March 1980: 7). The Hindko Batol Jirga, a private language planning organization, was also asked to prepare one (Swati 1986: 6; and letters in *Jamhoor*), and private individuals came up with their own systems (Gul 1982: 10; Sakoon Int: 20 August 1994). A standard script is still a matter of contention in Abbottabad as it is in Peshawar. The magazine *Parchol*, however, welcomes all the scripts of Hindko.

Another demand, which was repeated in every forum and featured again and again in the Press, was the need to give Hindko time on radio and television (*Nasheman* 18 April 1980). The establishment of a separate radio station in Abbottabad also became a major demand ('Editorial' Urdu-Hindi4 *Jamhoor* 25 March 1980). This was finally accepted and the relevant orders were passed in 1987 (*Jamhoor* 16 September 1987). Now Abbottabad has its own radio station and Hindko programmes are relayed from Peshawar, both on radio and the television. However, the activists of the Hindko movement demand more time on the electronic media (Yusufi 1990).

The other aspect of corpus planning—the creation of a modern vocabulary—is not being carried out in an organized manner. Even a dictionary is yet to be published, though Sultan Sakoon, like Nayyar in Peshawar, has published word lists in *Jamhoor* from 1981 to 1986, and has several volumes of a Hindko-Urdu dictionary ready for the press. Along with the Hindko translation of the Quran by Haider Zaman, it continues to await publication, because of lack of official patronage. Indeed, one of the bitterest complaints of the Hindko writers is that their language is neglected by the government.

The alleged discrimination by the NWFP government led to the formation of the Hazara Qaumi Mahaz (HQM) in July 1987. Its President, Asim Malik, alleges that Hindko speakers are denied their share of jobs in various government departments. Moreover, as Hindko is neither the language of schooling nor of competitive examinations (whereas Pashto is), the speakers of Hindko are at a disadvantage. As a reaction to this, he and his supporters want to create a separate province where Hindko would be the official language. Under the existing circumstances, the HQM supports the old demand of the Hindko movement that primary schooling should be in Hindko for Hindko-speaking children (Malik, A. Interview. 20 August 1994). The HQM contested the elections of 1990 and 1993 but did not win any seats.

The Hindko movement has succeeded in removing some of the stigma of using the language among members of the intelligentsia. However, this stigma has not died down completely as people continue to use Urdu in formal domains, even if everybody present knows Hindko (Durrani and Hyder 1994). Also, because it is seen as ghettoizing, people 'were considerably less enthusiastic about having their children learn to read and write in Hindko than they were about having books and magazines available in that language' (Rensch 1992 b: 73). This is only to be expected from people who have only just become conscious that their culture and language should be preserved, but have not ceased to acquiesce in the given state of affairs, which makes jobs available only through Urdu and English.

## Potohari

The Census of 1981 subsumed the language of the area of Azad Kashmir, Rawalpindi, and parts of Jhelum under Punjabi so that no separate official figures for the speakers of this language are available. There is, however, a Potohari language movement, whose activists are more active in England, where there are over 500,000 speakers of the language, than in Pakistan. Most of these people are immigrant workers from Azad Kashmir (especially Mirpur) and Pakistan. As mentioned earlier, local identity labels, both social and linguistic, are transcended under the impact of modernity to create a larger identity label. This process is in evidence among the Potohari speakers. The language itself was called Potohari, Mirpuri, Punjabi, Potohari Punjabi, and Pahari before the rise of the language movement. Now, however, the activists of the movement argue that a common name, such as Potohari, should be used (Mehmood. Int. 15 May 1995).

The British Potoharis brought out the first magazine in their language called *Chitka* in December 1993. They also created an Arabic-based phonetic script, which excluded letters which do not represent any sound of the language. The immediate goal of the activists of the language movement is to make people proud of their language and to learn to use it (Mehmood. Int. ibid.). In Pakistan, the magazine *Sang-e-Potohar*, although in Urdu, creates awareness about Potohar and its distinct culture. In short, a Potohari identity is now being forged in northern Punjab, as the Siraiki identity was created in southern Punjab in the 1990s.

## Gujrati

Gujrati is the official language of Gujarat state in India, with 42 million speakers. In India it is also spoken in Maharashtra and Rajasthan, but in Pakistan it is confined to the city of Karachi where the Bohras, Khojas, Memons, and Parsees speak it. The main occupation of all these communities being business, they are spread over some of the cities of Sindh and even in Africa and Burma.

Before Partition the city of Karachi had Gujrati-medium schools and a fairly active Gujrati Press. In the 1880s, the number of pupils who were taught in Gujrati in the primary schools of the Bombay presidency was 116,919 whereas those who were taught in Sindhi were 14,324 and Hindustani only 6,515 (Edn Comm: Bom 1884: 92). During the movement for the separation of Sindh from Bombay, politicized urban Muslims opposed Gujrati because it was associated with Bombay. In the debates in the Bombay Legislative Council, Vali Baksh Patel held that Muslim girls should get primary education in Gujrati, their mother tongue, in the Urdu-medium schools of Gujarat (LAD-Bom 30 November 1935: 2745). But this suggestion was opposed by other Muslims on the grounds that there were schools which taught only in Gujrati (ibid. 2750).

After the separation of Sindh from Bombay, the government of Sindh encouraged Sindhi, passing a resolution (No. 137 dated 27 July 1940) that the teaching of Sindhi would be compulsory in schools which taught in Gujrati, Marathi, and Urdu. R. K. Sidhwa, a Parsee, protested against this, pointing out that there were 100,000 Gujrati-speakers in Karachi whose children would not be able to learn their mother tongue if 'this compulsion is introduced in primary education' (LAD-S 26 February 1941: 60).

However, the use of Gujrati declined, although there were 17 Gujrati-medium primary schools in Karachi with 3,616 pupils in 1948 (ABE 1950: 59). This number decreased as the demand for Gujrati decreased in the Gujrati-speaking community, and only one Gujrati-medium middle school for boys was opened after 1954, as opposed to 25 schools for Urdu (LAD-S 20 December 1972: 55-6). After 1970, even private schools established by the Gujrati-speaking businessmen switched over to English or Urdu (Patel 1994), and the younger generation could no longer read Gujrati because it was written in a cursive variant of the Devanagari and not the Arabic script.

However, the Bohra community evolved an Arabic-based script for Gujrati called the Lisan-ud-Dawat. The script is said to have been made over four hundred years ago, and the religious books of the Bohras are written in it. Yet, Mrs Farida Tawawalla, the Head of the major Bohra school, Al Madrassatus Safyatul Burhania, said that the medium of instruction even in her school was English, and that the younger generation could not write or read Gujrati (Tawawalla. Int. 26 September 1994).

Indeed, all those whom the present writer interviewed agreed that young people, either for instrumental reasons or out of cultural shame, preferred to use Urdu and that their Gujrati was saturated with Urdu words. However, they could, and did, speak Gujrati at home, but were indifferent to its use in formal domains which involved writing and reading (Lakhani Int. 26 September 1994; Shahbaz Int. 24 September 1994; Patel Int. 10 October 1994).

Although the number of Gujrati publications has decreased since 1937, when the number of dailies alone was ten (LAD-S 7 August 1937: 8-12), they are still more in number than in most other Pakistani languages (see Appendix A). This may be because the Gujrati community is almost entirely urban and is financially strong. Moreover, the people who publish and read Gujrati publications are elderly or middle-aged people who know the script and are attached to their language.

These were the kind of people who formed organized bodies to preserve Gujrati and to promote its use. In 1951, the first poetry session in Gujrati was held in Karachi and this has become a yearly feature since then (Lakhani. Int. 26 September 1994). Organizations like the Pakistan Gujrati Ghazal Mandal, Anjuman Muslim Gujrati Adab, Gujrati Lekhat Mandal, Gujrati Sahitya Mandal, Gujrati Kavi Sangat, etc., tried to promote Gujrati but did not succeed beyond preserving it among older speakers. The Gujrati Kavi Sangat (Gujrati Poets Association) is perhaps the most active organization for the promotion of the language at present (Patel 1994: 3).

The Pakistan Writers' Guild did not initially include Gujrati among the regional languages of the country, but the efforts of Syed Fakhar Matsi and Usman Shabnam made the Guild accept it later (Patel 1994: 5). Gujrati was also represented for the first time in a national literary conference from 9-11 October 1994. However, most Gujrati-speaking people do not blame the government for neglecting their language. Some people do, however, complain of neglect in the media (see letter of Edhi in Jsrt 11 November 1982), but even they are aware that the decline of their language is mainly because young people, for whom it could have been a marker of identity, are indifferent to it (all interviewees).

## Languages of the Northern Areas and Kohistan

Shina, Burushaski, and Balti are the major languages of the Northern Areas of Pakistan whereas Wakhi and Domaaki are minor ones. Kohistan is a part of the NWFP but its languages, which are classified as minor in terms of the development of noticeable language movements, are different from Pashto and will be mentioned here in passing.

It appears that Shina was not an identity-marker of the Shina-speaking people. According to Leitner, one of the pioneering researchers on Shina, 'the Dards have no name in common, but call each Dard tribe that inhabits a different valley by a different name'

(Leitner 1889: 58-9). However, the modern intelligentsia gives language a more significant role in self-identification though religion—in this case Sunnism and Shiaism (including Ismailism)—is perhaps the most emotive identity-marker. Thus, although a recent linguistic survey suggests that the geographical criteria of identification may be giving way to linguistic ones, this cannot be accepted without reference to the religious tensions of the area. The survey carried out by Carlo Radloff claims that:

> Although the overall focus of identity for all the Shina-speaking areas is geographically oriented, this orientation appears to be stronger for the Kohistan participants. Most respondents from other areas seem to view their language group, if not their people group, as extending beyond their regional distinctiveness (Radloff 1992: 119).

Thus, concludes Radloff, 'the speaking of Shina is definitely part of their identity' (ibid. 115). This conclusion is not wrong but it may be qualified by adding that the religious component has the potential to become the major defining feature of these people in times of religious tension.

Shina is mostly used in homes and in informal domains, but it is also used, though less often, in such public domains as electioneering. Some of the speeches in the local elections of 1994 were in Shina. However, it is not used in the official domains of power. In the extreme north, it mixes with Burushaski, and in the east with Balti. Urdu is spoken for social mobility (Radloff 1992: 173).

Radio Pakistan began broadcasting in Shina from Rawalpindi in 1949 and from Gilgit in 1979 (Ali, U. 1991: 125; Appendix C). The standard Shina chosen is the Gilgiti dialect (Radloff 1992: 178). Some literature has also appeared in this variety and the Karakoram Writers Forum, a literary organization based in Gilgit, as well as talented individuals endeavour to publish in it (Alam 1990: 102-3). There is no standard script but M. S. Namoos, Amin Zia (1986), and Abdul Khaliq Taj (1990) devised orthographies by modifying the Persian letters (Ali, U. 1991: 120-31). Amin Zia's collection of verse *Sann* (1974) is a landmark in the development of the language. Despite this activity in Shina, young people tend to study Urdu for instrumentalist reasons. Thus, Urdu is spreading and 'opinion is strong that Urdu is the best language for writing things' (Radloff 185).

Burushaski, the language of the Brusho people, was not a written language in the Hunza and Nagar principalities, despite being the mother tongue of their rulers. In common with the other Muslim rulers of this part of the world, they used Persian as the court language and written literature was also in the same language. Folk literature, which was oral, was in Burushaski. It was written in the Latin script by European researchers such as Lorimer (see Lorimer 1936 vol. 2 for samples), till Naseeruddin Naseer used a modified form of the Urdu script to compose poetry in 1940 (Naseer 1979: 19). Since then, a number of such modifications have been suggested—such as that by Ghulamuddin Hunzai (1990), but no standard script has been agreed upon.

Naseeruddin Naseer has contributed to the development of the language by forming an organization called the Burushaski Research Academy in the late 1970s (BRA Questionnaire). It was first established in Hunza but then moved to Karachi, although there are branches in Skardu and Nagar because of the efforts of the Academy and its chief organizer, Naseeruddin, who is addressed by the title of *Allama* (most learned) by his admirers. His mystic poetry is available on audio cassettes and he has contributed towards a book of idioms (Tiffou 1993). Because of increased literary activity, there has been a change in the attitude of speakers towards it. Whereas in the past, it was considered vulgar and not suitable for writing, now some educated people have started taking pride in it (Naseer Int. 23 September 1994).

According to a recent survey, people now have a positive attitude towards Burushaski. 'No one foresaw their language dying out, even in Yasin where Khowar is very strong' (Backstrom 1992 b: 49). People also expressed interest in reading and writing in their language and were in favour of the production of Burushaski literature, especially poetry, and historical and religious material. More than half of those interviewed in this survey said they would send their children to a school which used Burushaski as the medium of instruction if one was available (ibid. 49). It is, indeed, a relatively strong language because the Doma people have adopted it to the extent that Domaaki is dying. Even Wakhi speakers, who are also neighbours of the Brusho, have learnt it (ibid. 49). In the Yasin valley, however, the Brusho speak Khowar, the dominant language of Chitral (ibid. 49).

Burushaski is, however, under strain as there are increasing trends towards bilingualism in Urdu, and in Khowar in the case of Yasin, as well as in the growing number of loan words from these languages being adopted into Burushaski (Backstrom 53; Naseer Int. 23 September 1994). This is perhaps inevitable because of increasing education and the availability of jobs in Urdu and English. However, because of conscious awareness about language, Burushaski seems in no imminent danger of extinction.

Balti speakers expressed positive attitudes towards Balti and thought that their children would continue using it. According to Backstrom's survey, 'All of the Balti men interviewed also expressed interest in learning to read their language. Most of them indicated that they would buy literature, especially poetry, in Balti if it was available' (Backstrom 1992a: 23). Although, according to some researchers, Balti did have a script of its own called *Age* in the eighth century (Yusuf 1990: 10; Rahman, K. 1973: 4), it is unknown now. An Englishman called A. F. C. Read wrote Balti in the Roman script in his grammar and lexicon of the language (Read 1934). From 1915 to 1938, Christian missionaries translated the Bible in Balti in a modified form of the Persian script (Rahman, K. 1973: 4). Later, Khalilul Rahman, himself a Balti speaker, wrote the first primer and grammar of the language in the Persian script (Rahman, K. 1973). In 1990, Muhammad Yusuf suggested further modifications to the script given in his primer, and gave a brief history of the script (Yusuf 1990: 29-38). However, even now, very few books are available in the new script. For lack of writing in Balti, and because it is ghettoizing, Urdu is preferred by the Baltis who consider it 'to be better than their own language; because of the wider possibility of social mobility in it' (Backstrom 1992a: 24). Urdu is learned in schools and through the electronic media. The fact that a language shift has been created is evidenced by the fact that Urdu words are much more in use in Balti than before (ibid. 24-5).

Wakhi, spoken by approximately 6,000 people in Pakistan, 7,000 in Afghanistan, and 12,000 in Tajikistan and China is a minor language even in the Northern Areas. It is mostly spoken in the following valleys: Gojal in Hunza, Ishkoman, Yasin and Yarkhan in Chitral (SSNP-2: 6¹-2). Apart from Lorimer's word list in the Roman script, there was no writing in Wakhi till the 1980s, when Haqiqat Ali wrote the first primer of the language in a modified form of the Roman script (Ali, H. n.d.). Ahmad Jami, however, devised a modified form of the Persian script and those who favour an indigenous or religious identity prefer it. In the 1980s, some Karachi-based students published a magazine entitled *Wakh* in the Persian Wakhi script. There is a Wakhi-Tajik Culture Association, first established by Haqiqat Ali and now headed by Ghulamuddin, which aims at developing the language and increasing its use. The PPP government (1993-1996) acceded to its old demand of giving time to Wakhi on the radio. The poetry of Mokhi Asmatullah and Amanullah Aman is also being published. These activities have made young people more serious about their language than before (Muzaffar, Q. November 1994). Thus, according to

Backstrom, Wakhi speakers who have a positive attitude towards their language, would like to educate their children in it; they read and write it and 'keep it in a pure form, without borrowing many words from other languages of wider communication like Urdu' (1992d: 73). However, for instrumental reasons, people are very keen to teach their children Urdu and English (Muzaffar, Q. November 1994).

Domaaki, the language of the Doma people in Mominabad (Hunza) and parts of Nagar and Gilgit, has only about 500 speakers. And these speakers have a negative attitude towards their language. According to Backstrom, 'No one expressed the least interest in developing their language, either for use in education or for literature. For these purposes, they far preferred Burushaski or Urdu' (Backstrom 1992c: 82).

Kohistani, spoken in Swat and Dir Kohistan as well as Indus Kohistan, is made up of various dialects. In Northern Swat and Dir, Kalami; in Bahrain (Swat), Torwali; and in Indus Kohistan, Kohiste or Mayan are spoken (Rensch 1992a: 5-6; Hallberg 1992b: 95-6). There are approximately 100,000 speakers of Kohistani (IFD 1984 and SSNP-1: 33). Although strongly influenced by Pashto, the speakers of these dialects have a positive attitude towards them. Rensch reports an alphabet of Kalami based on the Urdu script (1992a: 48). Shaheen, a local language planner, wrote Kalami without modifying the Urdu letters so that its distinctive sounds could not be represented (Shaheen 1989: 245). Baart showed the author a sample of Kalami written in a modified form of the Urdu alphabet, which he had made in collaboration with a local informant (Baart PC: 10 December 1994). There is said to be a local group dedicated to publishing literature in Torwali (Rensch 1992a: 62). A primer, using a modified form of the Persian script, has also been proposed for Torwali by Kareemi (1982). As for Indus Kohistani, Hallberg reports that 'almost every subject' wanted it to be used in local schools and to read books written in it. They did, however, appreciate the necessity of learning the languages of wider communication: Urdu and Pashto (Hallberg 1992b: 111). In short, although Kohistani is a symbol of identity (Rench 1992a: 62), there is also a widespread desire to learn other languages, especially Urdu, for utilitarian reasons.

**The Languages of Chitral**

According to Major W. Malleson, the compiler of a military report on Chitral, 'The Chitrali language, i.e., the language of the *Kho* [people], *war* meaning 'language' is the *lingua franca* of the Hindu Kush region and is understood by most of the leading men in Gilgit, but not by many persons in Hunza-Nagar' (Malleson 1904:173; also reported by Biddulph 1880: 62). Even nowadays, according to the sociolinguistic survey reports, it is the main language of the Chitral district, though there are Khowar speakers in the Gilgit district and pockets of immigrants in cities like Peshawar and Rawalpindi (Decker 1992 a: 32). When the British established their ascendancy over the Chitral state, its ruler, the Mehtar, used Persian as the official language. According to Malleson, 'Correspondence is conducted in Persian, but the people are practically illiterate' (1904:24). The idea that education could be a way of modernizing the people, to counteract the process of modernization in the USSR, Afghanistan, and even Swat, was rooted in a report of the Inspector of Vernacular Education, NWFP (August 1937). The Report goes on to say that the medium of instruction was discussed with the Mehtar and he agreed that 'Chitrali should be the medium of instruction in classes 1 and 2. In all other classes it should be Urdu. Persian, being the court language, should receive greater attention than it does in the NWFP' (Acc No. 772 in NDC). However, Khowar was not taught, possibly because of administrative difficulties. Nowadays, when there are many schools, the medium of instruction is Urdu but, since the teachers are generally locals, the explanation at the lower levels is often in Khowar (Decker 1992a: 39).

Because of this increase in education, exposure to the media, trade, travel, and service with the district administration and the militia (Chitral Scouts), many Chitralis know Urdu (Faizi 1986). According to the sociolinguistic survey's report:

> In Chitral District, men with some amount of education most commonly reported Urdu as their second language. In the areas outside of Chitral District there is some second language proficiency in the languages of their neighbours: Shina in Gilgit District, Kalami in Swat District, and Pashto in Peshawar (Decker 1992a: 42).

Traces of written literature date back to 1680 when Atalique Mohammad Shaheen Ghareeb wrote a few couplets in Khowar in his Persian collection of *ghazals*. He used the Persian *nastaleeq* script without modifying it, to express the distinctive Khowar sounds not found either in Persian or Arabic. It was, however, an individual effort, in fact, a literary curiosity and Khowar remained an unwritten language. In 1892, however, the British began to learn the language in pursuance of their policy of governing people through their languages.

Some of them, such as Captain D. J. T. O'Brien, made word lists in the Roman script in 1895 for this purpose (Sloan 1981: 20). Later, according to Inayatullah Faizi, Abdul Hakim Khan, an employee in the Political Agent's office, translated *Ganj-e-Pashto* in Khowar and used the Roman script to write it (Faizi Int: 27 July 1994). Nowadays, the most active proponent of the Roman script is Muhammad Ismail Sloan who has written a Khowar-English dictionary in which he describes his script (1981:22-36).

Most Chitrali language planners in Pakistan, however, stress the need to use a modified form of the Urdu script as it symbolizes the Islamic identity of Chitralis and is used in other Pakistani languages. Such a script was made in 1921 by Nasirul Mulk, the crown prince, and Mirza Muhammad Ghafran and it has been developing since then (Buddruss 1982: 17). A small book of verse and a primer were also written in an alternative script made by Wazir Khan. However, the one which is approved by the Anjuman-e-Taraqqi-e-Khowar (Association for the Promotion of Khowar) and which is used for its publications is based upon the Urdu script, with six modified letters to express the sounds of Khowar.

As mentioned earlier, it was part of imperial policy to encourage officers to learn the indigenous languages. Thus, the newly-posted British officers were required to learn Khowar within three months, otherwise an allowance, called the *gasht* allowance, would not be paid to them. A notification to this effect (No. 64, dated 18 April 1904) was issued by the Agent to the Governor-General and the Chief Commissioner of the NWFP and Khowar language examinations were held for Pakistani army officers serving in the Chitral Scouts even in the 1980s (see letters from Headquarters Frontier Corps in DC Chitral's office giving names of officers who passed these examinations from time to time). Like the British bureaucracy, the Pakistani bureaucracy was also aware of the political advantages of teaching Khowar to officers. A letter from the Secretary of Finance to the Secretary of Services and General Administration of the NWFP Government (3 September 1978) reads:

> Proficiency in local languages is an important requirement as otherwise such officers, not conversant with the local language, tend to be at a disadvantage in meeting the people, listening to their problems and explaining to them the Government policy in this behalf.

Thus, like their military counterparts, civilian bureaucrats too passed examinations and drew a 'language pay' (see letter No. 557, 27 March

1961 from the Additional Political Agent, Chitral to the Controller, Northern Areas West Pakistan, Peshawar in the office of the DC Chitral).

However, at present, neither military nor civilian officers in Chitral pass language examinations in Khowar (interviews of the DC Chitral and Commandant, Chitral Scouts with the author in August 1994). Military officers posted to the Frontier Corps are still given a *gasht* allowance and the *Guide for Officers* (n.d.) published by the Headquarters of the FC reads:

> The admissibility of gasht allowance consequent to acquisition of a working knowledge of Pashto has been made mandatory to enable officers to communicate and exercise effective command and control over troops (15).

The 'Joining Instructions' of officers also advise them to learn either Pashto or Khowar 'within three months' of arrival, but the orders concerning Khowar are no longer implemented.

The Anjuman-e-Taraqqi-e-Khowar points to the lack of official interest as a symptom of negligence. It appears, however, that the Anjuman is mistaken. Government functionaries, as we have noted, were not interested in Khowar for its intrinsic value but because it enabled them to exercise power more effectively. This basic policy has not been abandoned in theory, though there are times when individual officials do not seem to enforce it.

The government has never invested much money in Khowar, nor has it promoted it in the domains in which Urdu or English are used. In order to appease the local intelligentsia, however, some time was given to it in radio broadcasts from 1965 onwards. This has since been increased but no time is given on television (Faizi Int: 27 July 1994). In 1967, the Border Publicity Organization of the Ministry of Information started publishing the *Jamhoor-e-Islam*, a Pashto magazine, though it contained a section in Khowar also. In 1969, it became a Khowar-only magazine—the first of its kind to be published. The Chitral Students Association of the University of Peshawar also published an annual magazine called *Tirich Mir*, so as to introduce Khowar outside Chitral (Hasrat 1987: 114-9). The former has been closed down but the latter continues to date.

The Anjuman holds poetry sessions, conferences on language and culture (1987, 1988, 1992, and in 1995) and publishes books (Chughtai Int. 30 July 1994). It has offices in Chitral, Drosh, and Booni, and depends entirely on volunteers. According to its President, Inayatullah

Faizi, the government has not acceded to their demand for establishing a Khowar Adabi Board, nor is the language taught even in the primary classes. However, the Anjuman has published about twenty-six books and pamphlets in Khowar and provides a platform for writers and poets to come together. Its most important achievement, according to Faizi, is that it has given people pride in their language. Earlier, people would talk of doing away with Khowar, but now they are conscious that it is a symbol of their identity. It is this connection with ethnicity which the religious parties (JI, JUI, etc.) deplore. On the other extreme, some supporters of Khowar want to change non-Khowar titles like *Jamhoor-e-Islam* to Khowar ones (Faizi Int). Such views fall within the established pattern of ethnic politics in Pakistan: the rightists oppose ethnic languages; the ethno-nationalists support them. However, the Khowar-speaking members of the intelligentsia do not oppose Urdu (Faizi 1986: 9-15), though they do want their mother tongue to be used more extensively, so that it does not die out with the coming of modernization through Urdu and English.

The other languages of Chitral include Yidgha (5,000-6,000 speakers); Phalura (8,600): Dameli (5,000): Kalasha (2,900-5,700): and Eastern Kativiri (3,700-5,100) (Decker 1992 b: 11). Yidgha is spoken in the Lutkoh Valley of Western Chitral; Phalura near Drosh in Southern Chitral; Dameli south of Drosh in the Damel Valley; Eastern Kativiri at the far western ends of the Lutkoh, Rumbur, and Bumboret valleys. According to Decker, these languages are being preserved, though speakers of Phalura generally use Khowar, Pashto, and Urdu outside their own speech community. In general, the speakers of these very minor languages are positive towards them (Decker 1992 b). However, the case of the Kalasha speakers is different. They are not Muslims—that is why the negative term *kafir* (unbeliever) is used for them—being the followers of a pre-Islamic religion. Those who convert to Islam, however, also abandon their language and start using Khowar, the language of Chitrali Muslims, even within the family. However, 'some individual families in the Bumboret Valley who have converted still speak Kalasha' (Decker 1992 b: 109). Some people are interested in maintaining the language as part of the traditional non-Muslim Kalasha identity. It is reportedly taught in a primary school and 'a script has been developed for writing' it (Decker 1992 b: 112). Although the Muslim Kalasha speakers do use the language, it is associated with the traditional non-Muslim identity and they show little desire to maintain it (ibid. 113-4).

A parallel with Domaaki comes to mind here. In both cases the speakers of the language are keen to abandon it in order to be incorporated into a bigger, more prestigious community. The reason why they do not consolidate themselves as a pressure group using language as a symbol of solidarity may be because their community is generally pre-modern, illiterate, far too small in size, and too remote to gain power.

## Kashmiri

Kashmiri is a Dardic language spoken by the majority of the people of the Vale of Kashmir which is at present occupied by India. There are pockets of Kashmiri-speaking people in Azad Kashmir and elsewhere in Pakistan. According to a survey carried out by Yakubul Hasan, most of them are gradually shifting to other languages such as the local Pahari and Mirpuri which are dialects of Punjabi (Hasan 1991: 62). Most literate people use Urdu since, in both Azad and Indian-held Kashmir, Urdu rather than Kashmiri is the official language of government. According to a survey of the use of Kashmiri in Indian Kashmir by Rakesh Mohan, the 'Kashmiri language does not inspire favourable attitudes for functional attributes like "prestigious", "literary" and "useful for social gains" (Mohan 1989: 79). As social mobility is possible in English, Hindi, and Urdu—in that order—these results are understandable. Kashmiri Muslims have seen Urdu rather than Kashmiri as their identity symbol. The latter is written in the Sharda script by Kashmiri Hindus, while the Muslims write it in the Persian script. In the 1970s, under pressure from some Kashmiri writers, the government agreed to teach the language in schools and established a Cultural Academy and a department of Kashmiri at the University (Kishwar 1994: 4). Even after the anti-India movement started and Islam and the Kashmiri identity became its major symbols, language has not been stressed for identity purposes by any anti-Indian group (Kishwar 82).

In Pakistan, the Kashmiri-speaking community has been far too scattered and ineffective to organize a language movement. Individual members of it however, blame the government for neglecting their language (Hasan 1991: 30-61). They want it to be taught in schools and given more time in the media (Hasan 1991: 87-91; Jafri 1990). Decision-makers in Azad Kashmir are either Punjabi bureaucrats or locals who speak dialects of Punjabi. Thus, it is only for propaganda reasons that they pretend to patronize Kashmiri. One such effort was the setting up of the Kashmiri Language Committee in 1983. It was supposed to prepare courses in Kashmiri for classes 6 to 8 (Aziz 1983). However, as the Kashmiri speakers are scattered over a large area, the project failed to take off. Thus, in the words of Mir Abdul Aziz, a writer on Kashmir affairs, Kashmiri remains a 'stranger in its own country' (Aziz 1988). The fact, however, is that Kashmiri's 'own country' is not Azad Kashmir but the Vale of Kashmir which is occupied by India. If the Vale joins Pakistan or attains independence, Kashmiri would have a brighter chance of coming into its own. But that is a matter of speculation.

To sum up, language plays an important role in self-definition even in the case of linguistic minorities. However, purely local or tribal perceptions of identity are superseded by linguistic ones, when an intelligentsia develops scripts, begins the dissemination of the printed word in a language, and seeks to establish supra local solidarities. This process does not always follow a fixed pattern. Whereas this is the pattern in the case of the Hindko, Shina, Burushaski, and Khowar-speaking people, it is not in evidence among Gujrati speakers. The affluent Gujrati speakers are concerned with the instrumental advantages of becoming literate in languages of wider communication (LWCs) rather than their own, perhaps because, being affluent, they feel less threatened by the speakers of other languages. In fact, all speakers of minor languages, even in those in which language movements are going on, tend to accept LWCs (especially Urdu) much more enthusiastically than larger linguistic groups. Perhaps they feel that their language is ghettoizing since, even if their languages were used in certain domains, the small numbers of the communities would never allow them to become nationally important. Thus, the political advantages of forming a pressure group defined by language are non-existent or of little practical significance. Hence, the speakers of minor languages, rather than using their language to gain political and economic power, use it to preserve their identity, to avoid becoming deracinated, and to save themselves from becoming mere cyphers, under the onslaught of modernity.

### Notes

1. The figures for Gujrati-speaking people are not given anywhere. In his letter to the editor of *Jasarat* about Gujrati, Abdul Sattar Edhi gives a figure of 200,000 (11 November 1982). However, the census report (1981) of the Karachi division gives a figure of 87,707 households for the speakers of languages other than Urdu, Punjabi, Pashto, Sindhi, Balochi, Brahvi, Hindko, and Siraiki. On the assumption that 2,707 households speak the languages of Chitral, Swat, and the Northern Areas, Bengali, Persian, and English, the remaining 85,000 households speak Gujrati. If there are on average 8 persons per household, the number of Gujrati speakers in Karachi comes to 680,000.

# 13

# The Urdu-English Controversy

The English-vernacular controversy in pre-partition India took the form of the Urdu-English, or medium of instruction controversy in Pakistan. Essentially, the position in support of English is that it is used in the domains of power and is an international language. Thus, its use facilitates access to positions of power in Pakistan and abroad. This is why it is thriving in Pakistan and efforts are being made to improve its teaching (Abbas 1993). This situation is not unfamiliar in the former colonies of European powers. Let us look at the pattern of retention of the colonial language in some of the ex-colonies before discussing Pakistan.

**The Post-Colonial Situation**

In Kenya, the elite use English as a status symbol and in order to preserve its privileges (Harries 1983: 123-4). Such explanations have also been given for the retention of English in Ghana (Apronti 1974: 1), Nigeria (Emenyonu 1989: 88), the Philippines (Tollefson 1986: 177-98), and other ex-colonies.

The situation, however, is complex and varies from country to country in such a way that generalizations cannot be made. For instance, the ruling elites often want to stress authenticity and national identity for which an indigenous language would seem necessary. However, this comes into conflict with the desire for modernization, efficiency, and retention of a privileged status, for which the ex-colonial language is more important. Although Japan and Korea, to give two outstanding examples, carried out their modernization in their indigenous languages, such facts are ignored by westernized elites for their own interests. Thus, the ex-French Arab countries—Algeria, Tunisia, and Morocco in the Maghrib—are torn between Arabic and French (Gallagher 1968). In the Lebanon too, the ruling elite manifests contradictory aspirations (Wardaugh 1987: 186-90; Gordon 1985: 148).

In some countries, favouring any one indigenous language would privilege an ethnic group and hence lead to the intensification or rise of ethnicity (Wardaugh 1987: 164). In Nigeria, for instance, the major languages—Hausa, Igbo, and Yoruba—are associated with competing ethnic groups, and showing preference for one would create divisiveness in the country (Paden 1968: 199-213). In Ethiopia, Haile Sellasie's policy of privileging Amharic led to resistance from Ormo, Tigrinya, and Somali language groups (Bender 1985: 277). In the Cameroon, there are about 100 languages for more than 5 million people (Alexandre 1968: 120-1). It would be practically impossible to standardize all the languages, after making them the languages of governance and education (Todd 1983: 167-8). However, indigenous languages are given symbolic significance so that equilibrium is achieved. Such, indeed, is the 3 + 1 language policy of Ghana and India, in which English, a national language, and the mother tongue are taught to children (Laitin and Mensah 1991; Laitin 1988).

Only in a very few countries have the indigenous languages actually been privileged. One noteworthy case is the promotion of Swahili, mother tongue of only 10 per cent of the people, as the national language of Tanzania. It was acceptable to all the tribes, because it expressed anti-British sentiment and was not the language of any one tribe. It was used, therefore, as the 'language of national unity' by the ruling elite after independence in 1961 (Whiteley 1968: 331). In Indonesia too, the dominant Javanese used neither Dutch nor Javanese, but *Bahasa Melau*, or Indonesian as it is called, as a national language. This paradox is explained by Anderson who argues that Javanese was a rigid, formal, hierarchical, status-sensitive language, and because of this, it was unsuitable for the democratic and egalitarian aspirations of the anti-colonial Indonesian revolutionaries, who therefore chose to promote Indonesian, instead of Dutch and Javanese (Anderson 1990: 207). But since the Javanese use Indonesian, they do not thereby stand to lose power.

Sometimes, the ex-colonial language is reduced in status, in the interests of a powerful pressure group in the society. In Malaysia, for instance, where Malay (Bahasa Malaysia) was made the national language and the language of education after independence in 1957, it was the Chinese and not the Malay community which was more proficient in English. Thus, the privileging of Malay was a way of facilitating social mobility for the Malays (Mauzy 1985: 172; Watson 1983: 135).

Even in countries where indigenous languages are used in the domains of power, the ex-colonial one, mostly English, is the LWC. In this capacity, it facilitates access to science and technology and brings about modernization. However, as English is also the vehicle of Western culture, this dominance of English is described as linguistic and cultural imperialism (Phillipson 1992). Thus, at the international level, and even at the national one, English provides social mobility. It gives access to power and knowledge: it opens doors.

In some respects, the indigenous language is ghettoizing. To some extent such a situation exists in most Third World countries, especially those with strong links with English or French-speaking countries. Most of the literate inhabitants of these countries are drawn towards the privileged ex-colonial language, because it is an upper-class status-marker, and facilitates, or at least gives hope of, moving into the national or even the cosmopolitan elite. Even where the national language is supported as the emotional and rhetorical language, the possibility of moving into these elites is attractive. In the Philippines, for instance, the ordinary Filipino is drawn towards English because he wants his children to share in 'the good life' which 'is accessible, at present, through English' (Sibayan 1983: 94; also see Miller 1981).

**Urdu in the 1950s**

As we have seen earlier, Urdu was invested with special emotional significance by the founding fathers of Pakistan because it was part of the drive for Muslim separatism up to 1947. It was also symbolic of the Pakistani Muslim identity in the making. As the central government, dominated by Punjabis and Mohajirs, was most interested in creating this identity, so as to extend its power base over all the multilingual federating units and to prevent the rise of separatist ethnicity, the ruling elite at the Centre supported Urdu at the rhetorical level. Thus, questions were often asked in the Punjab Legislative Assembly as to what steps had been taken to popularize Urdu (LAD- Pun 1932: 628).

It was in the Punjab too that Sardar Abdur Rab Nishtar, the Governor, set up an Official Language Committee in 1949 for devising terms which would replace English ones in the official domains. This language planning initiative was also part of the ruling elite's general policy of appearing to support Urdu. Other such steps were the creation of the Chairs for Urdu in the universities of Malaya and Tehran (ABE 1955: 41); financial assistance to the Anjuman-e-Taraqqi-e-Urdu to the tune of Rs 20,000 in 1948-49 and Rs 50,000 in 1950-51; and promises to change the medium of instruction at all levels from English to Urdu. Moreover, courts of law, the provincial legislature, and some offices were ordered to conduct their work in Urdu (LAD-Pun 18 December 1952: 629; 25 February 1954: 240). However, at this time, only one office, the one creating Urdu terms for official use, actually functioned in Urdu (LAD-Pun 31 March 1955: 1228).

The first meeting of the Advisory Board of Education (7-9 June 1948) agreed that 'the mother-tongue should be the medium of instruction at the primary stage' (ABE 1948: 4), but left the question of the place of English to be determined by the Inter-University Board. In the second meeting, a committee was formed to develop Urdu—another LP initiative (ABE 1949: 25-7)—and was given the task of formulating a policy to replace English by Urdu in the universities (ABE 1949: 27). The Committee recommended, that Urdu should be used as the medium of instruction at the secondary stage from 1952 (ABE 1955: 220). The Inter-University Board had also agreed that 'English should cease to be the medium of instruction at the University stage' (ABE 1955: 261). However, the question whether 'selected schools (including Pre-Cadet Schools) be permitted to run parallel classes with English as the medium of instruction', posed by the fifth meeting of the Advisory Board (4-5 March 1953 in ABE 1955: 262), remained unanswered. In fact it was in contradiction of the government's professed desire to replace English with Urdu. These schools not only remained but they multiplied. For instance, the government spent Rs 4,000,000 in establishing a pre-cadet college at Chittagong to prepare students for 'commissions in the Armed Forces and the higher appointments in the Civil Services' (ABE 1958: 58).

Meanwhile, language planning activities in Urdu went on with great speed. In 1950, the Secretary of the Punjab Government's Official Language Committee reported that 2,284 new terms had been created (ABE 1955: 208-9), while in 1955, this number had reached 7,674 (LAD-Pun 31 March 1955: 1225). The Anjuman also gave a historical review of available work on this subject (ABE 1955: 45-85) and a list of publications, mostly on scientific subjects, in Urdu translation (ABE 1955: 81-142; for another such list see LAD-Pun 31 March 1955: 1225-7). The Majlis-e-Tarjuma (Society for Translation), working under the Punjab government in Lahore from 1950, translated and published 27 books in Urdu (Abdullah 1976: 210). The West Pakistan Urdu Academy, the brainchild of Syed Muhammad Abdullah, a leader of the Urdu lobby, was formed in 1955. Its major objective was the promotion of the teaching of science in Urdu (Sabir, A. 1985: 36-8). Other institutions for the promotion of Urdu are listed in Ayub Sabir's book on this subject (1985). A number of institutions, especially the

Urdu Science Board and the National Language Authority (Muqtadira Qaumi Zaban) kept coining new technical terms and published several glossaries (USB 1984; Durrani 1993: 24-68). At present, according to an estimate, there are about 250,000 technical terms in Urdu and more are being coined (Durrani 1993).

Despite the efforts of the Urdu proto-elite to promote the use of Urdu and the ruling elite's apparent support of these efforts, it was English which continued to be dominant till the end of the fifties, when democratic experimentation was replaced by General Ayub Khan's martial law. As we have seen, by 1956, Bengali was one of the national languages of Pakistan. Hence, the emphasis on Urdu was temporarily decreased in official rhetoric. Moreover, the expanding middle class found that their best chance of acquiring power, social prestige, and affluence was by joining the superior civil services, the officer cadre of the armed forces, or the professions. In all these, and especially the first two, English was crucial. Schools like Aitchison College (Lahore), Burn Hall (Abbottabad), and the numerous missionary schools catered for the children of the feudal lords, bureaucrats, and military officers, as well as other affluent people. The armed forces also started developing their own schools—cadet colleges and the PAF Model Schools—to cater for the children of their officers, who could thus get elitist English-medium schooling while spending less of their own money than their civilian counterparts. In other words, the elite of wealth (feudal and tribal lords; business magnates, etc.) and the elite of power (the military and the bureaucracy) made arrangements to facilitate the entry of their children into the same stratum of society by promoting elitist schooling, while professing to create equal opportunities for all through vernacularization.

**English in the Ayub Khan Era**

Ayub Khan was a Sandhurst-educated officer, who believed in the superiority of the army over politicians and in the rule of an elite in the country. He believed that this elite could be created in the English-medium schools. As the General Officer Commanding in East Pakistan, he urged the provincial government 'to start good public schools where intelligent young men' could be trained. With his usual contempt for politicians and their political constraints, he wrote that Khwaja Nazimuddin and Nurul Amin:

Seemed to understand what I was talking about but were unwilling or unable to do anything about it. I never quite understood what they were afraid of. Perhaps they thought that general reaction to the establishment of public schools would not be favourable (Khan, A. 1967: 25).

As Commander-in-Chief of the Army, he established 'a number of cadet colleges and academies' to train those who would one day administer the country (ibid. 43). As the armed forces encouraged the use of English even at the cost of all Pakistani languages—in fact the use of vernaculars was not allowed in the training institutions of the officer corps[1]—their officers picked up confidence and fluency in the language. Thus, in a report which was not made public, the army reported that the language of its internal use, at least among the officers, would have to remain English.[2]

As we have seen before, the other powerful partner of the army during the Ayub regime, the Civil Service of Pakistan (CSP), was not only traditionally anglicized, like the army, but had a larger number of people from the westernized elite in it.

Thus, despite the increased activities of the Urdu proto-elite which will be mentioned later, the government of Ayub Khan was more openly pro-English in its policies than governments up to 1958, when the politicians had to defer more often to public sentiment than was now necessary.

## The Sharif Commission Report

The Sharif Commission, whose report has been mentioned earlier, declared that both Urdu and Bengali would be the medium of instruction from class 6 onwards in the non-elitist schools. While this adversely affected the position of Sindhi, which was the medium of instruction in Sindhi non-elitist schools, as we have seen already, it had no effect on English. The English schools were defended as follows:

> While we feel that English must yield to the national languages the paramount position that it has occupied in our educational system so far, we are at the same time convinced that English should have a permanent place in that system (Edn Comm 1959: 288).

This attitude was criticized by the leaders of the Urdu proto-elite (Abdullah 1976: 59), although most of the criticism against it came from the supporters of the older indigenous languages (see Adil 1962;

Ahmad, S. 1968: 3; and editorial of *Mehran*, 31 October 1962 for Sindhi).

## The Hamoodur Rahman Report

The Commission on students' welfare and problems, generally called the Hamoodur Rahman Commission, was even more defensive of English than the Sharif Commission. Although it was constituted in response to student resistance to some of the recommendations of the Sharif Commission, it went out of its way to criticize the universities which had adopted Urdu as the medium of examination for the BA degree, a step which was popular with the large majority of students who came from the Urdu-medium schools and had average ability.[3] The Report said:

> We cannot help regretting that some of our universities should have preferred to be swayed more by sentiment than by a dispassionate judgment in accelerating the pace of changeover [to Urdu] beyond all reasonable proportion (RCSP 1966: 114).

The universities which were singled out were the Karachi University (which had allowed Urdu in 1963), Punjab University (in 1966), and the Sindh University (which had allowed Sindhi) (RCSP 1966: 114).

During the sixties, however, there was much criticism of English-medium elitist schools. In 1965, the government reported that it gave grant-in-aid, directly or through local bodies, to a number of such schools. The list provided in the West Pakistan Legislative Assembly consisted of 19 public schools, to which Rs 2,477,285 had been given in 1964-65, and on whose governing bodies there were 73 senior civil and military officers (LAD-WP 5 July 1965: Appendix 111, Question 529). There was some protest against Lahore Corporation's donation of Rs 1,000,000 to the Divisional Public School, whereas the corporation's own schools were in an impecunious condition. However, nothing was done to make amends, and a motion concerning this was not even allowed to be moved in the provincial legislature (LAD-WP 25 January 1965: 67-8).

The Commission, however, defended these schools—the missionary ones on grounds of religious freedom for Christians; and others on the grounds of excellence (RCSP 1966: 17-8). Disagreeing with the view that such schools produced snobs, the Commission took the paradoxical plea that they were meant to produce the military and civilian administrative elite. It declared that:

Such establishments are intended to produce some better type of students who would be more suitably disciplined and equipped for eventually entering the defence service of the country or filling higher administrative posts and other responsible executive positions in the government and semi-government bodies and private firms and corporations (RCSP 1966: 18).

The Commission did, however, agree that the existence of such schools violated the constitutional assurance that 'all citizens are equal before law' (Paragraph 15 under Right No. VI) and even recommended that the government 'should not build such schools any more' (RCSP 1966: 18). However, it stopped short of making any change in the status quo and recommended that the existing schools be allowed to continue and poor students be given scholarships to study in them (RCSP 1966: 18). Thus, despite the criticism levelled by students—such as the All-Pakistan Students Convention held at Lahore in 1966—against elitist schools (Abdullah 1976: 184), these schools continued to thrive during the Ayub Khan era.

In 1963, Allama Rahmatullah Arshad, and later Khwaja Muhammad Safdar, presented the West Pakistan National Language Bill demanding that Urdu be used as the official language instead of English. The Bill was sent to the commissioners of divisions and to heads of several educational institutions for comments. Although everyone agreed that Urdu should replace English in principle, not everyone felt that it could be done without adequate translation and planning (Zulfiqar and Akhtar 1986: 117-22; Abdullah 1976: 66-79). In a session of the National Assembly, Khurshid Ahmad, the Minister for Education, said that language planning was necessary to modernize Urdu and that the government had established two boards for this purpose at Lahore and Dhaka for Urdu and Bengali respectively. The actual replacement was shelved as follows:

> I would like to say that in the year 1972 the President shall constitute a commission to examine the report on the question of the replacement of English language for official purposes (LAD-P 8 Aug 1964: 465).

After this, the question was postponed for another decade.

The Urdu lobby was very active during the sixties, possibly because of Ayub Khan's pro-English bias. What was perhaps the first confrontation with the regime occurred when Ayub Khan suggested the adoption of the Roman script for writing both Urdu and Bengali, a suggestion which has been mentioned in the context of the Bengali language movement earlier (Khan, A. 1967: 85).

The issue of the script had been connected with the Islamic identity since the pre-partition Urdu-Hindi controversy days. In fact, all attempts at changing the Perso-Arabic Urdu script to either Roman or Devanagari had been regarded as anti-Islamic conspiracies (Barelvi 1989 and other articles in Majeed 1989). Thus, there was a sharp reaction to this proposal. Two meetings in Lahore took place, on the issue of the script, and Maulvi Salahuddin Ahmad declared that 'those who change the Quranic script will have to go over our dead bodies' (Abdullah 1976: 57). However, the Maulvi later appreciated Ayub Khan for having withdrawn this proposal (Ahmad, S. 1989: 362). The appeal to religious sentiment was not arbitrary. The Urdu proto-elite had always evoked religion along with Urdu as the integrative bonds of the country (after 1956, of West Pakistan) and the mainstay of the Pakistani identity. The linking of Islam and Urdu was to become more pronounced later, though the army, which at this period stood for westernization, was to change its own image during Ziaul Haq's martial law.

In 1961, there was a movement for replacing signboards written in English with Urdu ones (*PT* 21 February 1961). Greeting cards, visiting cards, and the number plates of cars were changed to Urdu. Syed Abdullah even walked out of a meeting in protest at its being conducted in English (Abdullah 1976: 145). The West Pakistan Youth Movement, which had been in existence since 1953, became active in support of Urdu and collected signatures in support of a change in the medium of instruction in the Punjab University to Urdu (Abdullah 1976: 183). Urdu conferences were held every year and processions were brought out, demanding that Urdu should replace English in every domain of life (Abdullah 1976: 144-9). Despite all this activity, the situation at the end of Ayub Khan's rule in 1969 was far from satisfactory, from the Urdu lobby's point of view. It was true that Urdu was compulsory in all schools up to matriculation and even at the intermediate level. The West Pakistan Urdu Academy, the Central Urdu Board, and the Majlis Taraqqi-i-Adab, (society for the advancement of literature) Lahore, were functioning; and the President delivered his monthly broadcasts to the nation in Urdu. However, these were merely cosmetic changes because entry to the most prestigious jobs was still facilitated by English. As for entry to the select circle of the fashionable and the sophisticated, which was in the process of moving to Islamabad from Karachi, it was impossible without fluency in English. The most committed members of the Urdu proto-elite, especially those who were also committed to Islam, opposed Ayub Khan in the disturbances against him in 1969 and waited for the changes which General Yahya Khan's government would bring about.

## Nur Khan's Radical Proposals

The proposals of Nur Khan, which have been mentioned earlier, stirred up much controversy. For the first time, an official document acknowledged the fact that there was 'almost a caste-like distinction between those who feel at ease in expressing themselves in English and those who do not' (PNEP 1969: 14). Moreover, it asserted that:

> Not only does the use of English as the medium of instruction at higher levels perpetuate the gulf between the rulers and the ruled, it also perpetuates the advantages of those children who come from the well-to-do families, (PNEP 1969: 3).

The perpetuation of the 'barriers of privilege', it was opined, was inextricably linked with English, the 'cadet colleges etc.' (PNEP 1969: 3; 15-6). Therefore, the following rather bold proposals were put forward:

1. The medium of instruction at all levels of education should be changed to Bengali in East and Urdu in West Pakistan.

2. The official languages of the provincial governments should be changed to Bengali and Urdu respectively by 1974. Both these languages should be brought into official use at the Centre by 1975.

3. Admission to cadet colleges should be made purely on merit and all those who cannot otherwise afford them should be offered full scholarships, including all living expenses.

4. 25 per cent of the admissions to private institutions which charge fees of Rs 30 per month or more should be on merit with free education for those who cannot otherwise afford them (PNEP 1969: 17).

The proposals were not radical in the real sense of the word, because the elitist schools were not to be abolished nor were the proto-elites of the provinces, who identified themselves with the indigenous languages in the Western wing, satisfied. However, after Ayub Khan's open elitism, the Urdu lobby regarded them as radical. The Urdu Academy of Lahore endorsed the proposals, and the leaders of the Urdu lobby showed their approbation (Abdullah 83). The supporters of the indigenous languages, especially those of Sindhi and Punjabi, opposed these proposals as we have seen.

Whether because of this opposition or because of the covert resistance of the westernized elite, the published version of the *New Education Policy* (1970) left the task of examining 'the question of the change over from English to the national languages' to a commission which would be established in 1972 (NEP 1970: 19). The egalitarian proposals were also withdrawn and a vaguely pious cliche, that it 'is important to safeguard against the division of society into several segments by ensuring equal access to educational opportunity' (NEP 1970: 2) was substituted instead. Thus, the incipient radicalism of Nur Khan was reversed as the status quo asserted itself. In the December 1970 elections, however, the people, opposing injustice, voted for political parties which promised to bring about social change. In West Pakistan, they voted for Zulfikar Ali Bhutto's PPP which promised them '*roti, kapra, aur makan*' (food, clothing, and shelter): in short, Islamic socialism.

### English Survives Bhutto's 'Socialism'

As the dethronement of English was an anti-elitist policy, it is not apparent at once why Bhutto did not enforce it. However, Urdu was supported by Bhutto's political enemies. In Balochistan and the NWFP, as we have seen, the NAP-JUI ruling parties opted for Urdu as the official language in 1972. In the Punjab, the Islamicists, especially those connected with the Jamaat-i-Islami, were more enthusiastic about Urdu than any other language. Thus, Bhutto found himself unable or unwilling to do away with English. Meanwhile, the Urdu lobby held several yearly Urdu conferences and the question of Urdu being made the national language of the country was raised in the National Assembly several times (LAD-P of 15 April 1972; 17, 30, 31 August 1972; 4, 7 April and 15 July 1975; 6 November 1975; 3 March 1976). Maulana Abdul Mustafa al-Zahri even objected to Abdul Hafeez Pirzada, a powerful minister of the PPP, making a speech in English (LAD-P 17 August 1972: 71). On 31 August 1972, Maulana Ghulam Ghaus, a member of the opposition, moved the 'Official Language Bill 1972' (LAD-P 1: 15, 31 August 1972: 743-4). This Bill went before a standing committee in 1975 (LAD-P 6 November 1975: 364) and had not been disposed of even in 1976, when Bhutto's government was about to come to an end (LAD-P 3 March 1976: 170).

The only concrete step the government did take was to give symbolic recognition to Urdu as the national language of the country in the 1973 Constitution. Article 251 said:

(1) The National Language of Pakistan is Urdu, and arrangements shall be made for its being used for official and other purposes within fifteen years from the commencing day.

(2) Subject to clause (1) the English language may be used for official purposes until arrangements are made for its replacement by Urdu.

English had got another fifteen-year reprieve. Meanwhile, Bhutto moved away from socialist egalitarianism (Wolpert 1993: 240-5) and thus from the only possible motive which may have encouraged him to introduce Urdu, or Urdu alongside the older indigenous languages, in the place of English. To please the Urdu proto-elite, he would have had to do away with elitist English schools and alienate the westernized elite. Such a policy would have also alienated the Sindhi, Balochi, Pakhtun, and Punjabi ethno-nationalist lobbies who were already fighting against the regime. Moreover, the Urdu lobby, which was opposed to Bhutto, was only loosely aligned to the religious right-wing parties and was not always part of them. As Islam had by far the greatest appeal for the strong religious lobby, Bhutto chose to placate it by announcing cosmetic Islamic measures rather than opting for the less emotive but more controversial strategy of giving Urdu the place of English.

Thus, despite the efforts at developing the technical vocabulary of Urdu (Abdullah 1976: 187-278); the Urdu conferences under the auspices of the Anjuman (Abdullah 1976: 110-34; Zulfiqar and Akhtar 1986: 327-45); and the identification of Urdu with Pakistani nationalism—the 1976 conference was named after the Quaid-i-Azam and that of 1977 after Allama Iqbal—the Urdu lobby did not succeed in improving the status of the language in the country. One thing was, however, more evident than ever before: the Urdu proto-elite identified with the religious right wing while the ethno-nationalistic proto-elites and the westernized elite were left of centre, being inclined towards socialism or liberalism. The fortunes of Urdu would from now on be connected more closely than ever before with the struggle between the religious and the secular strands of thought in Pakistani politics.

## Use of Urdu in Support of Martial Rule

General Ziaul Haq came from an urban lower middle class background, and, like most people of his class, had great emotional attachment to a non-mystic interpretation of Islam, which emphasized rituals, Puritanism, and a strict enforcement of the *shariat* (Azzam 1990: 1-3). Like many other members of this class, he was also attracted to Urdu. Islam and Urdu were the symbols which would legitimize his rule in the eyes of the religious parties, the Urdu proto-elite, the urban middle class, and the lower middle class in general.

Urdu, which had always been a part of the ruling elite's centrist ideology, was now exploited by the regime for its symbolic value. A Study Group on the Teaching of Languages, set up by Ziaul Haq, recommended that 'Arabic, a major symbol of Islam, should be taught as a compulsory subject from the earliest stage of schooling and should continue to be taught as such till the secondary stage' (UGC 1982: 15). It also asserted that 'a primary goal is that all Pakistani citizens should learn Urdu as a basic language', while leaving what it called the 'regional languages' for 'informal communication' (ibid. 14).

This cavalier dismissal of the indigenous languages was criticized in a note of dissent by Kemal A. Faruki, one of the members of the Study Group, who pointed out that this 'arrogant indifference to other people's sentiments and opinions has cost, and will continue to cost this country dearly' (UGC 99). However, the General went ahead with his Islamization and Urduization. In April 1978, he ordered that all official speeches should be made in Urdu (*PT* 17 April 1978). By the end of 1979, Urdu was being used in many offices of the Punjab (*PT* 8 October and 9 December 1978). In 1979, the National Language Authority (Muqtadira Qaumi Zaban, henceforth Muqtadira) was constituted:

> To consider ways and means for the promotion of Urdu as the national language of Pakistan and to make all necessary arrangements in this regard (Resolution 1979: 2).

The first chairman of the Muqtadira was I. H. Qureshi, one of the leaders of the pro-Urdu group in the Sindhi-Urdu controversy of 1972. Other supporters of Urdu were also against ethno-nationalism and, in their support of the military regime's Urdu policy, they even abandoned democratic norms. Thus, Ziaul Haq was declared the 'Patron of Urdu' by 100 organizations working with the Anjuman-i-Tahreeq-i-Urdu

(*PT* 13 April 1980). Moreover, in the two-day Annual Urdu Conference at Lahore (27-8 November 1981), the Urdu lobby demanded that Urdu should be imposed through a presidential ordinance (*PT* 28 November 1981).

Organizations like the Majlis Zaban-e-Daftari launched personal contact drives to make Urdu acceptable in official domains. However, as they were dominated by people with known rightist views—like Wahab Khairi, who had been sympathetic to the Jamaat and Brigadier Gulzar, whose passion for Islam and anti-communism were noted in a humorous biographical sketch by Zamir Jafri (1983: 64), they supported the rule of Ziaul Haq rather than the PPP brand of socialism or any Western idea of social justice. Thus, although the idea of doing away with the privilege of the English-speaking elite might have been considered an anti-elitist policy in other circumstances, it did not gain support among Pakistani leftists and liberals because Urdu was now associated with authoritarian rule and rightist views.

The most significant anti-English policy of Ziaul Haq was the order that Urdu would be the medium of instruction in all schools from 'class 1 or K. G. as the case may be from 1979' (*PT* 4 February 1979). Thus, all students appearing in the matriculation examination in 1989 would use only Urdu. Moreover, the Ministry of Education also said that the nomenclature 'English medium' schools would be abolished (*D* 18 February 1987). It was reported that several schools did adopt Urdu as the medium of instruction from class 1 and 2 (*D* 24 November 1980). Visible resistance came from the parents whose children studied in English-medium schools, and who were confronted with a change of language about which they had serious misgivings. Among these were the parents of the Badin PAF Model School (*D* 6 August 1986) and other parents (*MN* 15 December 1989 and *M* 19 April 1984). Some English language dailies also wrote editorials in favour of retaining English in the school system (*PT* 19 December 1986; *N* 22 February and 31 August 1987; *MN* 13 March 1980). The major argument of the English lobby was that Pakistan would fall behind other countries if English was abandoned (Ahmad, S. 1987; Letters to the Editor, *MN* 5 December 1980; 8 December 1980). To this, the Urdu lobby replied that sufficient books did exist in Urdu and more could be translated. Since parents preferred to teach the language of the domains of power, the Urdu lobby also recommended that all competitive examinations for government service be conducted in Urdu (*D* 28 December 1981).

However, the elitist schools continued to exist; indeed, they proliferated. By this time, however, most observers felt that the government was not sincere in its policy. An editorial of *The Muslim* (13 May 1987) voiced public opinion by reporting unofficial rumours which suggested that English would be allowed to continue. One minister in the government, Nasim Aheer, stated that Urdu was not fully developed and that the decision to eliminate English had been taken in a hurry (Editorial *M* 20 May 1987). Syed Sajjad Hyder, the Minister for Education, defended Urdu very strongly (*PT* 6 October 1987), although a press conference had been held earlier which proposed that the changeover to Urdu, due in 1988, be postponed (*NW* 13 September 1987; see editorials of *PT* 16 September 1987 and *M* 14 September 1987). The real change in policy occurred in 1983 when Ziaul Haq gave legal protection to the elitist English schools by allowing them to prepare students for the 'O' and 'A' levels examinations of the University of Cambridge through MLR 115 (*PT* 6 October 1987). On 28 October, *the Pakistan Times* reported:

> The Federal Ministry of Education has decided to continue the existing practice of allowing English as medium of instruction in the science subjects besides Urdu or provincial language in all the secondary schools of the country.

On 11 October, General Ziaul Haq himself allayed the fears of the English lobby by declaring that English could not be abandoned altogether (*PT* 12 November 1987). According to Lady Viqarunnisa Noon, the General had assured her earlier that she could continue to use English as the medium of instruction in her school. This suggests that the General was under pressure from the westernized elite and that he did not want to alienate them (Noon Int: 29 December 1994). Apart from a few comments against the continuation of the elitist system of schooling (Editorial *D* 18 December 1987), the reversal of the 1979 education policy, the most momentous step taken in favour of Urdu, was allowed to take place almost silently (see Editorials, *N* and *M* 13 November 1987).

Indeed, at the end of Ziaul Haq's rule, the Tehreek-e-Nifaz-e-Urdu (movement for the establishment of Urdu) as well as many independent observers agreed that, barring some cosmetic changes, the position of Urdu had not changed. English was still used in the domains of power. It was no wonder then that the growing middle class demanded more and more English-medium schools and these in fact proliferated. Among the most notable new elitist chains of schools which were established were the Beaconhouse and City School systems. They charged exorbitant fees (Rs 1000 per month on average in 1994) which excluded the lower middle class altogether. Even the middle and upper middle classes found it difficult to afford them, but kept sacrificing to buy power and prestige for their children.

**English for the Poor**

Being unable, or unwilling, to oust English from the domains of power, the PPP government of Benazir Bhutto, in both its tenures (the first from November 1988 to August 1990 and the second from October 1993 to November 1996) mooted the idea that English should be taught in all schools and not merely in elitist ones. The first PPP government's order (No. F.3-4/85-Eng of 2 May 1989) declared:

> It has been decided that option shall be given to adopt English as medium of Instruction in all subjects from class 1. It has also been decided that in the schools where the medium of instruction is Urdu or an approved provincial language, English be taught as an additional language from class 1.

During the second tenure, too, English was made part of the syllabus from class 1. These steps, said the government, would 'bring children of poor [sic] at par with privileged class' (Riaz Fatiana, then Adviser to the Chief Minister of the Punjab in *The News* 29 October 1993).

This was opposed on political grounds by the PPP's right-wing opponents such as the Institute of Policy Studies, 'one of the front organizations of the Jamaat-i-Islami' (*PT* and *J* 18 October 1989). Others of the same view denounced these decisions as dangerous conspiracies against the country (Saleem 1989; Hussaini 1989). However, it is clear that such a policy will not bring about any significant change in the existing system of the distribution of wealth, power, and prestige. First, Urdu-medium schools will not teach all subjects in English as elitist schools do. They will merely start teaching English from class 1 instead of from class 6 as formerly. Secondly, and this is the crucial point, the government will not provide teachers who can speak and teach English competently for all the schools in the country. Such teachers are from relatively affluent, urban backgrounds, and are unlikely to teach in the villages and poorer areas where the vernacular schools are located. To change this pattern, or even to make schools available for all children, the government would have to spend much more money.[4] This the government is neither prepared to do, nor is it indeed capable of doing, because the military, the higher bureaucracy, and the other members of the elite would be impoverished if such an enormous investment was made for the education of the common people. Thus, now as before, English remains the preserve of the elite and helps it to maintain its hegemony over the less privileged.

## The Supporters of English

We have seen that the spokesmen for the ruling elite, especially those who occupy powerful positions in the apparatus of the state, appear to support Urdu and call it the 'national language'. However, the state spends more money, even out of military funds (as in cadet colleges), on elitist English-medium schools than on Urdu ones. Recent figures are not available, but even in 1964-65 the government spent Rs 296.5 per pupil per year on the 8,355 pupils of the 19 elitist schools it aided (LAD-WP 5 July 1965). Yet these children could afford the high tuition fees of these elitist institutions even if the government had contributed nothing towards their upkeep. As we have seen, most reports on education, and even some very powerful decision-makers such as Ayub, Bhutto, and Ziaul Haq, have either overtly supported elitist institutions or made policies which would not undermine their position. Thus, even now elitist schools are being established at great cost (see Appendix G). Moreover, apart from writing letters in the press and pressurizing educational authorities as parents, members of the westernized elite have supported English in the name of efficiency and high standards. In their private capacities, senior bureaucrats and members of the fashionable upper class have come together in the British Universities Alumni Association and the English Speaking Union. The latter was formed in the fifties and its members include General Attiqur Rahman, Lady Viqarunnisa Noon, and several high-ranking bureaucrats, retired generals, and socialites (Noon. Int: 29 December 1994; Mooraj Int: 9 August 1994). Such clubs, however informal and small, have such powerful members that their influence is far in excess of their actual numbers. There is no doubt that this powerful upper class elite—which uses English as an identity-marker, a badge of distinction, the open sesame of an exclusive club—supports the continued use of English in all the domains of power. But even more significantly, the less affluent also support English.

Many people support English because they believe that it will also equip them with the means for entering the elite. According to Sabiha Mansoor's survey of students' attitude towards English, the situation is as follows:

> There is complete agreement between the Punjabi and Urdu speaking students regarding the usefulness of English and the need to study it both as a compulsory subject and medium of instruction. Almost all Punjabi students (98%) and Urdu speaking students (96%) consider the study of English useful. A desire to study English as a compulsory subject is seen in the responses of Punjabi (90%) and Urdu speaking students (96%) and as medium of instruction by 81% of Punjabi and 80% Urdu speaking students. In fact, more students want to study English than Urdu (Mansoor 1993: 141- 4).

It appears that, in practice, most students work on the assumption that the status quo will not change and, given this condition, it would be useful for them to learn English, so as to compete with the privileged elite which is taught this language from the beginning.

A Gallup Survey conducted in 100 villages and 75 towns of Pakistan concluded that 62 per cent of people wanted to send their children to Urdu-medium schools; 14 per cent to English-medium ones; 12 per cent to Sindhi; and 2 per cent to other languages (10 per cent gave no opinion) (Gilani and Rahman 1986: 25). The survey does not indicate whether the respondents assumed that English would cease to be used in the domains of power or not. It appears that they were expressing a wish or an aspiration, which assumed that they were being questioned about what change they would welcome. Hence, it is not surprising that they gave their vote against the dominance of English which has always made them feel inferior.

In the present state of affairs it would appear then that apart from the elite, the underprivileged also desire to learn English for upward social mobility. Thus, no matter what their notion of an ideal or reformed society may be, they remain supporters of English and the status quo out of pragmatism. Hence, movements against English are often emotionally charged but tend to quickly run out of steam. Even diehard supporters of Urdu do not take the risk of educating their own children in Urdu-medium schools, if they can afford English-medium ones.

Apart from rational considerations of loss and gain, people also have extra-rational motivations. Thus, in a society which accords great prestige to English, they give the same value to it in their minds. The term 'Urdu-medium' is often used on Pakistani TV to mean 'lacking sophistication'. Indeed, despite the widespread feeling that English is a symbol of social injustice, people are inordinately impressed by an Oxbridge accent or competence in written English.

Another argument advanced in support of English is that it is necessary for modernization and international interaction. English is, indeed, an international language used in aviation, commerce, and scholarship. Indeed, scientific scholarship, one of the means for gaining power, is mostly available in English. J. A. Laponce studied the *Chemical Abstracts* between 1977 and 1980 and concluded that 'English accounts for nearly 65 per cent of the total, Russian covers less than 20 per cent, and no other language reaches 6 per cent' (Laponce 1987: 71). Similarly, a study of the *Index Medicus* (1980) revealed that most scholars in the field of medicine publish in English (ibid. 73). In fact, even French scholars, notwithstanding the special affection the French are reputed to have for their language, often publish in English (Cans 1981). The following passage from a report on the teaching of language by the University Grants Commission mentioned earlier reflects the views of many educated Pakistani decision-makers:

> There is no escape for any country in the world from learning English well and thoroughly and it would be very unwise, in fact, almost suicidal for Pakistan to destroy by neglect all the advantages we already possess in respect of past knowledge of English (UGC 1982: 13).

Thus, recent years have seen an increasing concern with competence in the English language, so that courses in English language teaching rather than English literature have been supported by the British Council, the Pakistan American Cultural Center (Karachi), the United States English language programmes; private bodies like SPELT (Society for Pakistan English Language Teachers), the Teacher's Resource Centre (Karachi), the Aga Khan University, and the Lahore University of Management Sciences. Reluctantly, semi-government institutions such as the Allama Iqbal Open University, the University of Karachi, the English Language Centre at the Balochistan University, the University of Azad Jammu and Kashmir, and the International Islamic University have also shown the same concern (personal information; Abbas 1993: 152-3). The teachers involved in these programmes often oppose the teaching of English literature, or at least the traditional practices and texts used in that teaching, but are supporters of the English language. Thus, while they are willing to concede that the canonical texts of English literature may not be relevant for Pakistan, they are resistant to the idea—ably argued by Phillipson (1992: 136-69)—that the teaching of English by American or British organizations serves neo-imperialist interests or that 'ELT is integral to the functioning of the contemporary world order' (ibid. 318). If such a world order assumes American domination, then the domination rests on English in the realm of culture and the communication of ideas. Thus, any individual or country which is more competent than others in English stands a better chance of using the culture and ideas of the English-speaking world. In the process, the individuals or countries also risk losing their own indigenous culture, language, and world view (Banuri 1990: 82-8). English may be a means of modernization and may give power, but at the cost of making our society impersonal, breaking up the family, weakening human relations, and further alienating the elite from the masses. Moreover, English will maintain the present iniquitous domination of the westernized elite in the country.

**Notes**

1. The author was a cadet in the Pakistan Military Academy during 1970-71, when any cadet found speaking in the vernaculars was punished. The official language of communication in the officer-training military academies remains English and cadets are still forbidden to use any other language.
2. The author wishes to thank Professor Waheed Qureshi, former Chairman of the National Language Authority, for having shown him this report. Since the report is confidential, it can neither be referred to in full nor quoted from.
3. The following figures from Syed Abdullah (1976: 64) illustrate this:

*Number of students opting for a language as medium of instruction*

| Subject | 1964 Urdu | 1964 English | 1967 Urdu | 1967 English |
|---|---|---|---|---|
| Political Science | 1195 | 1887 | 4585 | 673 |
| History | 959 | 830 | 2835 | 211 |
| Economics | 919 | 1478 | 3492 | 716 |
| Social work | 8 | 35 | 97 | 12 |
| Geography | 74 | 213 | 163 | 67 |
| Sociology | 2 | 120 | 151 | 95 |
| Philosophy | 24 | 24 | 121 | 89 |
| Psychology | 15 | 15 | 82 | 146 |

The trend of taking examinations in Urdu increased because it was easier for students, the majority of whom had studied in Urdu-medium schools, to express themselves in this language rather than in English. It must be kept in mind, however, that the best students do not take the above subjects at the MA level. They either join professional colleges or study science subjects. For MA, they mostly prefer business administration, commerce, accountancy, or English literature to the subjects given above. This preference for Urdu is because of pragmatic short-term interests, i.e., doing better in examinations.

4. Out of the total population of 127,902,000 about 28 per cent are of school-going age (5 to 15) i.e., 35,812,560. The total number of pupils in government schools is 15,514,000 while that of pupils in private schools is 2,010,000 (Eighth Plan : 524). The total number of children not receiving any schooling is 18,305,360.

At present, the government spends Rs 17153.6 million per year (recurring cost) on government schools, which comes to Rs 1,105 per child per year. The tuition fees in these schools range between Rs 0.25 to Rs 12.75 or Rs 6.5 per month, i.e. Rs 78 per child per year on average, GOP 1993. If these tuition fees are charged from the children not being educated at present as well as those being educated in government schools (i.e., nearly 34 million children), it would signify a contribution of a little over 2.6 billion per year towards their education. However, if they are taught in English-medium schools with a fairly high standard, and an average fee of Rs 500 per month, the cost of educating them would be about Rs 204 billion per year. Even if the children contribute 2.6 billion in tuition fees per year, the government would have to spend over Rs 201 billion. But the total internal resources of Pakistan came to Rs 260 billion in the budget of 1994-95. This makes such an investment on education impossible, unless more resources are generated.

# Conclusion

Let us now attempt to answer some of the questions which were raised in the beginning. Firstly, are language movements created by enemy agents and Communists? This has always been the establishment view and many people still believe in it. There is, of course, some evidence that ethno-nationalist movements and the language movements associated with them have been supported off and on by India, Afghanistan, and sometimes the former Soviet Union. However, even official reports deny that the support has ever been serious or consistent. Most of these movements were created and sustained by indigenous elements. Were they then Communists? Or people who wanted to break up the country? All the evidence marshalled in the previous pages suggests that they were neither all Communists, as that term is understood, nor people who rejected the idea of Pakistan. Most of them wanted to be empowered within the federal or the confederal framework. Even in East Pakistan, it was only when power was not transferred to Sheikh Mujib and the army was used to crush the Bengalis that the very idea of Pakistan was rejected. In Sindh, the extremist supporters of an independent Sindhu Desh have never had much electoral support; while in the NWFP, as we have seen, the Pakhtunistan movement has actually weakened to the point of disappearing, and the ANP's vote bank has decreased (Waseem 1994: 174). Only in Balochistan is there such alienation from the Centre that separatist sentiment may be alive. This tells us that the causes of such a degree of alienation are part of the political situation rather than the work of enemy agents.

It is true, however, that whereas Communist parties themselves have been ineffective and badly organized in Pakistan, those who believe that subordinate classes and collectivities are dominated and exploited support ethno-nationalism and the assertion of linguistic identity. This is a leftist idea associated with parties like NAP in Pakistan. However, instead of being seen as a conspiracy, the idea can also be seen as part of a genuine desire for social justice. Its widespread appeal for subordinated collectivities lies in its promise of giving them power, wealth, security, and prestige. Since people desire the above, these ideas appeal to them. If people did not feel deprived, powerless, and marginalized, they would probably not be attracted to such ideas. So, unless it is assumed that only a few leftists can brainwash large numbers of people, it will have to be conceded that the unjust policies of the ruling elite make people receptive to salvationist ideas.

Let us now see what light is shed by the history of the language policies we have examined on the crucial issues of politics, identity-construction, ethnicity, modernity, and decentralization. We find that the advent of modernity, with the coming of the British, brought about radical changes in language policies and the distribution of power. In the beginning, the British developed the classical languages of India (Persian, Arabic, and Sanskrit) in order to conciliate the traditional elites and consolidate their rule. They also developed the vernacular languages, in order to rule Indians more effectively. Among these vernaculars were Bengali, Urdu, Hindi, and Sindhi. These were standardized and printed, and the standard varieties were given official patronage.

When Persian was replaced with the vernaculars, the traditional elite was marginalized. Since Persian was a symbol of Muslim rule, this was the death knell of the old order. This situation continues today in much the same fashion in Pakistan. The English-using elite does not only find easy access to prestigious and powerful positions in Pakistan but also has access to lucrative employment in the international job market. This is one major reason why, despite governmental rhetoric in support of Urdu, English continues to be the language of the domains of power and a symbol of elitist upbringing in Pakistan.

Even more interesting is the relationship of the vernaculars with ethnicity. The first result of giving a standard label to a number of mutually intelligible dialects was to create the possibility of imagining larger communities than before. Once jobs and educational opportunities were available on the basis of religious affiliation, the religious identity came to the fore. The major symbol of identification was, of course, the religious label: Muslim, Hindu, Sikh, etc. But the minor symbols were the newly created official vernaculars which partly superseded local names of languages in parts of India. Among the main languages which mobilized the Hindus and the Muslims were Hindi (in the Devanagari script) and Urdu (in the Arabic one). They both helped in the creation of new politicized identities. Whatever the sentiment for identity itself may have been, the symbols of these two languages were used to mobilize people politically. As we have seen, this political mobilization led to the partition of India into Bharat and Pakistan.

However, in Pakistan, once the fear of Hindu domination was removed, the federating units of the country were left to contend with the domination of the Punjabi-dominated ruling elite at the Centre. This elite, comprising the bureaucracy and the officer cadre in the armed forces, is English-using. However, Islam and Urdu are used by it as symbols of national integration and, indeed, to create a Pakistani identity. State-sponsored language policies and LP activities were, therefore, meant to make Urdu the dominant vernacular language.

The response of the vernacular proto-elites of the federating units was the assertion of language-based ethno-nationalism. It was language-based because language was the only symbol which had supra-local appeal and yet differentiated one community from the others. Thus, against the state's modernizing imperative of creating cultural uniformity through the hegemony of an urban Urdu-using culture, the Bengali, Pakhtun, Sindhi, Balochi, and Punjabi proto-elites asserted language-based ethno-nationalism. Among the most mobilized sections of the intelligentsia, which were also in competition for jobs and power with other collectivities, the old local identities were suppressed in favour of new ones. Thus, the Bengali, Sindhi, Pakhtun, Baloch, Siraiki, and Mohajir identities were asserted. This does not mean that pre-modern, local loyalties (biradaris, zats, and clans) disappeared. They are still used as badges of identity in the local context, but not in competition with larger external collectivities. In the Punjab, where this competition is not perceived as internal colonialism, it is arguable that the biradari is fairly strong, both socially and politically (Waseem 1994: 102-3). However, wherever there was a feeling of having been exploited or deprived of power, new ethnic identities were created. The common denominator in all of them was self-definition in non-religious terms. The Bengalis, Sindhis, and Mohajirs who had defined themselves primarily in religious terms when they competed with the Hindus in pre-partition days, now saw themselves primarily in ethnic terms. Language was the major symbol of ethnicity for Bengalis and Sindhis, while it was important, though not the sole symbol, for the Mohajirs. Bengali language-based ethnicity was strong enough to challenge the domination of the West Pakistani elite and contribute to the creation of Bangladesh. Sindhi ethnicity has led to a cultural and literary renaissance in Sindh and has mobilized Sindhis into a pressure group which questions the domination of the Centre. But the situation in Sindh is complicated by the rise of Mohajir ethnicity since the

1980s. Urdu is one of its defining features but not the only one. Its main feature is subjective and experiential—the experience of being non-local immigrants and settlers in urban Sindh. The experience is also confrontationist: thus, Mohajir ethnicity is a device to combat Sindhi ethnicity (as well as Punjabi domination) in the search for jobs, power, and security in Sindh. The clash between Urdu and Sindhi is really a dimension of the struggle for power between Mohajirs and Sindhis.

Pakhtun and Baloch ethnicity was tribal and seen in terms of belonging to a certain extended kinship collectivity, with a common culture, before modernity added the linguistic dimension. After this, the Pashto language rather than Pakhtunwali (the ideal behavioural norms) became the overt marker of Pakhtun identity. In the Baloch case, the language movement has succeeded in removing culture shame about Balochi and Brahvi, though the myth of common descent remains the major symbol of Baloch identity. Language not only helps to imagine the community—which was already imagined as a single kinship lineage—but also to create living cultural artefacts: literature, a heroic tradition, history, new words, etc. In short, language creates devices for increasing solidarity and for creating a pressure group. In political terms, the core of this pressure group agitates for autonomy (or even secession), increased power in the peripheries, a larger share of goods and services, or, at least, for recognition as a separate cultural collectivity. As we have seen, this is not because enemy agents or leftists seduce the people away from their allegiance to a caring and just Centre, but because the latter is seen as being coercive, unjust, and exploitative.

In the construction of the Bengali, Pakhtun, Baloch, Sindhi, Siraiki, and Mohajir ethnicities, the use of language as a symbol of mobilization is predominantly instrumental and rational. The leaders who chose the symbols felt politically powerless and economically exploited. They used these fears to mobilize people and believed that they would gain power if they rallied around one focal point. But this does not mean that no extra-rational factors came into play. In the case of Bengalis, Pakhtuns, Sindhis, and Mohajirs, the labels for their respective mother tongues were fairly old and sentiment about them either existed in some dormant form or could be built up. In the case of Siraiki, there was an ancient written tradition which needed only to be given the label of Siraiki to create sentiment. Even more importantly, the whole way of life of communities, for which there were extra-rational sentiments, was threatened by an alien culture. Language became the symbol for this way of life, and members of the intelligentsia and ordinary people both acted with strong emotion to preserve it. In fact, no matter how important jobs and power really were, or were consciously felt to be, it would be nearer to the truth to assert that the activists of the language movements felt they were fighting for intangibles: identity, honour, authenticity, culture.

The only language movement which appears to be solely about these extra-rational intangibles is the Punjabi language movement. It reacts to the subordination of the Punjabi identity to the national, Pakistani identity by the powerful Punjabi ruling elite. In supporting English and Urdu, this elite has marginalized Punjabi. This helps the elite to consolidate its rule over the provinces, but at the cost of keeping the Punjabis ashamed of their language. The activists of this movement want to reverse this trend, even if it means recognizing the claims of the other languages of Pakistan and giving more power to their speakers. Because of this possible disturbance in the pattern of the distribution of power, the elite ignores the Punjabi language movement more than any other in the country.

This is a matter which the ruling elite will have to confront. One possibility is to continue the existing language policies which keep power in the hands of the English-using elite at the Centre. This will continue to threaten the culture of the peripheries, keep them weak, and leave them feeling that they are being exploited. Such a policy may appeal to those who believe in a unitary system of rule or in the efficacy of the integrative potential of Islam and Urdu. But, in the face of perceived injustice, as we have seen, Islam and Urdu have not prevented the rise of militant ethnicity in Bangladesh, in Balochistan, or in Karachi.

The other possibility would be to divide the present provinces of Pakistan so as to form smaller units. The Ansari Commission, set up by Ziaul Haq, to examine the form of government conceded that the number of provinces should be increased, in view of the fact that Nigeria had raised the number of its provinces from three to nineteen as an aftermath of the Biafra ethnic conflict (Ansari 1983: 59). The Commission, however, did not endorse the idea of making provincial boundaries conform to ethno-linguistic ones. Such an idea has been proposed from time to time. In 1942, the election manifesto of the Communist Party of India advocated that power be transferred to seventeen different 'sovereign national constituent assemblies' defined by 'nationalities'. The Balochi nationality was added to the list in 1946 (Joshi 1946: 32-4). Ubaidullah Sindhi, an anti-British political figure in pre-partition

India, was also one of the exponents of nationalities. Sindhi proposed the establishment of ten republics in India: 'South Western Punjab including Bahawalpur with Multani Punjabi as its common language; 'Pushtania' having Pushtu as its common language; 'Baluchistan' where Baluchi language is spoken and Quetta and Kalat are the chief cities; 'Northern Punjab' with Pothwari Punjabi as its common language and Rawalpindi as its chief city and 'Sindh' with Sindhi as its common language and Karachi as its centre' (Shaikh 1986: 172).

If this is modified to take into account the demands of the speakers of Hindko, Khowar, Shina, and other minor languages, a Hindko-speaking province would be carved out of the NWFP. Moreover, Chitral and Kohistan would also become provinces. The Northern Areas could be divided into Burushaski and Shina-speaking provinces, though this may not be the best solution in those areas, due to the cleavage which exists there between Sunnis and non-Sunnis (Shias and Ismailis). In the elections of October 1994, the Tehrik-e-Jafria Pakistan (TJP), a Shia political party, got the maximum votes, and pressure groups mobilize with reference to religion rather than linguistic identities (Yusufzai 1994: 6).

The formation of Hindko, Siraiki, Punjabi, Pashto, and Balochi provinces will harm the Punjab most (for the possible boundaries of these provinces on the basis of the Census of 1981, see Map 4). For one thing, it will not remain a large province and its weight in the legislature will be reduced considerably. The Pashto-speaking province will not stand to lose because, while it will lose Chitral, Kohistan, Hazara, Mansehra, and Dera Ismail Khan, it will gain the Pashto-speaking areas of Balochistan. Balochistan will also lose some areas but the Pashtun-Baloch conflict will vanish. Likewise, in the NWFP the Hindko-Pashto conflict and in the Punjab, the Siraiki-Punjabi conflict will also disappear. Punjab will no longer be seen as dominant, and ethnic bitterness will be reduced. Above all, if the linguistic provinces desire to promote their language or culture, they would not have to struggle against the interests of powerful minorities as is now the case.

It is only in the province of Sindh that the consequences of creating an Urdu-speaking province may be even worse than the present state of high tension between the Sindhis and the Mohajirs. The supporters of the MQM have, of course, demanded such a province but the Sindhis do not accept this demand. This is understandable, considering that the Sindhis feel that the Mohajirs came as immigrants, not as conquerors. But now, if the most modernized part of Sindh is given to them, they would have conquered Sindh.

# MAP 3
## PAKISTAN
SCALE 1:5,000,000

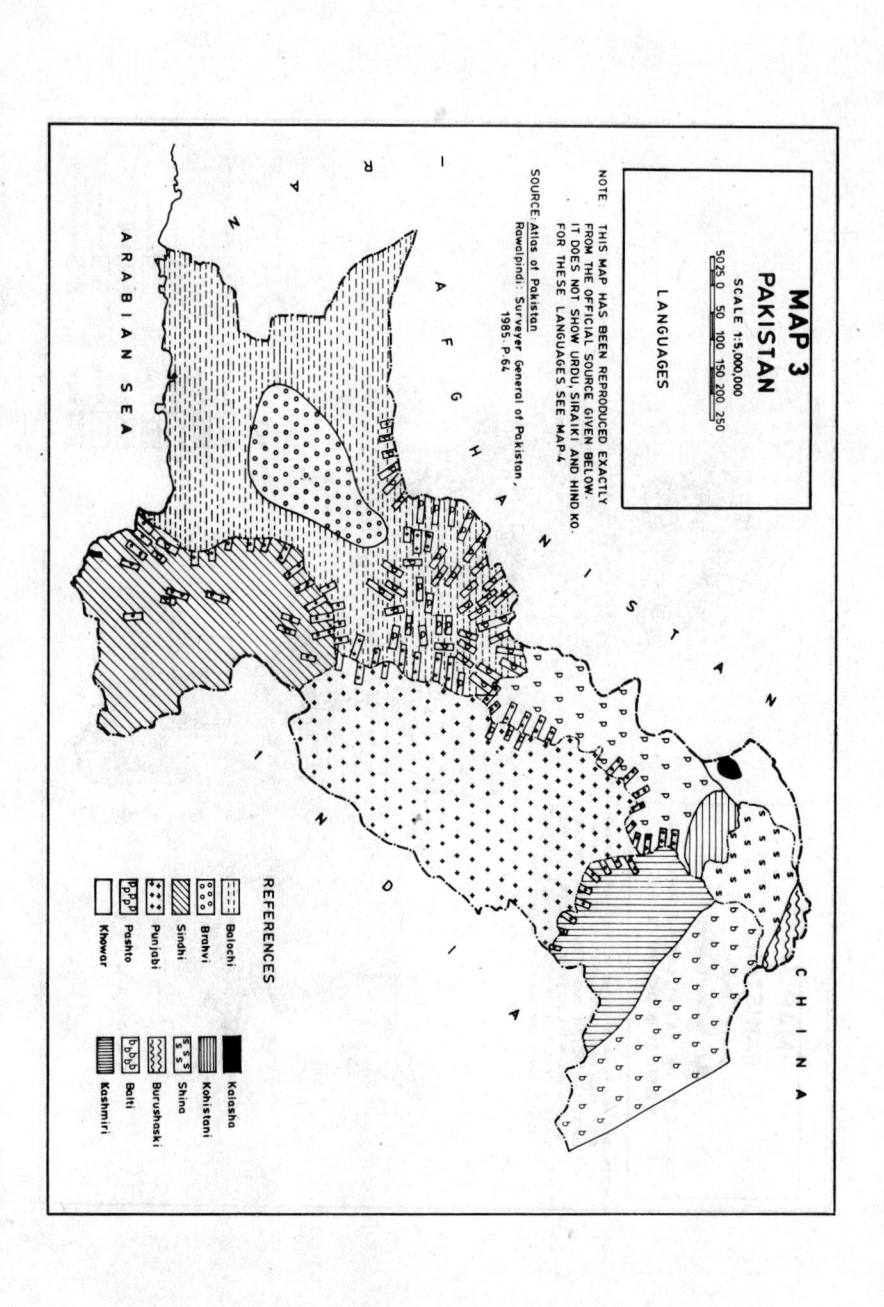

LANGUAGES

NOTE: THIS MAP HAS BEEN REPRODUCED EXACTLY FROM THE OFFICIAL SOURCE GIVEN BELOW. IT DOES NOT SHOW URDU, SIRAIKI AND HINDKO. FOR THESE LANGUAGES SEE MAP 4.

SOURCE: Atlas of Pakistan, Rawalpindi: Surveyor General of Pakistan, 1985. P. 64.

### REFERENCES

- Balochi
- Brahvi
- Sindhi
- Punjabi
- Pashto
- Khowar
- Kalasha
- Kohistani
- Shina
- Burushaski
- Balti
- Kashmiri

# MAP 4
# PAKISTAN

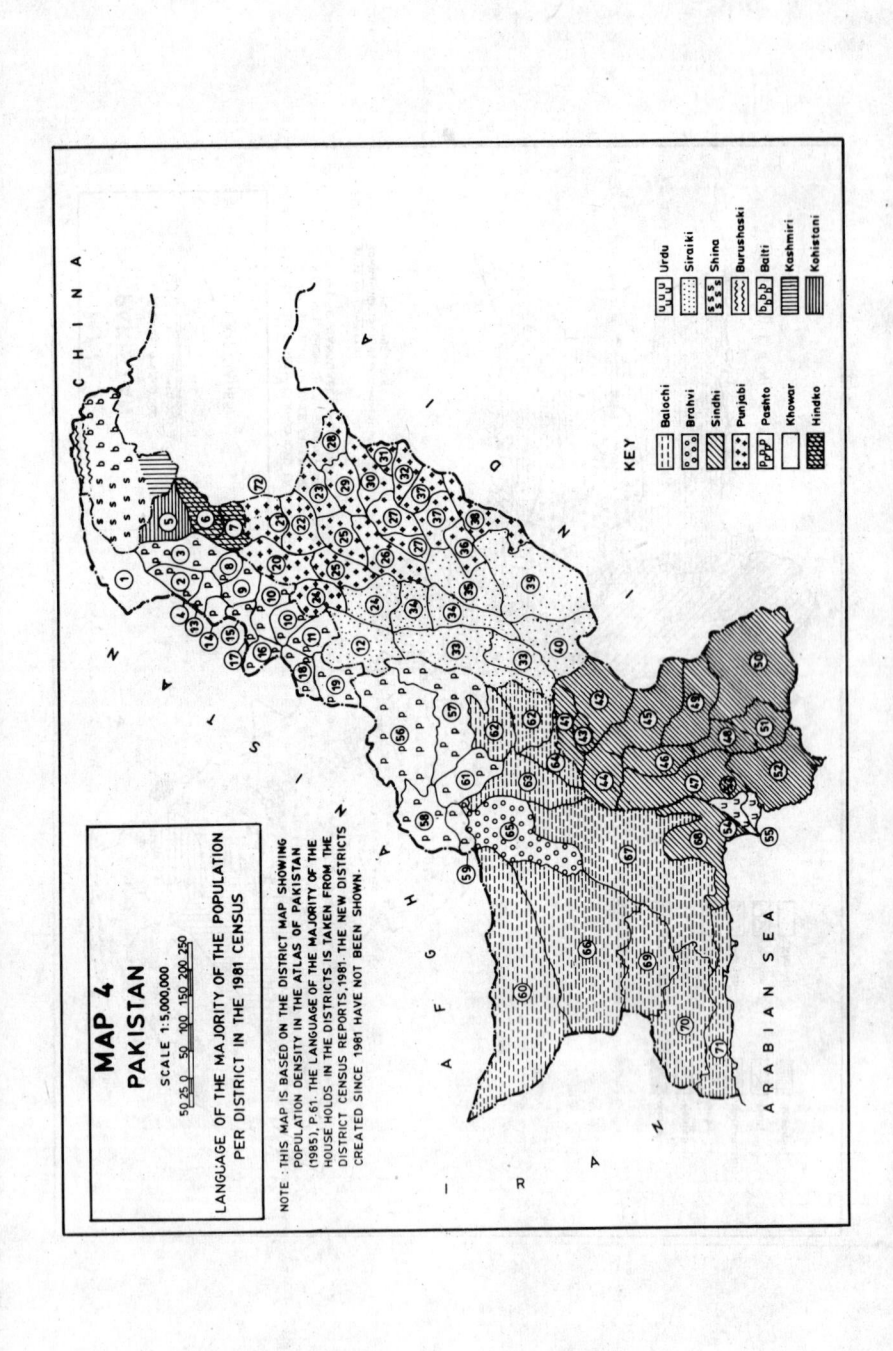

SCALE 1:5,000,000

50 25 0 50 100 150 200 250

LANGUAGE OF THE MAJORITY OF THE POPULATION PER DISTRICT IN THE 1981 CENSUS

NOTE : THIS MAP IS BASED ON THE DISTRICT MAP SHOWING POPULATION DENSITY IN THE ATLAS OF PAKISTAN (1985), P.61. THE LANGUAGE OF THE MAJORITY OF THE HOUSE HOLDS IN THE DISTRICTS IS TAKEN FROM THE DISTRICT CENSUS REPORTS,1981. THE NEW DISTRICTS CREATED SINCE 1981 HAVE NOT BEEN SHOWN.

KEY

- Balochi
- Brahvi
- Sindhi
- Punjabi
- Pashto
- Khowar
- Hindko
- Urdu
- Siraiki
- Shina
- Burushaski
- Balti
- Kashmiri
- Kohistani

The Mohajirs, for reasons given earlier, feel that they too have the right to preserve Urdu and their distinctive culture in the only part of Pakistan where they are in a majority. In practice, they have divided Sindh, since Karachi has remained separated from Sindh for many years as we have seen. If Karachi is now made a Mohajir province, it will only confirm and establish the *de facto* situation. However, on the basis of the 1981 census, only the city of Karachi and no other area of Sindh will be cut off from the province. But such a step cannot be advocated without taking the sentiments of Sindhis into account. The most important point is that bloodshed should be avoided; the tension between Sindhis and Mohajirs should not lead to a civil war and peace should be restored in Sindh. If the partition of Sindh can lead to these results, it may not be a bad idea. If, on the other hand, the level of violence increases, some other solution should be sought. There may still be the problem of fairly large groups of speakers of Urdu in the cities of the Sindh and speakers of Hindko in Peshawar, Kohat, and other cities of the NWFP. The new provinces will have to come to terms with these groups who might wish to preserve their languages and culture rather than integrate with the majority. However, the chances of the preservation of linguistic and cultural heritage will increase for most people.

These linguistic provinces could then promote their dominant languages in their domains of power, while using Urdu for interprovincial communication and English for international communication. This would facilitate major political change, because power would pass to the indigenous vernacular proto-elite. Once English ceases to be used in the domains of power, the English-using westernized elite will have to start using the vernaculars in order to survive. This will mean that there would be no English-medium schools and at least the linguistic basis for looking down upon people or keeping them out of elitist positions will be undermined. This, however, would not mean that English would not be taught or used in any domain. As mentioned in the chapter on the Urdu-English controversy, English is predominantly the language of the production of knowledge and its applications. It would have to be learned by research scholars, high-level technocrats, and those who communicate at the international level. However, the basis for teaching it would become academic merit and professional requirement, rather than the ability to buy elitist schooling. If all schools taught a uniform syllabus in the indigenous languages, charging tuition fees proportionate to the parent's income, elitist schooling need not be altogether eliminated, and the system would appear more just and humane. English and Urdu could then be taught as additional subjects in these schools. Such a step would also mean that Urdu would lose its dominant position in all the provinces except Karachi and the indigenous vernaculars would become passports for jobs and power, at least at the provincial level. This would go a long way towards empowering the peripheries, at the expense of the Centre and facilitate, amongst other things, decentralization and rule by local people.

According to Tariq Banuri:

> Legal decentralization would imply the transfer of legislative and executive powers to the decentralized units. Economic decentralization refers to the development of production systems which can facilitate direct participation in the economic decision-making by people involved in the production process. This is related to the notion that the knowledge as well as action should be responsive to the environmental, social as well as physical boundaries of the participants' world (Banuri 1990: 98).

The greatest impediment in the way of political decentralization are the conspiracy theories and the self-interest of the ruling elite. These factors prevent them from appreciating the hypothesis that satisfied federating units would have no urge to break away from the federation. As mentioned earlier, no matter what the level of enemy propaganda might be, it is only when people feel frustrated that they pay attention to it. A truly multi-ethnic, multilingual polity, like Switzerland, can live in equilibrium on the basis of perceived justice and equity. What is seen as unjust and forced is resented and even resisted with force.

As for Banuri's post-modernist suggestion that there can also be 'epistemological decentralization' (Banuri 1990: 99), it is indeed more likely if knowledge is obtained through indigenous languages rather than in English. The creation of knowledge is related in very complicated ways with the language in which it is created. One need not accept the extreme form of the Whorfian hypothesis that language determines thought, but it is difficult to deny that it does not influence it. So, when we use a language, we unconsciously see our reality through a grid which might well be distorting. One reason why Indonesian modernists use Bahasa Indonesia, is that it helps them discipline and unite 'the bureaucratic colonial vocabulary, the Western democratic-socialist vocabulary, the nationalist-revolutionary vocabulary' and indigenous, specifically 'Javanese tradition' (Anderson 1990: 126). The experiment has not fully succeeded but a beginning has been made. The use of local languages would prevent

Eurocentricism and allow scholars to be sensitive to areas of our experience such as colonial domination, white supremacy, and culture-specific interpersonal relations. Some exceptional scholars have already begun to be sensitive to these things, (see *Subaltern Studies*, Said 1993; Marglin and Marglin 1990, etc.) but much needs to be done. As already indicated, this is not an easy proposition, because English is the language of the dissemination of knowledge and it would have to be learned by scholars and technocrats. Whether people can master both English and the vernacular languages well enough to create knowledge and transfer it from one language to another is difficult to know.

If this does take place, the modernizing imperative will be accepted—as it is by all language planners who create terms for new concepts to express modern ideas—but the path towards modernization may be different from that of the post-Macaulay westernized elite. Pakistani modernization might then be more sensitive to the realities of the indigenous experience than that of the westernized elite, alienated as it is from indigenous cultures. These, however, are speculative thoughts for which no proof can be offered.

What is certain is that language policies are so intimately related with politics that, if they change, the political map of Pakistan will also change. Whether such a change occurs with or without violence, or whether the status quo continues, with the present low level of violence, is for the decision-makers to decide.

# Appendices

## Appendix A
## LANGUAGE-WISE PUBLICATIONS

|              | Urdu | English | Sindhi | Pashto | Punjabi | Siraiki | Gujrati | Balochi | Brahvi | Persian | Arabic | Total |
|---|---|---|---|---|---|---|---|---|---|---|---|---|
| Dailies      | 209  | 41      | 17     | 2      |         |         | 4       |         |        |         |        | 273   |
| Biweeklies   | 2    | 2       |        |        |         |         |         |         |        |         |        | 4     |
| Weeklies     | 341  | 65      | 42     | 4      | 1       |         | 2       | 1       | 1      |         |        | 457   |
| Fortnightlies| 57   | 34      | 2      |        |         |         | 1       |         |        |         |        | 94    |
| Monthlies    | 598  | 237     | 17     | 5      | 1       | 2       | 5       | 7       |        | 3       | 1      | 876   |
| Bimonthlies  | 3    | 11      |        |        |         |         |         |         |        |         |        | 14    |
| Quarterlies  | 75   | 136     | 1      |        |         |         | 3       |         |        |         |        | 215   |
| Biannuals    | 59   | 83      |        |        |         |         |         |         |        |         |        | 142   |
| Annuals      | 119  | 127     |        | 2      |         |         |         | 2       | 2      |         |        | 252   |
| All          | 1463 | 736     | 79     | 13     | 2       | 2       | 15      | 10      | 3      | 3       | 1      | 2,327 |

These figures are mainly based on *Pakistan Press Directory 1992* (Islamabad: Press Information Department, Ministry of Information and Broadcasting, 1992). Some have been changed after rechecking against the records of the provincial governments and independent sources. There are still minor discrepancies as publications are added to and taken off the list. However, the dominance of Urdu and English is established by these figures. The development of Sindhi, and the degree to which the Sindhi intelligentsia supports it, is also evidenced. As the publications in Khowar, Shina, and Burushaski are irregular they have not been included here.

## Appendix B

# LANGUAGE-WISE ALLOCATION OF TIME ON TELEVISION

| Language | TV Station | Number of programmes per week | Number of hours per week |
|---|---|---|---|
| Balochi | Quetta | 4 (25 minutes each) | 1 hr 40 mins |
| Brahvi | Quetta | 4 (25 minutes each) | 1 hr 40 mins |
| English | All | Many | 8 hrs |
| Hindko | Peshawar | 1 (50 minutes) 1 (25 minutes) | 1 hr 15 mins |
| Pashto | Peshawar Quetta | 2 (50 minutes each) 4 (25 minutes each) | 5 hrs |
| Punjabi | Lahore Islamabad | 3 (50 minutes each) 4 (25 minutes each) | 4 hrs 16 mins |
| Sindhi | Karachi | 3 (50 minutes each) 5 (25 minutes each) | 4 hrs 58 mins |
| Siraiki | Lahore Islamabad | 1 | 25 minutes |
| Urdu | All | Many | 49 hrs 18 mins |
| Urdu/Arabic | All | Many | 7 hrs 45 mins |

Source: Pakistan Television Headquarters, Islamabad, 1994

# Appendix C

## LANGUAGE-WISE ALLOCATION OF TIME ON RADIO

| Date of Commissioning of Radio Station | | Language used | Time given to each language Daily (All Stations) | |
|---|---|---|---|---|
| Peshawar | 16-7-1936 | Urdu, Pashto, Khowar, Hindko, Kohistani | Arabic | 10 min |
| Lahore | 16-12-1937 | Urdu, Punjabi, English | Balochi | 7 hrs 25 min |
| Rawalpindi | 16-4-1948 | Urdu, Kashmiri, Gojri | Balti | 2 hrs 5 min |
| Karachi | 16-4-1948 | Urdu, Sindhi, English, Gujrati | Brahvi | 5 hrs 35 min |
| Rawalpindi | 1-9-1950 | Urdu, Punjabi, Potohari, Kashmiri | Burushaski | 40 min |
| Hyderabad | 17-8-1955 | Urdu, Sindhi | English | 1 hr 9 min |
| Rawalpindi | 15-10-1960 | Urdu, Kashmiri, Pahari | Gojri | 5 min |
| Quetta | 16-10-1966 | Urdu, Balochi, Pashto, Brahvi, Hazargi | Gujrati | 1 hr |
| Multan | 21-11-1970 | Urdu, Siraiki, Punjabi, | Hazargi | 1 hr 7 min |
| Bahawalpur | 18-8-1975 | Urdu, Siraiki, | Hindko | 1 hr 50 min |
| Islamabad | 7-5-1977 | Urdu, English, Balti, Shina | Kashmiri | not available |
| Gilgit | 2-4-1979 | Urdu, Shina, Burushaski | Khowar | 2 hrs 5 min |
| Skardu | 16-4-1979 | Urdu, Balti | Kohistani | 25 min |
| Turbat | 4-1-1981 | Urdu, Balochi, | Pahari | Not available |
| D.I. Khan | 15-1-1981 | Urdu, Siraki, Pashto | Pashto | 11 hrs 42 min |
| Khairpur | 3-3-1981 | Urdu, Sindhi, | Potohari | 43 min |
| Khuzdar | 17-6-1981 | Urdu, Sindhi | Punjabi | 5 hrs |
| Faisalabad | 15-9-1982 | Urdu, Punjabi | Shina | 2 hrs 3 min |
| Abbottabad | 1-10-1989 | Urdu, Hindko | Sindhi | 11 hrs 42 min |
| Sibi | 1-10-1989 | Relay of Islamabad | Siraiki | 3 hrs 17 min |
| | | | Urdu | over 200 hrs |
| | | | Total (Home) | 270 hrs |

The general policy of the Ministry of Information and broadcasting is to give 60% time to Urdu and 40 % to all other languages. Column 3 gives the average time given to different languages from all the radio stations in column 1. These timings have been compiled from the programme of Radio Pakistan for 1994 and do not claim to be accurate because of overlap or lack of data

## Appendix D

### GRANT-IN-AID TO INSTITUTIONS FOR THE PROMOTION OF LANGUAGES FROM THE PAKISTAN ACADEMY OF LETTERS (1994-95)

| Organization | Pakistani rupees |
|---|---:|
| **Balochi** | |
| Balochi Academy, Quetta | 100,000 |
| **Khowar** | |
| Anjuman Taraqqi-e-Khowar (Chitral) | 5,000 |
| **Pashto** | |
| Pashto Academy (Peshawar) | 100,000 |
| Anjuman Adabiyat, Akora Khattak | 5,000 |
| **Punjabi** | |
| Punjabi Adabi Board, Lahore | 100,000 |
| Majlis Waris Shah, Multan | 25,000 |
| Punjabi Science Board | 30,000 |
| **Sindhi** | |
| Sindhi Adabi Board, Hyderabad | 100,000 |
| Institute of Sindhology, Hyderabad | 50,000 |
| Shah Abdul Latif Cultural Society, Karachi | 21,000 |
| Mansoor Academy, Hyderabad | 10,000 |
| **Siraiki** | |
| Siraiki Adabi Board, Multan | 10,000 |
| Siraiki Adabi Majlis, Bahawalpur | 20,000 |
| **Urdu** | |
| West Pakistan Urdu Academy, Lahore | 35,000 |
| Urdu Academy, Bahawalpur | 20,000 |
| Murree Literary Circle | 5,000 |
| Dame Iqbal Academy, Gujrat | 5,000 |
| Anjuman-e-Taraqqi-e-Urdu, Karachi | 1,500,000 |
| Idara-e-Yadgar-e-Ghalib, Karachi | 10,000 |
| Bazm-e-Ahl-e-Qalam, Abottabad | 2,500 |

Source: Budget statement of the Pakistan Academy of Letters, Islamabad

# Appendix E

## ANNUAL BUDGETS OF INSTITUTIONS FOR THE PROMOTION OF LANGUAGES

| Organizations | Pakistani rupees | |
|---|---|---|
| **Arabic** | | |
| Promotion of teaching Arabic | 764,000 | (1993-94) |
| **Balochi** | | |
| Balochi Academy | 212,000 | |
| **Brahvi** | | |
| Brahvi Academy | 30,000 | |
| Brahvi orthographic Committee | 15,000 | |
| **English** | 328,000 | (1993-94) |
| Strengthening of training programme in English as a foreign/second language | | |
| National English Language Institute | 4,000,000 | (1993-94) |
| **Pashto** | | |
| Khushal Khan Khattak Library, Akora Khattak | 1,811,000 | (1994) |
| Pashto Academy, Peshawar University | 1,773,456 | |
| Pashto Academy, Quetta | 30,000 | |
| **Punjabi** | | |
| Punjabi Adabi Board | 366,000 | |
| **Sindhi** | | |
| Award on Best Books on Shah Abdul Latif Bhittai and Sufism | 25,000 | (1994) |
| Sindhi Language Authority | 1,500,000 | (1993-94) |
| Institute of Sindhology | 3,500,000 | (1993-94) |
| Sindhi Adabi Board | 4,000,000 | (1993-94) |
| **Urdu** | | |
| Muqtadira Qaumi Zaban (National Language Authority) | 10,873,000 | |
| Iqbal Academy, Lahore | 2,310,000 | |

| | |
|---|---|
| Urdu Dictionary Board, Karachi | 4,410,000 |
| Urdu Science Board, Lahore | 3,009,000 |
| Lump provision for adoption of Urdu as Official Language | 1,000,000 |
| Grant of Hasrat Mohani Memorial Trust, Karachi | 50,000 |
| Pak Jamhuriat (weekly Urdu), Lahore | 1,021,000 |
| Presidential Award for Best Books on Iqbal and Iqbaliat | 190,000 |
| Urdu and other languages Pakistan Academy of Letters | 10,829,000  (C91994) |

Source: The source is CE 1994 : Vols. 1 and 2 for Arabic, English, Urdu and wherever indicated. Other budget statements were supplied by the individual institutions. The year is 1994-95 unless otherwise indicated.

## Appendix F

### DISTRICT-WISE DISTRIBUTION OF LANGUAGES

The percentage of the speakers of the languages given below are based on figures for languages commonly spoken in the household in the Census reports of districts (1981). In districts where one language does not dominate, others languages are also indicated. Minor languages have been ignored. The numbers of the districts given below are the same as in maps 2 and 4.

#### NWFP

| | | |
|---|---|---|
| 1. | Chitral | Khowar (95.34); Pashto (4.44) |
| 2. | Dir | Pashto (94.69) |
| 3. | Swat | Pashto (90.28): Kohistani (8.67) |
| 4. | Malakand | Pashto (98.09) |
| 5. | Kohistan | Kohistani (94.68): Pashto (4.89) |
| 6. | Mansehra | Hindko (46.84); Pashto (40.29) |
| 7. | Abbottabad | Hindko (92.32); Pashto (3.68) |
| 8. | Mardan | Pashto (97.17) |
| 9. | Peshawar | Pashto (87.54); Hindko (6.85) |
| 10. | Kohat | Pashto (86.75); Hindko (10.40) |
| 10. | Karak | Not given in the census 1981 |
| 11. | Bannu | Pashto (97.93) |
| 12. | D. I. Khan | Siraiki (64.87); Pashto (29.71) |

#### PUNJAB

| | | |
|---|---|---|
| 20. | Attock | Punjabi (93.4); Pashto (5.2) |
| 21. | Rawalpindi | Punjabi (85.0); Urdu (7.5) |
| 22. | Jhelum | Punjabi (97.5) |
| 23. | Gujrat | Punjabi (97.7) |
| 24. | Mianwali | Punjabi (83.9); Siraiki (8.3) |
| 24. | Bhakkar | Not given in the census 1981 |
| 25. | Sargodha | Punjabi (95.4) |
| 25. | Khushab | Not given in the census 1981 |
| 26. | Jhang | Punjabi (96.5) |
| 27. | Faisalabad | Punjabi (98.2) |
| 27. | Toba Tek Singh | Not given in the census 1981 |
| 28. | Sialkot | Punjabi (98.0) |
| 29. | Gujranwala | Punjabi (97.6) |

| | | |
|---|---|---|
| 30. | Sheikhupura | Punjabi (98.1) |
| 31. | Lahore | Punjabi (84.0); Urdu (13.4) |
| 31. | Okara | Not given in the census 1981 |
| 32. | Kasur | Punjabi (89.3) |
| 33. | D. G. Khan | Siraiki (73.4); Balochi (16.3) |
| 34. | Leiah | Not given in the census 1981 |
| 35. | Multan | Siraiki (44.7); Punjabi (43.8); Urdu (10.5) |
| 36. | Vehari | Punjabi (83.6); Siraiki (11.4) |
| 37. | Sahiwal | Punjabi (95.6) |
| 38. | Bahawalnagar | Punjabi (95.2) |
| 39. | Bahawalpur | Siraiki (66.7); Punjabi (27.0) |
| 40. | Rahim Yar Khan | Siraiki (65.0); Punjabi (27.9) |

## SINDH

| | | |
|---|---|---|
| 41. | Jacobabad | Sindhi (69.13); Balochi (21.34) |
| 42. | Sukkur | Sindhi (73.54); Urdu (12.66); Punjabi (6.37) |
| 43. | Shikarpur | Sindhi (86.48) |
| 44. | Larkana | Sindhi (78.43); Balochi (6.98) Brahvi (5.92); Siraiki (5.04) |
| 45. | Khairpur | Sindhi (80.48); Punjabi (8.50) |
| 46. | Nawabshah | Sindhi (66.18); Punjabi (10.58) Urdu (8.11); Siraiki (5.48) |
| 47. | Dadu | Sindhi (81.55); Balochi (7.39) |
| 48. | Hyderabad | Sindhi (56.48); Urdu (28.10) |
| 49. | Sanghar | Sindhi (56.10); Urdu (10.75); Punjabi (9.44) |
| 50. | Tharparkar | Sindhi (71.78); Urdu (8.39); Punjabi (5.78) |
| 51. | Badin | Sindhi (81.64); Punjabi (6.40) |
| 52. | Thatta | Sindhi (92.06) |
| 53. | Karachi Division | Urdu (54.3); Punjabi (13.6); Pashto (8.7) |

## BALOCHISTAN

| | | |
|---|---|---|
| 56. | Zhob | Pashto (98.09) |
| 57. | Loralai | Pashto (98.09) |
| 58. | Pishin | Pashto (97.55) |
| 59. | Quetta | Pashto (36.47); Punjabi (18.85); Brahvi (17.13); Urdu (11.17) |
| 60. | Chagai | Balochi (57.08); Brahvi (34.80) |
| 61. | Sibi | Pashto (49.77); Sindhi (20.12); Balochi (15.09) |
| 62. | Kohlu | Balochi (96.24) |
| 62. | Dera Bugti | Not given in the census 1981 |

| | | |
|---|---|---|
| 64. | Nasirabad | Balochi (41.73); Sindhi (26.10); Brahvi (17.81); Siraiki (12.57) |
| 65. | Kalat | Brahvi (87.20); Balochi (6.71) |
| 66. | Kharan | Balochi (69.85); Brahvi (29.39) |
| 67. | Khuzdar | Balochi (33.80); Brahvi (62.08) |
| 68. | Lasbela | Sindhi (56.23); Balochi (21.13); Brahvi (8.69) |
| 69. | Pangur | Balochi (99.41) |
| 70. | Turbat | Balochi (99.66) |
| 71. | Gwadar | Balochi (98.25) |

## Appendix G

### AID BY THE STATE TO ENGLISH-MEDIUM SCHOOLS
(The year is 1994-5 unless indicated otherwise)

| Institution | Pakistani rupees |
|---|---|
| Cadet College Hasanabdal (Construction of hostel building) | 3,389,000 |
| Cadet College Sanghar (Establishment of) | 9,056,000 |
| Cadet College Razmak | 8,926,000 |
| Cadet College Ghotki (Sukkur) | |
| (Construction in 1993-4) | 1,000,000 |
| (Budget in 1994-95) | 906,000 |
| Cadet College Palandri (Azad Kashmir) | 9,056,000 |
| Cadet College Larkana | |
| (Construction in 1993-4) | 31,630,000 |
| (Budget in 1994-5) | 9,056,000 |
| 4 Cadet Colleges in Punjab | 9,056,000 |
| Zam Public School (South Waziristan) | 100,000 |
| Public School Tank and Wana | 100,000 |
| Tochi Public School, Miranshah | 100,000 |

Source: *CE 1994: Vol. 1*

# Bibliography

This bibliography is in three parts. Part A: Manuscripts, typescripts, publications by corporate authors, reports, surveys, etc. Part B: Unpublished theses, books, articles, etc. Part C: Interviews, personal communications, questionnaires, etc.

## MANUSCRIPTS, TYPESCRIPTS, REPORTS, ETC.

ABE (1948). *The Advisory Board of Education: First Meeting 7-9 June.* Karachi: Manager of Publications, Ministry of Education.

— (1949). *The Advisory Board of Education: Second Meeting 7-9 February.* Karachi: as above.

— (1950). *Proceedings of the Fourth Meeting of the Advisory Board of Education for Pakistan, Lahore, 29 November-1st December.* Karachi: as above.

— (1955). *Proceedings of the Fifth Meeting of the Advisory Board of Education, 4-5 March 1953.* Karachi: as above.

— (1958). *Proceedings of the Seventh Meeting of the Advisory Board of Education, 27-9 January.* Karachi: as above.

Adm Rep B (1888.) *Administration Report of the Baluchistan Agency for 1886-87.* Calcutta: Printed by the Superintendent of Government Printing.

Adm Rep P (1853). *General Report on the Administration of the Punjab for the Year 1849-50 and 1850-51* London. In *PPP.*

— (1859). *General Report on the Administration of the Punjab Territories in the years 1856-57 and 1857-58.* London.

Anjuman (n.d). *Anjuman-e-Taraqqi-e-Urdu (Hyderabad): Sarguzasht Maqasid, Nizam-e-Amal* [Urdu: Organization for the development of Urdu: history, aims, and methods] Aurangabad: Secretary Anjuman.

Ansari (1983). *Ansari Commission's Report on Form of Government* (headed by Zafar Ahmad Ansari). Islamabad: Government of Pakistan, 4 August.

Appeal (1983). *Sindhi Language: An Appeal for Justice.* Hyderabad: Sindh Friends' Circle.

ARIB (1936). *Inter-University Board: Annual Report 1935-36.* Bangalore: Printed at the Bangalore Press.

— (1937). *Inter-University Board: Annual Report 1936-37.* Bangalore: Printed at the Bangalore Press.

— (1938). *Inter-University Board: Annual Report 1937-38.* Bangalore: Printed at the Bangalore Press.

— (1940). *Inter-University Board: Annual Report 1939-40.* Lucknow: Printed at the Lucknow Publishing House.

Baloch, Nabi B. (ed.) (1971). *Education in Sind Before the British Conquest and the Educational Policies of the Government*. Hyderabad: University of Sindh.

Basu, A. N. (ed.) (1952). *Indian Education in Parliamentary Papers: Part 1 (1832)*. Bombay: Asia Publishing House.

Bayley, E. C. BIA. (1867). The humble petition of the British Indian Association, North Western Provinces. In Malik 1989: 37-44.

Burton, Richard (1847). Memorandum on the Population of Sind by Lieutenant Burton, Sind Survey Dept. Kurrachee, 29 December. In *PPP* Vol. XLIX (1854), 340-2 IOL.

Butler (1903). Letter of Butler to his mother Florence Butler (13 May 1903). Harcourt Butler Collection, MSS. Eur. F. 116 (6). IOL.

CAPS (1993). *A Declaration for Peace and Amity in Sindh*, Karachi: Committee for Amity and Peace in Sindh.

Catalogue (1832). Tenth memoir of the Seharanpore press (1832). In the *Historical Catalogue of the Printed Editions of Holy Scripture in the Library of the British and Foreign Bible Society, Vol. II Part I*. London: 1911.

Census-B. *Census of Bengal*, dates and other details are given in the text.

CE (1944). *Current Expenditure: Details of Demands for Grants and Appropriations 1994-95*, 2 Vols. Islamabad: Government of Pakistan, Finance Division.

Census (1951). *Census of Pakistan 1951; Pakistan; Report and Tables* Vol.1 by E.H. Slade. Karachi: Manager of Government Publications. Table 7 A; Section 2.

—— (1961). *Census of Pakistan 1961; Pakistan; Population; Tables and Reports* by A. Rashid. Karachi: Ministry of Home and Kashmir Affairs. Chapter 5. Statement 5.1, IV-31 & IV-33.

Census (1961). *District Census Report Karachi*. Karachi: Office of the Census Commissioner, Ministry of Home and Kashmir Affairs, Home Affairs Division.

—— Karachi (1981). *1981 Census Report of Karachi Division*. Islamabad: Population Census Organisation, Statistics Division, Government of Pakistan, 1984.

—— Pakistan (1981). *Handbook of Population Census Data* by G. Mujtaba Mirza. Islamabad: Population Census Organization, Statistics Division, Government of Pakistan.

Census Sindh (1981). *1981 Census Report of Sindh Province*. Islamabad: Population Census Organisation, Statistics Division, Government of Pakistan, 1984.

Census Districts. District census reports with dates and other details.

Charter-P. (1985). *The Punjabi Charter of Demands*. Manuscript in Raja Rasalu's Private Collection [PC].

—— S. (1989). *Siraiki Lokan da Charter of Demands* [Siraiki]. Islamabad: Siraiki Lok Sanjh.

Chaudhry, Nazir A. (1977). *Development of Urdu as Official Language in the Punjab, 1848-1974* [Official letters and documents]. Lahore: Government of the Punjab.
Clerk, George (1848). Minute on Scinde, 10 August 1946. In *PPP: Accounts and Papers 1854* Vol. XLIX (1854), 15 IOL.
C.M.S. (1895). Punjab and Sindh mission. Letter No. 152, Church Missionary Society. Quoted from Shackle 1983: 25.
Curzon Correspondence (1900). Lord Curzon's correspondence with A.P. Macdonnell. Curzon Collection MSS. Eur. F. 111 (201), IOL.
—— (1903). Curzon's correspondence with La Touche. Curzon Collection MSS. Eur. F.111 (205), IOL.

Dunsterville, Lionel (1857). MSS Memorandum. Hyderabad, 16 June. In File 28 of 1858, General Dept [SA].

Edn Comm. (1883). *Report of the Indian Education Commission*. Calcutta: Superintendent of Government Printing.
—— B. (1884). *Appendix to Education Commission Report: By the Bengal Committee with Evidence Taken before the Committee and Memorials Addressed to the Education Commission*. Calcutta: Superintendent of Government Printing.
—— Bom (1884). *Report of the Bombay Provincial Committee: Appendix of the Education Commission Report*. Calcutta: Superintendent of Government Printing.
—— NWP and O. (1884). *Appendix to Education Commission Report: By the North West Provinces and Oudh Provincial Committee with Evidence Taken before the Committee and Memorials Addressed to the Education Commission*. Calcutta: Superintendent of Government Printing.
—— P. (1884). *Report of the Punjab Provincial Committee with Evidence Taken before the Committee and Memorials Addressed to the Education Commission*. As above.
Edn Comm. (1959). *Report of the National Education Commission*. Karachi: Government of Pakistan, Ministry of Education.
Edn Dept-F. (1991). *Evaluation Report on the Primary Pashto Text-Books Translation Project*. Peshawar: Education Department; Government of the NWFP.
Edn Ind. (1941). *Education in India in 1938-39*. Delhi: Manager of Publications.
Eighth Plan (1994). *Eighth Five Year Plan 1993-98*.Islamabad: Planning Commission.
Ellis, B.H. (1856). *Report on Education in Sind*, by B.H. Ellis to H.B.E. Frere, Commissioner in Sindh, 29 December 1854. In Baloch 1971: 7-30.
Ellis, (Justice). (1952). Report of the enquiry into the firing by the police at Dacca on 21 February 1952. In Umar 1986: 21-79.

Fisher, T. (1832). Memoir 'compiled from the records of the India Governments at the East India House, in pursuance of a Minute of th'

Committee of Correspondence of the 7th February 1826 . . .'. In Basu 1952: 1-143.

GAD-B. (1888). *Proceedings in the General Department: Bengal.* (August) Calcutta: Superintendent of Government Printing.
GAD-NWP. (1868). *Proceedings of the Honourable E. Drummond Lieutenant Governor of the North Western Provinces in the General Department.* Allahabad: Government Press 1868.
—— (1900). *North-Western Province, October, 1900: Proceedings of the Lieutenant Governor of the North Western Province in the General Department.* Allahabad: Government Press.
Gazeteer-B. (1907). *Baluchistan District Gazeteer Series: Makran and Kharan.* Bombay: Printed at the Times Press.
GCPI. (1832). Report on the Colleges and Schools for Native Education Under the Superintendence of the General Committee of Public Instruction in Bengal 1831. Calcutta: Bengal Orphan Press by G.A. Huttmann. IOL.
Gilani, S. Ijaz and Muttaqeenur Rahman. (1986). *The Language Question: Public Attitudes on Language of Education and Employment.* Islamabad: Gallup Pakistan and National Language Authority.
GOP. (1993). *Pakistan School Statistics.* Islamabad: Government of Pakistan, Ministry of Education.
Gungooli, Deena Nath (1868). Vernacular education in India 2. In GAD-NWP 1868.

Hastings, Warren (1781). The Governor General's Minute. Extract of Bengal Consultations, 18 April. In H M 487.
HBWI (1982). *History of Bangladesh War of Independence.* Dhaka: Government of Bangladesh, Ministry of Information.
HM. *Home Miscellaneous* (Followed by the relevant number). IOL.
Hussain, Zakir (ed.) (1938). *Basic National Education: Report of the Zakir Hussain Committee.* Sagaon, Wardha: Hindustani Talimi Sangh.

IB East Pakistan (1961). Intelligence Branch, East Pakistan Reports: 'Observance of "Shaheed Day" on 21 Feb 1961' and 'Confidential Report for the Fortnight Ended on 28 Feb 1961'. Secret. In HBWI 1982: Vol. 1. 62-8, 69.
IFD (1984). *Kalam On the Move: An Information Collection on Dardish Mountain Tribes in Upper Swat, NWFP.* Kalam/Bern: Integrated Forest Development Project, Kalam. Internal cyclostyled report.
IFH Report (1992). *Karkardagi Report Idara Farogh-e-Hindko di.* [Hindko: The report of activities of the Organization for the Promotion of Hindko] Peshawar: Idara Farogh-e-Hindko.

Jervis, G. (1847). Minute 24 February. In Richey 1922: 11-4. *Khelat Affairs (1872). The Khelat Affairs: Selections from Government Record.* Quetta: Gosha-e-Adab, 1977.

LAD-B. *Legislative Assembly Debates: Bengal.* [The abbreviation will remain the same though the debates are given different names. This is also true for the legislative assembly debate given below. Dates and page numbers are given in the text].
LAD-Bal. *Legislative Assembly Debates: Balochistan.*
LAD-Bom. *Legislative Assembly Debates: Bombay.*
LAD-F. *Legislative Assembly Debates: NWFP.*
LAD-P. *Legislative Assembly Debates: Pakistan.* LAD-Pun. *Legislative Assembly Debates: Punjab.*
LAD-S. *Legislative Assembly Debates: Sindh.*
LAD-WP. *Legislative Assembly Debates: West Pakistan.* [During One Unit, Sindh, Punjab, NWFP, and Balochistan did not have separate legislative assemblies].

Macaulay, T. B. (1835). Minute on the Necessity of English Education, 2 February. In Sharp 1920: 107-17.
Macdonnell Papers (1844-1925) (BO).
—— Letters as Lieutenant Governor of UP MS. English history c. 352.
—— Addresses to Macdonnell MS. English history c. 359.
—— Newspaper Cuttings MSS. English history c. 361, 363.
—— Correspondence (Letters to Macdonnell) MSS. English history c.350-1.
—— Correspondence (Letters from Macdonnell) MSS. English history c.354.
MCH (1965). Minute Book. Municipal Corporation, Hyderabad.
    Resolution No. 721 of 11 June 1965, 68.
Meeting (1914). Proceedings of a meeting held at Government House, Lucknow, 3 April 1914, Meston Collection 1914-1918. MSS. Eur. F.136 (15) IOL.
Memorandum (1969). Memorandum on the New Education Policy. *Punjabi Adab* 10: 9 (September). No pagination. Based on Malik, Rahat. 1969. The New Education Policy, *PT* 7 August.

Nagari Report (1900). An abstract report of the Nagari Pracharini Sabha, MSS. Eur. D. 641, 26 February. IOL.
Napier, Charles (1843). The Sind Battles 1843. Read out before the Sind Historical Society, 19 August 1843. MSS. Eur. F. 208/149 IOL.
NEP (1970). *New Education Policy.* Islamabad: Government of Pakistan, Ministry of Education.
NWFP (1991a). *Human Resources Survey: Teacher Supply and Distribution: Interim Report for Semi-Urban Villages.* Peshawar: Directorate of Primary Education, NWFP.
—— (1991b). *Kachi Study: NWFP.* Draft (November). Peshawar: Directorate of Primary Education, NWFP.

O'Brien, Edward (1882). Report on the Land Revenue Settlement of the Muzaffargarh District of the Punjab. Lahore: Government of the Punjab.

Parulekar, R.V. (ed.) (1955). *Selections from Educational Records (Bombay): Part II 1815-1840*. Bombay: Asia Publishing House. Pashto Academy (1957a). *Da Pakhto Academy*. [Pashto] Peshawar: The Pashto Academy.

—— (1957b). *Da Pashto rasmulkhat pa haqla aehme faesale* [Pashto: Important decisions about the Pashto script], *Pashto* 1: 1 (October), 18-23.

—— (1991). *Pakhto Leek Lar* [Pashto: The conventions of Pashto orthography]. Peshawar: Pashto Academy.

Pashto Tolane (1911-12). *Pashto Qamus* [Pashto: Pashto glossary]. Kabul: Pashto Tolane.

PEC (1947). *Pakistan Educational Conference held in Karachi from 27 November to 1 December 1947*. Karachi: Government of Pakistan.

PEI (1918). *Progress of Education in India 1912-1917: Seventh Quinquennial Review*. Calcutta: Superintendent of Government Printing.

—— (1939). *Progress of Education in India 1932-37: Eleventh Quinquennial Review*. Delhi: Manager of Publications.

Periodical (1800). *Periodical Accounts Relative to the Baptist Missionary Society*. Vol. 1. Chipstone.

Pirpur (1938). *Report of the Inquiry Committee Appointed by the Council of the All-India Muslim League to Inquire Into Muslim Grievances in Congress Provinces*. President, Raja Syed Muhammad Mehdi of Pirpur. No place: published by Liaquat Ali Khan, n.d. (The letter of Pirpur to Jinnah is dated 15 November 1938 and was written at Lucknow).

PNEP (1969). *Proposals for a New Educational Policy*. Islamabad: Ministry of Education and Scientific Research.

PPP. *Printed Parliamentary Papers* (volume and dates given as required). IOL.

Pringle, R.K. (1847). Commissioner's Report on the Conditions and Mode of Administration in the Province of Scinde, to G. Russell Clerk, Governor of Bombay, Kurachee, 31 December. No. 3, 886 of 1847, Political Department [SA].

—— (1848). General Queries submitted on 12 January 1848. Attached in 'List of Documents in Appendix' in Pringle 1847 [SA].

PSC (1888). *Report of the Public Service Commission 1886-1887*. Calcutta: Superindent of Government Printing.

PSC Bom. (1887). *Proceedings of the Public Service Commission Vol. IV: Proceedings Relating to the Bombay Presidency (Including Sindh)*. Calcutta: Superintendent of Government Printing.

—— Pun. (1887). *Proceedings of the Public Service Commission Vol. 1: Proceedings Relating to the Punjab*. Calcutta: Superintendent of Government Printing.

—— NWP and O. (1887). *Proceedings of the Public Service Commission Vol. II: Proceedings Relating to the North Western Provinces and Oudh*. Calcutta: Superintendent of Government Printing.

PUE. (1933). *Punjab University Enquiry Committee Report 1932-1933*. Lahore: Superintendent of Government Printing, Punjab.

Rashdi, Mahtab (1984). Letter to Dr Waheed Qureshi, 26 September. Institute of Sindhology.

RCC (1961). *Report of the Constitution Commission*. Karachi: Manager of Publications, Government of Pakistan.

RCSP (1966). *Report of the Commission on Student Problems and Welfare: Summary of Important Observations and Recommendations*. Islamabad: Government of Pakistan, Ministry of Education, Central Bureau of Education.

Resolution (1979). Resolution No. 275/CF/79 ordering the establishment of a National Language Authority, 4 October. Islamabad: Cabinet Division, Government of Pakistan.

Richey, J. A. (ed.) (1922). *Selections from Educational Records 1840-1859: Part II*. Calcutta: Superintendent of Government Printing.

RMEC (1934). *Report of the Muslim Education Advisory Committee*. Alipore: Bengal Government Press.

RPI-B (1876). *Report on the Progress of Education in Bengal 1875-1876 by the Director of Public Instruction*. Calcutta: Government Press.

RPI-B (1880). *Report on the Progress of Education in Bengal 1879-1880*. Calcutta: Government Press.

RPI-B (1883). *Report on the Progress of Education in Bengal 1882-1883*. Calcutta: Government Press.

RPI-B (1913). *Report on the Progress of Education in Bengal 1912-1913*. Calcutta: Government Press.

RPI-F (1907). *Report on Public Instruction: NWFP 1906-7*. Peshawar: Manager, Government Stationery and Printing.

—— (1927). *Report on Public Instruction: NWFP 1922-1927*. Calcutta: Government of India, Central Publications Bureau.

—— (1938). *Report on Public Instruction in the North West Frontier Province for the Quinquennium 1932-37*. Peshawar: Manager, Government Stationery and Printing.

—— (1939). *Report on Public Instruction: NWFP 1937-38*. Peshawar: Manager, Government Stationery and Printing.

—— (1941). *Report on Public Instruction in the North West Frontier Province: 1939-40*. Peshawar: Manager, Government Printing.

—— (1942). *Report on Public Instruction: NWFP 1940-41*. Peshawar: Manager, Government Stationery and Printing.

—— (1947). *Review on the Annual Report on Public Instruction in the NWFP for 1945-46*. Peshawar: Secretary to the NWFP Government, Home Department.

RPI-NWP (1868). *Report on the Progress of Education, North Western Provinces: 1867-68, by the Director of Public Instruction*. Allahabad: Government Press.

—— (1873). *Report on the Progress of Education: DPI-NWP, 1872-33*. As above.

RPI-O (1869). *Report of Public Instruction Oudh 1868-1869*. Lucknow: DPI, Oudh.

RPI-P (1860-61). *Report on Popular Education in the Punjab and Its Dependencies*. by Captain. A. R. Fuller, D. P. I. Punjab. Lahore: Government Press, 1864.

—— (1871). *Report on Popular Education in the Punjab and its Dependencies 1870-71*. Lahore: Director of Public Instruction.
—— (1877). *Report on Public Instruction in the Punjab and its Dependencies 1876-77*. Lahore: as above.
—— (1879). *Report on Public Instruction in the Punjab and its Dependencies 1878-79*. Lahore: as above.
—— (1881). *Report on Popular Education: Punjab and its Dependencies 1880-1881*. Lahore: as above.
—— (1888). *Report on Public Instruction in the Punjab and its Dependencies 1887-88*. Lahore: as above.
—— (1897). *Report on Public Instruction in the Punjab and its Dependencies 1896-1897*. Lahore: Civil and Military Gazette Press by DPI.
—— (1899). *Report on Public Instruction in the Punjab and its Dependencies 1898-99*. Lahore: as above.
—— (1900). *Report on Public Instruction in the Punjab and its Dependencies 1899-1900*. Lahore: as above.
—— (1907). *Report on Public Instruction in the Punjab and its Dependencies 1906-07*. Lahore as above.
—— (1911). *Report on Education in the Punjab: 1910-1911*. Lahore: Punjab Government Press.
—— (1912). *Report on the Progress of Education in the Punjab: 1911-1912*. Lahore: Punjab Government Press.
RPI-S (1938). *Quinquennial Report on Public Instruction in Sind 1932-37*. Karachi: The Government Press.
—— (1940). *Annual Report on Public Instruction in Sind for 1938-39*. Karachi: The Government Press.
—— (1943). *Annual Report on Public Instruction in Sind 1939-40*. Karachi: The Government Press.

Sangat. (n.d.). *Declare Sindhi as Official Language of West Pakistan*. [Pamphlet] Karachi.
Sath (1990). *Sindhi Boli Sath: Constitution*. Hyderabad: Hafeez Qureshi, Convener of the Sath.
SCIU (1930). *Second Conference of Indian Universities*. Cawnpore: Secretary, Inter-University Board.
Senate (1989). *Report of the Special Committee of the Senate on the Situation in Sindh*. Islamabad: The Senate of Pakistan.
Sharp, H. (1920). *Selections from Educational Records Part 1: 1781-1839*. Calcutta: Superintendent of Government Printing.
SLA (1991). *Sindhi Language Authority: Objectives and Conditions*. Karachi: Sindhi Language Authority.
SRSC (1852). *Sixth Report from the Select Committee on Indian Territories*, PPP Vol. 29 (1852-3).
Steedman, E. B. (1882). *Report on the Revised Settlement of the Jhang District of the Punjab*. Lahore.
Sunkersett, Juggonath (1847). Minute dated 1 May. In Richey 1922: 16-7.

TM (1947). *Pakistaner Rashtra Bhasha, Bangla na Urdu* [Bengali: Pakistan's state language, Bengali or Urdu?]. Dhaka:Tamaddun Majlis.

UGC (1982). *Report Study Group on the Teaching of Languages.* Islamabad: Government of Pakistan, University Grants Commission.

USAID (1990). *Socio-Economic Profile of South Waziristan Agency* by Lynn Carter and Shahzad Raza for Planning and Development Department, NWFP.

—— (1991a). *Socio-Economic Profile of Kurram Agency* by Lynn Carter, for Planning and Development Department, NWFP (Printed report).

—— (1991b). *Socio-Economic Profile of Orakzai Agency* for Planning and Development Department, NWFP.

—— (1991c). *Socio-Economic Profile of Bajaur Agency* for Planning and Development Department, NWFP.

—— (1993). *Socio-Economic Profile of Mohmand Agency* for Planning and Development Department, NWFP.

UPINR (1937). United Provinces Indian Newspaper Report 1934-37: notes on the press (Confidential) No. 14 of 1937. IOL.

Warden, F. (1828). 'Minute' 24 March. In Basu 1952: 221.
Wardha. (1939?). *Report of the Committee Appointed by the Council of the All-India Muslim League to Examine the Wardha Scheme.* Convenor: Raja of Pirpur. Lucknow: The Pioneer Press, n.d. (probably 1939).

Wellesley, Marquis (1800). Minute: with respect to the foundation of a College at Fort William. Appendix 2. In *Sixth Report from the Select Committee on Indian Territories* in PPP Vol.2 1852-1853: 11-22. IOL.

## PART B: UNPUBLISHED THESES, BOOKS, ARTICLES, ETC.

Abbas, Shemeem (1993). The Power of English in Pakistan. *World Englishes* 12; 2: 147-56.

Abdullah, Syed (1976). *Pakistan Mein Urdu Ka Masla* [Urdu: The problem of Urdu in Pakistan]. Lahore: Maktaba Khayaban-e-Adab.

Abeysekera, Charles and Gunasinghe, Newton. (1987). *Facets of Ethnicity in Sri Lanka.* Colombo: Social Scientists Association.

Adil Mukhtar (1962). Sindh ki diary. [Urdu: The diary of Sindh]. *J* 17 October.

Afzal, Rafique (1986). *Political Parties in Pakistan 1947-1958, Vol. 1.* Islamabad: National Institute of Historical and Cultural Research.

—— (1987). *Political Parties in Pakistan 1958-1969, Vol. 2.* Islamabad: as above.

Aggarwal, J.C. (1984). *Landmarks in the History of Modern Indian Education.* Delhi: Vani Educational Books.

Ahmad, Abul Mansur (1947). Bangla Bhashai Huevi Amadir Rashtro-bhasha. [Bengali: Bengali will be our state language]. *Azad* 30 June. In Umar. 1970: 31.

—— (1989). *Amar Dekha Rajniteer Ponchash Basar* [Bengali: Fifty years of politics as I saw it] Part 2. Dhaka: Srizon Prakashani Ltd.

Ahmad, Iftikhar (1976). *Pakistan General Elections: 1970.* Lahore: University of the Punjab.

Ahmad, Muneer (1964). *The Civil Servant in Pakistan.* Lahore: Oxford University Press.

Ahmad, Rafiuddin (1981). *The Bengali Muslims 1871-1906: A Quest for Identity.* Delhi: Oxford University Press (2nd. ed.) 1988.

—— (ed.) (1990). *Religion, Nationalism and Politics in Bangladesh.* New Delhi: South Asian Publishers.

Ahmad, S. (1987). What we may lose with English. *M* 7 March.

Ahmad, Saeed (1992). Siraiki suba aur Bahawalpur sube ki tehrik.[Urdu: Siraiki province and the movement for Bahawalpur]. *Jasarat* 6 May.

Ahmad, Salahuddin (1989). Hamari qaomi zaban aor us ka rasmul khat. [Urdu: Our national language and its script]. In Majeed 1989: 253-62.

Ahmad, Saleem (1968). *Oluh Pakistan men bolin jo maslo.* [Sindhi: the problem of languages in West Pakistan] Khairpur: Privately published.

Ahmad, Syed Iqbal (1992). *Balochistan: Its Strategic Importance.* Karachi: Royal Book Co.

Ahmad, Tajuddin (1948). 'Diary'. Handwritten entries reproduced in Umar 1984.

Ahmed, Akbar S. (1976). *Millennium and Charisma among Pathans: A Critical Essay in Social Anthropology.* London: Routledge and Kegan Paul.

—— (1991). *Resistance and Control in Pakistan.* London: Routledge. Reprint of *Religion and Politics in Muslim Society.* Cambridge: Cambridge University Press, 1983.

Ahmed, Azizuddin (1988). *Kya Hum Ekattha Reh Sakte Hain?* [Urdu: Can we live together?]. Lahore: Maktaba Fikr-o-Danish.

Ahmed, Emajuddin (1980). *Bureaucratic Elites in Segmented Economic Growth: Pakistan and Bangladesh.* Dhaka: University Press Limited.

Ahmed, Feroze (1992a). The language question in Sindh. In Zaidi 1992a: 139-55.

—— (1992b). Pakistan's problems of national integration: the case of Sindh. In Zaidi 1992 a: 156-79.

Ahmed, Shakeel (1989). *Sir Sahibzada Abdul Qaium: Life and Work.* Peshawar: Islamia College, University of Peshawar.

Akash, M. M. (1988). *Socioeconomic Background to the Language Movement. A Research Project* [Bengali] Vol.3. Dhaka: Bangladesh Development Research Institute.

Akbar, Muhammad (1957). Da jabe da taraqqi lare. [Pashto: The way of the progress of the language]. *Abaseen* (February), 32-6.

Alam, Said (1990). *Shimali Ilaqajat kc Lisani o Adabi Jaiza* [Urdu: Linguistic and literary survey of the Northern Areas] Islamabad: Privately printed.

Alam, Shamsul (1991). Language as political articulation: East Bengal in 1952. *Journal of Contemporary Asia* 21; 4: 469-87.
Alavi, Hamza (1972). The state in post-colonial societies Pakistan and Bangladesh. *New Left Review* No. 74 (July- August), 59-81.
—— (1987). Politics of ethnicity in India and Pakistan. Originally published in *Pakistan Progressive* 9: 1 (Summer). Quoted from Alavi, H. and Harriss, John (eds.). 1989. *Sociology of Developing Societies.* London: Macmillan Education Ltd. 222-46.
—— (1991). *Nationhood and the nationalities in Pakistan.* Donnan and Werbner 163-87.
Alexandre, Pierce (1972). *An Introduction to Languages and Language in Africa.* London: Heinemann.
—— (1968). Some linguistic problems of nation-building in Negro Africa. In Fishman *et al*. 1968: 119-27.
Ali, Babar (1992). Political forces in Sind. In Zaidi 1992a: 180-92.
Ali, Haqiqat (n.d.). *Wakhi Language Book* [Wakhi primer] Hunza: Wakhi Culture Association.
Ali, Muhammad (1942). Da Pakhto rasmul khat [Pashto: the Pashto Script]. *Nan Paroon.* 25 June, 13-5.
Ali, Muhammad (1987). Interview of G.M. Syed. In Siddiqui 1987: 63-7.
Ali, Nadir (1992). A daily that was. *FP: Weekend Post* 25 September.
Ali, Usman (1991). *Shinalogy* [Urdu]. Gilgit: Usmani Kutab Khana.
Alisjahbana, Takdir S. (1971). Some planning processes in the development of the Indonesian-Malay language. In Rubin and Jernudd, 1971:179-87.
Amin, Tahir (1988). *Ethno-National Movements of Pakistan: Domestic and International Factors.* Islamabad: Institute of Policy Studies.
Anderson, Benedict (1983). *Imagined Communities: Reflections on the Origin and Spread of Nationalism.* London: Verso (revised edition) 1991.
—— (1990). *Language and Power: Exploring Political Cultures in Indonesia.* Ithaca and London: Cornell University Press.
Anqa, Muhammad H. (1973). Balochi zaban u a'e nibishtanke war. [Balochi: The Balochi language and its orthographic norms] *Ulus* [Balochi] (November-December) 46-52.
Apronti, Eric O. (1974). Sociolinguistics and the question of a national language: the case of Ghana. *Studies in African Linguistics.* (October), 1-19.
Arif, Mazhar. (1992). The Other Punjab. *FP* (May) 28 August.
Armstrong, Robert G (1968). Language policy in West Africa. In Fishman *et al*. 227-37.
Aslam, Pir. (n.d.). *Sindhi zaban qaumi zaban* [Sindhi Pamphlet: Sindhi language, national language]. Hyderabad: Sindh National Students Federation.
Aslam, Talat (1987). Siraiki awakening. *Herald* (September), 87-92.
Awan, M.A. (1994). Hindko poet in distress. Letter to the Editor. *The News* 15 October.
Aziz, Mir Abdul (1983). The Kashmiri language in Azad Kashmir and Pakistan. *PT* 20 June.
—— (1988). Kashmiri language: stranger in its own country. *MN* 19 April.

Azzam, Salem (1990). *Shaheed ul Islam Muhammad Ziaul Haq*. London: Indus Thames Publishers.

Babar, M. Mashraf (1945). Zamung jaba o mung. [Pashto: We and our language]. *Pakhtun* (1 November 1945), 17-8.

Bachrach, Peter. (ed.) (1971). *Political Elites in a Democracy*. New York: Atherton Press.

Backstrom, Peter C. (1992a). Balti. In *SSNP-2*: 3-27.

—— (1992b). Burushaski. In *SSNP-2*: 31-54

—— (1992c). Domaaki. In *SSNP-2*: 77-83.

—— (1992d). Wakhi. In *SSNP-2*: 57-74.

Badal, Khan B. (1990). Balochi zaban e demrai e ur u janjal. [Balochi: Impediments in the development of Balochi]. *Labzank* (January-July), 11-22.

Baha, Lal (1978). *NWFP Administration Under the British Rule 1901-1919*. Islamabad: National Commission on Historical and Cultural Research.

—— (1979). The Khilafat movement and the North West Frontier Province. *Journal of the Research Society of Pakistan*. (16 July), 1-22.

Baksh, Khuda (1960). *Nisab-e-Zaroori* [Urdu]. Multan.

Baladi, Arif (1990). *Qaumi Ghulami* [Sindhi pamphlet: National slavery]. Hyderabad: Jagarta publications.

Baloch, Khair Muhammad (1993). *Motor Vehicle and Its Parts*. Hyderabad: Sindhi Language Authority.

Baloch, Khan (ed.). (n.d.). *Madri Zaban e Zaria-e-Taleem* [Sindhi pamphlet: The mother tongue as the medium of instruction]. Hyderabad: published privately by the editor.

Baloch, Nabi Baksh (ed.) (1993). *Sindhi Translation of Act IX of 1872: The Indian Contract Act*. Hyderabad: Sindhi Language Authority.

Banuri, Tariq (1990). Modernization and its discontents. In Marglin and Marglin 1990: 73-101.

Barelvi, I. (ed.) (1952). *Khutbat-e-Abdul Haq* [Urdu: the speeches of Abdul Haq]. Karachi: Anjuman-e-Taraqqi-e-Urdu, 1964 reprint.

Barelvi, Syed M. (1970). *Angrezon Ki Lisani Policy* [Urdu: The linguistic policy of the British]. Karachi: All-Pakistan Education Conference.

—— (1987). *Suba-e-Sindh Ki Taleemi Halat aur Hamare Masail 1852-1985* [Urdu: The province of Sindh's condition and our problems]. Typescript.

—— (1988). Suba-e-Punjab aur Urdu. [Urdu: The province of the Punjab and Urdu]. *Urdu Nama* (February), 24-7.

—— (1989). Zaban aur rasmul khat [Urdu: Language and script]. In Majeed 1989: 209-18.

Barth, Fredrik (1959a). Political leadership among Swat Pathans. LSE monograph. London: Athlone Press.

—— (1959b). Segmentary opposition and the theory of games: a study of Pathan organization. *Journal of the Royal Anthropological Institute* 89, part 1.

—— (1969a). *Ethnic Groups and Boundaries: The Social Organization of Culture Difference*. Boston: Little, Brown & Co.

—— (1969b). Pathan identity and its maintenance. In Barth 1969a: 117-34.
Basu, A.N. (1947). *Education in Modern India* Calcutta: Orient Book Co.
Baumgardner, Robert J. (ed.) (1993). *The English Language in Pakistan.* Karachi: Oxford University Press.
Bearce, G. D. (1961). *British Attitudes Towards India, 1784-1858.* London: Oxford University Press.
Beckett, J. C. (1966). *The Making of Modern Ireland 1603-1923.* London: Faber & Faber.
Beer, William. R and Jacob, James E. (eds.). 1985. *Language Policy and National Unity.* New Jersey, Totowa: Rowman & Allanhead.
Bender, M. Lionel (1985). Ethiopian language policy 1974-1981. *Anthropological Linguistics* 27: 3 (Fall), 273-79.
Berger, Peter L. and Berger, Brigitte (1976). Sociology: *A Biographical Approach.* (rev. ed.) Harmondsworth: Penguin Books.
Berghe, Pierre L.V.D. (1968). Language and nationalism in South Africa. In Fishman *et al.* 1968: 215-24.
Bhatt, Rakesh Mohan (1992). Sociolinguistic area and language policies. In Dimock *et al.* 1992: 47-69.
Bhutto, Muhammad Musa (1972). Balochi zaban ke rasmulkhat ka masla [Urdu: The problem of the script of the Balochi language]. *Jasarat* 14 September.
Biddulph, John (1880). *Tribes of the Hindoo Koosh.* Reprint. Karachi: Indus Publications, 1971.
Bizenjo, Tahir (1992). *Balochistan: siasat men utar charhao* [Urdu: Balochistan: The ups and downs of politics]. Karachi: Pakistani Adabi Publications.
Boman-Behram, B. A. (1943). *Educational Controversies in India: The Cultural Conquest of India Under British Imperialism.* Bombay: D.Y. Trana Porevala Sons and Co.
Bomford, Trevor (1895). Rough notes on the grammar of the language spoken in the Western Punjab. *Journal of the Royal Asiatic Society of Bengal* LXIV; Part 1: 296-335.
Bose, N. S. (1960). *Indian Awakening and Bengal.* Calcutta: Firma K. L. Mukhopadhyay.
Braibanti, Ralph (1966). *Asian Bureacractic Systems Emergent from the British Imperial Tradition* Durham, N. C.: Duke University Press.
Brass, Paul R. (1974). *Language, Religion and Politics in North India.* Cambridge: Cambridge University Press.
—— (1979). Elite groups, symbol manipulation and ethnic identity among the Muslims of South Asia. In Taylor and Yapp: 35-77.
—— (1991). *Ethnicity and Nationalism.* New Delhi and London: Sage Publications.
Bray, Denis (1913). *The Life History of a Brahvi.* Karachi: Royal Book Company.
Brohi, Nasser (1977). *Studies in Brahvi History.* Karachi: No information.

Broomfield, J. H. (1966). The regional elites: a theory of modern Indian history. *Indian Economic and Social History Review* III: 3 (September). In Metcalfe 1971: 279-90.

Buddruss, Georg (1982). *Khowar-Texte in Arabischer Schrift* [German: Khowar texts in the Arabic script]. Weisbaden: Akademie der Wissenschaften und der Literatur.

Bughio, Azizur Rehman (1991). The language, nationality issues. *FP* 3 May.

Bukhari, Tanvir (1989). *Punjabi Urdu Lughat* [Punjabi-Urdu dictionary]. Lahore: Urdu Science Board.

Bunting, B. (1966). *Education for the Apartheid*. London: South African Education Board.

Burgess, M. Elaine (1978). The resurgence of ethnicity: myth or reality. *Ethnic and Racial Studies*. 1 (July), 261-8.

Burton, Richard (1849). A Grammar of the Jataki or Belochki Dialect. *Journal of the Bombay Branch of the Royal Asiatic Society* III: Part 1: 84-125.

—— (1851). *Sindh and the Races that Inhabit the Valley of the Indus*. Lahore: Khan Publishers, Reprint 1976.

Calvet, Louis-Jean (1974). *Linguistique et colonialisme: petit traite de glottophagie*. Paris: Payot.

Cannon, Garland (ed.) (1970). *The Letters of Sir William Jones Vol.1*. Oxford: Clarendon Press.

Cans, R (1981). Le francais est-il encore une langue scientifique? [French: Is French once again a scientific language?]. *Le Monde*. 7 November.

Caroe, Olaf (1957). *The Pathans*. London: Oxford University Press.

Chamberlain, M.E. (1974). *Britain and India: The Interaction of Two Peoples*. Hamden, Connecticut: Aschon Books.

Chatterji, Saniti K. (1926). *The Origin and Development of the Bengali Language* Calcutta: This edition London: George Allen and Unwin, 1970.

Chikna Choor (pseudonym) (1963). Totay. [Punjabi: Parts]. *Punjabi Adab* (January-February), 4.

Chowdhury, Kabir (1992). *Of Ekushe and Other Essays*. Dhaka: Olat Palat Prokashani.

Chowdhury, Munier (1990). *Three Plays*. Translated from Bangla by Kabir Chowdhury. Dhaka: Bangla Academy.

Clark, Robert P. (1979). *The Basques: The Franco Years and Beyond*. Reno: University of Nevada Press.

Clive, J. (1973). *Macaulay: The Shaping of the Historian*. New York: Knopf.

Cohen, Stephen P. (1984). *The Pakistan Army*. Berkeley: University of California Press. Edition used: New Delhi: Himalayan Books, 1984.

Cohn, Bernard (1985). The command of language and the language of command. In Guha, Ranjit (ed.). *Subaltern Studies* IV. Delhi: Oxford University Press. 276-329.

Colebrooke, H. T. (1837). Discourse at the Royal Asiatic Society of Great Britain and Ireland. In Colebrooke, *Miscellaneous Essays*. London: William H. Allen and Co. Vol. 1.

Comrie, B. (ed.) (1987). *Languages of the World*. Cambridge: Cambridge University Press.
Connolly, William E. (1983). The politics of discourse. In Shapiro 1984: 139-67.
Connor, Walker (1993). Beyond reason: the nature of the ethno-national bond. *Ethnic and Racial Studies* 16: 3 (July), 373-89.
Cooper, Robert L. (1989). *Language Planning and Social Change*. Cambridge: Cambridge University Press.
Crafurd, Q. (1790). *Sketches Chiefly Relating to the Historical Learning and Manners of the Hindoos*. London.

Dahl, Robert A. (1958). A critique of the ruling elite model. *American Political Science Review* L 11 (June), 463-9.
—— (1961). *Who Governs? Democracy and Power in an American City*. New Haven: Yale University Press.
Dahrendorf, Ralf (1959). *Class and Class Conflict in Industrial Society*. London: Routledge and Kegan Paul. First published in German as *Soziale Klassen und Klassenkonflikt in der industriellen Gesellschaft*, 1957.
Dalby, David (1967). A survey of the indigenous scripts of Liberia and Sierra Leone: Vai, Mende, Loma, Kpelle and Bassa. *African Language Studies* 8: 1-51.
Das, Sirri Kumar (1966). *Early Bengali Prose: Carey to Vidyasagar*. Calcutta: Bookland Private.
Dashtiari, Saba (1992) Izzat mandeen Waja Shoonkar Mahtak *Balochi* [Balochi: To the honourable editor of the monthly *Balochi*]. *Balochi*. 6 December, 6-7.
—— (1993a). Shoonkar-e-nama. [Balochi: To editors]. *Balochi Labzank* (October), 7-10.
—— (1993b). Siasatdan, danishwar, sahafi tapin ut Chitthi [Brahvi: A letter to politicians, intellectuals and journalists]. *Tawar* (January), 45-46.
Davies, A. M. (1935). *Strange Destiny: A Biography of Warren Hastings*. New York: G. P. Putnam's Sons.
Davies, Thomas (1845). *Essays and Poems With a Centenary Memoir*. Dublin: Gill Reprint 1945.
Day, Richard R. (1981). ESL: A factor in linguistic genocide? In Fisher, J.C., Clarke, M.A and Schachter, J. (eds.) (1981) *On TESOL '80 Building Bridges: Research and Practice in Teaching English as a Second Language*. Washington D.C.: TESOL. 73-8.
—— (1985). The ultimate inequality: linguistic genocide. In Wolfson, Nessa and Manes (eds.) (1985) *Language of Inequality*. Berlin: Mouton.
De Francis, John (1977). *Colonialism and Language Policy in Vietnam*. The Hague: Mouton.
De Tassy, Garcin (1935). *Khutbat-e-Garcin De Tassy* [Urdu: Lectures of De Tassy 1850-69]. Aurangabad: Anjuman-e-Taraqqi-e-Urdu. Original French: *Histoire de la Literature Hindouie et Hindoustanie*. 2nd ed. Paris: Librarie de La Societe Asiatique.
Decker, Kendall D. (1992a). Khowar. In *SSNP-5*: 25-42.

—— (1992b) Yidgah (chapter 3), Phalura (chapter 4), Kalasha (chapter 5) Dameli (chapter 6), Eastern Kativiri (chapter 7). In *SSNP*-5: 43-150.

Denison, J. (1977). Language death or language suicide? *International Journal of the Sociology of Language*, 12: 13-22.

Deutsch, K. W. (1953). *Nationalism and Social Communication: An Inquiry into the Foundations of Nationality*. Cambridge: MIT Press, revised ed. 1966.

Dharmadasa, K. N. O. (1977). Nativism, diglossia and the Sinhalese identity in the language problem in Sri Lanka. *Linguistics* No. 193 (June), 21-32.

Dil, Afia (1993). *Two Traditions of the Bengali Language*. Islamabad: National Institute of Historical and Cultural Research.

Dil, Anwar (1966). *Shahidullah Presentation Volume*. Lahore: Linguistic Research Group of Pakistan.

Dimock, Edward C., Kachru, Braj B., and Krishnamurti, B. (1992). *Dimensions of Sociolinguistics in South Asia: Papers in Memory of Gerald Kelly*. Lahore: Vanguard Books; New Delhi: American Institute of Indian Studies.

Dittmer, Kerrin (1972). *Die Indischen Muslims und die Hindi-Urdu-Kontroverse in den United Provinces* [German: The Indian Muslims and the Urdu-Hindi controversy in the United Provinces]. Wiesbaden: Otto Harrassowitz.

Donnan, Hastings and Werbner, Pnina (eds.) (1991). *Economy and Culture in Pakistan: Migrants and Cities in a Muslim Society*. London: Macmillan.

Dow, Hugh (1976). A note on the Sindhi alphabet. *Asian Affairs* 63: 1 (February), 54-6.

Dressler, W. (1972). On the phonology of language death. In Peranteau, P. M., Levi, J. N., and Phares, G. C. (eds.) (1972) *Papers from the Eighth Regional Meeting: Chicago Linguistic Society*. Chicago: Chicago Linguistic Society.

Dupree, Louis (1978). Language and Politics in Afghanistan: an essay in sociolinguistics through time. In Maloney, Clarence (ed.) *Language and Civilization Change in South Asia*. Leiden: E. J. Brill.

—— (1973). *Afghanistan*. New Jersey: Princeton University Press, 1978.

Durrani, Atash (1993). *Urdu Istalahat Nigari* [Urdu: The making of technical terms in Urdu]. Islamabad. Muqtadira Qaumi Zaban.

Durrani, Mariam and Hyder, Najia (1994). Unpublished survey of language attitudes in Rich Bhen, Abbottabad. Department of Anthropology, Quaid-i-Azam University, Islamabad.

Eidheim, Harold (1969). When ethnic identity is a social stigma. In Barth 1969a: 39-57.

Elfbein, Josef H. (1983). *A Baluchi Miscellany of Erotica and Poetry: Codex Oriental Additional 24048 of British Library*. Naples: Institute Orientale di Napoli 43: 2.

—— (1963). Baluchi manuscripts in the British Museum. *In Proceedings of the XXV International Congress of Orientalists*. Moscow.

Embree, Ainslee (1962). *Charles Grant and British Rule in India*. London: George Allen and Unwin Limited.
Emeneau, Murray B. (1962). *Brahvi and Dravidian Comparative Grammar*. Berkeley and Los Angeles: University of California Press.
Emenyonu, Ernest M. (1989). National language policy in Nigeria: Implications for English teaching. In Kennedy (1989). *Language Planning and English Language Teaching*. Hertfordshire: Prentice Hall International. 82-9.
Esman, Milton J. (1985). The politics of official bilingualism in Canada. In Beer and Jacob (eds.) (1985): 45-6.

Fainberg, Yaffa Allong (1983). Linguistic and sociodemographic factors influencing the acceptance of Hebrew neologisms. *International Journal of the Sociology of Language*, 41: 9-40.
Faizi, Inayatullah (1986). *Chitral Mein Urdu* [Urdu: Urdu in Chitral] Islamabad: Muqtadira Qaumi Zaban.
Faqir, M. (1956). Punjabi Conference. *Punjabi* (May), 3.
Faridi, Qais. (n.d.). *Chand Siraiki Istalahat o Mutradifat* [Siraiki: Some Siraiki terms and usages] Khanpur: Dehareech Adabi Academy.
Fatehpuri, Farman (1977). *Urdu-Hindi Tanaza* [Urdu: Urdu-Hindi Controversy]. Islamabad: Qaumi Committee Barai Sadsala Taqribat Paidaish-e-Quaid-i-Azam.
—— (1989). *Pakistan Movement and Hindi-Urdu Conflict*. Lahore: Sang-e-Meel.
Fazal, Abul (n.d.). *Ain-e-Akbari* [Urdu] trans. from Persian by Fida Ali. Vol. 1, Part 2 and Vol.2 Lahore: Sang-e-Meel.
Fellman, Jack (1974). *The Revival of a Classical Tongue: Eliezer Ben Yehuda and the Modern Hebrew Language*. The Hague: Mouton.
Fellman, Jack and Fishman, Joshua A. (1977). Language Planning in Israel: Solving terminological problems. In Rubin *et al* 1977: 79-95.
Fierman, William (1985). Language development in Soviet Uzbekistan. In Kriendler (1985a): 205-33.
Fishman, Joshua (1972). *Language and Nationalism: Two Integrative Essays*. Rowley, Massachusetts: Newbury House.
—— Ferguson, Charles A., and Gupta, Jyotirindra Das (eds). (1968). *Language Problems of Developing Nations*. New York: John Wiley.
—— (1977a). Advances in the creation and revision of writing systems. In Fishman 1977b: xi-xxviii.
—— (ed.) (1977b). *Advances in the Creation and Revision of Writing Systems*. The Hague: Mouton.
—— (1989). Language and Ethnicity. In *Minority Sociolinguistic Perspective*. Cleveden, Avon (UK): Multilingual Matters.
—— (1991). *Reversing the Language Shift*. Clevedon, Avon: Multilingual Matters.
Franda, Marcus F. (1970). Communism and regional politics in East Pakistan. *Asian Survey* (May), 588-606.

Fuller, A. (1815). Brief View of the Baptist Missions and Translations. In Shackle 1983: 3.
Foucault, Michel (1976). Disciplinary power and subjection. In Lukes 1986: 229-43.
Fox, Richard G. (1971). *Kin, Class, Raja and Rule: State Hinterland Relations in Pre-Industrial India*. Berkeley: University of California Press.

Gair, James W. (1983). Sinhala and English: the effects of a Language Act. *Language Problems and Language Planning* 7: 1 (Spring), 43-59.
Galbraith, John K. (1984). Power and organization. In Lukes (1986) 211-2.
Gallagher, Charles F. (1968). North African problems and prospects: language and identity. In Fishman *et al.* (1968): 129-5.
―― (1971). Language reform and social modernization in Turkey. In Rubin and Jernudd (1971) 157-78.
Galtung, J. (1980). *The True Worlds: A Transnational Perspective*. New York: The Free Press.
Ganadiah (pseudonym) (1984). *Siraiki Qaumiat* [Urdu:Siraiki nationality]. Multan: Siraiki Lok Sanjh.
Gandhi, M. K. (1922) *Young India (1919-1922)*. Quoted from Nurullah and Naik, Part 2 1943: 564.
―― (1942). *Our Language Problem*. Anand T. Hingorani (ed.) Karachi.
Gankovsky, Yuri V. (1964). *The Peoples of Pakistan: An Ethnic History*. Trans. from Russian by Igor Gavrilov. Moscow: Peoples' Publishing House, 1971.
Geertz, Guido (1963). The integrative revolution: primordial sentiments and civil politics in the new states. In Geertz, G. (ed.) 1963. *Old Societies and New States: The Quest for Modernity in Asia and Africa*. New York: Free Press.
―― (1979). History as language planner: The Netherlandic language area. *Word* 30: 1-2 (April-August), 58-75.
Gellner, Ernest (1983). *Nations and Nationalism*. Oxford: Blackwell, 1992.
Ghaffar, Khan Abdul (1929a). Da sarkar madrase o Pukhtana: Part 1 [Pashto: the government schools and the Pukhtuns]. *Pakhtun* (August), 49-50.
―― (1929b). Da sarkar madrase o Pukhtana: Part 2. *Pakhtun* (September), 35-9.
―― (1969). *My Life and Struggle: Autobiography of Badshah Khan*. Delhi: Hind Pocket Books Ltd.
Ghamshad, Akbar (1992). Awali jamat e Balochi wangi kitab. [Balochi: Balochi textbook for class 1]. *Balochi* (March), 18-20 & 97.
Ghose, M. M. (ed.) (1912). *Selections from the Writings of Girish Chandra Ghosh*. Calcutta: India Daily News Press.
Giles, Howard, Bourhis, Richard R.Y., and Taylor, D.M., (1977). Towards a theory of language in ethnic group relations. In Giles, H. (ed.) *Language, Ethnicity, and Intergroup Relations*. London: Academic Press. 307-48.

Glazer, N., and Moynihan, D. P. (1975). Introduction. In. Glazer, and Moynihan D. P. (eds.) *Ethnicity: Theory and Experience*. Cambridge, Mass: Harvard University Press. 1-26.
Gohar, Mumtaz. (ed.) (1988). *Muntakhabat-e-Tahzeeb-e-Niswan* [Urdu: Selections from *Tahzeeb-e-Niswan*]. Lahore: Maghribi Pakistan Urdu Academy.
Goodnow, Henry F. (1969). *The Civil Service of Pakistan: Bureaucracy in a New Nation*. Karachi: Oxford University Press.
Gordon, David C. (1985). The Arabic language and national identity: the cases of Algeria and of Lebanon. In Beer and Jacob (1985). 134-50.
Gorman, Thomes P. (1973). Language allocation and language planning in a developing nation. In Rubin and Shuy 1973: 72-82.
Grant, Charles (1792). *Observations on the State of Society Among the Asiatic Subjects of Great Britain Particularly with Respect to Morals; and on the Means of Improving it*. In *PPP* Part 4, Vol. 10 (1812-13).
Grierson, George (1903-1921). *Linguistic Survey of India*. Reprinted as *Linguistic Survey of Pakistan*, 5 Vols. (subtitles are given below). Lahore: Sang-e-Meel (n.d.).
—— *Introductory*, Vol. 1.
—— *Aryan Family*, Vol. 2.
—— *Indo-Aryan Family (Central Group)*, Vol. 3.
—— *Ando-Aryan Family (North Western Group)*, Vol. 4.
—— *Aryan Family: kafir, khowar, etc.*, Vol. 5.
Grillo, R.D. (1989). *Dominant Languages: Language and Hierarchy in Britain and France*. Cambridge: Cambridge University Press.
Gul, Ismat Ara (1982). Hindko zaban ke huroof taehji. [Urdu: The alphabet of the Hindko language]. *Jamhoor* 30 March.
Gulati, Chandrika J. (1988). *Bangladesh: Liberation to Fundamentalism*. New Delhi: Commonwealth Publishers.
Gumperz, T. J. (1977). Language problems in the rural development in North India. *Journal of Asian Studies* 16: 2 (February) 251-9.
Gupta, Jyotirindra Das (1970). *Language Conflict and National Development: Group Politics and National Language*. Berkeley and London: University of California Press.
—— and Gumperz, John J. (1968). Language, communication and control in North India. In Fishman *et al.* 1968: 151-66.

Hai, M. Abdul (1971). The development of Bengali since the establishment of Pakistan. In Rubin and Jernudd 1971: 189-92.
Haideri, Muhammad H. (1971). Siraiki adab [Urdu]. In *Tarikh Adbiyat Musalmanan Pakistan o Hind* [Urdu: History of the literature of the Muslims of Pakistan and India]. Lahore: Punjab University. XIV; 2.
Halbfass, Wilhelm (1988). *India and Europe: An Essay in Understanding* [German ed. 1981]. New York: State University of New York Press.
Hali, Altaf Hussain (1901). *Hayat-e-Javed* [Urdu: Life of the immortal]. Edition used: English translation by Qadiri, K. H. and Matthews, David J. Delhi: Idarah-i-Adabiyat-i-Delhi, 1979.

Hallberg, Daniel G. (1992a). Pashto: a sociolinguistic and dialect study. In *SSNP-4*: 1-44.
—— (1992b). The languages of Indus Kohistan. In *SSNP-1*: 83-141.
Hamdam, Naguman (1992). Nadrahen Balochi meuseum e zaban joriyat? [Balochi: Is Balochi becoming the language of the museum?]. *Balochi Labzank* (November), 21-31.
Hameed, A. (1964). Punjabi Government College wich [Punjabi: Punjabi in the Government College]. In Malik, Naseer. 1964. *Ravi Diyan Challan: Government College de Likhari 1914-1964* [Punjabi: The waves of Ravi: the writers of Government College]. Lahore: Government College.
Hameed, Abdul (1972a). Balochi rasmulkhat ka masla. [Urdu: The problem of Balochi script]. *H* 15 September.
—— (1972b). Balochi zaban ke rasmulkhat ka convention. [Urdu: The convention for the script of the Balochi language]. *J* 1 October.
Hamid, Shahid (1988). *Autobiography of a General*. Lahore: Ferozsons Ltd.
Hampton, H.V. (1947). *Biographical Studies in Modern Indian Education*. Madras: Oxford University Press.
Haq, Abdul (1940). Presidential address in Urdu Conference Lahore. [Urdu]. 8 December. In Barelvi 1952: 221-34.
—— (1945). *Marhoom Dilli College* [Urdu: The deceased Delhi College]. Karachi: Anjuman-e-Taraqqi-e-Urdu, 1962.
—— (comp) (1952). *Pre-eminence of Urdu as Appraised by Several Distinguished Publicmen of East Bengal*. Karachi: Anjuman-e-Taraqqi-e-Urdu.
—— (1961). Presidential speech on the 92nd birth anniversary of Ghalib, *Hamari Zaban*, 16 February.
—— (1964). *Khutbat-e-Abdul Haq*. In Barelvi, I, 1952.

Haq, Fazlul (1905). Proceedings of the Mahomedan Educational Conference, Barisal, 19 December. *General Proceedings: East Bengal and Assam 1906* (June), 3. *Report of the Calcutta University Commission*, 1917-1919, i-xiii. Calcutta.
Haq, Mehr A. (1967). *Multani Zaban aur Uska Urdu se Ta'aluq* [Urdu: The Multani language and its relationship with Urdu]. Bahawalpur: Urdu Academy.
Haque, Enamul (1968). *Nawab Bahadur Abdul Latif: His Writings and Related Documents*. Dhaka: Samudra Prokashani.
Harrison, Selig S. (1981). *In Afghanistan's Shadow: Baluch Nationalism and Soviet Temptations*. New York and Washington: Carnegie Endowment for International Peace.
Harries, L. (1983). The nationalisation of Swahili in Kenya. In Kennedy 1983: 118-27.
Hartig, Matthias (1985). The language situation and language policy in Belgium. In Beer and Jacob (eds.) 1985: 67-78.
Hasan, Yaqubul (1991). Azad Kashmir main Kashmiri zaban ke masail aur us ka mustaqbil. [Urdu: The problems of the Kashmiri language and its future

in Azad Kashmir]. Unpublished MA Dissertation, Allama Iqbal Open University, Islamabad.
Hasanabadi, Hafeez (1991). Gol Urdu a che kung ba baet? [Balochi: what should be done with Urdu?] *Balochi* (May), 18-22.
Hashmi, Riaz (1972). *Brief for Bahawalpur Province*. Bahawalpur: Bahawalpur Suba Mahaz.
Hashmi, Sayyid (1962). *Balochi Siahug Rast Baneesag* [Balochi: The correct norms for Balochi orthography]. Privately printed. No details.
—— (1973). Baluch zaban aur us ka rasmulkhat [Urdu: The Baluchi language and its script]. *Musawat* (6, 9, 10, and 11 January).
Hasrat, Gul Murad (comp. and ed. ) (1988). *Aeena-e-Khowar* [Urdu: The mirror of Khowar]. Chitral: Anjuman-e-Taraqqi-e-Khowar.
Haugen, Einar (1959). Planning for a standard language in modern Norway. *Anthropological Linguistics*, 1;3: 8-21.
—— (1972). Dialect, language, nation. In Dil, Anwar S. (ed). *The Ecology of Language: Essays by Einar Haugen*. Stanford: Stanford University Press. 237-54.
Heath, Shirley B. (1981). English in our language heritage. In Ferguson, Charles A. and Heath, Shirley (eds.) (1981). *Language in the U.S.A*. New York: Cambridge University Press. 6-20.
Hechter, Michael (1971). Towards a theory of ethnic change. *Politics and Society*. 2: 21-45.
—— (1975) *Internal Colonialism: The Celtic Fringe in British National Development*. London: Routledge and Kegan Paul.
Helal, Bashir al. (1985). *Bhasha Ondolaner Ittihash* [Bengali: The History of the Language Movement]. 3 Vols. Dhaka: Bangla Academy.
—— (1986). *Bangla Akademir Ittihash* [Bengali: *A History of the Bengali Academy*]. Dhaka: Bangla Academy.
Helbock, R.W. and Naqvi S. N. H. (1976). Inter-district variation in social well-being in Pakistan. Unpublished paper, Pakistan Institute of Development Economics, Islamabad.
Heyd, Uriel (1954). *Language Reform in Modern Turkey*. Jerusalem: Israel Oriental Society.
Hirson, B. (1981). Language in control and resistance in South Africa. *African Affairs* 80; 319: 219-37.
Hornberger, Nancy H. (1988). Language planning orientations and bilingual education in Peru. *Language Problems and Language Planning* 12: 1 (Spring), 14-29.
Huda, M. Nurul (1994). Shahid Minar as a poetic image. In Islam 1994: 90-8.
Hudson, R. A. (1980). *Sociolinguistics*. Cambridge: Cambridge University Press.
Humayun, Khalid (1986). Nazriyati dhare bandi, ik vaddi rukavat. [Punjabi: Ideological polarisation, a major impediment]. In Qaisar and Pal 1988: 227-33.
Hunter, W. W. (1871). *The Indian Musalmans. Are they Bound in Conscience to Rebel Against the Queen*? Lahore: Premier Book House, 1974.

Hunzai, Ghulam Uddin (1990). *Diwan-e-Kareemi* [Burushaski: The poetic works of Hunzai]. Gilgit: Privately printed.
Husain, A. Sultan (trans.) (1962). *The story of Swat as told by the Founder Miangul Abdul Wadud Badshah Sahib to Muhammad Arif Khan.* Peshawar: Printed at Ferozsons Ltd.
Hussain, Asaf (1979). *Elite Politics in an Ideological State: the Case of Pakistan.* Folkestone, Kent: WM Dowson and Sons.
Hussaini, Yusuf B. (1985). Akhir Angrezi he kyun? [Urdu: Why only English after all?]. *Jsrt* 1 July.
Inden, Ronald (1990). *Imagining India.* Oxford: Blackwell.
Ingram, D.E. (1988). Language policy in Australia. *Babel* 23; 1: 16-24.
Insha, Insha Allah Khan (1803). Rani Ketki. In Tufail, Muhammad (ed.) (1955). *Naqoosh: Afsana Number* [Urdu: Short story edition]. Lahore: Idara Farogh-e-Urdu.
Iqbal, Arshad A. (1991). Sajjan band kyun hoeya [Punjabi: Why did *Sajjan* close down?]. *Ravael* 2: 10.
Isajiw, Wesvolod W. (1974). Definitions of ethnicity. *Ethnicity* (July), 111-24.
Ishaque, Muhammad (1972). *Musalli* [Punjabi: Sweeper] Lahore: Punjabi Adabi Markaz.
—— (1976). *Ququnus* [Punjabi: Phoenix] Lahore: Punjabi Adabi Markaz.
Islam, Manzoorul (1994). *Essays on Ekushey: The Language Movement 1952.* Dhaka: Bangla Academy.
Islam, Rafiqul (1986). The language movement. In Chakravorty, S. R. and Narain, V. (eds.). 1986. *Bangladesh History and Culture. Vol.1.* New Delhi: South Asian Publishers. 147-61.
Jacob, James E., and Gordon, David C. (1985). Language policy in France. In Beer and Jacob 1985: 106-33.
Jafar, Iqbal (1992). The parting of ways. *Dawn Magazine* 4 August.
Jafri, Jawad (1990). Zaban-o-adab Kashmiri. [Urdu: Kashmiri language and literature]. *J* 5 March.
Jafri, Zamir (1983). Koh-e-namak ka meetha pani [Urdu: The sweet water of the Salt range]. *Urdu Digest* Vol. 23: No. 1 (January), 65-72.
Jahan, Rounaq (1972). *Pakistan: Failure in National Integration.* New York and London: Columbia University Press.
Jahani, Carina (1989). *Standardization and Orthography in the Balochi Language.* Upsalla, Sweden: Almqvist and Wiksell International.
Jalal, Ayesha (1990). *The State of Martial Rule: The Origins of Pakistan's Political Economy of Defence.* Cambridge: Cambridge University Press.
Jampuri, Kaifi (1969). *Siraiki Shairi* [Urdu]. Multan: Bazm-e-Saqafat.
Janmahmad (1989). *Essays on Baloch National Struggle in Pakistan.* Quetta: Gosha-e-Adab.
Janowitz, Morris (1975). *Military Conflict: Essays in Institutional Analysis of War and Peace.* London: Sage Publications.
Jatoi, Hyder Baksh (1957). *Shall Sindhi Language Stay in Karachi or Not?* Hyderabad: Sind Hari Committee.
Javed, Qazi (1992). Jawab. [Urdu: Reply]. *Pakistan* 2 August.
Jeffrey, Robin (1986). *What's Happening to India.* London: Macmillan, 1994.

Jinnah, Mohammad Ali (1947). Text of broadcast by Mr Jinnah on 3 June 1947. In Shah, S. W. 1992: 182-6.
—— (1948a). Speech at a public meeting at Dacca, 21 March. In *Quaid-i-Azam Mohammad Ali Jinnah: Speeches and Statement 1947-8*. Islamabad: Government of Pakistan, Ministry of Information and Broadcasting, 1989. 175-85 [henceforth *Speeches*].
—— (1948b). Speech at the Dacca University Convocation, 24 March 1948. In *Speeches*. 191-7.
Jones, Kenneth W. (1966). The Bengali elite in post-annexation Punjab. *The Indian Economic and Social History Review*, 3: 4 (December), 376-95.
Jones, William (1786). Third annual discourse. In *The Works of Sir William Jones*, 6 Vols. London: Robinson and Evans, 1799. Vol. 1: 19-34.
Josh, Shabbir Hasan (1964). *Yadon Ki Barat* [Urdu: The wedding procession of memories] Lahore: Maktaba-e-Sher-o-Adab.
Joshi, Kantilal (1962). *Rajat Jayanti Granth* [Hindi]. Wardha: Rashtrabhasha Prachar Samiti.
Joshi, P. C. (1946). *For the Final Bid for Power*! Bombay: People's Publishing House.
Joyo, Ibrahim (comp.) (1985). *Asan Ji Boli, Asan Ji Taleem* [Sindhi: our language, our education]. Hyderabad: Sindh Friends' Circle.
JSSF. (n.d.) *Sindhi Boli Qaumi Boli* [Sindhi: Sindhi language, national language]. Hyderabad: Jeay Sindh Student's Federation.

Kabir, M.G. (1987). Religion, language and nationalism in Bangladesh. *Journal of Contemporary Asia* 17; 4: 473-487.
Kaefvi, H. (1979). *Kashmir Mein Urdu* [Urdu: Urdu in Kashmir] Lahore: Markazi Urdu Board.
Kahut, Chaudhry N. (1992). *Avo! Punjabi Nun Katal Kariye*! [Punjabi: Come let us murder Punjabi]. Karachi: Waris Shah Publications.
Kalanchvi, Dilshad (1974). Khud Punjabi Siraiki da hik lahja hai [Siraiki: Punjabi itself is a dialect of Siraiki]. *Siraiki* 8: 31 (Jul).
Kalichbeg, Mirza (1900). *The Chachnama: An Ancient History of Sindh*. Trans. from the Persian. Hyderabad; Lahore: Vanguard, 1985.
Kalgi, Dilpal B. (1992). Domi jama'at e Balochi wangi kitab [Balochi: Balochi book for class 2]. *Balochi* (December), 45-7.
Kamal, Omar (1975). Siraiki Adabi Conference Multan [Urdu]. Multan: Privately Printed.
—— (1988). *Bain ul Aqwami Sindhi Conference 4 February 1988*. [Urdu: Narrative of the International Sindhi Conference] Multan: Bazm-e-Saqafat.
Kammi, Saeed F. (1988). *Punjabi Zaban Naheen Maray Gi* [Urdu: The Punjabi language will not die]. Jhelum: Majidia Maktab.
Kamran, Jilani (1992). *Qaomiat Ki Tashkil aor Urdu Zaban* [Urdu: Nationalism and the Urdu language] Islamabad: Muqtadira Qaumi Zaban.
*Kanayat* (1972). *Kanayat Goli Number* [Urdu] 27: 150 (3 July).
Kareemi, Abdul Hameed (1982). *Urdu Kohistani Bol Chal* [Urdu/Kohistani: Conversation in Urdu and Kohistani] Swat: Kohistan Adab Academy.

Kausar, Inamul Haq (1986). *Balochistan Men Urdu ki Qadeem Daftri Dastawezat* [Urdu: Historical documents about Urdu in Balochistan] Islamabad: Muqtadira Qaumi Zaban.
Kearney, Robert N. (1978). Language and the rise of Tamil separatism in Sri Lanka. *Asian Survey* 17: 5 (May), 521-34.
Kejariwal, O.P. (1988). *The Asiatic Society of Bengal and the Discovery of India's Past.* Delhi: Oxford University Press.
Kennedy, Charles H. (1984). Policies of ethnic preference in Pakistan. *Asian Survey* 24: 6 (June), 688-703.
—— (1987). *Bureaucracy in Pakistan.* Karachi: Oxford University Press.
Kennedy, Chris (ed.) (1983). *Language Planning and Language Education.* London: George Allen and Unwin.
Khaleeq, Hamesh (1966). Shaheed-e-Pashto Nasr Sahib. In Khaleeq. H. (ed.) (1966). *Nasrullah Khan Nasr.* Peshawar: Nasr Academy.
Khalid, Chaudhry M. (1993). Punjabi zaban nal dharu [Punjabi: Injustice with Punjabi]. *Ravael* 4: 2 (15-31 January).
Khan, Asif (1973). Punjabi zaban odian bolian te duje nan. [Punjabi: The Punjabi language, its dialects and other names]. In Salahuddin, Iqbal (ed.) 1973. *Lalan di Pand* [Punjabi: A treasure of rubies] Lahore: Aziz Book Depot.
—— (1994). Pakistan wich maan boli laher [Punjabi: The mother tongue wave in Pakistan]. *Maan Boli* (January), 66-82.
Khan, Ayub (1967). *Friends Not Masters: A Political Biography.* Karachi: Oxford University Press.
Khan, Gul Hassan (1993). *Memoirs of Lt. Gen Gul Hassan Khan.* Karachi: Oxford University Press.
Khan, Hamid Ali (1900?). *The Vernacular Controversy.* Lucknow: no details.
Khan, M. Hasan, and Iqbal, Mahmud (1982). Socio-Economic indicators in rural Pakistan: some evidence. In Nabi 1986: 93-108.
Khan, Muin-ud-Din A. (1965). *History of the Faraizi Movement in Bengal 1818-1906.* Karachi.
Khan, Nabi A. (1983). *Multan: History and Architecture.* Islamabad: Institute of Islamic History, Culture and Civilizations.
Khan, Sheereen (1990). Hindko Journalism. Unpublished MA Thesis. Department of Journalism, University of Peshawar, 1989-90.
Khan, Syed Ahmad (1872). Translation of the report of the members of the Select Committee for the Better Diffusion and Advancement of Learning among Muhammadans of India. In Malik, H. (1989): 138-40.
—— (1869). Strictures upon the present educational system in India. In Malik, H. (1989): 100-16.
Khattak, Pareshan (1977a). Da Pakhto rasmul khat: Part 1. [Pashto: The Pashto script]. *Pashto* (April), 18-2.
—— (1977b). Pakhto rasmul khat: Part 2 [Pashto: The Pashto script]. *Pashto.* (February-March), 32-4.
Khattak, Raj Wali (1991). *Nave Imla.* Peshawar: Pashto Academy, University of Peshawar.

Khuhro, Ayub (1930). *A story of the sufferings of Sind: A case for the separation of Sind from the Bombay Presidency*. In Khuhro, H. (1982.
Khuhro, Hamida (1978). *The Making of Modern Sind: British Policy and Social Change in the Nineteenth Century*. Karachi: Indus Publications.
— (ed.) (1982). *Documents on Separation of Sind from the Bombay Presidency*, Vol. 1. Islamabad: Institute of Islamic History, Culture and Civilization.
Khurshid, Abdussalam (1986). Punjabi sahafat: farsi lippi wich [Punjabi: Punjabi journalism in the Persian script]. In Qaisar and Pal 1988: 381-8.
Kishwar, Madhu (1994). Kashmiri and Kashmiriyat. *Manushi* No. 82 (May-June), 2-6.
Kloss, Heinz (1969). *Research Possibilities on Group Bilingualism: A Report*. Quebec: International Center for Research on Bilingualism.
Kopff, David (1969). *British Orientalism and the Bengal Renaissance: The Dynamics of Indian Modernization 1773-1835*. Berkeley and Los Angeles: University of California Press.
Kriendler, Isabelle T. (ed.) (1985a). *Sociolinguistic Perspectives on Soviet National Languages: Their Past, Present and Future*. Berlin: Mouton de Gruyter.
—— (1985b). The non-Russian languages and the challenge of Russian: the Eastern versus the Western tradition. In Kreindler (1985a): 345-67.
—— (1985c). The Mordvinian languages: a survival saga. In Kriendler (1985a): 237-63.
Krishna, Lajwanti R. (1977). *Punjabi Sufi Poets AD 1460-1900*. Karachi: Indus Publications.

La Porte, Robert (1975). *Power and Privilege: Influence and Decision-Making in Pakistan*. Berkeley: University of California Press.
Laitin, David D. (1988). Language policy and political strategy in India. *Policy Sciences*, 22: 415-36.
—— Mensah, Edward. 1991. Language choice among Ghanaians. *Language Problems and Language Planning*, 15; 2: 139-55.
Lambrick, H. T. (1975). *Sindh: A General Introduction*. Hyderabad.
Langah, Taj M. (1990). Lecture on the Siraiki demands. *Jang Forum* [Urdu] 15 January.
Laponce, J. A. (1987). *Languages and their Territories*. Trans. from French by Martin Sperry. Toronto: University of Toronto Press.
Leitner, G. W. (1882). *History of Indigenous Education in the Punjab Since Annexation and in 1882*. (Reprint) Lahore: Republican, Books, 1991.
—— (1889). *Dardistan in 1866, 1886 and 1893*. Repr. Karachi: Indus Publications 1985.
Lelyveld, David (1993). Colonial knowledge and the fate of Hindustani. *Comparative Studies in Society and History*, Vol. 35; No. 4: 665-82.
Lewis, G. L. (1981). Oh! No! we never mention her (thoughts on Turkish language reform). *Asian Affairs*, 12: 2 (June), 155-166.
Lorimer, David L. R. (1935-8). *The Burushaski Language*, 3 volumes. Oslo Institute for Sammenlignende Kulturforskning. Vol 2. (1936).

Lorimer, E. O. (1938). *Language Hunting in the Karakoram*. Karachi: Indus Publications, 1989.
Lukes, Steven (ed.) (1974). *Power: A Radical View*. London: Macmillan.
—— (1986). *Power* Oxford: Basil Blackwell.

Mackenzie, D. N. (1987). Pashto. In Comrie (1987): 547-65.
Macnamara, John (1971). Successes and failures in the movement for the restoration of Irish. In Rubin and Jernudd (eds.) (1971): 65-94.
Magsi, Qadir (1990). *Vatan ya Kafan* [Sindhi pamphlet: Country or shroud] Hyderabad: Jagarta publications.
Mahmood, Sohail (1989). *The Sind Report: A Province in Turmoil*. Lahore: Classic publishers.
Mahmud, S. (1895). *A History of English Education in India 1781-1893*. Aligarh: MAO College.
Majeed, Javed (1992). *Ungoverned Imaginings: James Mill's The History of British India and Orientalism*. Oxford: Clarendon Press.
Majeed, Sheema (ed.) (1989). *Urdu Rasmul Khat: Intikhab-i-Maqalat* [Urdu: The Urdu script, selection of articles]. Islamabad: Muqtadira Qaumi Zaban.
Malaviya, Madan M. (1897). *Court Character and Primary Education in the N.W. Provinces and Oudh*. Allahabad: The Indian Press. [BM: the document is ascribed to Malaviya in the BM catalogue].
Malik, Fateh M. (1988). *Punjabi Identity*. Lahore: Sang-e-Meel.
Malik, Hafeez (ed.) (1989). *Sir Syed Ahmed Khan's Educational Philosophy: A Documentary Record*. Islamabad: National Institute of Historical and Cultural Research.
Malik, Manzoor (1975). Siraiki ilaqe ke haqooq-o-masail. [Urdu: The rights and problems of the Siraiki area]. *Lail-o-Nahar* [Lahore] 13 November.
Malik, Shahbaz (1985). *Goer: Khoj te Prakh* [Punjabi: Insight: research and evaluation]. Lahore: Taj Book Depot.
Malleson, W (comp.) (1904). *Military Report on Chitral*. Simla: Intelligence Branch: Printed at the Government Press.
Mangan, J. A. (1986). *The Games Ethic and Imperialism*. New York: Viking Penguin.
Manglori, Mumtaz (1959). Hazara ke lok geet. [Urdu: The folk songs of Hazara]. *Jamhoor* 17 March.
Mansoor, Sabiha (1993). Punjabi, Urdu, English in Pakistan: *A Sociolinguistic Study*. Lahore: Vanguard.
Marani, Akram (1991). *Greater Thal* [Urdu]. Leiah: Leiah Kitab Ghar.
Marglin, Frederique A., and Marglin, Stephen A. (eds.) (1990). *Dominating Knowledge: Development, Culture, and Resistance*. New York: Oxford University Press.
Marri, Mir Khuda Baksh (1974). *Searchlights on Baloches and Balochistan*. Karachi: Royal Book Company.
Matin, H. M. (1954). *National Language of Pakistan*. Karachi: Marsh Publishing House.

Maudoodi, Syed Abul Ala. (1942). *Tehreek-e-Azadi-e-Hind aur Musalman* [Urdu: The freedom movement of India and Muslims] Vol. 1. Lahore: Islami Publications Ltd, 1974 edition.

Mauzy, Diane K. (1985). Language and language polcy in Malaysia. In Beer and Jacob 1985: 151-77.

Mayhew, A. (1926). *The Education of India*. London: Faber and George.

McConnell, Grant D., Daoust-Blais, Denise, and Martin, Andre. (1979). Language Planning and language treatment in Quebec. *Word* 30: 1-2 (April-August), 87-104.

McDonald, Ellen E. (1966). English education and social reform in late nineteenth century Bombay. *The Journal of Asian Studies* 25: 3 (May), 453-70.

McLynn, Frank (1990). *Burton: Snow Upon the Desert*. London: John Murray.

Medhurst, Kenneth (1977). *The Basques and the Catalans*. London: Minority Rights Group.

Mengal, Mir Aqil K. (1993). Interview by Saleem Kurd, Shahjahan Raisani, and Khadim Lehri on behalf of *Tawar* [Brahvi]. (January), 13-28.

Metcalfe, Thomas R. (1971). *Modern India: An Interpretive Anthology*. London: Collier-Mcmillan.

Mill, J. (1817). *The History of British India*. abridged and introduced by William Thomas. Chicago: University of Chicago Press.

Miller, Jacob R. (1981). The politics of Philippine national language policy. *Language Problems and Language Planning* 5; 2: 137-52.

Mills, C. Wright (1956). *The Power Elite*. New York: Oxford University Press.

Miran, M. Alam (1977). The functions of national languages in Afghanistan. *Afghanistan* [Kabul] 30: 1 (June), 67-77.

Mirza, Shafqat (1969). Nayi Taleemi Policy: Punjab aur Punjabi, [Urdu: The New Educational Policy: Punjab and Punjabi]. *Punjabi Adab* 19: (September), 46-53.

—— (1985). Privation and deprivation, *Viewpoint* 15 August.

—— (1989). 'Will Punjabi language die?', *PT* 31 March.

—— (1993). Punjabi and the PPP. *FP*: *Weekend Post* 17 December.

—— (1994). Pakistan wich man boli laher. [Punjabi: The mother tongue wave in Pakistan]. Interview by Maqsood Saqib *Maan Boli* (January), 83-96.

Mitra, H. N. and Mitra, N. N. (eds.) (1990). *The Indian Annual Register 1937* Vol. 11. New Delhi: Gian Publishing House.

Mobbs, Michael C. (1991). *Languages as identity symbols*: An investigation into language attitudes and behaviour amongst second generation South Asian schoolchildren in Britain, including the special case of Hindi and Urdu. Unpublished Ph.D thesis, University of London.

Mohammad, Akhund Saleh (1659). *Koord Gal Namik*. Trans. from Persian to Urdu. Abdullah Jan Jamaldini and Nadir Qambrani. Quetta: Balochi Academy, 1994.

Mohan, Rakesh (1989). Language planning and language conflict: the case of Kashmiri. *International Journal of the Sociology of Language*. 73-85.

Moraes, Dom (1968). *My Son's Father: An Autobiography*. New Delhi: Penguin India, 1990.

Mosca, G. (1939). *The Ruling Class*. Livingston. New York: Mc Graw Hill.
Mujeeb, M. (1967). *The Indian Muslims*. London: George Allen and Unwin; New Delhi: Munshiram Manoharlal, 1985.
Mujtaba, Hasan (1992). Sindhi separation. 38-55, containing 'We think the slogan of Sindhu Desh is too extreme'. Interview of Qadir Magsi. *Newsline* (February), 51-5.
Mukherjee, S. N. (1968). *Sir William Jones: A Study in Eighteenth Century British Attitudes to India*. Cambridge: Cambridge University Press.
Munir, Ahmad Munir (1972). Sind ke quaid-e-hazb-e-ikhtilaf Shah Faridul Haq se ek mulaqat [Urdu: A meeting with Shah Faridul Haq, Sindh's Leader of the Opposition] *Chattan* 14 August.
Muniruzzaman, Talukdar (1973). Radical politics and the emergence of Bangladesh. In Brass, Paul, and Franda, Marcus F. (eds.) *Radical Politics in South Asia*. Cambridge, Mass. and London: MIT Press.
Murshid, T. M. (1985). *The Bengal Muslim intelligentsia, 1937-77: the tension between the religious and the secular*. Unpublished D.Phil thesis, University of Oxford.
Muzaffar, Nawab Hussain (1972). Letter to Shorish Kashmiri [Urdu]. *Chattan* (Lahore) 26 June.

Nabi, Ijaz (ed.) (1986). *The Quality of Life in Pakistan*. Lahore: Vanguard.
Nadira (pseudonym) (1989). Letter from Bahawalpur. *N* 11 February.
Naeem, Hidayatullah (1986). *Islamic literature in Pashto*. Unpublished Ph.D thesis, University of Peshawar.
Naqvi, Aftab (1986). Speech at the Punjabi Conference, 1986. In Qaisar and Pal (1988): 116-20.
Naseem, Nabeela (1991). *Mukhtar Ali Nayyar*. Unpublished MA Thesis, Department of Journalism, University of Peshawar, 1990-1.
Naseer, Naseeruddin (1979). *Diwan-e-Naseeri* [Burushaski/Urdu: The poetic works of Naseer]. Karachi: Khana-e-Hikmat.
Naseeruddin, M. (1984). Da Pashto zane Arabi ul asl alfaz. [Pashto: Some words of Arabic origin in Pashto]. *Pashto* (February-March), 26-34.
Naushahi, Gauhar (1988). *Qaumi Zaban ke Bare Men Ahem Dastavezat* [Urdu: Important documents about the national language]. Islamabad: Muqtadira Qaumi Zaban.
Nayar, Baldev Raj (1969). *National Communication and Language Policy in India*. New York: Frederick A. Praeger.
Nayyar, Mukhtar A. (1965). *Hindko Nasr di Kahanri* [Hindko: The story of Hindko Prose]. Peshawar: Idara-e-Farogh-e-Hindko, Revised ed. 1992.
—— (1976). *Hindko Qawaid* [Hindko: Hindko grammar]. Peshawar: Maktaba Hindko Zaban.
—— (1977). *Tarikh-e-Hindko* [Urdu: The history of the Hindko language]. Peshawar: Maktaba Hindko Zaban.
Nehru, Jawaharlal (1936). *Jawaharlal Nehru: An Autobiography*. London: John Lane, Bodley Head.
—— (1937). *The Question of Language*. Allahabad: Political and Economic Information Department of the All India Congress Committee.

Niedzielski, Henry (1979). Language consciousness and language policy in Poland. *Word* 30: 1-2 (April-August), 134-59.
Nurullah, Syed, and Naik, J. P. (1943). *A History of Education in India*. Bombay: Macmillan, 1951. Vols. 1 and 11; Parts 1 and 2.

Obhari, Diwan Chand (1938). *The Evolution of North West Frontier Province*. Peshawar: London Book Company.
Ozolini, U. (1985). The national language policy issue in Australia. In Clyne, M. G. (ed.) (1985). *Australia, Meeting Place of Languages*. Canberra: Department of Linguistics, A.N.U.
Pachori, S. S. (1990). The language policy of the East India Company and the Asiatic Society of Bengal. *Language Problems and Language Planning*, 14: 2 (Summer) 104-18.
Paden, John N. (1968). Language problems of national integration in Nigeria: the special position of Hausa. In Fishman *et al*. 1968: 199-213.
Panipati, M. I. (ed.) (1962). *Muqalat-e-Sir Syed* [Urdu: The dissertations of Sir Syed]. Lahore: Majlis Taraqqi-e-Adab.
—— (ed.) (1976). *Maktubat-e-Sir Syed* Vol. 1 [Urdu: The Letters of Sir Syed]. Lahore: Majlis Taraqqi-e-Adab.
Pareto, Vilfredo (1935). *The Mind and Society*. New York: Harcourt-Brace.
Parry, Geraint (1969). *Political Elites*. London: George Allen and Unwin.
Parsons, Talcott (1951). *The Social System*. New York: The Free Press.
—— (1966). *Societies: Evolutionary and Comparative Perspectives*. Englewood Cliffs: Prentice-Hall.
Pasha, Hafeez A., and Hasan, Tariq (1982). Development ranking of districts of Pakistan. *Pakistan Journal of Applied Economics* 1: 2 (1986). Quoted from Zaidi (1992a): 43-89.
Patel, Khatri Asmat (1994). *Gujrati adab aur Pakistan* [Urdu: Gujrati literature and Pakistan]. Paper read out at the National Conference of Writers and Intellectuals, Pakistan Academy of Letters, Islamabad, 10 October 1994.
Pazhwak, Rahman (1960). *Pakhtunistan: A new state in Central Asia*. New York. [Pamphlet]
Pearce, R. R. (comp.) (1846). *Memoirs and Correspondence of Wellesley, Vol. II*. London: Richard Bentley.
Peddie, Roger A. (1991). Coming ready or not? Language policy development in New Zealand. *Language Problems and Language Planning*. 15: 1 (Spring), 25-42.
Pema, Tameez (1960). Hindko boli ki tareekh. *Jamhoor* 23 February.
Phadnis, Urmila (1984). Ethnic movements in Pakistan. In Nayak, Nandev (ed.) *Pakistan: Society and Politics*. New Delhi: South Asian Publishers Pvt. Ltd.
—— (1989). *Ethnicity and Nation Building in South Asia*. New Delhi and London: Sage Publications.
Philips, C. H. (1961). *The East India Company 1784-1834*. Bombay: Oxford University Press.
—— (ed.) (1977). *The Correspondence of Lord William Cavendish Bentinck Vol. 1*. Oxford: Oxford University Press.

Phillipson, Robert (1992). *Linguistic Imperialism.* Oxford: Oxford University Press.
Piracha, A. Halim (1970). Pakistan ka lisani masla 2. [Urdu: The language problem of Pakistan] *J* 11 November.
Pirzada, S. Sharifuddin (ed.) (1969). *Foundations of Pakistan All-India Muslim League Documents 1906-1924, Vol. 1.* Karachi: National Publishing House. (ed.) (1970). *Foundations of Pakistan All-India Muslim League Documents 1925-1947 Vol. 2.* Karachi: National Publishing House.
Prasad, Siva (1868). A Memorandum on court characters in upper India. In Malaviya 1897: 29.
—— (1870). Strictures upon the strictures of Sayyad Ahmad Khan Bahadur, C. S. I. Benares: E. J. Lazarus and Co. In Malik, H. 1989: 117-32.
*Poems on 21st* (1992). Dhaka: Bangla Academy.
Polome, Edgar C. (1968). The choice of official languages in the Democratic Republic of the Congo. In Fishman *et al.* 1968: 295-311.
Poullada, Leon B. (1973). *Reform and Rebellion in Afghanistan: 1919-29 King Amanullah's Failure to Modernize a Tribal Society.* Ithaca and London: Cornell University Press.

Qadir, Abdul (1942). Da Pakhto rasmul khat [Pashto: The script of Pashto]. *Nan Paroon* (25 Jun), 20-5.
Qaisar, Iqbal (1992). *Ratan Huyian Vadyan* [Punjabi: The nights got longer] Lahore: Ravel Publications.
Qaisar, Iqbal, and Pal, Jamil A. (eds.) (1988). *A'almi Punjabi Conference 1986* [Punjabi: World Punjabi Conference, 1986] Lahore: Classic.
Qambrani, Nadir (1990). Brahvi adabi akabereen [Urdu: Brahvi literary exemplars]. *Pakistan Studies* Vol. 1: No. 1: 13-21.
Qasmi, Ataul Haq (1986). Punjabi Conference aur Porus ke hathi. [Urdu: Punjabi conference and the elephants of King Porus]. *NW* 15 May.
Qazi, I. I. (1956). Sindhi boliyun ji baqa-e-bacha. [Sindhi: The Sindhi language its existence and defence]. *Mehran* 2.
Quraishi, M. S. H. (1967). Recruitment to Central Services in Pakistan. *NIPA Journal* [Karachi] No. 1.
Qureshi, Ishtiaq Hussain (1972). Presidential address in the Urdu Conference, Karachi. *J* 25 July.

Rabbani, Ghulam (1939). *Anjuman-e-Taraqqi-e-Urdu Ki Kahani* [Urdu: the story of the Organization for the Development of Urdu]. Delhi: Anjuman.
Radloff, Carla F. (1992). The dialects of Shina. In *SSNP-2*: 89-203.
Rahman, Anisur (1968). *East and West Pakistan: A Problem in the Political Economy of Regional Planning.* Cambridge: Center for International Affairs, Harvard University.
Rahman, Ataur (1986). Lahore mein pahli almi conference [Urdu: The first World Conference in Lahore]. *NW* 1 May.
Rahman, Ataur (1984). *O Zaratir dui Bochhor* [Bengali: Two years of my ministership]. Dhaka (4th ed.) First published in the 1960s.

—— (1990). The Language Movement and Bengali nationalism In Ahmad, R. (1990): 166-77.
Rahman, Azizur (1944). *Diwan-e-Farid* [Siraiki and Urdu: The poetical works of Farid]. Bahawalpur: Azizul Mutabeh Press.
Rahman, Khalilur (1973). *Balti ka Qaida* [Urdu-Balti: Primer of Balti]. Gujranwala: Asghar Ali Chaudhury.
Rai, Amrit (1984). *A House Divided: The Origin and Development of Hindi/Hindavi*. Delhi: Oxford University Press, 1991.
Rai, Lajpat (1920). *The Problem of National Education in India*. London: George Allen and Unwin.
Raleigh, T. (1906). *Lord Curzon in India: Being a Selection from His Speeches as Viceroy and Governor General 1898-1905*. London: Macmillan.
Ramay, Hanif (1985). *Punjab Ka Muqaddama* [Urdu: The trial of the Punjab]. Lahore: Jang Publishers.
Rashdi, A. (1970). Bahawalpur. *J* [Urdu] 4 May.
Rasheed, Rao Abdul (1985). *Jo main ne dekha*: interview of Rao Rasheed by Munir Ahmad Munir [Urdu: What I saw] Lahore: Atish Fishan Publications.
Rashid, Ahmed (1994). *The Resurgence of Central Asia: Islam or Nationalism*. Karachi: Oxford University Press; London: Zed Press.
Rashid, Harun al (1987). *The Foreshadowing of Bangladesh: Bengal Muslim League and Muslim Politics 1936-1937*. Dhaka: Asiatic Society of Bengal.
Rashiduzzaman, M. (1982). East-West conflicts in Pakistan: Bengali regionalism 1971-1970. In Jeyaratnam and Dalton (1982). *The States of South Asia: Problems of National Integration*. London: C. Hurst and Co. 111-30.
Rasoolpuri, Aslam (1976). *Siraiki Rasmulkhat ki Mukhtasar Tareekh* [Urdu: A brief history of the Siraiki script]. Multan: Bazme Saqafat.
Raverty, H. G. (1860). *A Dictionary of the Pukhto, Pushto or Language of the Afghans*. Peshawar: Saeed Book Bank, 1982.
Read, A. F. C. (1934). *Balti Grammar*. London: The Royal Asiatic Society.
Reetz, Dietrich (1993). Ethnic and religious identities in colonial India.
—— (1920-1930s): a conceptual debate, *Contemporary South Asia*, 2; 2: 109-22.
Rensch, Calvin R. (1992a). Patterns of language use among the Kohistanis of the Swat valley. In *SSNP-1*: 3-62.
—— (1992b). The language environment of Hindko-speaking people. In *SSNP-3*: 3-88.
Rial, James (1985). Spain: Regional languages in a lingua franca-dominant state. In Beer and Jacob (eds.) 1985: 97-105.
Risley, Herbert (1908). *The People of India*. Lahore: Al-Biruni, 1977.
Rittenberg, Stephen A. (1977). *The Independence movement in India's North West Frontier Province: 1901-1947*. Ph.D Thesis. Columbia University.
Robertson, William (1791). *An Historical Disquisition Concerning the Knowledge the Ancients Had of India*. Dublin.

Robinson, Francis (1974). *Separatism Among Indian Muslims: The Politics of the United Provinces' Muslims 1860-1923*. Cambridge: Cambridge University Press.
—— (1979). Islam and Muslim separatism. In Taylor and Yapp 1979: 78-112.
Rooman, H. A. (1987). *Balochistan Mein Urdu Zariya-e-Taleem*. [Urdu: The Urdu medium of instruction in Balochistan] Islamabad: Muqtadira Qaumi Zaban.
Roy, Asim (1987). The Bengal Muslim cultural mediators and the Bengal Muslim identity in the nineteenth and early twentieth centuries. *Journal of South Asian Studies* 10; 1: 11-34.
Royce, A. Peterson (1982). *Ethnic Identities: Strategies of Diversity*. Bloomington: Indiana University Press.
Rubin, Joan, and Jernudd, Bjorn H. (eds.) (1971). *Can Language Be Planned? Sociolinguistic Theory and Practice for Developing Nations*. Honolulu: University Press of Hawaii.
—— and Shuy, Roger (eds.) (1973). *Language Planning: Current Issues and Research*. Washington: Georgetown University Press.
—— Jernudd, B., Das Gupta, J., Fishman, J., and Ferguson, C. (eds.). (1977). *Language Planning Processes*. The Hague: Mouton.
Rudnyckyj, J.B. (1976). *Linguicide*. Winnipeg: Ukrainian Technical University.

Sabir, Ayub (1985). *Pakistan Mein Urdu Ke Taraqiati Idare* [Urdu: The institutions for the development of Urdu in Pakistan] Islamabad: Muqtadira Qaumi Zaban.
Sabir, Razzaq (1990). Balochi aur Brahvi zaban men huroof o harkat ka ishtirak [Urdu: The common letters and phonemes of Balochi and Brahvi]. *Pakistan Studies* Vol. 1: 36-45.
Sabir, Sultan M. (1986). Pashto sahafat [Urdu: Pashto journalism]. In Tair 1986: 185-96.
Saeed, Ahmad (1972). *Maulana Ashraf Ali Thanvi aur Tehreek-e-Azadi* [Urdu: Maulana Ashraf Ali Thanvi and the freedom movement] Rawalpindi: Khalid Nadeem Publications.
Saib, Abdul Qaiyyum (n.d.) *Sindhi zaban aur Dr Abdur Rahim Piracha* [Urdu pamphlet: The Sindhi language and Dr Abdur Rahim Piracha]. Hyderabad: Sindhi Zaban Publications.
Said, Edward (1978). *Orientalism*. London and Henley: Routledge and Kegan Paul.
—— (1993). *Culture and Imperialism*. New York: Alfred A. Knopf.
Sajid, Wasim (1972). Mukhlisur Rahman Report. [Urdu] In *Kanayat* 1972: 51-2.
Salahuddin, Sheikh (1972). Bahawalpur ka iqtisadi ehstihsal. [Urdu: The economic exploitation of Bahawalpur]. *Kanayat* 1972: 32-3.
Saleem, Ahmad (1986). *Jadeed Punjabi Adab: Ek Savalia Nishan?* [Urdu: Modern Punjabi literature: a question mark?]. Karachi: Riktab.
Saleem, Syed M. (1989). English talim: sazish [Urdu: English education: conspiracy]. *Jasarat* 19 May.

Salik, Abdul M. (1956). Khutba-e-Sadarat [Punjabi: Presidential address] *Punjabi* (May), 4-8.
Saqib, Maqsood (1986). Punjabi zaban di rah diyan okran. [Punjabi: Impediments in the way of Punjabi]. In Qaisar and Pal 1988: 121-7.
Sardar, Muhammad (1977). *A Literary History of the Baluchis* (2 Vols.). Quetta: Balochi Academy.
Sayeed, Khalid Bin (1968). The role of the military in Pakistan. In Van Doorn, Jacques (ed.) (1968). *Armed Forces and Society*. The Hague: Mouton.
—— (1964). Pathan regionalism. *The South Atlantic Quarterly*, 63:4.
Seal, Anil (1971). *The Emergence of Indian Nationalism: Competition and Collaboration in the Later Nineteenth Century*. Cambridge: Cambridge University Press.
Shackle, Christopher (1970). Punjabi in Lahore. *Modern Asian Studies* 4; 3: 239-67.
—— (1976). *The Siraiki Language of Central Pakistan: A Reference Grammar*. London: School of Oriental and African Studies.
—— (1977). Siraiki: a language movement in Pakistan. *Modern Asian Studies* 11; 3: 379-403.
—— (1979). Language and Cultural Identity in Pakistan Punjab. In Krishna, Gopal (ed.) (1979). *Contributions to South Asian Studies*. Delhi. 137-60.
—— (1980). Hindko in Kohat and Peshawar. *Bulletin of the School of Oriental and African Studies*, 63; 3: 482-510.
—— (1983). *A Century of Siraiki Studies in English*. Multan: Bazm-e-Saqafat.
—— (1985). Language, dialect and local identity in Northern Pakistan. In Zingel, Wolfgang P. and Lallemant, Stephanie A. (eds.) (1985). *Pakistan in the 80s: Ideology, Regionalism, Economy, Foreign Policy*. Lahore: Vanguard. 311-33.
Shad, Ubaid (1991). Balochi mae wati . . . [Balochi: Our own Balochi . . .]. *Balochi* (February), 1-21.
Shah, Bulleh (pseudonym) (1986). The World Punjabi Conference. *D* 22 June.
Shah, Qeemat (1945). Zamung jaba [Pashto: Our language]. *Pakhtun* (17 October), 21-4.
Shah, Syed Waqar (1992). *Muslim League in NWFP*. Karachi: Royal Book Company.
Shahbaz, A. Majeed (1972). Alaehda sube ki tehreek. [Urdu: The movement for a separate province]. In *Kanayat* 1972: 21-8.
Shahbaz, M. (1977). *Punjabi Lisaniyat* [Urdu: Punjabi linguistics]. Lahore.
Shaheen, M. Parvesh (1989). *Kalam Kohistan: Log aur Zaban* [Urdu: People and language]. Mingora: Academy of Swat Culture.
Shahidullah, Muhammad (1947). Pakistanir Rashtro Bhasha Shamosh. [Bengali: The language problems of Pakistan]. In Umar 1970: 19-20.
Shahwani, Abdul Qadir (1993). Maktaba Darkhani [Brahvi: The Darkhani School]. *Tawar* (June), 60-76.
Shaido, M. Nawaz (1942). Pakhto rasmulkhat: 1. [Pashto: Pashto script]. *Nan Paroon* (25 December), 17-9.
—— (1943). Pakhto rasmulkhat: 2. In *Nan Paroon* (17 January), 8-10.

Shaikh, Muhammad Hajjan (1986). *Maulana Ubaid Allah Sindhi: A Revolutionary Scholar*. Islamabad: National Institute of Historical and Cultural Research.

Shamsuddin, Abul Kalam (1968). *Otit Diner Sriti* [Bengali: Reminiscence of the past]. Dhaka: Nauroz Kitabistan.

Shapiro, Michael (ed.) (1984). *Language and Politics*. Oxford: Basil Blackwell.

Shardadevi, Veralankar (1955). Development of Hindi prose literature. Unpublished Ph.D Thesis, School of Oriental and African Studies, University of London.

Shelley, Habibur Rahman (1951). Language problem. *PO* 12 June.

Shils, E. A. (1957). Primordial, personal, sacred and civil ties. *British Journal of Sociology*, 8: 130-45.

Shorish, Mobin M. (1984). Planning by decree: the Soviet language policy in Central Asia. *Language Problems and Language Planning* 8; 1: 35-49.

Sibayan, B. P. (1983). Survey of language use and attitudes towards language in the Philippines. In Kennedy 1983: 80-95.

Siddiqui, Ishrat Ali (ed. and trans.) (1980). *Gandhi Ji aur Zaban Ka Mas'ala* [Urdu: Mr Gandhi and the language problems]. Trans. from articles in English. Lucknow: Uttar Pradesh Urdu Academy.

Siddiqui, Javed Ahmad (1987). *G.M. Syed Ki Masbat aur Manfi Siasat* [Urdu: G. M. Syed's positive and negative politics] Karachi: Shel Publications Ltd.

Siddiqui, M. A. (1993). Sindhi and Urdu-speaking intellectual's declaration. *N* 21 May.

Sindhi, Haider (1980). *Pakistan je subai-e-ilaqi zabanan men Sindhi zaban ji ilmi-e-lisani haisiat*. [Sindhi: The position of Sindhi among the regional languages of Pakistan]. Unpublished Ph.D thesis, University of Sindh.

Skinner, Quentin (1974). Some problems in the analysis of political thought and action. *Political Theory* 2: 3 (August), 277-303.

Sloan, M. Ismail (1981). *Khowar-English Dictionary*. New York: Privately published.

Smith, Anthony D. (1981). *The Ethnic Revival*. Cambridge: Cambridge University Press.

—— (1986). *The Ethnic Origins of Nations*. Oxford: Basil Blackwell.

Spear, Percival (1932). *The Nabobs: A Study of the Social Life of the English in the Eighteenth Century India*. London and Dublin: Curzon Press Limited, 1980.

—— (1938). Bentinck and Education. *The Cambridge Historical Journal Vol. I*. 78-100. Quoted from Metcalfe 1971: 169-86.

—— (ed.) (1958). *Oxford History of India* (3rd. ed.). Oxford: Clarendon Press.

SSNP-1 (1992). *Sociolinguistic Survey of Northern Pakistan. Volume 1: Languages of Kohistan*. Calvin R. Rensch, Sandra J. Decker and Daniel G. Hallberg (eds.). Islamabad: National Institute of Pakistan Studies, Quaid-i-Azam University, and Summer Institute of Linguistics.

SSNP-2 (1992). Vol. 2: *Languages of Northern Areas*. Peter C. Backstrom, and Carla F. Radloff (eds.). Islamabad: as above.

SSNP-3 (1992). Vol. 3. *Hindko and Gujari*. Calvin R. Rensch, Calinda E. Hallberg, and Clare F. O'Leary (eds.) as above.
SSNP-4 (1992). Vol. 4: *Pashto, Waneci, Ormuri*. Daniel G. Hallberg (ed.) as above.
SSNP-5 (1992). Vol. 5. *Languages of Chitral*. Kendall D. Decker(ed.)as above.
Stephens, Meic (1976). *Linguistic Minorities in Western Europe*. Landysul, Dyfed (Wales): Gomer Press.
Stock, A. G. (1973). *Memoirs of Dacca University 1947-1951*. Dhaka: Green Book House Ltd.
Stokes, Eric (1959). *The English Utilitarians and India*. Oxford: Clarendon Press.
Swati, Niaz (1986). Hindko haroof taehji: Hindko likharion ke liye dawat-e-fikr. [Urdu: The Hindko alphabet: invitation for thought to Hindko writers]. *Jamhoor* 16 December.
Syed, Anwar H. (1988). Political parties and the nationality question in Pakistan. *Journal of South Asian and Middle Eastern Studies Vol. XII:* No. 1 (Fall), 42-75.
Syed, G. M. (1949). *Struggle for New Sind: A Brief Narrative of the working of Provincial Autonomy in Sind During a Decade (1937-1947)*. Karachi: Sindh Observer Press. [The spelling of Syed is Sayed in this book but it has been altered in the interest of uniformity here].
—— (1990?). *Sindhu Desh: A Study in Its Separate Identity Through the Ages*. Karachi: G. M. Syed Academy (the date is not given but the Accession number is of early 1991).

Tajfel, H. (1981). *Human Groups and Social Categories*. Cambridge: Cambridge University Press.
Talpur, M. Yusuf (1969). *A Memorandum on Proposals for a New Educational Policy and Sindhi Language*. Hyderabad: Jeay Sind Naujawan Mahaz Publication 3.
Tair, M. Nawaz (n.d.). *Pashto Academy: Ek Ilmi aur Tehqiqi Idara* [Urdu: an educational and research organization]. Peshawar: Pashto Academy.
—— (ed.) (1986). *Suba-e-Sarhad Par Paehli Lisani aor Saqafati Conference* [Urdu: The first linguistic and cultural conference on the NWFP]. Peshawar: Pashto Academy.
Taizi, Sher Zaman (1989). Letter to the Editor. *FP* 9 February.
Taj, Abdul Khaliq (1989). *Shina Qaida* [Shina primer]. Rawalpindi: Privately printed.
Tambiah, S. J. (1967). The politics of language in India and Ceylon. *Modern Asian Studies* 1: 3 July, 215-40.
Taylor, David, and Yapp, Malcolm (eds.). (1979). *Political Identity in South Asia*. London and Dublin: Curzon Press.
Tendulkar, D. G. (1967). *Abdul Ghaffar Khan: Faith is a Battle*. Bombay: Popular Prakashan.
Tiffou, Etienne (1993). *Hunza Proverbs*. Calgary, Canada: University of Calgary Press.

Tigri, Piral She (1993). Balochi zaban man vang Jahan [Balochi: Balochi language in educational institutions] *Balochi* (August), 5-8.
Todd, L. (1983). Language options for education in a multi-lingual society. In Kennedy 1983: 160-71.
Tollefson, James W. (1986). Language policy and the radical left in the Phillipines: the new people's army and its antecedents. *Language Problems and Language Planning*, 10; 2: 177-89.
Trevelyan, C. (1838). *On the Education of the People of India.* London: Longmans.
Troup, F. (1976). *Forbidden Pastures: Education Under Apartheid* London: International Defence and Aid Fund.

Ulfat, Gul Bacha (1961). *Leekwali: Imla-o-Insha* [Pashto: Writing, spelling and essays] Kabul: Pukhto Tolana.
Umar, Badruddin (1970) *Purba Banglar Bhasha Ondolan-o-Tatkalin Rajniti* [Bengali: Language movement of East Bengal and contemporary politics of the time]. Dhaka: Mowla Brothers (rev. ed.) (1989). Vol. 1.
—— (1984). *Bhasha Ondolan Prasanga: Katipay Dolil Vol. 1* [Bengali/English: The language movement: some documents]. Dhaka: Bangla Academy.
—— (1986). *Bhasha Ondolan Prasanga: Katipay Dolil Vol. 2,* Dhaka: Bangla Academy (1st. ed.)
—— (1973). *Politics and Society in East Pakistan and Bangladesh.* Dhaka: Mowla Brothers.
USB. (1948). *Farhang Istalahat* [Urdu: A glossary of terms]. 3 Vols. Lahore: Urdu Science Board.

Viswanathan, Gauri (1987). The beginning of English literary study in British India. *The Oxford Literary Review* 9: 1-2, 2-26.
—— (1989). *Masks of Conquest.* New York: Columbia. This ed. London: Faber and Faber, 1990.
Vittachi, Varindra T. (1987). *The Brown Sahib (Revisited).* Harmondsworth: Penguin Books.

Wadud, Kazi Abdul (1963). *Banglar Jagaram* [Bengali: Renaissance in Bengal]. No details.
Wagha, Ahsan (1990). *The Siraiki Language: Its Growth and Development.* Islamabad: Derawar Publications.
Wardaugh, Ronald (1987). *Languages in Competition: Dominance, Diversity and Decline.* Oxford: Basil Blackwell in association with Andre Deutsch.
Waseem, Muhammad (1994). *The 1993 Elections in Pakistan.* Lahore: Vanguard Books.
Watson, J. K. P. (1983). Cultural pluralism, nation-building and educational policies in Peninsular Malysia. In Kennedy 1983: 132-50.
Weinstein, Brian (1980). Language planning in Francophone Africa. *Language Problems and Language Planning* 4 (1): 55-77.

—— (1982). Noah Webster and the diffusion of linguistic innovations for political purposes. *International Journal of the Sociology of Language* 38: 85-108.
Whiteley, W. H. (1968). Ideal and reality in national language policy: a case study from Tanzania. In Fishman *et al.* 1968: 327-44.
Wierzbicka, Anna (1990). Antitotalitarian language in Poland: some mechanisms of linguistic self-defence. In *Language in Society* 19: 1 (March), 1-59.
Wilberforce, Robert, and Wilberforce, Samuel (eds.) (1838). *The Life of William Wilberforce*, 5 Vols. London: John Murray.
Williams, Colin H. (1984). More than tongue can tell: linguistic factors in ethnic separatism. In Edwards, John (ed.) (1984) *Linguistic Minorities: Policies and Pluralism*. London: Academic Press.
Wilson, James (1894). Note on primary education in the Punjab and the teaching of Punjabi in the Roman character. 21 April. In Chaudhry 1977: 169-77.
—— (1899). *Grammar and Dictionary of Western Punjabi; as Spoken in the Western Shahpur District with Proverbs, Sayings, and Verses*. Lahore.
Wolpert, Stanley (1984). *Jinnah of Pakistan*. New York: Oxford University Press.
—— (1993). *Zulfi Bhutto of Pakistan: His Life and Times*. New York and Oxford: Oxford University Press.
Woodfall, William (ed.) (1793). *Debates at East India House*. London.
Woolard, Kathryn A., and Gahng, Tae-Joong (1990). Changing language policies and attitudes in autonomous Catalonia. *Language in Society*, 19: 311-30.
Yar, Mehram (1963). Adabi sargarmian [Punjabi: Literary activities]. *Punjabi Adab* (July), 49-54.
Yar, Mir Ahmed (1975). *Inside Balochistan: Political Autobiography of Khan-e-Azam Mir Ahmed Yar Khan Baloch ex-Ruler of Kalat State*. Karachi: Royal Book Company.
Yinger, J. M. (1981). Towards a theory of assimilation and dissimilation. *Ethnic and Racial Studies* 4; 3: 249-64.
Yusuf, Muhammad (1990). *Balti Zaban* [Urdu: The Balti language]. Skardu: Privately printed.
Yusufi, Ahmad F. (1990). Hindko. Letter to the Editor, *M* 12 March.
Yusufzai, Rahimullah (1994). New provinces: do it yourself. *The News* 26 October.
Zaheer, Hasan (1994). *The Separation of East Pakistan: The Rise and Realization of Bengali Muslim Nationalism*. Karachi: Oxford University Press.
Zaidi, M. Abbas (1993). Interview with Agha Babar. *N* 4 February.
Zaidi, S. Akbar (ed.) (1992a). *Regional Imbalances and the National Question in Pakistan*. Lahore: Vanguard Books.
—— (1992b). Sindhi vs Muhajir contradictions, conflict, compromise. In Zaidi 1992a: 334-61.

Zaidi, Zawwar H. (ed.) (1993). *Quaid-i-Azam Mohammad Ali Jinnah Papers: Prelude to Pakistan 20 February – 2 June 1947 Vol. 1.: Part 1*. Islamabad: Quaid-i-Azam Papers Project, National Archives of Pakistan.

—— (ed.) (1994). *Jinnah Papers, 3 June – 30 June 1947 Vol. 2*. As above.

Zami, Bashir (1970). *Siraiki Zaban Ka Irtiqa* [Urdu: The evolution of the Siraiki language]. Bahawalpur.

Zeno (Safdar Mir) (1969). Urdu and Punjabi. *Punjabi Adab* 10: 9 (September). Original in *PT* 9 August 1969.

—— (1986). A sense of distinct identity. *PT* 15 July.

Zia, M. Amin (1986). *Shina Qaida aur Grammar* [Urdu: Shina primer and grammar]. Gilgit: Zia Publications.

Zulfiqar, Ghulam H., and Akhtar, Naseem (eds.) (1986). *Qaumi Zaban Ke Bare Men Ahem Dastavezat* [Urdu: Important document concerning the national language] *Vol. 2, Part 1*. Islamabad: Muqtadira Qaumi Zaban.

## PART C. INTERVIEWS, PERSONAL COMMUNICATION, LETTERS, QUESTIONNAIRES

### (A) INTERVIEWS.

The language given in brackets below the place of interview is the language about which information was sought. Not all the interviews are cited in the text.

| | |
|---|---|
| Abid (7 June 1994, Quetta) (Pashto) | Abid Shah Abid, ex-President of the Pashto Academy, Quetta. |
| ADEF (22 December 1993, Peshawar) (Pashto) | Assistant Director of Education, FATA (Federally Administered Tribal Areas). |
| Akram (4 June 1994, Quetta) (Balochi) | Mir Muhammad Akram, ex-member of the BSO and presently of BNM. Speaker of the Balochistan Assembly in 1994. |
| Ali (18 January 1993, Multan) (Siraiki) | Omar Ali, former member of Riaz Hashmi's Siraiki Students Federation and presently the editor of the monthly *Siraiki Adab*. |
| Arif (19 January 1993, Multan) (Siraiki) | Mazhar Arif, active member of the Siraiki Lok Sanjh and a journalist. |

| | |
|---|---|
| Asif (2 February 1993, Lahore) (Punjabi) | Muhammad Asif Khan, Secretary of the Punjabi Adabi Board and a well known writer of Punjabi. |
| Baloch (3 June 1994, Quetta) (Balochi) | M. Ayub Baloch, General Secretary of the *Balochi* Academy, Quetta. |
| Bandiq (8 June 1994, Quetta) (Balochi) | Abdul Wahid Bandiq, editor of the monthly Balochi from Quetta. |
| Chowdhury (30 September 1994, Dhaka) (Bengali) | Professor Kabir Chowdhury, one of the most eminent Bangladeshi intellectuals and translators from Bengali to English. His sister and his brother, Munier Chowdhury, were both in the Bengali language movement. Munier Chowdhury was killed on 14 December 1971. |
| Chughtai (30 July, 1994, Chitral, Drosh) (Khowar) | Anisur Rahman Chughtai, President of the Anjuman-e-Taraqqi-e-Khowar in Drosh. |
| Dashtiari (5 June 1994, Quetta) (Balochi) | Saba Dashtiari, Professor of Islamic Studies at the University of Balochistan and a leading writer of Balochi. |
| Dillon (23 November 1994, Rawalpindi) (Punjabi) | Sardar Iqbal Dillon, organizer of the Punjabi Morcha who believes in writing Punjabi in the Gurmukhi script. |
| Faizi (28 July 1994, Booni-Chitral) | Inayatullah Faizi, President of the Anjuman-e-Taraqqi-e-Kho-war. |
| Ghani (2 November 1993, Utmanzai) (Pashto) | Khan Ghani Khan, son of Khan Abdul Ghaffar Khan. A famous Pashto poet and the founder of Pakhtun Zalmay, who were young men ready to use force whereas Ghaffar Khan's Khudai Khidmatgars were under oath not to. |
| Ghumman (31 January 1993, Lahore) (Punjabi) | Ilyas Ghumman, an activist of the Punjabi language movement and the author of scientific books in Punjabi. |

| | |
|---|---|
| Haider (19 August 1994, Abbottabad) (Hindko) | Haider Zaman Haider, a well-known Hindko poet and the first translator of the Quran in that language. |
| Haq (26 December 1992, Multan) (Siraiki) | Mehr Abdul Haq, well-known historian of Siraiki language and literature. |
| Imdad (3 January 1995, Peshawar) (Hindko) | Sabir Husain Imdad, a Hindko poet and compere on television. One of the activists of the Hindko movement in Peshawar. |
| Jamaldini (5 June 1994, Quetta) (Balochi) | Abdullah Jamaldini, one of the pioneers of the Balochi language movement and a leading Baloch intellectual. |
| Joyo (26 January 1993, Hyderabad) (Sindhi) | Ibrahim Joyo, well known activist of the Sindhi language movement. |
| Kanju (6 February 1993, Rawalpindi) (Siraiki) | Abdul Majeed Kanju, President of the Siraiki National Party. |
| Kazi (24 January 1993, Hyderabad) (Sindhi) | Abrar Kazi, General Secretary of the Sind Democrats Group which makes efforts to create amity between Mohajirs and Sindhis. |
| Khalid (19 August 1994, Abbottabad) (Hindko) | Yahya Khalid, a pioneer of the Hindko literary movement and a well-known writer of Hindko. |
| Khattak (1 November 1993, Peshawar) (Pashto) | Dr Raj Wali Khattak, a language planner and research scholar in the Pashto Academy, University of Peshawar. |
| Khuhro (22 January 1993, Karachi) (Sindhi) | Hamida Khuhro, well-known scholar and Sindhi nationalist. |
| Lakhani (26 September 1994, Karachi) (Gujrati) | Akbar Lakhani, on the editorial staff of the Gujrati daily *Millat*. |
| Langah (27 December 1992, Multan) (Siraiki) | Taj Muhammad Langah, President of the Pakistan Siraiki Party. |
| Malik, A. (20 August 1994, Abbottabad) (Hindko) | Asim Malik, the pioneer and head of the Hazara Qaumi Mahaz, a political party which demands that Hazara should be made a separate province. |

## Bibliography

Malik (4 June 1994, Quetta) (Balochi) — Muhammad Malik, member of the BNM and the Minister of Education in the Balochistan Government in 1994.

Marri (2 June 1994, Quetta) (Balochi) — Surat Khan Marri, writer of Balochi and a civil servant in Quetta.

Mehmood (15 May 1995, Rawalpindi) — Tariq Mehmood, one of the founding editors of Chitka, the first Potohari magazine, published from Manchester.

Mirza (16 October 1991, Lahore) — Shafqat Tanwir Mirza, editor of the Urdu daily *Imroze* and a well-known writer of Punjabi.

Mooraj (9 August 1994, Rawalpindi) (English) — Executive Director of the Pakistan American Cultural Center (Karachi) and a member of the English Speaking Union, Karachi.

Murshid (28 September 1994, Dhaka) (Bengali) — Dr Khan Sarwar Murshid, ex-Vice Chancellor of Rajshahi University edited *New Values*, a prestigious magazine of the fifties.

Naeem (19 October 1993, Peshawar) (Pashto) — Hidayatullah Naeem, a research scholar at the Pashto Academy, University of Peshawar.

Naseer (23 September 1994, Karachi) (Burushaski) — Allama Naseeruddin, the father of Burushaski poetry and founder of the Burushaski Research Academy.

Nayyar (3 January 1995, Peshawar) (Hindko) — Mukhtar Ali Nayyar, the father of Hindko (Baba-e-Hindko), who is the leading intellectual of the Hindko language movement in Peshawar.

Noon (29 December 1994, Islamabad) (English) — Lady Viqarunnisa Noon, President of the Islamabad Chapter of the English Speaking Union.

Patel (10 October 1994, Islamabad) (Gujrati) — Khatri Ismat Ali Patel, well-known translator from Gujrati to Urdu.

| | |
|---|---|
| Rasalu (1 February 1993, Lahore) (Punjabi) | Raja Rasalu, *nom de plume* of Muhammad Sadiq, a pioneer of the Punjabi language movement. |
| Sabir (2 June 1994, Quetta) (Balochi/Brahvi) | Razzak Sabir, Assistant Professor of Brahvi at the University of Balochistan, Quetta. |
| Sakoon (20 August 1994, Abbottabad) (Hindko) | Sultan Sakoon, a Hindko language planner who has compiled an unpublished dictionary of the language. |
| Sarwar (25 September 1994, Karachi) | Zakia Sarwar, founder member of the Society of Pakistani English Language Teachers (SPELT). |
| Shahbaz (24 September 1994, Karachi) | Ibrahim Shahbaz, Editor of the Gujrati edition of *Dawn*. |
| Shahwani (8 June 1994, Quetta) (Brahvi) | Abdul Qadir Shahwani, General Secretary of the Brahvi Academy, Quetta. |
| Shaukat (3 January 1995, Peshawar) (Hindko) | Sheen Shaukat, one of the activists of the Hindko language movement in Peshawar and founding President of the Hindko Arts Council. |
| Siddiqui (3 October 1994, Dhaka) (Bengali) | Professor Zillur Rahman Siddiqui, ex-Vice Chancellor of Jahangirnagar University, was a student in Salimullah Hall at the time of the Bengali language movement. |
| Sindhi (24 November 1993, Islamabad) (Sindhi) | Ghulam Haider Sindhi, Associate Professor of Sindhi, National Institute of Pakistan Studies, Quaid-i-Azam University, Islamabad. |
| Syed (17 October 1991, Lahore) (Punjabi) | Najam Hussain Syed, the founding chairman of the Department of Punjabi at the University of the Punjab, Lahore. |
| Tawawalla (26 September 1994, Karachi) (Gujrati) | Farida Tawawalla, Head of a Bohra (Gujrati) community school, called Al Madrassah Tus Safya Tul Burhania in Karachi. |

Yusuf (5 August 1994, Chitral) — Muhammad Yusuf, Deputy Commissioner of Chitral.
    (Khowar)

## (B) PERSONAL COMMUNICATION (PC)

Baart (10 December 1994, Islamabad) — Dr Johann Baart, a linguist, at the Summer Institute of Linguistics studying Kohistani (Kalami).

Saleem (8 December 1994, Islamabad) — Ahmad Saleem, a writer on Punjabi literature and politics.

## (C) LETTERS (LTR)

Rahman, U 6 February 1993 From Bahawalpur (Siraiki) — Seth Ubaidur Rahman, a leader of the Bahawalpur Province Movement.

## (D) QUESTIONNAIRES (Q)

(This questionnaire contained questions on language planning, attitude towards the language, and its domains of use.)

Barcha (Gilgit) (Shina) — Sherbaz Khan Barcha, writer and member of the Karakoram Writers Forum.

BRA Hunza (Burushaski) — Burushaski Research Academy which was established as the Burushaski Research Committee by Naseeruddin Naseer in the late 1970s.

Muzaffar (Gilgit) (Wakhi) — Muhammad Muzaffaruddin, a member of the Wakhi-Tajik Cultural Association.

Zia (Gilgit) (Shina) — Amin Zia, writer and member of organizations meant for promoting Shina.

# Index

Abdul Haq, 57, 71, 73-4, 93, 95.
Abdul Latif, 48, 81.
Afghanistan, 4, 134-5, 137-8, 141-5, 147, 149-50, 152, 154-5, 161, 170, 206, 211, 222, 249.
Africa, 23-4, 40, 228-9.
Anglicist/anglicism, 24-38, 40-1, 46, 54.
Anglicist-Orientalist Controversy, 24*ff*.
Anjuman-e-Punjab, 45.
Anjuman-e-Taraqqi-e-Khowar, 223-4.
Anjuman-e-Taraqqi-e-Urdu, 71, 73, 93, 230, 239-40.
Arabic, 11, 24, 31, 33, 47-8, 61, 80, 81-2, 88, 94, 99-100, 104-5, 129.
*Ashraf*, 2, 69, 76, 79-83.
*Atrap/Ajlaf*, 80.
Awami League, 94, 101.
Awami National Party (ANP) 147, 152, 185, 249, 295.
Ayub Khan, 86, 95-6, 99, 101, 116-18.
Bahawalpur Province Movement 181-4.
Balochi Academy, 163.
Balochi language, 1, 6, 58, 155*ff*, 210, 227, 255.
Balochistan, 51, 55, 58, 121, 130, 155-90, 238, 249, 253.
Balti language, 217-20.
Bangladesh, 55, 79, 95, 100, 101.
Bengal, 17, 28, 37, 46-7, 61, 63, 67, 78-102.
Bengali, 2, 31, 47, 78, 102, 115, 118-9, 227, 232-4, 237, 250.
Bengali Language Movement, 2-3, 6, 79-102, 118.

Bengalis, 2, 16, 30, 35, 79-102.
Bentinck, Lord William, 31-2, 36.
Bhutto, Benazir, 168, 187, 188, 205, 207, 243.
Bhutto, Z. A., 21, 123, 125, 165, 182, 191, 238-9, 244.
Brahvi Academy, 158, 163.
Brahvi language, 1, 58, 155-90, 210, 227.
Brahvi-Balochi Controversy 157-8.
British Language Policy, 3, 5, 6, 23-38, 44, 49, 55, 62-3, 72-3, 81, 103, 105-7, 135, 137, 141, 192, 194, 222-3, 250.
Bureaucracy (Civil Service), 13, 14, 20, 21-2, 29-30, 42, 47, 53, 81, 86-8, 99, 103, 108, 113, 121, 130, 163-4, 169, 171, 179-80, 191, 202, 223, 226, 231-4, 243, 244, 251, 255.
Burushaski language, 27-8, 210, 217-9, 226, 254.
Chitral, 210, 219-25, 227, 254.
Civil Service (*see* Bureaucracy).
Colonialism/anti-colonialism, imperialism, etc.), 4, 5, 6, 10, 16, 23-41, 43, 47, 49, 53, 58, 86, 135-9, 201, 228-30, 251, 255.
Communism/Socialism/left-wing, 4-5, 11, 40, 54, 88, 92-3, 95, 102, 119-20, 122, 147, 162, 166, 182, 185, 187, 201, 204-6, 238-9, 241, 249-50, 252-3, 255.
Congress, Indian National, 46-7, 54, 71, 73-5, 137, 140, 143.
Corpus Planning (*see* Language Planning).
Curzon, Lord, 49-50, 56, 70-2.
Darkhani School, 159-60, 165.
Domaaki language 211, 217, 218-20.
Domains of power (*see* Power).

Devanagari script, 2, 27, 61, 64, 66, 69-70, 72-3, 107, 196, 216, 235, 250.
Education Commission (1882), 53, 56, 66, 81, 107, 195, 197.
Education Commission (1959), 99, 116, 233.
Education Policy (1969-70), 118, 203-4, 237-8.
Education Policy (1979), 242-3.
Ellis Report, Sindhi, 105; Police firing, 105.
Elite, 10-13, 15, 19-20, 24, 38, 47, 55, 58, 67-8, 77, 79-80, 142, 150, 203, 228, 247; ruling, 2, 11, 13-5, 40, 42, 91-2, 94-5, 102, 112, 119, 122, 132, 146, 169, 229-30, 232, 234, 240, 244, 246, 250-1, 253-4, 256; westernized, 3, 13-4, 22, 24, 32-3, 40-1, 48-55, 58, 64, 67, 228-9, 232-4, 238-9, 244, 247, 251, 255, 257.
English, 1, 4, 10, 12, 15, 38, 47, 85, 86, 88, 104, 119, 123, 128, 129, 141, 143, 147, 148, 153, 161, 171, 196, 209, 224, 227-48, 250, 256-7; education in, 5, 24, 28, 30, 31, 33-4, 39-59, 150, 153, 168, 216, 219, 229, 249, 256; elitism in, 3, 14, 22, 40, 42, 46, 48, 49-58, 168, 208, 228, 231, 233, 235, 240-1, 244-5, 250-1; and colonialism/neo-colonialism, 23, 28, 33, 35, 40, 41, 44, 55, 228-30, 246; and social mobility, 9, 27, 30, 31, 33, 40, 47, 48, 150, 191, 209, 214, 219, 220, 226, 236, 245.
English-Urdu Controversy, 3, 228-48, 255.
English-Vernacular Controversy, 5, 39-58, 228.
Ethnicity/ethno-nationalism, 2-7, 14-5, 18-20, 37, 40, 46, 57, 58, 79, 86, 88, 93, 99-100, 102-3, 108, 115-8, 124, 126-7, 131, 133, 135, 139, 146, 151, 155, 166, 174, 180, 183, 185, 205, 209, 224, 228-9, 239, 249-50, 251-5; in Balochi/Brahvi, 2, 155-64, 167, 170-71, 239, 253; in Bengali, 2, 79, 99-102, 161, 251; in Hindi, 65; in Mohajir, 2, 127, 252; in Pakistan, 2-4, 70, 93, 99, 167, 189, 202, 208, 239, 251; in Pakhtun, 2, 134, 137-8, 142, 145, 151, 153-4, 156, 239; in Punjabi, 2, 207, 239; in Sindhi, 2, 103, 113, 117, 124, 127, 129, 131-2, 137, 180, 183, 239; in Siraiki, 2, 157, 174, 180, 183, 185-6, 189.
Extra-rational factors (Primordialist), 14, 19, 59, 69, 72, 77-8, 85, 209, 245, 252, 253.
French, 10, 15, 18, 24, 40, 223, 246.
Gandhi, M. K., 46-7, 73-5, 77.
Ghaffar Khan, 55, 134, 137-8, 140, 143, 145-6, 150.
Ghettoizing languages, 10, 12, 35, 46, 149-50, 165, 168, 170, 195-6, 198, 202, 214, 220, 227.
Gujrati language, 58, 108, 109, 210, 215-7, 226-7.
Gurmukhi, 140, 192, 194-8, 202, 204.
Hamood-ur-Rehman Report, 234.
Hazara, 140-1, 146, 214.
Hindi, 1, 12, 16, 27, 40, 44, 47, 57, 59-78, 84, 109, 140, 173, 175, 198, 207, 226, 250.
Hindko language, 1, 140, 146, 150, 173, 178, 210-4, 226-7, 254, 255
Hindu/Hinduism, 2, 4, 16-7, 19, 25-6, 29-30, 35-6, 44, 46-8, 60, 63-4, 66-8, 70-72, 77-8, 80-6, 92, 103-7, 109, 113, 119, 132, 140, 195, 197, 199, 226, 250-1.
Hindustani language, 27, 31, 39, 60, 62, 72-5, 77, 215.
Identity, 6, 10-1, 16-8, 20, 39, 46, 78, 85-6, 217-8, 226-7, 250, 254; as Baloch/Brahvi, 2, 157, 159, 161, 163, 166-72, 251; as Bengali, 2, 16, 79, 82-4, 86, 88-9, 96, 99-101, 161, 251; construction of, 3, 5-7, 11, 20,

37, 46, 59, 60, 62, 73, 78, 82, 98, 134, 152, 170-1, 174, 176, 179-80, 199, 215, 218, 226-7, 250-2, 254; language as marker of, 5, 18, 39, 46, 47, 75, 77, 133, 138, 145-56, 151-2, 154, 156, 161, 166, 168, 175, 206, 209, 214, 215, 217, 218, 221-2, 226-7, 244, 250, 350; as Hindu, 1, 59-60, 62, 78, 107, 195; local, 16-8, 39, 215, 226, 250; as Mohajir, 2-3, 112, 116, 126-7, 129-31, 251; as Muslim, 1-2, 11, 16-7, 19, 46-7, 59-60, 75-9, 82-4, 86, 88-9, 98, 110, 112, 130, 145, 152, 157, 195, 199, 205-6, 217-8, 220, 222, 230, 236, 251; as Pakhtun, 2, 16, 82, 133, 134-5, 138-9, 145-6, 150-7, 169, 251, 252; as Pakistani, 16, 86, 112, 127, 145, 152, 166, 202, 206, 220, 230, 236, 251-3; as Punjabi, 2, 190, 195, 198-202, 205-6, 253; as Sindhi, 2, 103, 113, 115, 117-8, 120, 130, 131, 251; as Siraiki, 2, 16, 174-6, 180-1, 184, 190, 215, 251; other identities in Pakistan, 214-5, 217-8, 221, 224-7, 251.

Inayatullah Faizi, 222, 224.

India/Indian, 2, 4, 6, 12-13, 16-17, 19, 23-59, 63, 64-5, 75, 77, 88, 92-3, 115, 119-20, 137, 141, 144, 210-11, 225-6, 228-9, 249, 251, 253.

Instrumentalism, factors in, 2, 14, 19-20, 59, 77, 85, 113, 208, 216, 218, 220, 226, 245, 252.

Islam/Islamic, anti-Islamic, 2, 4-5, 11, 13, 19, 21, 31-2, 36, 43, 55, 56, 58-9, 63-4, 72-3, 75-81, 83, 85, 88-9, 93, 100, 103, 119, 122, 128, 138, 143, 153, 159-60, 166-7, 170, 186, 203, 207, 225-6, 235-6, 238, 240-1, 243, 254.

Islamization, 80, 88, 147, 240.

Jamaldini Brothers, 158, 162, 165-6.
Jeeay Sindh, 123, 127.
Jinnah, M. A., 54, 74, 87-8, 90, 108, 109, 143, 160.
Kalasha language, 211.
Kalat (also Khan of) 156-8, 160-2, 164.
Kanju, Abdul Majeed, 178, 182-3, 186-9.
Karachi, 50, 58, 110-7, 121, 123-6, 128, 130, 132, 157, 161, 187, 210, 215-7, 220, 227, 236, 246, 254-5.
Karakoram Writers' Forum, 218.
Kashmir, 58, 121, 130, 178, 210-1, 225-6.
Kashmiri language, 173, 210-1, 225-6.
Khowar language, 210, 219, 221-6.
Kohistani language, 211, 221-2.
Langha, Taj Mohammad, 178, 183, 187.
Language, death of, 178, 183, 187.
Language Planning/Corpus Planning, 7, 11, 23, 28, 39, 61, 88-9, 99-100, 105-6, 130, 133, 136, 142, 150-3, 157, 166, 169-70, 175-6, 177, 184, 194, 204, 208, 218, 222-3, 230-1, 235, 239, 251; planning in Balochi/Brahvi, 166,170-1; in Bengali, 80-2, 88-9, 99-100; in Hindi, 61-2, 64; in Hindko, 212-4; in Pashto, 142, 150-3; in Punjabi, 204, 206-7; in Sindhi, 105-6, 128-9; in Siraiki, 176-7; in Urdu, 60, 231-2, 239.
Language riots, 3, 6, 12, 91-2, 120-7.
Latin, 11, 15, 41.
Liaquat Ali Khan, 76, 86, 113.
Linguistic Provinces, 253-5.
Macaulay, T. B., 32-6, 40-1, 46, 53, 257.
Macdonnell, A. P., 69-72.
Medium of Instruction, 3, 5, 21, 43, 45, 47, 50, 55-7, 65-6, 74, 84-5, 88, 94, 101, 106, 109-10, 116, 118, 122, 128, 139, 141, 185, 195, 212, 228-48; in Balochi, 58, 168-9; in Brahvi 58, 168-9; in Bengali, 88; in English, 21, 48, 55, 228-48; in Hindi, 65, 74;

in Pashto, 138-41, 144, 147-50, 152-3, 168-9; in Punjabi, 195-6, 200, 203, 206, 208; in Sindhi, 58, 116-8, 245; in Siraiki, 185; in Urdu, 43, 50, 58, 65, 74, 110, 116-7, 139, 149, 222, 228-48.
Military, 1, 3, 13, 20-2, 27, 49-50, 54, 81, 86, 98, 101, 104, 113, 121, 123, 127, 130, 147-8, 161-3, 167, 182, 187, 189, 191, 193, 197, 205, 222-4, 231-4, 237, 240, 243-4, 247, 293.
Mill (James and Jones), 25, 28-9, 36, 54.
Modernity/Modernization, 13-4, 18-20, 29-30, 38-9, 47, 81-2, 99, 151, 199, 209, 215, 222, 228-9, 235, 245-6, 250-2, 257.
Mohajirs, 1, 4, 5, 6, 103, 110-32, 134, 182, 202, 230, 254, 255.
MQM, 3, 127, 132, 187, 254.
Muslims, 2-3, 11, 16-7, 25-6, 29, 31, 35, 43-8, 55-6, 58-9, 60, 62-75, 77-83, 85, 89, 99-100, 103, 106, 107-9, 132, 166, 173, 176, 194-6, 198-9, 218, 225-6, 230, 250.
Muslim League, 2, 59, 74-6, 83-4, 88, 91, 94, 113-4, 143, 160, 197.
Nasir, Gul Khan, 161, 165-6.
Nasir, Nasiruddin, 218-9.
Nasrullah, Nasr, 144, 150-1.
Nationalism/Nationalities, 18, 37, 40, 46, 135; in Baloch/Brahvi, 2, 155, 156, 157, 158, 159; in Bengali, 2, 79, 99-102, 161, 251; in Hindu, 66; in Mohajir, 2, 127, 252; in Pakistani, 2-4, 90, 93, 99, 167, 189, 202, 208, 239, 251; in Pakhtun, 2, 134, 137-8, 142, 145, 151, 153-4, 156, 239; in Punjabi, 2, 207, 239; in Sindhi, 2, 103, 113, 117, 124 127, 129, 131-2, 180, 183, 239; in Siraiki, 2, 157, 174, 180, 183, 185-6, 189.

NAP, 93, 146-7, 162, 164-5, 250.
National language, 1, 9, 12, 39, 84-5, 88, 94-5, 99, 115, 118-9, 122-3, 125, 127, 131, 134-5, 140, 146, 161, 164-5, 192, 100, 221, 229-30, 232-3, 235, 237-9.
Nawab Muzaffar Khan, 122-4.
Nayyar, Mukhtar Ali, 211-2.
Nazimuddin, Khawaja, 29, 86-8, 90, 232.
Northern Areas, 16, 121, 130, 210, 217-21, 227, 254.
Nurul Amin, 115-6, 123, 232.
One Unit, 115-6, 123, 146, 181, 190.
Orientalism, 24-38, 43, 45-6, 48, 53, 71, 136.
Pashto language, 1, 6, 37, 133*ff*, 159, 165, 172, 203, 210, 213, 217, 221-7, 252, 254.
Pashto Academy, 139, 142, 145, 152-3, 156.
Pashto Organizations, 144, 151.
Pakhtuns, 17, 37, 82, 121, 130, 133*ff*, 155-6, 164-5.
Pakhtunistan, 137, 143-6, 150, 249.
Pakistanis, 1-6, 13-4, 17-20, 37, 50-1, 65, 75, 77, 79, 83, 85, 88, 93, 96, 135, 143, 146, 152, 154, 156, 158, 161-2, 165-7, 170, 181, 188, 191, 195, 198, 201-2, 211, 224, 228, 232, 234, 237-8, 249-51, 254-5, 257; and ethno-nationalists, 2, 4-5, 101, 113, 116, 118, 123, 134, 143, 155, 162, 164, 166, 170, 186, 189, 202-3, 205-6, 224, 249, 252, 254; languages of, 1, 3, 119, 155, 166, 182, 185, 100, 203, 205, 210, 217, 222, 228, 233, 235, 238, 240.
Perso-Arabic script, 1, 62, 66, 74, 75, 81-2, 89, 104-7, 151-2, 165-7, 173, 176, 196, 205, 212-3, 215, 218, 220-3, 226, 235-6.
Perso-Arabic vocabulary, 60, 62, 63-4, 80, 88, 99-100, 152, 170, 207, 210.
Persian, 19, 24, 25, 27, 31, 35, 37, 48, 60, 61-3, 66, 69, 80-3, 88, 99-100, 103-4, 129, 134, 136-7, 142, 155,

159-60, 164, 192-4, 199, 218, 221-2, 227, 250.
Potohari language, 214-5, 254.
Power, 3-5, 7-12, 20, 22-3, 26, 30, 36, 39, 42, 46-7, 72, 93, 96-7, 103, 113, 120, 125-6, 130, 133, 135-7, 146, 150, 153-4, 183, 208, 224-5, 228, 241-4, 247, 249, 253; domains of, 1, 7-8, 11, 13, 35, 39, 46, 101, 103, 142, 144, 147, 153-5, 163, 169-70, 192, 209, 214, 216, 218, 224, 228-9, 242-5, 250, 255.
Press, 32, 75, 88, 246-7, 249, 253; Balochi/Brahvi, 158, 160-3, 170; English, 2, 70, 133, 205; Hindi, 61; Pashto, 138-9, 145, 149, 153, 224; Punjabi, 198-9, 201, 204, 207-8; Sindhi, 109, 115, 117-8, 122, 133; Siraiki, 180, 182; Urdu, 70, 75, 122-5, 133, 212; Other Languages, 212, 215-6, 224.
Primordial (*see* Extra-rational).
Proto-elite, 2, 11-2, 14, 39-40, 48, 55, 58, 79, 86, 94, 96, 98, 188, 233, 236, 239-40, 252, 255.
Punjabi, 3, 4, 112, 114, 119, 121, 130, 132, 175, 177, 179, 189, 191-209, 230, 253.
Punjabi language, 3-4, 6, 18-9, 31, 51, 56-8, 60, 63, 66, 70, 76, 113, 152, 155, 173-5, 177-8, 180-1, 188, 191-210, 215, 225-7, 253.
Punjabi Organizations, 191-2, 198-203, 208.
PPP, 122, 131, 146, 145, 182, 187, 188, 191, 205, 207, 220, 238, 241-2.
Roman script, 10, 27, 99, 152, 159, 166-7, 196, 218-20, 222, 235.
Riaz Hashmi 178, 181, 182, 183, 186, 188.

Sanskrit, 24-5, 30-1, 33, 35, 44, 47, 60, 64, 73, 77-8, 80-1, 88-9, 100, 177, 207, 250.
Schools, languages in: English, 14, 21, 42, 44, 48, 49-53, 148, 168, 228-48, 255; Sindhi, 56-7, 103-4, 109, 116-8, 127, 215-6, 233, 245; Urdu, 56-8, 74, 109, 117, 143, 148, 150, 164, 198, 215-6, 220-2, 228-48; Other Languages, 12, 44, 56-8, 104, 136, 138-40, 143-4, 148, 150, 164, 167-9, 171, 185, 192, 196, 198, 202-4, 213-16, 219, 221-2, 225-6.
Shaheed Minar, 92, 94-6.
Sharif, Nawaz, 188-9, 207.
Shina language 17, 210, 217-8, 222, 226, 254.
Sindhi language, 1, 3, 6, 58, 103, 133, 159-60, 174, 176, 203, 210, 214-6, 227, 240, 245, 250, 254.
Sindhi Organizations, 127-8.
Sindhu Desh, 119-20, 122, 249.
Siraiki Language, 4, 6, 155, 157, 159, 173-4, 210-11, 227, 252, 254.
Siraiki Organzations, 176, 178, 180-1, 183-6.
Soviet Union, 4, 11, 120, 149, 222, 249.
Swat, language in, 135, 142-3, 227.
Syed Ahmed Khan. 31, 35, 43, 45-56, 48, 65-6, 109, 113, 118-20, 122, 131.
Syed Hashmi, 166, 170-1.
Syed, G. M., 103, 108-9, 113-4, 118, 120, 127, 131.
UP (including Oudh and NWP), 42, 55-6, 59-60, 62-4, 66-9, 71, 77-8, 112, 192-3.
Universities, 42, 44-6, 48, 50, 57, 108-10, 114, 118, 123-4, 186, 197, 199, 230; language in, 43-6, 48, 56-7, 65, 83-4, 86, 92, 110, 114, 125, 148, 171, 199, 203-4, 226, 234, 246.
Urdu, 2-6, 13, 19, 31, 40, 43-5, 47-8, 50, 56, 58*ff*, 81, 83-4, 95-6, 100, 103, 110, 112-9, 123-6, 128-9, 131-2, 136-7, 139, 141-2, 145-51, 153, 155, 159-61, 164-5, 167-8, 170-2, 174-5,

180, 191-5, 197-206, 208-10, 212-6, 218-22, 224-47, 250, 252-3, 255.

Urdu-Hindi Controversy, 2-3, 6, 46, 59-78, 112, 195-7, 207, 235.

Vernacular, 5, 14-5, 18, 22, 26, 28, 33-4, 36-7, 39-58, 62, 76, 79, 94, 98, 104, 136-7, 143, 164, 192-4, 198, 228, 232-3, 243, 245, 250-2, 255-6.

Vernacular-English Controversy (*see* English-Vernacular controversy)
Wakhi Language, 211, 217, 219-20.
Wakhi-Tajak Organization, 220.
Yahya Khan, 101, 118, 182, 236.
Ziaul Haq, 13, 147, 67, 168, 186-7, 204-5, 236, 240-2, 244, 253.